Praise for *Understanding Organ Donation*

"This work represents thousands of hours of effort in the understanding of individual decision-making and the promotion of positive outcomes in organ donation. The variety of approaches used with different populations in different settings that have been found to be more or less effective based on sound field-based research and evaluation is the hallmark of this work. Practitioners can get great insight into promoting better health behaviors and the greatest human to human gift of all and researchers can get great insight into the complexities of conducting research and evaluation in the messy real world."

J. Jackson Barnette, Colorado School of Public Health,
University of Colorado Denver

"Over a relatively short period of time, a relatively small group of dedicated professionals have sought to accomplish a great purpose . . . to eliminate deaths on the transplant waiting list. This book chronicles the breadth and depth of their research into changing human behaviors which in many cases have never been studied, or even fully described, before. As such, it is a wonderful contribution to an ever-growing field still pursuing the ultimate goal of eliminating deaths on the waiting list."

Jeffrey P. Orlowski, Chief Executive Officer, Center for Donation and
Transplant, Albany, NY

"Siegel and Alvaro have gathered the experience and perspectives of some of the field's most respected professionals and scholars. For anyone seeking to apply recent developments and contribute research in their own right, *Understanding Organ Donation* goes a long way toward delivering on the promise of its title."

Bryan Stewart, President, Donate Life California

"With hundreds of thousands of lives on the line, we don't have the luxury of guesswork. This book shows us how to apply evidence-based theory with life-saving outcomes."

G. David Fleming, President and CEO, Donate Life America

"*Understanding Organ Donation* is a groundbreaking volume on the topic of vital importance to the public and scientific community. The book is informative in its overview of the current approaches, it is insightful in its detection of the challenges, and it is extremely useful in providing guidance to researchers and activists for meeting those challenges."

Radmila Prislin, San Diego State University

THE CLAREMONT SYMPOSIUM ON APPLIED SOCIAL PSYCHOLOGY

This series of volumes highlights the important new developments on the leading edge of applied social psychology. Each volume focuses on one area in which social psychological knowledge is being applied to the resolution of a social problem. Within that area, a distinguished group of authorities present chapters summarizing recent theoretical views and empirical findings, including the results of their own research and applied activities. The preface frames the material, pointing out common themes and varied areas of practical applications. Each volume brings together trenchant new social psychological ideas, research results, and fruitful applications bearing on an area of current social interest. This volume will be of value not only to practitioners and researchers, but also to students and lay people interested in this vital and expanding area of psychology.

The Changing Realities of Work and Family: A Multidisciplinary Approach
Edited by Amy Marcus-Newhall, Diane F. Halpern, and Sherylle J. Tan

Understanding Organ Donation: Applied Behavioral Science Perspectives
Edited by Jason T. Siegel and Eusebio M. Alvaro

Understanding Organ Donation

Applied Behavioral Science Perspectives

Edited by

Jason T. Siegel and Eusebio M. Alvaro

A John Wiley & Sons, Ltd., Publication

This edition first published 2010
© 2010 Blackwell Publishing Ltd

Blackwell Publishing was acquired by John Wiley & Sons in February 2007. Blackwell's publishing program has been merged with Wiley's global Scientific, Technical, and Medical business to form Wiley-Blackwell.

Registered Office
John Wiley & Sons Ltd, The Atrium, Southern Gate, Chichester, West Sussex, PO19 8SQ, United Kingdom

Editorial Offices
350 Main Street, Malden, MA 02148-5020, USA
9600 Garsington Road, Oxford, OX4 2DQ, UK
The Atrium, Southern Gate, Chichester, West Sussex, PO19 8SQ, UK

For details of our global editorial offices, for customer services, and for information about how to apply for permission to reuse the copyright material in this book please see our website at www.wiley.com/wiley-blackwell.

The right of Jason T. Siegel and Eusebio M. Alvaro to be identified as the authors of the editorial material in this work has been asserted in accordance with the Copyright, Designs and Patents Act 1988.

Library of Congress Cataloging-in-Publication Data
Understanding organ donation : applied behavioral science perspectives / edited by Jason T. Siegel and Eusebio M. Alvaro.
        p. ; cm.
    Includes bibliographical references and index.
    ISBN 978-1-4051-9213-2 (hardcover : alk. paper)   1. Donation of organs, tissues, etc—Psychological aspects.   2. Clinical health psychology.   I. Siegel, Jason T.   II. Alvaro, Eusebio M.   III. Claremont Symposium on Applied Social Psychology (24th : 2007)
    [DNLM: 1. Tissue and Organ Procurement.   2. Cultural Diversity.   3. Health Promotion.
4. Program Development.   5. Program Evaluation.   6. Tissue Donors—psychology. WO 660
U55 2010]
    RD129.5.U53 2010
    617.9′56—dc22

                                                                                    2009020182

A catalogue record for this book is available from the British Library.

Set in 10/12.5pt Minion by Graphicraft Limited, Hong Kong
Printed and bound in Malaysia by Vivar Printing Sdn Bhd

1   2010

To Satoko, Maya, and Shaw—JTS
To Jack—EA

Contents

List of Contributors

G. Caleb Alexander, MD, MS, Assistant Professor, Department of Medicine, University of Chicago
E-mail: galexand@uchicago.edu

Margaret D. Allen, MD, Research Member, Benaroya Research Institute, and Affiliate Professor of Surgery, University of Washington
E-mail: mallen@benaroyaresearch.org

Eusebio M. Alvaro, PhD, Research Professor, School for Behavioral and Organizational Sciences, Claremont Graduate University
E-mail: Eusebio.alvaro@cgu.edu

Ashley E. Anker, PhD, post-doctoral Research Associate, Department of Communication, University at Buffalo, State University of New York
E-mail: aeanker@buffalo.edu

David Bosch, MA, Communications Director, Gift of Hope Organ & Tissue Donation
E-mail: dbosch@giftofhope.org

William D. Crano, PhD, Oskamp Professor of Psychology, School for Behavioral and Organizational Sciences, Claremont Graduate University
E-mail: William.crano@cgu.edu

Diane Dodd-McCue, DBA, Associate Professor, Program in Patient Counseling, Virginia Commonwealth University
E-mail: ddoddmccue@vcu.edu

Kimbertey Downing, PhD, Co-Director, Institute for Policy Research, Affiliated Research Associate Professor, Department of Political Science, University of Cincinnati
E-mail: kim.downing@uc.edu

Kelly Eng, Community Relations Specialist, New York Organ Donor Network
E-mail: keng@nyodn.org

Nancy L. Fahrenwald, PhD, RN, Associate Professor, College of Nursing, South Dakota State University
E-mail: nancy.fahrenwald@sdstate.edu

Thomas Hugh Feeley, PhD, Associate Professor, Department of Communications, University at Buffalo, State University of New York
E-mail: thfeeley@buffalo.edu

Robert L. Fischer, PhD, Center on Urban Poverty and Community Development, Mandel School of Applied Social Sciences, Case Western Reserve University
E-mail: fischer@case.edu

Mary Ganikos, PhD, Chief, Public and Professional Education Branch, Division of Transplantation, Health Resources and Services Administration, U.S. Department of Health and Human Services
E-mail: mganikos@hrsa.gov

Jackie Gnepp, PhD, President, Humanly Possible, Inc.
E-mail: Jackie@HumanlyPossible.com

Kate Grubbs O'Connor, BS, Chief Operating Officer, National Kidney Foundation of Illinois, 215 W. Illinois Street, Suite 1C, Chicago, IL 60610
E-mail: koconnor@nkfi.org

Susan Gunderson, MHA, CEO, LifeSource
E-mail: info@life-source.org

Paul L. Hebert, PhD, Investigator and Research Associate Professor, Health Services Research and Development, Mount Sinai School of Medicine, and Department of Health Services, University of Washington School of Public Health
E-mail: Paul.Hebert2@va.gov

Zachary P. Hohman, MA, Graduate Student, School for Behavioral and Organizational Sciences, Claremont Graduate University
E-mail: Zachary.hohman@cgu.edu

Diane Hollingsworth, BBA, Manager of Transplantation and Organ Donor Awareness Education, National Kidney Foundation of Illinois
E-mail: hollingsworthdm@aol.com

Carolyn C. Johnson, PhD, FAAHB, NCC, LPC, Professor, Department of Community Health Sciences, Tulane University School of Public Health and Tropical Medicine
E-mail: cjohnso5@tulane.edu

Clarence Jones, MA, Outreach Director, Southside Community Health Services
E-mail: clarence.jones@southsidechs.org

Linda L. Jones, RN, Emetitis CEO, Lifeline of Ohio Organ Procurement Organization
E-mail: ljones0625@sbcglobal.net

Sara Pace Jones, Director, Donor Program Development, Donor Network of Arizona
E-mail: sara@dnaz.org

Joshua Klayman, PhD, Professor Emeritus of Behavioral Science, Booth School of Business, University of Chicago
E-mail: joshk@uchicago.edu

Willa Lang, MSW, Executive Director, National Kidney Foundation of Illinois, 215 W. Illinois Street, Suite 1C, Chicago, IL 60610
E-mail: wlang@nkfi.org

Susan Mau Larson, APR, Director of Public Affairs, LifeSource
E-mail: info@life-source.org

Regina Lee, JD, Chief, Development Officer, Charles B. Wang Community Health Center
E-mail: rlee@cbwchc.org

David Meltzer, MD, PhD, Associate Professor, Department of Medicine, University of Chicago
E-mail: dmeltzer@medicine.bsd.uchicago.edu

Susan E. Morgan, PhD, Professor, Department of Communications, Purdue University
E-mail: semorgan@purdue.edu

Stuart Oskamp, PhD, Emeritus, Claremont Graduate University
E-mail: stuart.oskamp@cgu.edu

Catherine Paykin, MSSW, Transplant Services Programs Director, National Kidney Foundation
E-mail: cathyp@kidney.org

Gigi Politoski, BA, Senior Vice President of Programs, National Kidney Foundation
E-mail: gigip@kidney.org

Anita Pomerantz, PhD, Professor, Department of Communication, University at Albany, The State University of New York
E-mail: apom@albany.edu

Michael T. Quinn, PhD, Associate Professor, Department of Medicine, University of Chicago
E-mail: mquinn@medicine.bsd.uchicago.edu

David M. Radosevich, PhD, RN, Assistant Professor, University of Minnesota
E-mail: davidmr@umn.edu

Julia Rivera, MHS, Director of Communications, New York Organ Donor Network
E-mail: Jrivera@nyodn.org

James R. Rodrigue, PhD, Psychologist, Beth Israel Deaconess Medical Center, The Transplant Center
E-mail: jrrodrig@bidmc.harvard.edu

Tiffany Scott, LifeSource
E-mail: info@life-source.org

Susan Seto-Yee, RN, Clinical Director, Charles B. Wang Community Health Center
E-mail: syee@cbwchc.org

Jason T. Siegel, PhD, Research Professor, School for Behavioral and Organizational Sciences, Claremont Graduate University
E-mail: Jason.siegel@cgu.edu

Linda Singleton-Driscoll, MBA, Principal, Chléire Consulting, Inc.
E-mail: linda@chleire.com

Barbara Stillwater, PhD, RN, Director, Diabetes Prevention and Control Program, Division of Public Health, State of Alaska
E-mail: barbara.stillwater@alaska.gov

William Tendle, MS, Executive Director, Southside Community Health Services
E-mail: bill.tendle@southsidechs.org

Donald E. Vincent, MA, Doctoral Candidate, Department of Communications, University at Buffalo, State University of New York
E-mail: vincent4@buffalo.edu

Amy D. Waterman, PhD, Assistant Professor, Department of Internal Medicine, Washington University School of Medicine
E-mail: amywaterman@wustl.edu

Larry S. Webber, PhD, Professor, Department of Biostatistics, Tulane University School of Public Health and Tropical Medicine
E-mail: lwebber@tulane.edu

Carla Williams, Former Executive Director, New York Alliance for Donation, Inc.
E-mail: crw03@health.state.ny.us

Preface

Jason T. Siegel and Eusebio M. Alvaro

Being researchers fortunate enough to be funded as part of the Social and Behavioral Science grant program of the Health Resources and Services Administration (HRSA), we attend several yearly meetings where fellow grantees presented their findings. Year after year we listen to our colleagues' presentations of intervention calamity and recovery. Reports of campaigns leading to increases in hospital consent rates and workplace interventions increasing the number of registered workers are commonplace. Gains in knowledge about organ donor registration behavior are rivaled only by the lessons learned as researchers and practitioners teamed up to apply social science and behavioral theories to a domain with great need. One project was interrupted by Hurricane Katrina (Johnson & Weber, this volume), another by a funeral home tissue scandal (Hebert et al., this volume). We knew that a book highlighting these studies and showing off the range of applied studies that this area is built upon could benefit both the organ donation field and psychologists and other behavioral scientists interested in domains where their skills can be put to use with saving lives as the goal.

This volume, the 24th in the long-standing series of books drawn from Claremont Graduate University's Annual Applied Social Psychology Symposium, serves as a comprehensive introduction to, and survey of, social and behavioral science perspectives on organ donation. It should be noted that, with the exception of a single chapter, this volume focuses on nonliving organ donation. This emphasis reflects the field as a whole as it is only recently that intervention research on living donation has begun in earnest. In selecting chapters and contributors, great care was taken to include insights from organ donation professionals, policy makers, scientists conducting organ donation research, and the broader social and behavioral science community. Chapters were selected so as to provide valuable information on one or a number of areas of interest. These areas include the role of mass media, the importance of theory, working with unique and difficult-to-reach populations, the indirect impact of interventions, motivating individuals to become strong advocates, and the use of quasi-experimental designs. As such, we believe this book should be of value to a broad array of audiences, including professionals and practitioners working in the field of organ donation and/or transplantation; graduate students in the social, behavioral, or health sciences; as well as social and behavioral scientists involved in applied research.

Introduction and Overview

The volume begins with introductory chapters by Drs. Stuart Oskamp and Mary Ganikos. Dr. Oskamp, author of the first introductory chapter, has long been recognized as a pioneer of applied research, particularly in the domain of social psychology. Dr. Ganikos, author of the second introductory chapter, is chief, Public and Professional Education Branch, Division of Transplantation (DoT), at the HRSA. Her considerable efforts to keep the HRSA/DoT grant programs alive and vital have been essential in driving the research discussed herein.

Drawing on decades of social psychological experience, Dr. Oskamp offers insight into "many of the characteristics of field research and health interventions that may become issues in conducting research on organ donations." In doing so, he highlights the complexities and challenges of research in this domain.

The chapter authored by Dr. Ganikos, provides an overview of organ donation and transplantation to facilitate readers' understanding of subsequent chapters. A review of the benefits of transplantation as well as the dire need to increase the number of donated organs is followed by information pertaining to what can be donated, how to register to donate, the advantages and disadvantages of living donation, as well as living donation barriers and challenges. An overview of the different social and behavioral interventions follows. The overview includes efforts to increase hospital referral, increase family consent, and increase public commitment to donation. Subsequently, the role of donor registries is addressed along with overviews of national organizations such as Donate Life America. The chapter concludes with Dr. Ganikos pondering a not-so-simple question: "Have we made a difference?"

Organ Donation Interventions

The second section represents a wealth of applied research projects targeting organ donation. Common to each of these chapters is insightful examination of the challenges and issues faced when conducting applied research. Media and community campaigns are presented first. Targets of these efforts range from the general population to specific subgroups including American Indians, African Americans, Alaska Natives, and Hispanics. Each chapter in this section begins with a discussion of the need of the specific population in regard to donated organs and ends with lessons learned as a result of the intervention(s).

Part 1: Media and Community Campaigns

This section begins with our chapter on media campaigns. The chapter presents broad perspectives on mass media effects, reviews 3 decades of organ donation mass media campaigns, and provides insights gleaned from nearly a decade of experience creating, implementing, and assessing the impact of media and community campaigns designed to reach Hispanics. This chapter is designed to provide readers with a broad understanding of the capabilities and limitations of media and community campaigns. Key issues, highlighted throughout by examples from theory and research, include the appropriate role of media campaigns, successful campaign implementation, measurement of campaign impact, and specific campaign materials and approaches that work.

Next, beginning with a description of the need and the unique challenges of organ donation for the African American population, Dr. David Radosevich along with Susan Mau Larson and colleagues turn to a presentation of the outcomes of a media and grassroots campaign implemented in the Twin Cities of Minneapolis and St. Paul, Minnesota. This campaign, guided by the theory of reasoned action, was designed to educate and increase the propensity to donate as well as the actual rate of donor designation among African Americans. Results of the intervention include increases in awareness of the need for organs within the African American community and more favorable attitudes toward organ donation. This chapter offers insights on the importance of fidelity checks and provides a model for those looking to evaluate similar efforts.

Drs. Margaret D. Allen and Barbara Stillwater follow with a chapter describing a broad, multicomponent intervention to increase awareness of organ donation and transplantation among Alaska Natives. They begin with a discussion of the need for organs among Alaska Natives as well as the barriers and challenges in implementing organ donor interventions for this population. This chapter provides a detailed look at the development and implementation of a number of interventions including community education, training of rural health care providers and health educators, and development of educational curricula for schools. Some outcome data are presented, including pre-post knowledge increases for high school students: "Knowledge scores on donation and transplantation increased significantly following the intervention ($p < 0.001$), with the mean percentage of correct answers increasing from 58% on the pretest to 95% on the posttest."

Subsequently, Dr. Kim Downing and Linda Jones focus on an intervention designed to increase awareness of Ohio's new state organ registry via two statewide efforts: a media campaign and one based at Ohio Bureau of Motor Vehicles locations. This chapter begins with a brief history of Ohio's first-person consent organ donor registry and a historical perspective on first-person consent–donor designation implementation. Afterward, the development, implementation, and assessment of a campaign guided by Horton and Horton's model of organ donation willingness are described. The ability to track organ donation registrations at the Ohio Buteau Motor Vehicles provided an ideal outcome measure of campaign impact—a key feature of this chapter. An increase of registrations among younger individuals is particularly noteworthy.

Dr. Paul Hebert, along with Julia Rivera and colleagues, follows with a chapter describing efforts to increase donation within Chinese American communities that have been underserved when it comes to donor interventions. The purpose of the study was to expand the pool of willing organ donors in Asian communities in New York City by focusing educational efforts on Chinese Americans. Chinese American communities are traditionally isolated from donation campaigns by language and other cultural barriers. The intervention was hindered by a scandal involving a funeral home and a tissue bank. The scandal had the impact one would expect of something described by the cable news network CNN as a "body-snatching ring." Few interventions could overcome a nationwide scandal with the control group serving as ground zero. This was not one that could.

The closing chapter of this section, written by Dr. Nancy Fahrenwald, gives readers insight into organ donation research with American Indian, Alaska Native, and First Nations Communities. It describes features such as the long-term commitment and collaboration needed to engage in successful research with these communities. Readers are warned to avoid being seen as "helicopter researchers" and are provided with practical advice for intervention development and implementation. Dr. Fahrenwald presents process and outcome data from an intervention, guided by the transtheoretical model, that serves as an excellent example of community-based participatory research. As reported by the author, key outcomes include findings such as the following: "Over 50% of all of the participants progressed in their intention to serve as an organ or tissue donor, whereas just over 40% remained unchanged in their intentions."

Part 2: Organizational Interventions

This section focuses on organizational interventions. These interventions do not target an entire community but rather a specific organization or group of organizations such as home care workers, students, nurses, or funeral directors.

Dr. Diane Dodd-McCue kicks off this section with a chapter focused on behavioral research in hospital settings. She begins with an introduction of the Family Communication Coordinator Protocol, which is designed to improve the level of care provided to potential donor families. As stated by Dodd-McCue, "Evaluation of the protocol required examination of theoretical frameworks and constructs rarely considered in the organ donation realm. These approaches are unique in that the focus is not on typical outcome measures such as donor conversion rates, but rather on what can be considered collateral outcomes feeding back into the system." These perspectives include role stress and work attitudes with an individual focus, stakeholder analysis with the organizational environment as the level of analysis, and systems theory with the organ donation team as the level of analysis.

Dr. Michael Quinn and colleagues offer additional insight and outcomes associated with organ donor workplace interventions. The chapter begins with a presentation of the benefits as well as the real-world challenges in the design and evaluation of worksite organ donation efforts. The narrative then turns to Quinn et al.'s brief, multicomponent, multisite workplace study. Grounded in the transtheoretical model, the intervention, designed as a randomized controlled trial with three treatment conditions, sought to raise social consciousness, highlight personal benefits, refute myths, and provide specific action strategies regarding organ donation. Among the outcomes presented, "Over baseline, increases in organ donation intention in the basic and enhanced intervention groups were approximately 30%, whereas control group increases were only 17%."

Drs. Carolyn C. Johnson and Larry S. Webber provide the next chapter, which "describes the development, implementation, and evaluation of a Donate Life Workplace Partnership for the purpose of increasing intent to donate through participation in the Louisiana donor registry." A catastrophic event in the form of Hurricane Katrina challenged the evaluators and project directors, but the project persevered. Guided by the diffusion of innovation theory and teamed with the Home Care Association of Louisiana (HCLA), Drs. Johnson and Webber describe Donate Life Workplace Partnership programs followed by the specific path they took in implementing their intervention and adjusting to natural disasters. As stated by the authors, "To date, almost 700 completed registrations have been obtained from individuals in the home health care industry through the efforts of the HCLA Donate Life Workplace Partnership." They conclude their chapter with a brief but poignant mention of the lack of recognition of organ donation research at national conferences and meetings of professional health organizations.

The next chapter, penned by Dr. Tom Feeley and colleagues, presents evaluative data for a 3-year multicampus classroom intervention designed to promote organ and tissue donation. This unique intervention uses active learning as a persuasive technique by targeting members of a college class who are challenged with increasing an organ donor campaign for their college campus. Presented in this chapter is information about the design and implementation of the course as well as outcomes in the form of registration behavior and survey results. This approach is intriguing not least for the potential it offers for those interested in developing a cadre of trained and enthusiastic donation advocates. The authors note key outcomes such as the following: "Over the course of the semester . . .

students reported demonstrable gains in knowledge, increases in positive attitudes toward donation, and greater intentions to become organ donors."

The volume turns next to the tension between funeral directors and organ procurement professionals. Catherine Paykin and colleagues present an explanation for the conflict and describe an intervention designed to improve relations between the two groups. A detailed description of the intervention highlights the challenges of applied research. Lessons put forth as a result of this intervention are useful for working with any group of professionals whose cooperation can help or hinder the donation process.

Dr. Morgan closes the section with a chapter drawing exclusively from her prior experiences in intervention implementation. She offers a detailed presentation of her perspective on challenges associated with collaborations with community partners, gaining and maintaining intervention site access while weathering varied difficulties, and maintaining intervention fidelity. The lessons learned from Dr. Morgan's spirited discussion of her experiences with community partners can guide others seeking to maximize the successful implementation of organ donor campaigns, particularly in the workplace context.

Broad Perspectives and Future Directions

This final section includes chapters devoted to pursuing issues of broad import to organ donation and other applied research endeavors. Key issues in theory, measurement, and research methods are addressed in detail, and future directions for organ donation research are highlighted.

The section commences with a chapter coauthored by Sara Pace Jones and Dave Bosch. They present a view of organ donation research from the perspective of two experienced organ donation education professionals. They highlight important considerations such as the benefits of grant-funded research, community organization perspectives on applied research, and collaborating with researchers. This chapter is highly relevant for community professionals seeking involvement in research as well as for researchers involved with community partners.

Dr. Rob Fischer follows with a review of the state of the art regarding the evaluation of organ donation promotion strategies. Organ donor interventions are diverse in their range of targeted populations, venues, and modalities. Evaluating these strategies requires attention to a wide range of methodological and contextual factors. Dr. Fischer offers a comparison of intervention models and a discussion of different intervention settings. The chapter wraps up with a discussion of the challenges of conducting evaluation research on interventions aimed at increasing organ and tissue donation.

Dr. Anita Pomerantz offers a compelling argument for greater use of qualitative studies in organ donor research. The chapter begins with a discussion of the importance of studying interpersonal discussions about sensitive health-related topics, including the functions served by interpersonal discussions about health topics. An introduction to qualitative methods, with particular emphasis on conversation analysis, follows. The chapter concludes with the results of a conversation analytic study of family discussions of organ and tissue donation. Research questions such as "What practices did the participants use to comfortably raise the topic of donation?" are answered based on a conversation analysis of 57 taped conversation of families discussing donation.

Drs. Waterman and Rodrigue present information on an area of organ donation that has received minimal attention from social and behavioral scientists: living organ donation. This chapter begins by addressing ethical issues and then moves on to discuss current approaches for advancing living donation. Attempts to increase living donation such as paired exchange and reimbursement of living donor expenses are explained, and a framework based on Uri Bronfenbrenner's ecological systems theory is presented. The authors conclude by drawing attention to the need for "a strong theoretical and research foundation, in partnership with health professionals and agencies serving kidney recipients and donors," in order to maximize the likelihood for success in living donation.

In the penultimate chapter, we bring together several years of research conducted with the Donor Network of Arizona. The main project focused on organ donor registration via computer kiosks. Efforts to motivate registrations led to rates from .0005% to 50%. Four factors are proposed as determining the success of the different projects: (a) immediate opportunity, (b) information, (c) favorable activation, and (d) focused engagement. We draw to a close by suggesting donor registration rates would benefit if studies can pinpoint the contexts where the three factors can simultaneously exist as well as identify the underlying patterns of activation leading to maximum registrations.

The book concludes with reflections by Dr. William D. Crano, Oskamp Professor of Psychology at Claremont Graduate University. Dr. Crano brings wisdom from his 40-plus-year career to bear on the past and future of organ donor research. Discussing the writings of Kurt Lewin and Don Campbell, a historical perspective on science and theory is presented. Touting the success of the past and the potential for the future, Dr. Crano offers sage advice regarding the dire opportunity that is the field of organ donation.

Acknowledgments

This book is the result of a one-day symposium on applied social psychology. Researchers and practitioners came together from across the United States to discuss the latest findings and developments in the field of organ donation research. The words of the presenters, as well as other leaders in the field, are found within.

First and foremost, we thank the contributors. Some contributors come from academia, some from the "real world," but all took time and effort to create a volume that will draw attention to the need for applied research directed at resolving the organ donation crisis faced by the United States and many other countries. Special thanks to those who contributed to the peer review process: Drs. Margaret Allen, Diane-Dodd McCue, Kim Downing, Nancy Fahrenwald, Thomas Feeley, Anita Pomerantz, and Amy Waterman.

It also gives us pleasure to acknowledge the support of Claremont Graduate University (CGU) and particularly the School of Organizational and Behavioral Sciences, Dean Stewart Donaldson, Allen Omoto, and the founder of the Applied Social Psychology Research Symposium, Dr. Stuart Oskamp. We are honored to be part of this prestigious tradition of scholarship.

The symposium itself would not have occurred without the dedication of Paul Thomas and a host of hardworking graduate students. We are particularly grateful to Zachary Hohman and Dana Turcotte for their assistance in planning and implementation. Thanks to Erica Rosenthal for her willingness to share her knowledge, experience, and materials with us.

We were also the beneficiaries of assistance provided by the graduate students of the Health Psychology and Prevention Science Institute at CGU: Crystal Coyazo, Lori Garner, Ian Johnson, Amelia Gonzalez, Andrew Lac, Chris Lamb, Erin Keely O'Brien, Valerie Okelola, Neil Patel, David Rast, Benjamin Seifert, Jessica Skenderian, and Erica Wedlock.

Our appreciation goes to Chris Cardone and Constance Adler for their persistence and patience. Our editorial assistant, Zachary Hohman, will hopefully take pride in his ability to keep us on track and organized. The project would not have been possible without his help.

We would also express gratitude to Sara Pace Jones for introducing us to the world of organ donation and transplantation nearly a decade ago and for being an incredible partner across a number of collaborative research projects. Our appreciation is also directed at Mary Ganikos and her team at the Division of Transplantation, Health Resources and Services Administration (HRSA/DoT), for their continued support and for helping us round up a decade's worth of project reports and other documents related to the Social and Behavioral Grant Program at HRSA.

Lastly, our sincere thanks go to Dr. William D. Crano for his unwavering support and mentorship.

Introduction and Overview

Applying Psychology to Health Behavior Interventions

Not Last Decade's Approach

Stuart Oskamp

The focus of this volume is on organ donation, an emergent area in health psychology. My goal in this introductory chapter is to provide some historical and disciplinary context for this new field. I had originally considered as a subtitle "Not Your Dad's (or Mom's) Research Approach." However, as I delved into the literature, I soon realized that this field began much more recently than a generation ago—indeed, mostly in the last decade.

As a social psychologist with a strong applied orientation, but not a health psychologist per se, I sought a source that would provide some background on the area of organ donation. Hence, I consulted two classic volumes on health psychology. The first was Shelley Taylor's seminal textbook, *Health Psychology* (2nd ed.), published in 1991. I found that its index had no listing of *organ* or of *donation*. It did list *liver* and *kidney*, but only in a brief section that explained how these organs work in the processes of digestion and excretion. However, I reasoned, that book is now over 15 years old, so perhaps a newer volume might give a summary of research on organ donation.

So next I consulted the massive, multivolume series entitled *Handbook of Psychology*, published by Wiley in 2003—specifically, volume 9, *Health Psychology*, which is over 660 pages in length (Nezu, Nezu, & Geller, 2003). But again I found that its index did not list either *organ* or *donation*. Also, its chapter headings gave no indication that research on organ donation would fit within any of their purviews. Hmmm! I began to wonder—maybe *there is no research* in this field. Can that be true?

Thus, to begin the process of contextualization, I retreated to the broader area of applied social psychology—specifically, my own text in that field (Oskamp & Schultz, 1998). Of course, its subject index didn't list *organ* or *donation* either! However, its chapters on various research methods and on health and health care did help me begin to fit the topic of organ donation into a broader perspective.

First of all, our topic is one area of applied psychological research on health behavior. Applied psychological research can and often does use any of the research methods of psychology. These methods include

- laboratory experiments, which manipulate independent variables in highly controlled situations and use precise measurements of their dependent variables, with the goal of showing clear-cut causal relationships between a treatment and an outcome.
- correlational studies, which measure and compare the levels of two or more variables that may or may not be causally related, but do not manipulate either one.
- evaluation research, conducted to determine the operation and effectiveness of a treatment program or policy as it functions in everyday practice.
- sample surveys, which study the levels of variables in a (we hope) carefully chosen and representative sample of individuals.
- epidemiological reviews, which survey vast numbers of people to determine what proportion have had a given medical or physical condition.

Whatever the particular research method that is used, most research on health psychology and health care issues is *field research*—that is, it studies human behavior directly as it occurs in natural, real-life settings. That feature often adds a considerable level of difficulty, as health researchers can unhappily attest.

But our topic of organ donation is not merely one area of field research. It is special in that it involves *an intervention*. It not only studies people's behavior as it naturally occurs but also tries to persuade people to volunteer for a medical procedure, and aspects of that procedure can be emotionally charged and highly important both to them and to others.

Issues in Conducting Field Research on Health Behavior

Let's consider in greater detail many of the characteristics of field research and health interventions that may become issues in conducting research on organ donations:

- An initial issue is simply *obtaining respondents* to survey studies of health behavior—for instance, epidemiological studies on the extent of organ donation needs or organ donorship.
- Next, it is important to insure that these respondents are *representative* members of some group of interest, rather than self-selected, atypical individuals, who would not yield valid, useful data.
- Then, how should instructions be worded and organized for data collectors and for respondents in order to obtain the most useful and valid information?

- In an intervention to persuade people to become organ donors, what persuasive techniques are acceptable, and how should they be framed, both for clarity and for maximum effectiveness?
- Should an intervention be designed as a direct test of a theoretical viewpoint, or, alternatively, should it be a "big-bang" or "kitchen sink" kind of intervention, which includes several different types of influencing factors?
- What *control conditions* should be used for comparison to see whether the intervention had a significant effect? Related to this, are there any *artifacts*, stemming from the research procedure or comparisons, which would distort the meaning of the obtained significant findings? A similar question considers the likelihood of *interaction effects* between the intervention and other variables (which may often be unstudied ones)—such as the intervention working well for one type of target person but not for others (e.g., highly educated versus less educated, or individuals from different ethnic or cultural backgrounds).
- Beyond significance, what was the *size* of the obtained effect? In practical terms, what would be its degree of payoff, for instance in number of additional donors or their appropriateness?
- It is also important to consider possible problems of *self-report inaccuracy* and *attitude versus behavior differences*. It may be much easier to agree to donate an organ than to actually follow through, despite the best of intentions. What evidence is there about the behavioral follow-through of people who register as potential donors?
- What are the *costs*—both financial costs and nonquantitative social and personal costs—of the intervention program? And, in a cost–benefit analysis, do the benefits appear to outweigh or justify the costs?
- Going beyond the immediate effects, what *long-term effects* of the intervention can be determined—both effects on the organ donors (or even on people exposed to the intervention who remained nondonors) and effects on donation recipients (and possibly on their families as well)?
- What *ethical issues* are raised by the research—for instance, the possibility of harmful consequences, the question of truly informed consent, and the issue of deception in the procedures? Particularly important for research on organ donation is the possibility of negative impacts of the intervention, and the severity of any such impacts.

The questions listed above are ones that stem from research methodology and research ethics. However, there are other questions that arise because of the nature of the U.S. health care system—or *nonsystem*, as if has often been called. Of course, we are all aware that the United States has no program of universal health care for all citizens, and as a result well over 40 million of our citizens have no medical insurance or other means of accessing regular medical care. In the absence of a federal health care system, many states apply different decision standards, and greatly different levels of funding, to their residents' medical care. In addition, socioeconomic levels of geographic areas have a great influence on the number and quality of hospitals there and the accessibility of medical care in general. For people who do have medical coverage within any given area, different competing systems of managed care often have widely different standards and costs for the same medical procedures. Undoubtedly, all of these factors have major impacts on the availability and the costs of such high-tech procedures as organ donations.

Persuasion Approaches and Framing of the Intervention Appeal

Now let us change the topic and consider approaches to persuasion. Getting a person to sign an organ donation register is certainly a high-stakes persuasion task, and accomplishing it should be aided by following principles of persuasion that have been developed in the past 70 years of social psychological research. Some of the main theories of persuasion and attitude and behavior change are briefly described below, and a succinct summary of some of the research findings about persuasion principles has been provided by Nicholson (2007).

A theory that describes the process of behavioral change in general, rather than variables that produce it, is the transtheoretical model of behavior change (Prochaska, DiClemente, & Norcross, 1992). Two of its main contributions are the propositions that behavior change is a continuum rather than a single discrete action, and that different interventions may be needed for moving individuals forward who are lower on the continuum than for those who are higher on the continuum. The model specifies five stages that form a continuum of change that is applicable in any realm of health behavior. The stages are (a) *precontemplation*, where individuals have no thought or intention of adopting a healthprotective behavior (e.g., using condoms during vaginal intercourse); (b) *contemplation*, where they form an intention to adopt the behavior sometime in the future; (c) *preparation*, where the intended adoption date is imminent, and exploratory or trial attempts may be made; (d) *action*, where the new behavior is adopted; and (e) *maintenance*, where it becomes a routine part of life. When research is done with large samples, a difference as small as one quarter of a stage of change may be statistically significant; and with small samples, even seemingly small differences may be statistically significant. This is equivalent to one fourth of the respondents moving, for instance, from contemplation to preparation, a degree of change that is far short of most of the sample reaching the action stage (e.g., Fishbein et al., 1996).

Two other widely used and closely related theories of attitude and behavior change are the theory of reasoned action (TRA; Fishbein & Ajzen, 1975) and the theory of planned behavior (TPB; Ajzen, 1991). As its name implies, the theory of reasoned action holds that people normally take actions that seem reasonable from their point of view. It posits that the only important determinant of someone's volitional behavior is the person's *intention* to take a particular action at a particular time. Two main components are specified as contributing to intentions: the person's *attitude* toward the behavior, and his or her *subjective norm* about what relevant other people think he or she should do. In turn, each of these components is a compound of the person's salient beliefs about the behavior and his or her evaluations (e.g., evaluations of various specific consequences of his or her acting in that way).

Ajzen's (1991) theory of planned behavior revised the TRA by adding one other factor—*perceived behavioral control*—that helps to determine whether individuals will act in accordance with their attitudes and subjective normative pressures. As an example, if you don't think your behavior has a chance of accomplishing a desired goal (i.e., you feel you have no behavioral control over losing 100 pounds), you are not likely even to try to reach the goal. In some situations, research has found that perceived control can be an independent predictor of behavior, rather than acting only through intentions (Armitage & Conner, 2001). Much research on health behavior, including studies on organ donation, has used the TRA and/or the TPB as a basis for interventions and predictions of outcomes.

A central theory in recent persuasion research is the *elaboration likelihood model*, advanced by Richard Petty and John Cacioppo (1981). It proposes that people are not just passive targets of persuasion, but rather they react actively to persuasion attempts, generating cognitive responses (that is, thoughts) that are favorable or unfavorable to the incoming message. Importantly, the theory holds that it is not the incoming message per se, but rather the balance of the recipient's favorable and unfavorable elaborations of its points, that determines whether the person will be persuaded or not.

Moreover, the theory proposes two routes that both lead to persuasion, but in different ways. The *central route* focuses on the information and arguments contained in the persuasive message, which are analyzed logically by the recipient. If the source is a credible one and the arguments seem strong, the recipient's cognitive responses are likely to be favorable, and persuasion will occur. The *peripheral route* relies much less on logical thinking and more on the recipient's emotions and feelings about the message. It is more likely to be used if the recipient is low in information, interest, motivation, or ability to analyze the message content. Then peripheral cues, rather than the arguments in the message, assume more importance. These may include the source's attractiveness or likeability, the slick production or humorous content of the message, or the happy or exciting emotions that it arouses. Because the peripheral route is cognitively "lazy," a cute slogan or a sexy model may have more persuasive effect than a strong, well-reasoned argument.

Since the goal of organ donation is an important one to both parties in the exchange—often one involving life-or-death consequences—we should hope that people will make their decisions concerning it by the central route of reasoned thought. That fact determines that our interventions should be aimed *primarily* at the recipient's central processing reactions, not at his or her casual peripheral responses such as transitory feelings. This focus is also desirable because persuasion via the central route is usually *stronger, more lasting,* and *more resistant to counterattack* than is peripheral-route persuasion. Nevertheless, it is wise to maximize peripheral cues in the persuasive message as well, such as the attractiveness of the communicator and the artistic quality and clarity of the message.

In this brief overview, it is worth mentioning two other books that offer additional ways of looking at the persuasion process. Robert Cialdini's *Influence: Science and Practice* (1993) suggests six categories of psychological principles that underlie persuasive influence. They are as follows:

1. Consistency: following through on our own public commitments or past behavior
2. Reciprocation: doing things for others who have rewarded us, or who we think will do so
3. Social proof: following the example set by others around us
4. Authority: trusting and complying with people we think are experts or legitimate authorities
5. Liking: agreeing with and following people whom we like
6. Scarcity: preferring and desiring things that seem to be less available or time limited.

Another book is *Made to Stick* by Chip Heath and Dan Heath (2007). It describes six qualities that are evident in communications that "stick" in the listener's mind, such as highly effective stories or communications. As described by Nicholson (2007, p. 19), they are

1. Simplicity: the message should be as brief as possible but still be profound;
2. Unexpectedness: the message should surprise the audience so that they pay attention;
3. Concreteness: the message should not contain meaningless jargon, but rather use concrete details and examples that are based in real experience;
4. Credibility: the message should be delivered by a trustworthy source;
5. Emotions: the message should make the audience feel something; and
6. Stories: the message should be in narrative form, something that can be retold and imagined.

Another important consideration in persuasion research is how to *frame* the advantages stated in the persuasive message. Alex Rothman and Peter Salovey (1997) have done extensive research on what they call gain-framed or loss-framed messages. Their findings show that persuading someone to undertake a *preventative* behavior, such as getting a flu shot, will be most effective if the message emphasizes the *benefits* of getting the shot. But in persuading someone to engage in *detection* of a disease, such as cervical cancer, the message will be most effective if it highlights the potential *loss* or *negative consequences* of not getting tested.

These research findings grew out of the model of human decision making that has been termed *prospect theory* (Kahneman & Tversky, 1988). Kahneman and Tversky's research findings showed that people are usually more likely to take risks (that is, to choose an option whose chance of paying off is less than 100%) when the options are stated in terms of losses "but less likely to take risks when they are given options in terms of gains. . . . Basically, people tend to take risks when there is something to lose, but tend not to take risks when there is something to gain" (Nicholson, 2007, p. 18).

Unfortunately, it is not clear how to apply these findings to the area of organ donation. First of all, there are two classes of donations: ones after the donor's death, and ones made while the donor is living. Donating an organ seems to be neither a preventative act (for the donor) nor a detection act, because the disease state of the potential recipient is already well-known. Receiving the organ transplant *is* clearly a preventative act *for the recipient*. Perhaps, therefore, if the donor is highly identified with the donee, such as the donee being a nuclear family member or a close friend, donation of an organ might be considered a preventative act *for the donor* (i.e., to the extent that his or her identity overlaps with that of the donee). In that case, Rothman and Salovey's (1997) findings would indicate that the persuasive message should be stated in terms of possible gain to the recipient (as well as to the donor), rather than in terms of the loss to the potential donee without a transplant. This point leads to a simple research question: Is that what is usually done in soliciting donors?

In the case of donations after death, one might extend this reasoning to donations to any recipient, not just family members or friends—that is, there may be some overlap of identities because both parties are human beings, with feelings and hopes and dreams in common. However, the case of *living donation* of organs seems more complex than just suggested, for there the donor clearly is accepting some risk of bad consequences to him or herself. In that situation, Kahneman and Tversky's (1988) findings seem to suggest that the persuasive appeal should *not* be framed in terms of gains to the donee (or to the donor), but rather in terms of the losses that the potential donee will suffer without a donation. However, because there is some risk to the donor, it would seem that the losses to the potential donee without a donation should be described as much greater than the possible losses to the donor. Again, these points lead to a simple research question: Which of these opposing approaches is usually used in soli-citing organ donations, or is there any established practice in this area? And furthermore, is there any research evidence about which approach is more successful? These and many other questions about "best practices" in the field of organ donation seem ripe for research.

Some Findings of Research on Organ Donation

Now let's return briefly to the initial question in this chapter of when research on organ donation began. In my literature search, I found that the U.S. Health Resources and Services Administration's (HRSA) program of extramural grants to increase organ and tissue donations began in 1999. Among the researchers who have worked in this area, my colleagues at Claremont Graduate University, Professors William Crano, Eusebio Alvaro, and Jason Siegel, began conducting research on organ donation almost 10 years ago, so my subtitle "Not Last Decade's Approach" seems just about right.

During this time, these researchers from Claremont, California, have studied a number of aspects of organ donation extensively and produced many replicated and useful findings. For instance, they have launched donor registries, and used experimental and quasi-experimental methods to test what medium and type of appeal were most effective in increasing registrations. They have tested TV ads, radio ads, billboards, kiosks placed in a variety of institutional locations, e-mails, and hotline calls as ways of generating donor registrations. They have compared the effectiveness of several different types of message appeals, as well as of messages produced by the National Coalition on Organ Donation. They have used several major cities as control communities to assess the success of appeals, and replicated their campaign findings in other cities. They have studied dependent variables of donation beliefs and family discussions on the topic, as well as donor registrations. They have studied both Hispanic and Anglo populations, are currently adding groups of African Americans and Asian Americans, and have conducted campaigns for both nonliving and living organ donations with Hispanic Americans. That is an impressive list of research topics and populations.

To add to these research findings, let me cite some bits of knowledge that I picked up recently from television programs. It is certainly gratifying that major TV programs are beginning to present useful information about the need for organ donations and the process of donating. In February 2007, a program in the PBS series *California Connected* reported on organ donations, particularly liver donations, in California. It stated that less than one third of the 92,000 people then on the national waiting list for a new organ would have a transplant opera-tion within a year, and that typically one third of those on the waiting list would die before having an operation. In some California hospitals, as many as 58% of waiting list patients had to wait for *3 years* before an operation, whereas in other hospitals the figure was as low as 14%. The program also discussed patients going overseas for transplants, and stated that in China the care was good and the cost only one third of that in California. Obviously, that information is selective and may not be reliable, but it dramatically illustrates how far some patients are willing to go to get a transplant.

Another program, in March 2007 on ABC, had a number of discussions with the anchor, who was planning to donate a kidney to someone; and then a few days later, the anchor returned to the program and reported on his own experience and that of the person who received his kidney. Certainly this kind of empathic discussion on TV should be a help in raising awareness of the need for organ donations and of the safety of the operation. I have not learned whether any empirical research was done on public responses to the program, but such findings might be a profitable indication of public response to the issue of organ adoptions.

The chapters that follow provide many additional examples of research approaches and valuable findings concerning the process of organ adoption.

References

Ajzen, I. (1991). The theory of planned behavior. *Organizational Behavior and Human Decision Processes, 50,* 179–211.

Armitage, C., & Conner, M. (2001). Efficacy of the theory of planned behaviour: A meta-analytic review. *British Journal of Social Psychology, 40,* 471–499.

Cialdini, R. B. (1993). *Influence: Science and practice* (3rd ed.). New York: HarperCollins.

Fishbein, M., & Ajzen, I. (1975). *Belief, attitude, intention, and behavior: An introduction to theory and research.* Reading, MA: Addison-Wesley.

Fishbein, M., Guenther-Grey, C., Johnson, W. D., Wolitski, R. J., McAlister, A., Rietmeijer, C. A., et al. (1996). Using a theory-based community intervention to reduce AIDS risk behaviors: The CDC's AIDS community demonstration projects. In S. Oskamp & S. C. Thompson (Eds.), *Understanding and preventing HIV risk behavior* (pp. 177–206). Thousand Oaks, CA: Sage.

Heath, C., & Heath, D. (2007). *Made to stick: Why some ideas survive and others die.* New York: Random House.

Kahneman, D., & Tversky, A. (1988). Prospect theory: An analysis of decision under risk. In P. Gardenfors & N. Sahlin (Eds.) *Decision, probability, and utility: Selected readings* (pp. 183–214). New York: Cambridge University Press.

Nezu, A. M., Nezu, C. M., & Geller, P. A. (Eds.) (2003). *Handbook of psychology: Vol. 9. Health psychology* (I. B. Weiner, Ed.). New York: Wiley.

Nicholson, C. (2007, January). Framing science: Advances in theory and technology are fueling a new era in the science of persuasion. *APS Observer, 20*(1), 16–21.

Oskamp, S., & Schultz, P. W. (1998). *Applied social psychology* (2nd ed.). Upper Saddle River, NJ: Prentice Hall.

Petty, R. E., & Cacioppo, J. T. (1981). *Attitudes and persuasion: Classic and contemporary approaches*. Dubuque, IA: Brown.

Prochaska, J. O., DiClemente, C. C., & Norcross, J. C. (1992). In search of how people change: Applications to addictive behaviors. *American Psychologist, 47*, 1102–1114.

Rothman, A., & Salovey, P. (1997). Shaping perceptions to motivate healthy behavior: The role of message framing. *Psychological Bulletin, 121*, 3–19.

Taylor, S. E. (1991). *Health psychology* (2nd ed.). New York; McGraw-Hill.

2

Organ Donation

An Overview of the Field

Mary Ganikos

Introduction

I am delighted to provide the overview chapter for this foundational text on organ donation research as it is an honor to be asked by these accomplished editors. To my knowledge, this is the first book that focuses exclusively on rigorous and methodologically sound applied research on increasing donation. It is an exciting milestone that there now exists a sufficient number of sophisticated data-based investigations on increasing organ donation to assemble a book of this nature. The publication of this book is a testament to the dedication of these editors, authors, and others to resolving the problem of insufficient organ donation.

The intent of this chapter is to provide an overview of organ donation and transplantation. A snapshot of basic issues in the transplant field may help readers better understand the studies and strategies in this book. If this is your first foray into the exciting field of donation and transplantation, all the new names, organizations, acronyms, terms, and concepts might be challenging (see Appendix 2.1).

I hope that this chapter will provide a smooth transition to the main content of this book and that the book as a whole will leave you with a greater appreciation for the miracle that is transplantation. I also hope that the scientists among you will share our excitement and will join the relatively small cadre of social and behavioral researchers who are using scientific methods to confront the challenge of increasing donation.

Transplantation has come a long way, from initial experimentation to the daily practice of life-saving surgery. What began with the ability to transplant a single kidney from one identical twin to the other has evolved into the ability to transplant eight organs from one deceased donor into as many as nine distinct people, saving each of their lives. More than 400,000 transplant procedures have been performed since 1988, and approximately 200,000 organ recipients are alive today (U.S. Organ Procurement and Transplantation Network [OPTN], 2007), enjoying family and friends, having babies, pursuing careers, climbing mountains, and running marathons. One young man, for example, won an Olympic bronze medal in snowboarding 18 months after a liver transplant. A kidney recipient helped his team win the National Basketball Association 2006 championship game. People of all ages, ethnicities, cultures, socioeconomic backgrounds, and religions are now living healthy lives through transplantation. Organ transplantation, although a complex surgical practice, is a routine and effective procedure for terminally ill patients with no other alternative.

Why Are Transplants Needed?

People need transplants because an organ that they need to continue living is failing to function. Many diseases and conditions can lead to end-stage organ failure. For example, diabetes and hypertension can result in kidney failure. Liver failure can be caused by acute or chronic hepatitis, cancer, or alcohol abuse. Hypertension, congenital disorders, and valvular heart disease can lead to heart failure. Lung failure can result from chronic obstructive pulmonary disease and/or pulmonary hypertension.

In addition to enhancing the quality of life, transplantation can give many years to a recipient who otherwise would have died. Immunosuppressive drugs and technological advances have improved recipient longevity: 80.6% of patients who received a deceased donor kidney in 2000 were still living 5 years later, as were 73.6% of liver and 74.4% of heart recipients (ustransplant.org, 2007).

Quality of life is also enhanced by tissue transplantation. Corneas give vision to a blind person. Ligaments restore mobility. A heart valve replacement restores function to a defective heart. Skin can repair burns and scars. Bone mends a broken or malformed jaw. In all, more than 900,000 tissue transplants are performed each year (Musculoskeletal Transplant Foundation, 2006).

The benefits of each transplant procedure extend beyond providing life anew for the organ recipient; transplantation affects families, friends, colleagues, and others. Considering that one deceased organ donor can potentially save nine lives, and improve 50 or more lives with donated tissues, the number of people affected by any one donor is substantial.

Anecdotal and reported evidence (National Kidney Foundation, 2000) indicates that, besides benefits to recipients and their families and friends, organ donation and transplantation help the donors' surviving loved ones. Knowing that their loved one's gift saved or enhanced the life of even one other individual provides comfort to the bereaved. They can appreciate and treasure the thought that something positive resulted from an otherwise traumatic situation, creating a legacy for their loved one.

Despite its far-reaching benefits, transplantation is not available to all who need it. The potential of this life-saving procedure is limited by an insufficient supply of donated organs. As of August 2009, nearly 103,000 patients were on the national waiting list for organs (OPTN, 2009). However, the total number of deceased donors in 2008 was 7,984 (OPTN, 2009). In 2008, 14,198 living and deceased donors enabled 27,958 transplants to occur. Another 6,782 patients died waiting for an organ (OPTN, 2009).

The donor shortage is simultaneously simple and complex. The simplicity lies in that it is easily identified as the most crucial problem in transplantation today. It is complex due to the need to understand the attitudes, beliefs, and motivation that prevent people from committing to be donors, and to identify, implement, and rigorously evaluate strategies to combat those barriers and increase public donor enrollment (see Siegel, Alvaro Hohman, this volume).

What Can Be Donated?

Organs and tissues can be donated from deceased donors. Organs – and in rare cases, tissues – also are donated by living individuals. Deceased donors can provide more organs and tissues than living donors can (OPTN, 2009). Not everyone who dies, however, is eligible to donate. Only deaths that occur in a hospital where organs can be kept viable by artificial means may be considered for organ donation (OPTN, 2009). Tissues and corneas can be obtained from deaths that occur both inside and outside the hospital setting. Some health conditions may preclude donation.

Deceased donors can provide six types of organs: kidney, heart, lung, liver, pancreas, and small bowel (small intestine) (OPTN, 2009). Tissues that can be provided by deceased donors include: bone, skin, corneas, middle ear, heart valves, veins, cartilage, tendons, and ligaments. Unlike organs, most tissues can be stored and used when needed (OPTN, 2009).

Living donors can provide a kidney or a lobe (section) of a lung or a liver. When a liver lobe is donated, the donor's liver regenerates, quickly regaining its original size (OPTN, 2009). When a living donor provides a kidney, the remaining kidney will increase in size and perform about 80% of the function of two kidneys (OPTN, 2009). Tissues that can be donated by living donors include amnion after childbirth, skin after certain surgeries (e.g., abdominoplasties), and bone after hip or knee replacements. While living, people also can donate life-saving blood, blood stem cells and cord blood; however, while vitally important, they are not the focus of this book.

Deceased Donation: Who Makes It Happen?

Many organizations are involved in the donation trajectory and are described in Appendix 2.1. Before reading on, it may be useful to review Appendix 2.1 to familiarize yourself with the public and private organizations enabling the donation and transplantation process.

How Does It Happen?

Deceased donation takes place in a hospital after an individual has been declared dead. An important point to remember is that the team of medical professionals trying to save an individual's life in the hospital differs from the transplant team. The former has one goal, to save that life. When all possible attempts have been exhausted and death is imminent or declared, the hospital notifies the local organ procurement organization (OPO) while continuing to mechanically oxygenate the organs pending consideration for donation.

OPO professionals determine whether the deceased is medically suitable to be a donor and obtain consent for donation. A transplant team may not recover organs without legal consent, which is obtained in one of two ways. In states that practice *first-person consent*, the deceased's predeath designation as a donor serves as legal consent authorizing the transplant team to proceed. Common tools for indicating one's predeath donor designation are donor registries and driver's licenses. In states where first-person consent is not practiced or where a pre-authorization tool, such as a driver's license, is unavailable, OPO staff must obtain consent from next of kin (OPTN, 2009).

Once consent is obtained, OPO professionals let the surgeons and other recovery team members know that there is a donor. The OPO submits critical information about the donor (e.g., blood type, height, weight, gender, and age) to the Organ Procurement and Transplantation Network (OPTN), the national system that facilitates organ matching and allocation administered by the United Network for Organ Sharing (UNOS) under contract to the U.S. Department of Health and Human Services. The donor's information is entered into the OPTN computer system which contains the same type of information for each wait-listed patient. The computer identifies compatible patients and generates a "match list" prioritizing patients for each donated organ. Patients who are to receive the organs are notified by their transplant team that an organ is available and told when to go to their hospital to prepare for surgery. Transplant surgeons remove the donor's organs in an operating room under standard sterile surgical conditions. OPOs prepare each organ for transport according to standard preservation procedures for that organ and arrange for ground or air transportation of viable organs to appropriate transplant hospitals. Surgical teams then implant the organs into the intended recipients.

Registering to Be a Deceased Organ Donor

For many years, the only means people had for indicating their wish to donate was to sign and carry a donor card, indicate their wish on their driver's license or will, and notify their family, doctor, faith leader, or friends of their intentions. Although it is important to cover all those bases, they share one key liability: Availability at the individual's time of death is questionable. Wallets carrying donor cards and driver's licenses may be lost. A will is usually unavailable at the time of death, and next of kin may be difficult to locate. The unfortunate result is that some people who stipulated their donation wish in these ways may not at the critical moment have the authorization needed for donation. Once death is declared, there is a short window of opportunity for recovering organs, so a reliable method for obtaining consent is essential.

The most reliable method of obtaining, storing, and retrieving an individual's wish to donate is a donor registry (an electronic database). Introduced in Illinois in 1993 and then in Pennsylvania in 1994, today all states, the District of Columbia, and Puerto Rico have registries capturing residents' donation decisions, which are available to appropriate recovery personnel on a 24/7 basis (Organ Donor, 2009). Most registries are affiliated with the state's department of motor vehicles (DMV), enabling enrollment when residents obtain or renew their license. Although many states also support an online enrollment capability, the majority of enrollments occur at licensing agencies. LifeNet Health in Virginia, for example, has reported that monthly online registry enrollments reach a high of about 150, whereas DMV enrollments average about 10,000 to 12,000 per month (organdonor.gov 2009). Colorado and Utah both report that 97% to 100% of people on the registry who die and are medically eligible actually become donors (organdonor.gov 2009).

Living Donation

During the past 15 years, living donation has become an increasingly frequent alternative to deceased donation (OPTN, 2009). In the majority of cases, each donor provides one organ: a kidney or a lobe of a lung or liver. Some organs, such as the heart and a set of lungs, can be provided only by deceased donors. In 2001, the number of living donors (6,610) surpassed the number of deceased donors (6,080) for the first time and continued to outpace deceased donation until 2004 (OPTN, 2009). Despite a recent downturn, living donation remains a viable alternative. Several factors have contributed to the increase in living donation: the expanding gap between the number of patients needing a transplant and the number of deceased donors, greater public awareness of living donation, and an increase in laparoscopic (camera-assisted) surgeries. Before laparoscopy, removal of a kidney involved a major incision partially around the donor's abdominal area and an extended and uncomfortable recovery period. Laparoscopic kidney recovery requires a few small incisions and a substantially shortened and easier recovery.

Advantages of Living Donation

The availability of a willing and medically suitable living donor offers several advantages for a recipient. Most notably, the recipient is assured of receiving a life-saving transplant. Moreover, because the organ spends less time outside the body (ischemic time), its integrity is better maintained (OPTN, 2009). Also, recipients with living donors can usually be transplanted sooner thereby increasing the likelihood of a successful outcome (OPTN, 2009). These patients do not have to be wait-listed for an organ and endure the mental anguish of wondering whether an organ will become available. Also, by the time an organ becomes available, the potential recipient might be too sick to with-stand the transplant surgery and recovery process. Lastly, wait-listed patients may die before an organ becomes available; more than 6,000 per year usually do (OPTN, 2009).

In addition to helping recipients, living donors themselves experience benefits (e.g., Johnson et al., 1999). Most living donors are relatives or close friends of recipients and generally express gratification in being able to, literally, give of themselves to save a loved one's life.

Risk to Living Donors

Major surgery has potential risks, such as those associated with anesthesia or surgical error. Surgery to remove an organ for transplant is no exception (Elliott, 1995). Donors electively subject their body to a major surgical procedure with no physiologic benefit for themselves. The transplant field has only begun tracking living donors over time, so potential long-term consequences for living donors are unknown (OPTN, 2009).

Becoming a Living Donor

Once someone decides to become a living donor, a meeting is arranged with the transplant team for physical and psychological evaluation. Only individuals in good health are considered. High blood pressure and diabetes are two disqualifying conditions (OPTN, 2009). The psychological evaluation is for the donor's safety—making sure donors have thought through the commitment, understand risks and benefits, and are not being coerced into the procedure.

Living Donation: Obstacles and Options

Not all patients pursue living donation. Patient obstacles include lack of awareness of living donation, reluctance to ask relatives and friends to be donors, and the difficulty of finding a matched donor (Horton & Horton, 1990).

Various outreach efforts have been created to overcome these obstacles (see Waterman & Rodrigue, this volume), including programs to educate dialysis patients of their opportunity for living donation and to help them develop the ability to broach the issue with others (Horton & Horton, 1990). Another strategy is called *paired exchange*. This involves a group of potential recipients and their willing but incompatible donors (pairs). Within the group of pairs, there must be one matching donor for each potential recipient, which allows each recipient to receive an organ from the donor in the group who is a match. Paired exchanges occur among any number of donor–recipient pairs and can involve any combination of relatives or nonrelatives as long as each pair contains a donor and a recipient and every recipient gets an organ.

Can You Be Paid to Be an Organ Donor?

No. Any exchange of "valuable consideration" for donor organs is prohibited by federal law (the National Organ Transplant Act, or NOTA). Violators can be fined up to $50,000 or imprisoned for up to 5 years. See the discussion of financial incentives later in this chapter.

The Organ Shortage

Figure 2.1 provides some perspective on the donor shortage. The national waiting list for organs at year's end 2008 was 100,775 (OPTN, 2009). As deceased donors provide multiple organs (3.05 per donor on average), the 14,198 living and deceased donors that year resulted in 27,958 transplants (OPTN, 2009). However, 6,782 wait-listed patients died waiting (OPTN, 2009). Although the number of donors has increased in most years since 1993 (OPTN, 2009), many more are needed.

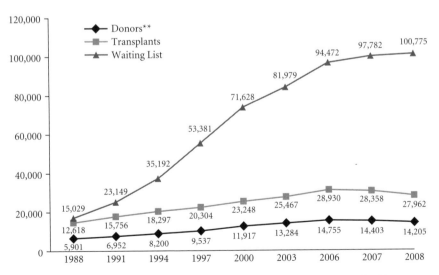

Figure 2.1 Donor shortage: The national waiting list for organs compared with transplants and donors.

The Need for Greater Ethnic Diversity among Minority Donors

The organ shortage is a particular concern for non-Caucasian ethnic groups (e.g., Siegel, Alvaro, Lac, Crano, & Alexander, 2008), who at year's end 2008 comprised 53.1% of the national waiting list. Due to disproportionately high rates of diabetes and high blood pressure, African Americans (Davis et al., 2005), Hispanics (Alvaro, Jones, Robles, & Siegel, 2005), Native Americans (Fahrenwald & Stabnow, 2005), and Asian/Pacific Islanders (Hebert et al., this volume) are at particular risk for kidney disease, resulting in greater need for transplants. In 2008, for example, African Americans comprised 35% of the kidney waiting list, 14% of kidney donors, and 24.5% of kidney transplants (OPTN, 2009).

Although organs are not matched according to ethnicity, and people of different ethnicities frequently match one another, all individuals waiting for an organ will have a better chance of receiving one if there are large numbers of donors from their ethnic background. This is because compatible blood type and tissue markers – critical qualities for donor/recipient matching – are more likely to be found among members of the same ethnicity. A greater diversity of donors may potentially increase access to transplantation for diverse populations.

Why Is There an Organ Shortage?

Clinical issues

To begin with, few deaths result in donation. Although there are about 2.5 million deaths in the United States annually (Centers for Disease Control and Prevention, 2005), clinical and social factors whittle away at that figure, considerably reducing the number potentially available for organ donation.

Since the 1980 Uniform Determination of Death Act recognized cessation of brain function as a legal form of death, transplanting organs from individuals declared brain dead became the norm. The estimated number of U.S. brain deaths, however, is small, and not all those declared brain dead are potential donors. Some are medically unsuitable, afflicted with diseases like active cancer. Although federal regulation requires hospitals to refer every death to the local OPO, some deaths are not referred at all or in time for donation to occur. Sometimes, the deceased left no predeath authorization for donation, and the family cannot be located in time to provide consent or the deceased's medical and social history. Families may refuse consent. Sometimes potential donors are lost due to inadequate medical care. These factors combine to yield an actual annual number of brain-dead donors that is substantially less than the estimated number of potential brain-dead donors—approximately 11,000 per year. Most recently, a growing number of surgical-OPO teams are pursuing donation after cardiac death, a former standard practice from the first successful use of a deceased donor in 1962 until the field began using brain-dead donors in the 1980s.

Social-psychological issues

Social-psychological factors contribute to the donor shortage. For example, positive attitudes aside, many people simply do not register as donors. Data from two national surveys conducted by the Gallup Organization—one in 1993 for the Partnership for Organ Donation, and another in 2005 for the Health Resources and Services Administration (HRSA)—illustrate this point. The percentage of respondents who supported or strongly supported donation was 93% in 1993 and 95% in 2005. In contrast, the percentage having granted permission for donation, such as on a driver's license or donor card, was 28% and 52.7%, respectively.

Why Don't More People Register to Become Donors?

A key issue, especially for donation professionals involved in public education and for social and behavioral scientists investigating ways to increase donation, is to understand why people do not register as donors. Some people simply may not have thought about donation (Siegel, Alvaro & Hohman, this volume). Others may be willing but have not had an opportunity to register (Siegel, Alvaro, & Hohman, this volume). In the 2005 HRSA–Gallup survey (HRSA, 2005), 19% of the uncommitted said they were, however, willing to sign up. With more information and/or an easy and convenient registration opportunity, this group might sign up as donors. An accessible donor registry available at the DMV or online might make the difference.

For the remaining 81% of the uncommitted, other factors may be preventing them from registering. Various barriers to donor registration identified over the past 20+ years continue to apply. These include false beliefs about organ donation held by the general population and subpopulations (for a list of commonly held beliefs, see Mayo Clinic, n.d.). For example, Clive O. Callender, director of transplant at Howard University Hospital, invoked such myths as key reasons why African Americans choose not to donate (Callender, Bayton, Yeager, & Clark, 1982).

The Quest for Organs: A Social and Behavioral Challenge

It is unique and challenging in this field of sophisticated and miraculous medicine that the major impediment to life-saving treatment is not science, but rather the human element—the critical organ shortage. Despite clinical hurdles left to cross, especially in preventing organ rejection, transplantation science continues to advance. Expanding the human contribution, however, remains a challenge. It is a public health challenge whose resolution rests predominantly with social and behavioral scientists as well as community educators, hospital development specialists, and concerned citizens.

The challenge to increase donation is a relative newcomer to the public health and behavior change arena. The first successful transplant in the United States took place at Boston's Brigham and Women's Hospital in 1954 (Hume, Merrill, Miller, & Thorn, 1955). Later, the 1978 discovery and 1983 U.S. Food and Drug Administration (FDA) approval of the immunosuppressive drug Cyclosporin made transplantation possible between genetically dissimilar individuals. This momentous discovery enabled many more transplants to be performed, rendered almost any healthy individual a potential donor, and stimulated a quest to increase donation.

The American organ donation system has always been an opt-in system. As noted earlier, operationally and legally, this means a transplant team may not remove organs from a deceased donor unless legally authorized by (a) the individual prior to death (e.g., via a driver's license or donor registry), or (b) the family at the time of a relative's death. In parallel fashion, the quest to increase donation has encompassed two complementary approaches:

1. A focus on promoting individuals' commitment to, and registration for, organ donation through education and outreach efforts (e.g., Alvaro, Jones, Robles, & Siegel, 2006)
2. A focus on creating a donation-friendly hospital environment to increase death referrals to OPOs, and family consent for a deceased loved one's donation by improving discussions and encounters with potential donors' families (Dodd-McCue & Tartaglia, 2005)

These goals involve a constellation of knowledge, attitudes, emotions, and behaviors, providing ample opportunities for social and behavioral research (Quinn, Alexander, O'Connor, & Meltzer, 2006). Hospital referral, family consent, and public commitment to donation—along with some related milestones—are discussed below.

Efforts to Increase Hospital Referral

During the late 1980s and early 1990s, with partial support from HRSA Division of Transplantation (DoT) grants, OPOs in Pennsylvania, Colorado, and New Jersey performed a retrospective study of their hospital records to determine the number of potential donors. The data suggested there were 12,000–15,000 potential donors per year nationwide. Comparisons with actual donation revealed that hospitals did not identify or refer (to an OPO) 25–30% of potential donors (Nathan et al., 1991).

Armed with that information and the knowledge that approximately 50% of families declined to donate a relative's organs, Pennsylvania passed a law

(PA-102) in 1994 requiring hospitals to refer all deaths to the local OPO or be fined $500 for each occurrence. Three years later, the actual number of donors increased by 43%; 5 years later, by 61% (OPTN, 2009).

Considering Pennsylvania's results, when DHHS's Centers for Medicare and Medicaid Services (CMS; U.S. Department of Health and Human Services [DHHS], CMS, 1997) issued its 1998 *Conditions of Participation in Medicare and Medicaid Programs*, they required hospitals participating in Medicare and Medicaid to refer every death and imminent death to the relevant OPO. They also required all requesting to be done by the OPO or a "designated requester" trained by the OPO. Noncompliant hospitals could lose their ability to participate in Medicare and Medicaid.

In 1995, LifeGift, the Houston-based OPO, with DoT grant support, increased hospital–OPO collaboration, potential donor identification, referral, and consent rates by locating OPO recovery personnel in level I trauma centers, hospitals with large donor potential (Shafer et al., 1997). These in-house coordinators (IHCs) worked closely with, and became more visible to and trusted by, hospital staff, and were instrumental in promoting substantial change. In 1999, LifeGift obtained another DoT grant and replicated the IHC strategy in Los Angeles, New York, Seattle, and two additional hospitals in Houston, again obtaining impressive results. Referrals in IHC hospitals increased by 26% compared to 12% in non-IHC hospitals (Shafer et al., 1997). Organ donors increased by 26% (vs. no change in non-IHC hospitals). IHC hospital consent rates increased by 13% (vs. no change in non-IHC hospitals). The IHC strategy has been adopted nationwide and is now standard practice (Shafer et al., 1997).

Efforts to Increase Family Consent

Many practices and projects have been implemented to improve interactions with decedents' families, thereby increasing consent rates (Dodd-McCue & Tartaglia, 2005). In 1988, the Health Care Financing Administration issued a regulation requiring hospitals participating in Medicare and Medicaid to establish protocols to identify potential donors, assure families are offered the option of donation, and notify OPOs of potential donors. For years, the norm was to "offer families the option of donation"—meaning assuming a neutral posture on the decision.

In 1991, the National Kidney Foundation (NKF), collaborating with the American Association of Critical Care Nurses, implemented the first national program of workshops to help nurses with their feelings about donation and their skills for offering families the donation option (Politoski & Boller, 1994). OPO requestors—often clinically trained staff (e.g., nurses) assisting in organ recovery—also offered families the donation option. Later, many OPOs trained separate staff for requesting consent and performing organ recovery, necessitating the identification of skills and traits typifying successful requesters. Some OPOs provided training in interpersonal skills and bereavement support to help develop family rapport.

During the mid-1990s, timing of donation requests was recognized as significant with respect to its proximity to informing families of their relative's death (Gortmaker et al., 1998). "Decoupling" these two discussions became the norm, allowing the bereaved time to accept the reality of death before being approached about donation.

In 1999, HRSA launched a new applied research grant program (discussed later) enabling teams of practitioners and researchers to implement and evaluate strategies for increasing consent (e.g., Jacoby, Breitkopf, & Pease, 2005). Some engaged specific types of people in the consent process and provided emotional support to potential donor families (e.g., Dodd-McCue, Tartaglia, Veazey, & Streetman, 2005). Examples include enabling mothers of donors (MOD Squads) to provide supportive assistance to families. Some projects provided simulated training experiences (sometimes using professional actors) for requesters.

Two of the most recent and widely adopted strategies for approaching families are the "presumptive" and "dual advocacy[sm]" approaches (e.g., Mulvania, 2008). Unlike traditionally neutral offers of donation, often presented to families as one close-ended question (i.e. "Would you like to consider donating your loved one's organs?"), these strategies incorporate a proactive approach.

Another promising consent strategy is the practice of first-person consent, honoring the predeath donor commitment of the deceased as legal consent to recover organs. The legal tools for donor designations vary by state, but the most common are driver's license donation indicators and donor registries. The legal foundation for first-person consent stems from the promulgation of the first Uniform Anatomical Gift Act (UAGA) in 1968, which endorsed donor cards as legal documents for expressing one's wish to donate, authorizing organ recovery. The UAGA also identified kin who could serve as a proxy for a decedent without a document of gift. Some states adopted a version of the 1968 UAGA, and most states and the District of Columbia adopted a later, 1987 version of the UAGA, thereby incorporating the legal foundation for first-person consent. In deference to surviving family, however, the practice of seeking family consent continued to be the norm.

In the mid-1990s, the practice of first-person consent debuted in the procurement community. The Center for Organ Recovery & Education (CORE), the OPO serving western Pennsylvania and part of West Virginia, began upholding deceased persons' legally expressed donation wishes, even in the face of family objection. This radical deviation from the family-centered approach was viewed with curiosity by some and with skepticism by those assuming legal suits would soon be brought against CORE by families whose objections went unheeded. Some also argued preference should be given to the wishes of the living. CORE has continued this approach with no suits to date.

An increasing number of OPOs have adopted first-person consent, some in its unadulterated form and others giving preference to a family's wishes under extreme circumstances. For example, some OPOs will yield to families presenting a convincing argument that, although not documented, the deceased's donation decision had changed. Some states have recently passed legislation strengthening legal requirements favoring first-person consent. Even when a deceased's predeath authorization for donation is available, however, families continue to play a critical role in providing the medical and social history of loved ones. This information helps recovery staff determine the risk of transmittable but dormant diseases such as Hepatitis C or HIV and the deceased's suitability for donation.

Disseminating Best Practices

Effective practices for increasing referral and consent have been used in different areas of the country and contribute to high performance. Several evolved from HRSA's research grant program. Although it is important to expand research efforts identifying ways to increase referrals and consent in hospital settings, it also is important to broadly implement strategies shown to be effective through research and practice.

In September 2003, HRSA launched the Organ Donation Breakthrough Collaborative (ODBC) with the goal of raising the organ donation conversion rate in the nation's largest hospitals from an average of 50% to 75% (OPTN, 2009), a level already achieved by several hospitals. A conversion rate is the percentage of medically eligible donors in a hospital that become actual donors. Conversion depends on optimal conduct of referral, consent, and medical management of potential donors after consent and prior to transplant. Because an individual's predeath donation decision informs the consent process, public commitment to donation also has an impact on conversion rates.

The Breakthrough Collaborative model was developed by the Institute for Healthcare Improvement to stimulate goal-oriented change (Shafer et al., 2006) using a series of intense, highly interactive meetings to disseminate effective practices in a specific health care area. The model tests proposed changes (Shafer et al., 2006) and systematically integrates successful strategies into institutional practices.

Another collaborative was introduced in 2005 with the goal of increasing the average number of organs transplanted per donor from 3.06 to 3.75, and subsequently the two collaboratives merged. By October 2007, the national organ donation conversion rate rose to 69% from 51.5% (United Network for Organ Sharing, 2004). Equally important, however, are the hospital–OPO relationships that were strengthened through this process and the bridges built between the transplant community and other organizations that can positively influence donation. For example, as a result of the collaboratives, the Joint Commission, a hospital accreditation organization, emphasized conversion rates as an integral part of hospital performance and recommended improvement plans as part of the accreditation process. The collaborative process has evolved to a local and regional effort that continues to function, encouraging additional hospitals to become involved and promoting successful strategies.

In January 2009, the National Kidney Foundation launched its "End the Wait!" campaign, a national initiative to eliminate the kidney waiting list in 10 years, NKF proposes to work with other organizations and government agencies to implement tested and proven strategies to improve transplant outcomes and reduce the need for second transplants, increase deceased donation and the number of living donors, and improve the donation and transplantation system in the country, including the elimination of regional and ethnic disparities related to transplantation.

Financial Incentives and Presumed Consent: Untried but Often Debated Strategies

No overview of efforts to increase consent would be complete without reference to frequently discussed yet untried strategies of financial incentives and presumed consent.

Financial incentives are the proposed use of "valuable consideration" to encourage donation and consent (Schlitt, 2002). Coverage of funeral expenses, gifts to charities, and direct payments to donor families are some suggested incentives (Cohen, Siminoff, Arnold, & Virnig, 1991). The 2005 HRSA–Gallup survey (HRSA, 2005) indicates 16.5% of the population would be more likely to donate their own organs if paid an incentive; 72.2% said a financial incentive would have no effect on their decision. Similarly, 18.7% said they would be more likely to donate a relative's organs if paid an incentive (HRSA)—up from 12% in 1993. As noted earlier, however, the National Organ Transplant Act (NOTA) prohibits the exchange of human organs for valuable consideration, eliminating the possibility of empirically testing the concept.

Unlike the American opt-in donation system, some European countries practice an opt-out system of *presumed consent* where people are considered potential donors unless they take legal means indicating they do not wish to donate. Whether presumed consent would work in this country also is unknown (see Institute of Medicine, 2006, for further discussion). The 2005 HRSA–Gallup data (HRSA, 2005) indicate that 85.9% of respondents thought presumed consent would increase organs for transplant; 43.2% supported such a system.

Efforts to Increase Public Commitment to Donation

The 1968 UAGA triggered early outreach efforts to increase public commitment by endorsing a donor card as a legal document of gift, thereby enabling advocacy groups to promote an action step in their outreach efforts. In the 1970s, groups like the NKF and the American Medical Association began widespread distribution of donor cards in mail campaigns, health fairs, and other venues. Other outreach efforts emerged along with publicity sponsored by families hoping to stimulate donation for loved ones needing an organ.

In September 1983, the U.S. Congress designated the third week of April as National Organ and Tissue Donor Awareness Week (P.L. 98-99), which continued to be observed annually until 2003, when then HHS Secretary Tommy G. Thompson designated the month of April as National Donate Life Month. Each year since 1984, presidential proclamations recognize this commemorative occasion.

The 1984 passage of NOTA further legitimized this young field and helped solidify a national system of organ sharing through the OPTN. Among other provisions, the act enabled the establishment, operation, and expansion of OPOs whose function includes increasing donation, and authorized a federal grant program to increase donation. The act also created a Federal Task Force on Organ Transplantation to report on public education initiatives. The Task's Force's 1986 report indicated that public education and outreach efforts were uncoordinated, were localized, lacked goals, and were not well evaluated (DHHS, Public Health Service, 1986). This is not surprising given that few donation professionals at that time had experience in public relations or health education, and little funding for public outreach was available.

As the field grew, and transplantation became increasingly accepted as a surgical procedure, the need for organs escalated, as did the search for ways to increase organ availability. The late 1980s saw the proliferation of public outreach. Speakers' bureaus, outreach to faith-based organizations, schools, social and civic organizations, and other programs were implemented by OPOs, eye banks and tissue banks, the NKF and affiliates, national health organizations, and private nonprofits. In 1988, DoT began a program of 1-year demonstration grants to promote outreach activities. The 1990s saw a sustained evolution of donation education and outreach. Increasingly, OPOs began hiring staff with experience in public relations, communication, and health education, enabling the development of more sophisticated outreach programs. The increase in the number and variety of programs has been significant. Gospel concerts, theatrical programs, DMV staff training, parade floats, and donor kiosks exemplify the diversity of these efforts. Community outreach professionals in OPOs and other organizations work with state legislatures in promoting legislation to enhance donation infrastructure by incorporating tools such as registries, trust funds for public education, and first-person consent practices.

These professionals and organizations have played a major role in promoting the positive changes in public attitudes and practices related to donation.

In 1991, the need to increase donation took center stage when then U.S. Surgeon General Antonia Novello conducted a national workshop on the subject—itself an endorsement of the community's responsibility to increase donation. The workshop led to a compilation of papers on donation-related topics and a book of proceedings containing recommendations for increasing donation. The recommendations ranged from implementing clinical approaches to increasing community education targeting the general public and diverse ethnic populations (DHHS, Public Health Service, 1991).

In 1992, Kentucky became the first state passing legislation to raise funds for public donation education via the Trust for Life. The trust enables residents, when obtaining or renewing a driver's license, to contribute $1 to a fund administered by Kentucky's circuit court clerks. By 2000, 50% of Kentucky drivers had contributed, over $3,000,000 was raised, and organ donation increased by 62% (DHHS, HRSA, 2001).

The 1992 launch of the Coalition on Donation, now Donate Life America (DLA), enabled donation professionals to coalesce around a national leadership organization of donation-related organizations focused solely on the mission of increasing organ and tissue donation. Nationwide, local donation-related organizations (i.e., OPOs, eye and tissue banks, and sometimes blood banks and marrow donor centers) came together as DLA affiliates to cooperatively implement community-level outreach and to rally around a common theme. The national DLA worked with The Advertising Council, Inc., and other advertising companies to develop 11 national campaigns that included TV and radio ads with coordinated print materials (see Alvaro & Siegel, this volume). The DLA was among early groups stressing the importance of research-based campaigns and outreach. From its inception until 2000, DLA's campaign materials used the call to action "Share Your Life. Share Your Decision," encouraging Americans to make a personal donation commitment and to inform their families of that decision. This theme was in response to the tradition of seeking family consent for donation based on knowledge that, without awareness of their loved one's wishes, families often defaulted to "no" when asked for consent. For several years, this focus on family discussions predominated. In 2000, DLA launched its current call to action, Donate Life. A major effort has been made by DLA and the donation community to consistently use this slogan and its corresponding trademarked logo to promote a common brand.

Shortly after the coalition's inception, another critically important trend began in 1993, when Illinois implemented the nation's first statewide donor registry. This electronic database enabled Illinois residents to record their donation decision with the assurance that it would be available at their time of death. Now all states, the District of Columbia, and Puerto Rico have implemented registries. Besides providing safe storage and reliable reporting of individuals' donation wishes, registries provide useful data that other registration methods cannot. Specifically, registries provide an unprecedented accurate account of the number of organ donation registrants. Additionally, analysis of registry data by zip codes yields important information for planning and evaluating outreach efforts. Prior to registries, donation education staff had few ways to gauge outreach effectiveness barring a rigorous evaluation and research study. Although registry enrollment per se may be insufficient to demonstrate cause and effect, it provides a valid impact measure of changes over time and in targeted locations and populations.

In 2001, former DHHS Secretary Tommy G. Thompson's National Gift of Life Donation Initiative was begun to increase organ, tissue, marrow, and blood donation. Three of his campaign elements remain in practice today: the Workplace Partnership for Life; Decision: Donation; and the Organ and Tissue Donation Collaborative. The Workplace Partnership for Life is a public-private collaboration wherein businesses and organizations educate employees and members about donation and encourage registration. This program currently sponsors an intense effort to increase donation in postsecondary institutions of various types. Decision: Donation is an educational package for teachers of driver's education and other classes designed to ensure high school students make an informed donation decision when applying for their driver's license. It continues to be used in high schools throughout the United States and Canada. For a complete list of these programs, see www.organdonor.gov.

Most recently, the Donor Designation Collaborative (DDC), modeled after HRSA's successful Collaborative, was launched by DLA in 2006 as a national effort to promote registry development and increase U.S. registry enrollment from 60 million to 100 million. Local OPOs and DLAs continue to implement an array of strategies to meet this goal. By April 2009, the number of registry enrollments increased to nearly 80 million. The efforts of the DDC—along with strategies implemented by other groups, such as the NKF and its affiliates, other national and local organizations, HRSA, HRSA and NIH grantees, and others—have all contributed to the increase in registry enrollments that hopefully will continue.

National Events and Observances

Two recurring events that often elicit significant national attention are the U.S. Transplant Games and the Donate Life float in the New Year's Day Tournament of Roses Parade. Coordinated by the NKF, the Transplant Games is an Olympic-style event where transplant recipients of all ages compete in various athletic events. The games trigger enormous media attention with national and local outlets featuring stories on participating recipients.

Coordinated by OneLegacy, the OPO serving greater Los Angeles, the donation community has featured an annual Rose Parade float since 2004. The 2008 float was awarded the prestigious Judges' Special Trophy as the most spectacular in showmanship and dramatic impact, and the 2009 float was awarded the Queen's Trophy for most effective use and display of roses in concept, design, and presentation.

Numerous national observances provide a common synchronized focus for donation outreach efforts in communities across the nation (see www.organdonor.gov). Examples of national annual observances are National Donor Day (February 14), Donate Life Month (April), National Minority Donor Awareness Day (August 1) and National Donor Sabbath (a November weekend).

Local Efforts

From the 1990s to the present, the local and regional donation organizations have implemented an increasingly sophisticated agenda of strategies to promote donation in communities nationwide (e.g., Siegel, Alvaro, Jones et al., 2008). Donation professionals share best practices (through meetings, listservs, etc.). Although the costs of TV and radio advertising are generally prohibitive for most donation organizations, many communities are served by multiple grassroots efforts targeting various audiences, settings, events (see Allen & Stillwater, 2009), and institutions. Culturally diverse populations are a common focus, building on pioneering work by Howard University and the National Minority Organ Tissue Education Program.

Division of Transplantation Grant Programs

In 1999, DoT launched the first in a series of more sophisticated grant programs to increase donation. Two programs are research based, aiming to identify successful replicable interventions. These programs span the donation continuum from encouraging the public to sign up as donors to the clinical management of donors to ensure organ viability.

Three programs have provided support for replicating projects found to be successful through the research grant program or other research. Another program supports the development and improvement of state donor registries and helps build an infrastructure to ensure donation wishes are legally documented, safely stored, and readily accessible (see www.organdonor.gov for a list of grant programs).

Have We Made a Difference?

Countless community- and hospital-based activities have been conducted to promote organ donation: some as part of national efforts, and others location specific. Some have been evaluated; others have not. Subsequent chapters provide project results—here, we examine some overall outcomes.

Hospital-based activities

Conversion rates have increased along with actual donation rates. Since the collaboratives began in late 2003, the national conversion rate increased from 51.5%

to 66.2% (OPTN, 2008), and the annual number of deceased donors has increased from 6,457 (2004) to 7,985 (2008)—an annual average rate of growth of 7.5% as compared to 2.5% in prior years (OPTN, 2009). Certainly, the collaboratives, with their multifaceted, positive, and comprehensive approach, have had a major impact on conversion and donation rates and hospital-based activities. They have also galvanized the hospital–OPO community to work together in unprecedented fashion.

Other efforts also have contributed to the increase in conversion rates. For example, some OPOs and hospitals not participating in the collaborative continued hospital development efforts and demonstrated positive results. OPO–hospital teams supported by DoT's social and behavioral research grants also demonstrated positive results. Further, public education efforts stimulating previous increases in organ donation continued to have an impact. Without controlling for such additional influences, it is difficult to determine the precise contribution of the collaboratives, but the results have been dramatic—in terms both of numbers and of expanding the base of individuals and organizations promoting donation in the nation's hospitals.

There are strong indicators that public outreach and education also have had a substantial impact on donation knowledge, attitudes, and, most important, behavior. Donor registry enrollment, for example, has increased to about 80 million. Especially with more states honoring the donor's wishes as consent for donation to occur, this is a particularly important outcome.

Figure 2.2 provides an empirical testament to the success of the donation community's efforts to increase public commitment to donation and registry enrollment. There is a steady increase in the number of actual deceased donors having written documentation of their wish to donate: from 20% in 2005 to nearly 28% in 2008. As noted, documentation of donation wishes is pivotal in converting potential donors to actual donors.

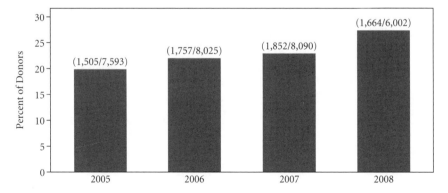

Figure 2.2. Donors with written documentation of intent to donate, 2005–September 30, 2008.
Source: OPTN database as of 11/2008.

National surveys also provide interesting data on the impact of public education. Bearing in mind that other factors (i.e., news and entertainment media) also influence public perceptions and behaviors, comparison of the 2005 HRSA–Gallup survey (HRSA, 2005) with the 1993 Partnership–Gallup survey (Partnership for Organ Donation, 1993) yields interesting comparisons.

Both surveys randomly selected respondents (1993, $N = 6,127$; 2005, $N = 2,341$) with minorities oversampled. The data in Appendix 2.2 illustrate some findings. Some indicate success in changing donation practices. Other findings are instructive, suggesting new avenues for outreach efforts (Appendix 2.2). Overall, data suggest that collective public education efforts of the donation community have made a difference. For example, dramatic increases in family donation discussions—intensely promoted by the donation community—highlight the potential of combined media and grassroots outreach for influencing donation attitudes and practices.

Results also indicate the need for continued and strategically targeted outreach to convert unregistered yet willing individuals into registered donors while bolstering efforts to reach those who are more skeptical and reluctant with compelling messages. Correcting false beliefs may be particularly helpful; for example, identifying effective strategies to inform those aged 55+ that organ viability, not age, is the most important factor for donor suitability. Although progress is evident, so is the escalation of the transplant waiting list and the continued need to search for creative ways to save lives through donation.

Conclusion

Ideally everyone would be aware of organ transplantation as an effective treatment for an otherwise terminal illness. Everyone would have made a personal commitment to donation and registered as a donor. Although this is not yet the case, progress is evident.

According to the popular transtheoretical model of behavior change (Prochaska & Velicer, 1997), modification of health behavior follows a path from unawareness of an issue to actually taking action and maintaining behavior. Although Americans are undoubtedly at all stages along this continuum, it is exciting to see increases in action and maintenance as evidenced by increases in registrations, and more subtle changes discerned with well-designed surveys such as the two Gallup surveys (Partnership for Organ Donation, 1993; HRSA, 2005) and measures described in this volume.

Even though people began experimenting with transplanting bones as early as 400 BC, modern-day successful transplantation is a relatively young, although sophisticated and stimulating, field of medicine. Social and behavioral research on increasing organ donation is just evolving as a body of empirically based literature. There is ample room for new and inquisitive researchers in this exciting field: researchers who have the skills to construct sound and meaningful studies, the fortitude to carry them out even when research meets reality and the road gets bumpy, and the wisdom to understand that it is equally important to find out what doesn't work as it is to discover what does.

Appendix 2.1 Key Organizations in the Donation and Transplantation Process

- **U.S. Department of Health and Human Services (DHHS)**: DHHS is one of the 15 departments in the president's Cabinet. DHHS itself consists of 11 major agencies. Although three of these have some role in donation and transplantation, the Health Resources and Services Administration (HRSA), through its Healthcare Systems Bureau (HSB), Division of Transplantation (DoT), is the focal point for transplantation within DHHS. As charged by Congress, DHHS, through HRSA/HSB/DoT, provides support for and oversight of the transplant system in the United States through its contracts with the Organ Procurement and Transplantation Network (OPTN) and the Scientific Registry of Transplant Recipients (SRTR). DHHS is responsible for ensuring that the transplant system in this country is fair, efficient, and equitable. Congress also charges the department with increasing organ donation by implementing various national initiatives, both directly and through grants and contracts.
- **State governments**: State governments pass laws and policies that have an impact on organ donation and transplantation in various ways. For example, laws may identify who has legal authority to make a donation decision for a deceased individual, facilitate the creation of a voluntary trust fund for donation education efforts, or require implementation of a donor registry.
- **State motor vehicle departments or offices**: These are the places in most states where the majority of state residents register to be organ donors, usually on a driver's license, in a donor registry, or both. In many states, the motor vehicle offices actually house the donor registry, making information available to the transplant community when residents die.
- **Organ Procurement and Transplantation Network (OPTN)**: The OPTN maintains the computerized national transplant waiting list, runs matches when donor organs become available, and works with the transplant community and the public to develop and provide to DHHS policy recommendations for improving the efficiency, equality, and effectiveness of the organ allocation (matching) and distribution system. The OPTN has been operated since its inception in 1986 by the United Network for Organ Sharing (UNOS) under contract to HRSA.

- **Scientific Registry of Transplant Recipients (SRTR)**: The SRTR provides analytic support to the OPTN in the development and evaluation of organ allocation and other OPTN policies. The SRTR also provides analytic support to the DHHS, including the Secretary's Advisory Committee on Organ Transplantation. It conducts research on various aspects of organ donation and transplantation, including survival rates of recipients of different organs and from different transplant centers. The SRTR, also operated under contract to HRSA, has been administered since 2000 to the present by Arbor Research Collaborative for Health and from 1987 to 2000 by UNOS.
- **Acute care hospitals**: Hospitals where most donation-eligible deaths occur. Most deaths that can result in donation occur in large acute care hospitals that have the equipment to artificially maintain the body and keep the organs viable for donation. A hospital, by federal law, must refer all deaths that occur in its facility to the OPO serving that hospital.
- **Transplant programs**: These are surgical units within a hospital that perform organ transplants. A transplant hospital may have one or more transplant programs (e.g., a kidney program, heart program, and lung program). In addition to implanting organs into their wait-listed patients, transplant program surgeons also recover organs from donors in their donation service area (DSA).
- **Organ procurement organizations (OPOs)**: There are 58 nonprofit organizations that implement strategies to increase donation in their exclusive DSAs. OPOs also orchestrate the donation process when notified of a death in their local hospitals. At notification of a death, an OPO does the following:
  - Determines whether the deceased is medically eligible to be a donor
  - Secures family consent for donation or documents first-person consent
  - Identifies potential organ recipients through an OPTN "match list"
  - Coordinates management of the donor before surgical recovery of the organs
  - Arranges for and assists with surgical recovery and preservation of organs
  - Arranges transportation of organs to the transplant program where they will be implanted into recipients
- **Eye banks**: These organizations recover and distribute donated corneas for transplantation and research. U.S. life banks enable about 46,000 cornea transplants a year to treat conditions such as keratoconus and cornea scaring.
- **Tissue banks**: Such organizations recover, process, store, and distribute donated human tissue (e.g., bone, veins, and skin) for transplantation. Unlike organs that can be maintained out of the body for varying but limited times depending on the organ, tissues can be stored, some indefinitely.
- **Histocompatability laboratories**: These laboratories have the specialized capability of determining whether the tissues of donors and potential recipients are compatible, thus decreasing the possibility of organ rejection.

Other National Donation and Transplant Organizations

- The **American Association of Tissue Banks (AATB)** makes available a safe supply of tissues and cells of high quality for transplantation (aatb.org, 800-635-2282).
- The **American Society for Histocompatibility and Immunogenetics (ASHI)** is an association of clinical and research professionals dedicated to the advancement, education, and application of immunogenetics and transplant immunology (ashi-hla.org, 856-638-0428).
- The **American Society of Multicultural Health and Transplant Professionals (ASMHTP)** serves a diverse group of transplant professionals in the community by providing national leadership and increased multicultural initiatives and opportunities (asmhtp.org, 866-276-4871).
- The **American Society of Transplant Surgeons (ASTS)** is an association of transplant surgeons that fosters and advances the practice and science of transplantation for the benefit of patients and society (asts.org, 703-414-7870).
- The **American Society of Transplantation (AST)** consists of transplant physicians and other professionals dedicated to research, education, advocacy, and patient care in transplantation offering knowledge, scientific information, and expertise about transplantation (a-s-t.org, 856-439-9986).
- **Arbor Research Collaborative for Health** conducts major studies in epidemiology and public health and administers the SRTR under contract to HRSA (ArborResearch.org, 734-665-4108).
- The **Association of Organ Procurement Organizations (AOPO)** supports OPOs to increase the availability of organs and tissues and to enhance the quality, effectiveness, and integrity of the donation process (aopo.org, 703-556-4242).
- **Donate Life America (DLA)** is an alliance of national organizations and local coalitions in the United States, dedicated to inspiring donation of organs, eyes, and tissue (donatelifeamerica@donatelife.net, 804-782-4920).
- The **Eye Bank Association of America (EBAA)** is a national organization of eye banks dedicated to the restoration of sight through the promotion and advancement of eye banking. It is the oldest transplant association in the United States and the nationally recognized accrediting body for eye banks (restoresight.org, 202-775-4999).
- The **National Kidney Foundation (NKF)** seeks to prevent kidney and urinary tract diseases and to increase organ and tissue availability for transplantation (kidney.org, 800-622-9010).
- The **National Minority Organ Tissue Transplant Education Program (MOTTEP)** educates minority communities about organ and tissue transplantation and promotes healthy living (nationalmottep.org, 202-865-4888/800-393-2839).

- The **North American Transplant Coordinators Organization (NATCO)** supports, develops, and advances the knowledge and practice of a diverse group of transplant professionals and influences the effectiveness, quality, and integrity of donation and transplantation (natcol.org, 913-492-3600).
- **Transplant Recipients International Organization (TRIO)** improves the quality of life of transplant candidates, recipients, their families, and the families of organ and tissue donors (trioweb.org, 800-874-6386).
- **United Network for Organ Sharing (UNOS)** advances organ availability and transplant through education, technology, and policy development and administers the OPTN under contract to HRSA (unos.org, 804-782-4800/800-292-9547).

Appendix 2.2   Indicators of Success

Some Indicators of Outreach Success: A Comparison of 1993 and 2005 National Probability Survey Data

- The percentage of Americans who have granted permission on a driver's license or a donor card for their organs to be donated nearly doubled from 28% in 1993 to 52.7% in 2005.
- The percentage of Americans who talked to a family member about their wish to donate increased significantly from 52% in 1993 to 70.8% in 2005.
- The percentage of Americans who would donate a family member's organs even if they did not know the family member's wishes increased significantly by 24.2%, from 47% (1993) to 71.2% (2005).

Some Indicators for Further Outreach and Research:
Lessons from the 2005 Survey

- With respect to having granted permission to donate one's own organs:
  - Whites (61%) were most likely to have granted permission to be a donor, with Blacks (31%) least likely, and Hispanics (39%) and Asians (39%) in between.
  - Among age groups, the 55 and older group was least likely to have granted permission (44.3%) compared with people in the other two age groups, 35–54 (59%) and 18–34 (51.1%).
  - College graduates were more likely to have signed up to donate (63.8%), followed by those with some college (55.1%), and those with a high school education or less (28.6%).
- Of those who had not granted permission:
  - Overall, 43.2% said they would be willing to do so.

∘ Hispanics (49.2%) were most willing, Blacks (30%) were least willing, and Asians (46%) and Whites (44.8%) were in the middle. When controlled for educational level, willingness to donate among Blacks with college degrees is similar to that of other races with college degrees.

∘ People 55 and older (37.4%) were least willing to grant permission versus the other age groups, 35–54 (44.4%) and 18–34 (50.6%).

Acknowledgments

The author appreciates the assistance of many people who reviewed and/or provided input to this chapter. Appreciation is extended to Remy Aronoff, Jim Bowman, Dave Bosch, Jim Burdick, Rich Durbin, David Fleming, Tommy Frieson, Rusty Kelly, Bernie Kozlovsky, Monica Lin, Ginny McBride, Lin McGaw, Patty Mulvania, Howard Nathan, Catherine Paykin, Linda Ohler, Teresa Shafer, Bryan Stewart, and Sarah Taranto. Very special thanks are extended to Teresa Beigay, Joy Demas, Debbie Gibbs, Jan Howard, Rita Maldonado, and Venus Walker.

References

Alvaro, E. M., Jones, S. P., Robles, A., & Siegel, J. T. (2005). Predictors of organ donation behaviors among Hispanic Americans. *Progress in Transplantation, 15*, 149–156.

Alvaro, E. M., Jones, S. P., Robles, A. S., & Siegel, J. T. (2006). Hispanic organ donation: Impact of a Spanish-language organ donation campaign. *Journal of the National Medical Association, 98*, 28–35.

Callender, C., Bayton, J. A., Yeager, C., & Clark, J. E. (1982). Attitudes among Blacks toward donating kidneys for transplantation: A pilot project. *Journal of the National Medical Association, 74*, 807–809.

Centers for Disease Control and Prevention. (2005). Deaths: Final data for 2005. *National Vital Statistics Reports, 56*, 1–5.

Cohen, A., Siminoff, L., Arnold, R., & Virnig, B. (1991). Increasing organ and tissue donation: What are the obstacles, what are the options? *The surgeon general's workshop on increasing organ donation: Background papers* (pp. 199–232). Washington, DC: U.S. Department of Health and Human Services.

Davis, K., Holtzman, S., Durand, R., Decker, P. J., Zucha, B., & Atkins, L. (2005). Leading the flock: Organ donation feelings, beliefs, and intentions among African American clergy and community residents. *Journal of Transplant Coordination, 15*(3), 211–216.

Dodd-McCue, D., & Tartaglia, A. (2005). The role of relatedness' in donation discussions with next of kin: An empirical study of the common wisdom. *Progress in Transplantation, 15*(3), 249–256.

Dodd-McCue, D., Tartaglia, A., Veazey, K., & Streetman, P. (2005). The impact of protocol on nurses' role stress: A longitudinal perspective, *Journal of Nursing Administration, 35*(4), 205–216.

Elliott, C. (1995). Doing harm: Living organ donors, clinical research and "The Tenth Man." *Journal of Medical Ethics, 21,* 91–96.

Fahrenwald, N. L., & Stabnow, W. (2005). Sociocultural perspective on organ and tissue donation among reservation-dwelling American Indian adults. *Ethnicity and Health, 10*(4), 341–354.

Gortmaker, S. L., Beasley, C. L., Sheehy, E., Lucas, B. A., Brigham, L. E., Grenvik, A., et al. (1998). Improving the request process to increase family consent for organ donation. *Journal of Transplant Coordination, 8*(4), 210–217.

Health Resources and Services Administration (HRSA). (2005). *2005 national survey of organ and tissue donation attitudes and behaviors.* Rockville, MD: Author.

Horton, R. L., & Horton, P. J. (1990). Knowledge regarding organ donation: Identifying and overcoming barriers to organ donation. *Social Science and Medicine, 31,* 791–800.

Hume, D. M., Merrill, J. P., Miller, B. F., & Thorn, G. W. (1955). Experiences with renal homotransplantations in the human: Report of nine cases. *Journal of Clinical Investigation, 34,* 327–382.

Institute of Medicine. (2006). *Organ donation: Opportunities for action.* Washington, DC: National Academies Press.

Jacoby, L. H., Breitkopf, C. R., & Pease, E. A. (2005). A qualitative examination of the needs of families faced with the option of organ donation. *Dimensions in Critical Care Nursing, 24,* 183–189.

Johnson, E. M., Anderson, J. K., Jacobs, C., Suh, G., Human, A., Suhr, B. D., et al. (1999). Long-term follow up of kidney donors: Quality of life after donation. *Nephrology Dialysis Transplantation, 67*(5), 717–721.

Mayo Clinic. (N.d.). *Organ donation: Don't let these 10 myths confuse you.* Retrieved January 2, 2009, from http://www.mayoclinic.com/health/organ-donation/FL00077

Mulvania, P. A. (2008). *Dual advocacy: A value-positive approach to obtaining consent for organ donation: A skills practice workshop.* Unpublished paper, Gift of Life Institute, Philadelphia.

Musculoskeletal Transplant Foundation. (2006). [Home page]. Retrieved January 8, 2009, from http://mtf.org

Nathan, H. M., Jarrell, B. E., Broznik, B., Kochik, R., Hamilton, B., Stuart, S., et al. (1991). Estimation and characterization of the potential renal organ donor pool in Pennsylvania: Report of the Pennsylvania Statewide Donor Study. *Transplantation, 51,* 142–149.

National Kidney Foundation. (2000). *KDOQI Guidelines 2000.* Retrieved January 2, 2009 from http://www.kidney.org/professionals/kdoqi/guidelines_updates/doqi_uptoc.html#va

Organ Donation Breakthrough Collaborative. (N.d.). *About the collaborative.* Retrieved January 4, 2009, from http://www.organdonationnow.org/index.cfm?fuseaction=Page.viewPage&pageId=471

organdonor.gov (2009). *Donor registry.* Retrieved January 4, 2009, from http://organdonor.gov/donor/registry.shtm

Partnership for Organ Donation. (1993). *The American public's attitudes toward organ donation and transplantation.* Boston: Author.

Politoski, G., & Boller, J. (1994). Making the critical difference: An innovative approach to educating nurses about organ and tissue donation. *Critical Care Nursing Clinics of North America, 6,* 581–585.

Prochaska, J. O., & Velicer, W. F. (1997). Behavior change: The Transtheoretical model of behavior change. *American Journal of Health Promotion, 12,* 38–48.

Quinn, M. T., Alexander, G. C., O'Connor, K. G., & Meltzer, D. (2006). Design and evaluation of a workplace intervention to promote organ donation. *Progress in Transplantation, 16*(3), 253–259.

Schlitt, H. J. (2002). Paid non-related living organ donation: Horn of Plenty of Pandora's box. *Lancet, 359,* 906–907.

Shafer, T. J., Wagner, D., Chessare, J., Zampiello, F. A., McBride, V., & Perdue, J. (2006). Organ donation breakthrough collaborative: Increasing organ donation through systems redesign. *Critical Care Nurse, 26,* 33–48.

Shafer, T. J., Wood, R. P., Van Buren, C. T., Guerriero, G., Davis, K., Reyes, D. A., et al. (1997). A success story in minority donation: The LifeGift/Ben Taub general hospital in-house coordinator program. *Transplantation Proceedings, 8,* 3753–3755.

Siegel, J. T., Alvaro, E., Jones, S. P., Crano, W. C., Lac, A., & Ting, S. (2008). A quasi-experimental investigation of message appeal variations on organ donor registration rates. *Health Psychology, 27,* 170–178.

Siegel, J. T., Alvaro, E., Lac, A., Crano, W. D., & Alexander, S. (2008). Intentions of becoming a living organ donor among Hispanics: A theoretical approach exploring differences between living and non-living organ donation. *Journal of Health Communication, 13,* 80–99.

United Network for Organ Sharing. (2004). Chapter 3: Organ donation and utilization in the U.S., 2004. Table III: 1. Eligible, actual and additional donors, 2002–2003. In *OPTN/SRTR Annual Report.* Richmond, VA: Author. Retrieved January 4, 2009, from http://www.optn.org/AR2004/Chapter_III_AR_CD.htm?cp=4

U.S. Department of Health and Human Services (DHHS), Centers for Medicare and Medicaid Services, (CMS). (1997). *Conditions of participation in Medicare and Medicaid programs.* Washington, DC: Author.

U.S. Department of Health and Human Services, Health Resources and Services Administration. (2001). *State strategies for organ and tissue donation: A resource guide for public officials.* Washington, DC: Author.

U.S. Department of Health and Human Services, Public Health Service. (1986). *Organ transplantation: Issues and recommendations, report of the Task Force on Organ Transplantation.* Washington, DC: Author.

U.S. Department of Health and Human Services, Public Health Service. (1991). *The surgeon general's workshop on increasing organ donation: Proceedings.* Washington, DC: Author.

U.S. Organ Procurement and Transplantation Network. (2004). *OPTN/SRTR annual report.* Washington, DC: Author.

U.S. Organ Procurement and Transplantation Network. (2007). *Welcome to the 2007 OPTN/SRTR annual report: Transplant data 1997–2006.* Retrieved January 8, 2009, from http://www.ustransplant.org/annual_reports/current

U.S. Organ Procurement and Transplantation Network. (2009). *Donation and transplantation.* Retrieved January 3, 2009, from http://www.optn.org/about/

Part I

Media and Community Interventions

3

Where Have We Been and Where to Next

A Review and Synthesis of Organ Donation Media Campaigns

Eusebio M. Alvaro and Jason T. Siegel

Recent decades have witnessed a burgeoning interest in using the mass media to champion social causes and general improvements to the human condition. The bulk of these efforts have focused on changing a variety of behaviors affecting our health. The organ donation domain has not been exempt from this general trend. Following the development of antirejection drugs and improvements in transplantation techniques (see Ganikos, this volume), the encouragement of organ donation registration and consent became core issues for those involved in saving and improving lives through organ transplants. As a result, mass media campaigns focusing on public awareness and knowledge of transplantation and donation became routine in the 1980s. As with other campaigns addressing health-promoting behaviors, earlier atheoretical campaigns soon gave way to more sophisticated theory-based efforts evaluated with considerable input from behavioral and social scientists. This evolution gained more momentum following the development of the Health Research Services Administration Division of Transplantation's Social and Behavioral Grant Program.

The goal of this chapter is to provide the reader with an overview of research on mass media campaigns designed to improve organ donation outcomes such as awareness, attitudes, intentions, and actual behaviors. Moreover, readers will be provided with a broader theoretical understanding of the outcomes that one can expect as a result of a mass media campaign and how research on organ donation campaigns may benefit from such an understanding. In pursuit of this aim, the first section of the chapter reviews theoretical perspectives addressing mass media effects. Implications of each perspective for the study of organ donation campaigns are addressed. The second, and main, section of this chapter consists of a decade-by-decade overview of organ donation mass media campaigns implemented both in the United States and internationally. Key features and outcomes of these campaigns are discussed with an eye toward delineating the current knowledge base and identifying possible directions for future research and evaluation efforts. This review culminates with a section outlining challenges and issues for organ donation campaign research.

Theoretical Approaches to Mass Media Effects

Theories of how mass media influences human behavior can be of considerable use in informing investigations of mass media campaigns targeting organ donation behavior. Rather than pitting these theories against each other, we look for complementary insights that can be applied to organ donation campaigns.

Hypodermic Needle or Magic Bullet Model

The "hypodermic needle" or "Silver Bullet model" (Schramm, 1982) is the idea, around since the 1930s, to explain the power of Nazism: that the mass media have such power that they "inject" a message into a passive audience unable to resist the impact of the "injection" or "bullet." From a populist perspective, this reflects the idea that creators of media messages can directly manipulate audiences. In fact, proponents of this approach tend to be present more in pop circles rather than in academic ones—and are usually visible following the occurrence of some horrific crime supposedly "caused" by some media depiction.

Following this perspective, the challenge to creating effective organ donation media campaigns is in developing the appropriate message, then simply delivering it to a mass audience; and, given exposure to the message, all message recipients will register as organ donors. Although message variation deserves substantial research and has shown promise (Siegel Alvaro, Crano, Lac, Ting & Jones, 2008), it is highly unlikely that any one message type will, simply via exposure, result in mass organ donation registration.

Two-Step Flow Model

In the 1940s, public opinion researcher Paul Lazarsfeld (Lazarsfeld, Berelson, & Gaudet, 1948) proposed that mass media effects can be best explained via a two-step flow model that posits a system whereby mass media messages influence opinion leaders, who then influence others in their social group via direct contact. Thus, information is channeled to the "masses" through opinion leadership. The people with most access to, and understanding of, media explain and diffuse the content to others. In short, this perspective conceptualizes media as having quite limited *direct* effects on audiences. Two general findings emerged: Mass media is more likely to reinforce existing audience opinions than to change them (Klapper, 1960), and audiences expose themselves to media messages congruent with their predispositions (Berelson & Steiner, 1964). Perhaps most importantly, research supports the view that interpersonal communication about mediated messages may be more important to attitude formation and change processes than the messages themselves. For example, evaluations of antitobacco media campaigns (Durkin & Wakefield, 2006; Gunther, Bolt, Borzekowski, Liebhart, & Dillard, 2006; Hafstad & Aaro, 1997) found interpersonal discussion to be associated with positive campaign effects, whereas experimental research has found that mass and interpersonal communication act together to enhance general health risk perceptions (Morton & Duck, 2001).

Interestingly, organ donation public education efforts have had a historical emphasis on encouraging individuals to discuss their donation decision with loved ones. Given the potential importance of the role played by interpersonal communication in maximizing the impact of mass media campaigns, messages aimed at increasing donation discussion may find fertile ground in these campaigns. Increases in discussion also function to keep the topic of organ donation salient among target audiences until an opportunity for donation registration presents itself—an important facet in any behavior change effort (for more detail on salience, see Siegel, Alvaro, & Hohman, this volume).

Agenda Setting

Although support for a limited effects model of mass media grew from the 1940s onward, there were also indications that some powerful media effects existed. As summarized by Schramm (1982): (a) Media confer status on organizations and individuals, (b) media reaffirm social norms by noting deviations, and (c) media act as a social narcotic where, overwhelmed by information, audiences may be lulled into inaction. This research helps support what became known as the agenda-setting model (McCombs & Shaw, 1972) whereby the mass media are conceptualized as a tool for telling audiences what to think *about*, not what to think. Mass media set the order of importance for issues and also set the terms of debate on these issues. This theory, only recently being applied to health campaign research, shows considerable promise.

In combining the above-mentioned two-step flow approach with the agenda-setting model, it could be suggested that mass media campaigns may be best suited to introduce a novel idea to a population, creating a social context wherein this idea becomes the focus of discussion. This discussion then supplements any direct impact on issue-relevant behaviors. It may be that the largest impact of a mass media campaign is to make organ donation a topical issue perceived as worthy of and garnering public debate. Increased registration behavior then arises largely as a result of such discussion. This approach argues for the use of more vivid messaging that attracts attention or a focus on some novel aspect of organ donation stimulating considerable discussion.

Cultivation

Yet another perspective on media effects is offered by Gerbner's (1969; Gerbner, Gross, Morgan, & Signorielli, 1980) cultivation analysis. This approach is concerned with *cumulative* exposure to mass media and gradual shifts in societal perceptions rather than outright direct change. From this perspective, mass media dominate our symbolic environment, and the image of reality found in the mass media shapes our conceptions of reality. Mass media "cultivate" or reinforce certain values and beliefs in audiences. A key finding is that heavy viewers of TV tend to believe that the TV world accurately reflects the real world. Moreover, heavy viewing creates a homogenous view of the world—a concept known as *mainstreaming*. The end result of these processes is social legitimization of the "reality" depicted in the mass media, which then influences behavior.

From this perspective, the best use of mass media is to introduce or reinforce the idea that being a registered organ donor is normative. One current approach (see Ganikos, this volume) is the encouragement of organ donation story lines in television programs. If organ donation registration is portrayed on television as normative, viewers could, in the long term, be motivated to register when given the opportunity. A more subtle approach may be to use the media to foster values that are found to underlie organ donation behavior.

Uses and Gratifications

Raymond Bauer (1964) was an early proponent of what came to be called the *uses and gratifications approach* to media. Far from being passive recipients of media messages, audiences are seen as active, purposive, and goal directed. They seek out media and use media to achieve desired goals and satisfy specific needs. An initial set of audience needs was identified early on (McQuail, 1971): surveillance, personal identity, personal relationships, and diversion. However, it does behoove one to note that audience needs may themselves be partially influenced by societal processes—including mass media.

Applied to organ donation, this approach posits that audiences must be taken seriously. As active consumers of media, audiences bring with them values, expectations, needs, and goals. Thus, one recommendation may be to seriously consider the placement of organ donation messages when making media buys. Different organ donation messages may work best in different programs. Perhaps it would be best to imbed relatively straightforward information appeals in news and information programming targeting older adults. Alternatively, it may be better to relegate pallid information-only messages to the historical dustbin and come up with more visually and sonically interesting ads.

It is worth noting that care needs to be taken with message placement. Serious audience analysis is required as different audience needs may be addressed by the same programming. For example, viewers watching soap operas to learn about romantic relationships may be positively influenced by a character questioning another's charitable values upon finding out that that individual is not an organ donor. On the other hand, viewers watching for pure escapism may resent attempts to elicit guilt in the audience—especially if such attempts are heavy-handed. At minimum, a uses and gratifications perspective should lead organ donation message developers to expend considerable effort in formative research in order to understand target audience perspectives and viewing habits.

Summary of Theoretical Perspectives: What Can Mass Media Do?

Numerous theoretical perspectives converge on the idea that mass media are most useful if used as an avenue for (a) maintaining issue salience, (b) shaping public perceptions of issue importance, (c) creating perceptions of normative behavior, (d) shaping the terms of debate on an issue, and, ultimately, (e) encouraging and facilitating both public and interpersonal discussion. Given this knowledge, much more attention should be paid to maximizing the salience, prioritization, and discussion of organ donation. For example, approaches should be invest-igated to ensure that organ donation should have a frequent and enduring presence in the mass media. Moreover, it is worth examining possible benefits that may accrue from playing off media coverage of controversial events involv-ing organ donation and transplantation. Controversy makes issues salient and engages audiences—two features that need to be exploited instead of avoided (see Siegel et al., this volume).

It is crucial to remember that organ donation mass media campaigns lack an immediate mechanism for registration. In other words, most television viewers do not have a mechanism for registration at hand. Even if they are inspired, it is unlikely that registration will occur absent opportunities to do so (see Siegel et al., this volume). Thus, the five outcomes of mass media discussed above are especially valuable in the case of organ donation registration. The combination of high issue salience, positive public perceptions of organ donation as a socially normative behavior, and frequent interpersonal discussion of donation should go far in encouraging actual registration once an opportunity presents itself.

Organ Donation Mass Media Campaigns

We turn now to a review of organ donation mass media campaigns implemented on a broad community level in one or more media markets primarily using broad-cast media (television and radio). Such an emphasis is in keeping with traditional conceptualizations and research on mass media campaigns and their effects (i.e., Noar, 2006; Snyder, 2007). Moreover, studies lacking any outcome data other than campaign reach (i.e., Allen et al., this volume) are excluded, as are mass media efforts addressing living organ donation. Lastly, although there has been considerable research activity wherein media channels make up one or more aspects of an intervention (i.e., Feeley, Anker, Vincent, & Williams, this volume; Siegel et al., 2008), such studies are not the focus of this review. These efforts are typified by interventions targeting a very specific and localized population contextualized within a particular setting. Although providing valuable information on the use of organ donation messages, these studies reflect different dynamics than those conceptualizing mass media effects in more traditional terms.

A search of three databases (Communication and Mass Media Complete, PsychINFO, and MEDLINE) using the search term *organ donation* resulted in 1,750 articles published between 1970 and 2009 that included *organ donation* in the title. Perusal of the search results as well as a citation review of articles found following the study criteria noted above resulted in 17 publications reporting on 14 unique campaigns (see Table 3.1). Two other campaigns are reported on in chapters in this volume, and a third is currently under review. A number of key observations can be made about these studies: (a) Hispanic and African Americans have received approximately as much attention as the general population; (b) with two exceptions (Alvaro, Siegel, Crano, & Pace Jones, under review; Sanner, Hedman, & Tufveson, 1995), evaluation has been conducted largely following quasi-experimental pretest–posttest designs lacking a control or comparison group; (c) behavioral outcomes are reported in about half of the studies; and (d) most studies have been conducted in the United States. A detailed decade-by-decade review points to considerable variation in scientific rigor as well as a need for more research.

The 1980s

The use of mass media campaigns to foster public education about organ donation and transplantation is a relatively recent phenomenon, and rigorous examination of such efforts is more recent still. Early campaigns launched in the 1980s— the District of Columbia Organ Donor Program (DCODP) in Washington, DC (Callender, 1987); the Dow Chemical Company Take Initiative Program (DOWTIP) from 1986 to 1992 (Callender, 2001; Callender, Burston, Yeager, & Miles, 1997); a program in St. Louis, Missouri (Kappel, Whitlock, Parks-Thomas, Hong, & Freedman, 1993); and a Saudi Arabian campaign (Aswad, 1991)—certainly are to be commended for their prescience, innovation, and attention to minority communities. Both of Callender and colleagues' efforts and the St. Louis campaign spearheaded an ongoing emphasis on minority populations by targeting African Americans. Data on campaign outcomes largely reflect the marketing and public education considerations driving campaign development and implementation.

Published assessments of Callender and colleagues' campaigns (Callender, 2001; Callender et al., 1997) and the St. Louis project (Kappel et al., 1993) are to be commended for the inclusion of pre- and post-campaign measures. Moreover,

Table 3.1 Published OD mass media campaign studies

Study	Target Audience	Research Design	Behavior Outcome	Campaign Location
Alvaro et al. (2006) Study 1	Hisp Amer	Pre/post	No	USA/AZ
Study 2	Hisp Amer	Pre/post	No	USA/AZ
Alvaro et al. (under review)	Hisp Amer	Pre/post and control	No	USA/NV
Aswad (1991)	General	Post only	No	Saudi Arabia
Callender (1987)	Af Amer	Pre/post	Yes	USA/DC
Callender (2001)	Af Amer+	Pre/post	Yes	USA/DC
Callender et al. (1997)	Af Amer+	Pre/post	Yes	USA/DC
Cosse et al. (1997, 2001)	General	Pre/post+	No	USA/VA
Downing and Jones (this volume)	General	Pre/post+	Yes	USA/OH
Frates et al. (2006)	Hisp Amer	Pre/post+	Yes	USA/CA
Kappel et al. (1993)	Af Amer	Pre/post+	Yes	USA/MO
Lauri and Lauri (2005)	General	Pre/post	No	Malta
McLoughlin et al. (1991)	General	Pre/post	Yes	Australia/NSW
Persijn and van Netter (1997)	General	Pre/post	Yes	Netherlands
Radosevich et al. (this volume)	Af Amer	Pre/post	No	USA/MN
Sanner et al. (1995)	General	Pre/post and control	Yes	Sweden
Wolf et al. (1997)	General	Post only	No	USA

even at this early stage, campaign assessments took behavioral organ donation indicators such as organ donation consent and registration statistics into account. For example, in reporting on a campaign launched in 1982, Callender (1987) was able to report increases in DMV registration of 25 per month pre-campaign to 600 per month postcampaign. In the St. Louis study (Kappel et al.), referrals of African American donors increased from 30 in 1988 to 61 in 1990. This was a good foundation for the increasing methodological sophistication to follow (see Fischer, this volume).

The 1990s

The 1990s saw the launch of the National Minority Organ/Tissue Transplant Education Program (MOTTEP) in the United States (Callender, 2001; Callender et al., 1997). In 1993 the program targeted African Americans in three cities and was expanded to 15 cities in 1995 with the focus expanded to include other minorities. A second major development in organ donation efforts at public education initiated during this time was the National Coalition on Organ Donation's (now Donate Life America) "Share Your Life. Share Your Decision" campaign. Launched in July 1994, this first phase of the campaign was supported by $33.4 million in donated media for television, radio, and print advertisements. Future incarnations of the campaign saw the use of actual donor families and celebrities and continued funding.

Unfortunately, evaluations of campaign impact are flawed, but the results are promising. A post-campaign survey (Wolf, Servino, & Nathan, 1997) found 59% of respondents reporting exposure to a TV or radio commercial about organ and tissue donation—10% of whom reported signing a donor card. Cosse and colleagues (Cosse & Weisenberger, 2000; Cosse, Weisenberger, & Taylor, 1997) assessed the impact of the national campaign on local audiences in Richmond, Virginia. Yearly cross-sectional tracking surveys from 1994 to 1997 reveal statistically significant increases in self-reported organ donation registration. From a base rate of 39% in 1994, rates increased in subsequent years to 37% in 1995, 50% in 1996, and then 44% in 1997 (Cosse & Weisenberger). Limitations of this study include small sample sizes for each survey (i.e., N = approximately 150), no control or comparison group, and no assessment of campaign exposure. As the authors note, at the time of these studies, much non-campaign publicity about organ donation was generated by transplants received by such famous recipients as Mickey Mantle and David Crosby (as well as other stories). Such publicity may have accounted for some of the observed differences. A comparison or control group would have been valuable. The methodological sophistication of these studies was an improvement over the research of the 1980s, but there was still considerable room for improvement.

Major developments in organ donation campaigns during the 1990s were not limited to the United States. International efforts included campaigns in Australia, the Netherlands, and Sweden. The 2-month-long Australian campaign (McLoughlin et al., 1991), designed to increase the number of drivers registering as organ donors while obtaining or renewing licenses at local motor vehicles locations, was launched in August 1990 and consisted of a 30-second television ad complemented by posters, bus ads, and interviews on TV and radio. A total of 21 television and radio interviews were conducted, and 16 newspaper articles were published immediately following the launch. Data gathered at local motor vehicles offices indicate that, prior to the campaign, 28% of drivers' license applicants registered as organ donors and 34% registered following the campaign. No statistical tests are reported, and no further information is provided. The lack of a control group allows for a secular trend as an alternative explanation for the increase in registrations.

The Dutch Foundation for the Information/Education of Organ and Tissue Donors opened its office in 1991 and immediately implemented a number of community outreach efforts (Persijn & van Netter, 1997). A television and radio campaign was launched shortly after a 15-minute film on organ donation premiered on Dutch television during National Donor Week in October 1993. Television spots (1 minute and 4 minutes long) were created from this film and aired throughout the next 2 years—supplemented by other television and radio programs and, in 1994, by radio ads. Large surveys (i.e., $N = 1,000+$) were conducted in 1988, in 1992, and postcampaign in 1994. Donor registrations were also tracked. The latter provide the most interesting data—revealing identical registrations in 1988 and 1992 (2,050,000) and a considerable increase in 1994 (2,625,000). The evaluation report provides much process information—revealing a host of outreach efforts beyond the media campaign—but presents no statistical analyses or assessments of campaign exposure. This is problematic in that observed differences could be due to efforts other than the campaign, and there is no indication that the campaign was seen or heard by all.

As noted, the evaluation design of the Swedish campaign (Sanner, Hedman & Tufreson, 1995) is considerably improved by the addition of a control group to multiple campaign conditions. This decidedly more rigorous approach is an early indicator of the behavioral-science orientation that will typify the evaluation of subsequent organ donation campaigns. The central aim of the study is to evaluate public education campaigns implemented in three geographical areas of Sweden in the winter of 1992–1993. One key contribution of this study, beyond the inclusion of a no-intervention control group, is the stated secondary aim of testing the effects of different *kinds* of information. Three interventions were compared: (a) an intensive intervention, including advertising donor cards, training key groups, and lecturing at meetings and exhibitions; (b) simply distributing a brochure with two donor cards to each household; and (c) Intervention 1 combined with 2.

Data from large ($N = 700$) pre- and post-intervention surveys indicate increased awareness in intervention areas (vs. control) yet no differences in organ donation attitudes. Registration data reveal the most important findings—donors more than doubled (3% to 13% and 5% to 12%) in the two areas where brochures were provided (Interventions 2 and 3) yet remained the same (5%) in the control area and the area receiving Intervention 1. This provides evidence for the efficacy of providing people with a registration mechanism (for more discussion, see Siegel et al., this volume). Moreover, the results support the need for behavioral indicators, as focusing only on attitudes leaves out an important piece of the equation.

The evaluation of another international organ donation campaign—this one implemented in Malta (Lauri & Lauri, 2005)—is an example of a creative approach to examining campaign effects. The central goal of the campaign was to publicize organ donation and increase registration. The month-long campaign used ads aired on national television and radio stations as well as newspaper ads. The ads featured kidney transplant recipients as well as donor family members providing testimonials about organ donation benefits. Considerable formative research including surveys, interviews, and focus groups was undertaken to assist in campaign development.

The unique aspect of the evaluation of this campaign is a focus on people's social representations of organ donation. Five focus groups were used to assess pre- to post-campaign differences in such representations. To do this, precampaign focus group participants were shown 60 photographs depicting a variety of people, then asked to choose photographs of people who would donate their organs and of those who would not. Word associations elicited by the photographs comprised the core data. Results indicate that, prior to the campaign, donors were perceived to be young, caring, and active professionals or public figures, whereas following the campaign, donors were perceived to be more ordinary working-class people with families who are generous and informed about current affairs.

2000–Present

The close of the 1990s saw the creation of the Health Resource Services Administration Division of Transplantation's (HRSA/DoT) Social and Behavioral Sciences Grant program (see Ganikos, this volume). This program has provided the motivation and funding for numerous research projects investigating the impact of organ donation media campaigns. A key feature of these efforts is a distinct behavioral-science approach reflected in improved methodology along with strong collaboration between organ donation professionals and researchers. A noteworthy aspect of these projects is a focus on minority communities; in fact, as seen in Table 3.1, of the published studies funded by this program, only one (Downing & Jones, this volume) targets the general market. All the projects to follow have received HRSA/DoT funding.

The establishment of the Ohio Donor Registry provided the impetus for launching, in January 2005, a statewide mass media campaign including television and radio ads, billboards, posters, brochures, and a new Web site. The "Hero" campaign was implemented throughout 2005 and highlighted individuals of all ages, races, and ethnicity, using the tag line "Be a hero. Be an organ and tissue donor. Join the Ohio Donor Registry. www.donatelifeohio.org" (see Downing & Jones, this volume). During the same time frame, an Ohio Bureau of Motor Vehicles (OBMV)–based campaign launched, with all OBMV locations provided with marketing materials.

Campaign evaluation (Downing & Jones, this volume) was conducted using registry data and data from three large cross-sectional surveys conducted in 2001, 2003, and 2005. Registrations increased from 46% to 51%. Youth rates were most dramatic—with a 14 percentage point difference. Survey results indicate statistically significant increases in registry awareness, attitudes toward donation, willingness to donate, and self-reported registration. The absence of a control group precludes solid conclusions, and the impact of the media campaign is difficult to differentiate from that of the DMV outreach; however, the use of multiple data sources and sensitive measures lends some confidence to the interpretation of results. The richness of the data derived from this project exemplifies the increased emphasis on measurement and research methodology characterizing the evaluation of these more recent interventions.

A second intervention (Radosevich, Larson, Scott, Jones, Tendle, & Gunderson, this volume) involves a more focused effort in terms of both geography and audience. The media campaign, using materials from a national campaign developed by the Coalition on Donation/Donate Life America, included radio spots, television spots, brochures, and posters emphasizing the importance of organ donation—developed specifically for African Americans. Local print ads and press kits supplemented these materials. Public relations efforts in the form of interviews with health care professionals, recipients, and donor families on local radio and television stations were also part of the campaign.

The evaluation used a quasi-experimental pretest–posttest study design with pretest ($N = 278$) data collected 6 months prior to the campaign and posttest data ($N = 187$) collected 6 months post-campaign. Analyses revealed significant pretest–posttest differences: increased awareness of the campaign and donation information sources, increased knowledge, and more positive attitudes. A self-reported 7 percentage point increase in registration behavior was not statistically significant. However, donor authorization rates for African Americans increased from 29% to 63% over the course of the campaign. Rates for Whites remained stable, whereas those for other races declined. Lastly, although the study did not include a comparison group, analyses assessing the relationship between campaign exposure and outcomes were conducted. Results indicate a significant relationship between exposure and donation attitudes. In total, the results are positive.

Hispanic Campaigns: California, Arizona, and Nevada

Although African Americans have traditionally been, and continue to be, targeted by donation media campaigns, interventions directed at an emerging minority group, Hispanic Americans, have gained momentum. In 2001, Frates and colleagues (Frates, Bohrer, & Thomas, 2006) implemented and evaluated a Spanish-language campaign in Los Angeles stations composed of three television and radio ads. Two of the television ads feature children—one ostensibly in need of a transplant, and another who grows to become a physician informing a family about the need for a donor. The third features a young patient in need of a transplant. Radio ads lasted a year.

Campaign impact was assessed via hospital consent rates and telephone surveys. Four telephone surveys ($N = 500$ each) assessed organ donation attitudes and behaviors. One survey was implemented precampaign, whereas another followed media flights for each of the next 3 years. Analyses of survey data point toward considerable campaign exposure as well as changes in donation beliefs but no changes in self-reported registration. Consent data reveal increases in hospital consents from baseline through subsequent years. However, the study authors noted that, during the time frame of the study, additional bilingual and bicultural requesters were hired—potentially having a direct impact on consent rates. Adding to the difficulty of assessing campaign impact was local publicity attending the death of a young Hispanic heart transplant recipient (from medical errors). This may have mitigated against positive campaign impact.

One of our own programs of research has been concerned with the assessment of Spanish-language mass media campaigns targeting organ donation. Sara Pace Jones at the Donor Network of Arizona drew us in as collaborators in 2000, and together we have continued this HRSA/DoT–funded work through to the present. In our initial media project (Alvaro, Jones, Robles, & Siegel, 2006, Study 1), a campaign was implemented in Tucson, Arizona, from January through June 2001. Data from a pre-campaign telephone survey (Alvaro, Jones, Robles, & Siegel, 2005) and focus groups were used as formative research informing message development and campaign implementation tactics.

The campaign consisted of four Spanish-language 30-second television ads and two Spanish-language 60-second radio ads. One of the television ads emphasizes the considerable efforts taken by medical personnel to try to save the life of potential donors while also addressing the impact of transplantation. The other three television ads share a theme—the positive impact of organ donation on local Hispanic organ recipients—and feature a montage of the life events of an organ recipient narrated by that recipient. The two radio ads used the local bishop to convey the Catholic Church's position on organ donation. Using paid media (approximately $30,000), the campaign achieved substantial airtime—the television ads aired 697 times, and the radio ads aired 1,368 times. The considerable airtime was possible due to the relatively inexpensive cost of Spanish-language media in the Tucson market. Value-added airtime from stations with an interest in promoting prosocial behaviors to their audience also added measurably to the airtime for our ads.

Campaign impact was evaluated via a quasi-experimental pretest–posttest design with telephone surveys ($N = 500$) of Spanish-speaking adult residents of Tucson. A number of noteworthy findings emerged. First, considerable campaign exposure was reported with 45.5% of respondents reporting recall of at least one television ad following a description of the ads (aided recall). Aided-recall data reveal that approximately 30% of respondents report recalling at least one ad. Second, pre–post differences in specific beliefs about religion opposition, family opposition, medical care, and morbidity emerged. The differences suggest a more favorable orientation toward donation. Third, post-campaign family discussion of organ donation was greater than precampaign levels.

We followed this initial study with a replication implemented in Phoenix, Arizona, from September 2001 through July 2002. The same television ads were used in both studies. Two new radio ads were developed for Phoenix—and the test of the radio ads was the same as for those aired in Tucson except that the source was the bishop of Phoenix. As with Study 1, considerable airtime was purchased (approximately $50,000) for the campaign: combined, the television ads aired 1,855 times, and the radio ads aired a total of 1,264 times.

As in Study 1, campaign impact was assessed using a quasi-experimental pretest–posttest design. Procedures were exactly the same as those used in the earlier study. The results are similar but not identical to those of Study 1. Aided recall was high, with nearly two thirds of respondents recalling at least one television ad and one third recalling at least one radio ad. As in Study 1, pro-donation pre–post differences were observed for beliefs about religious and family barriers; however, perceptions of medical care and issue morbidity did not differ. Importantly, and in keeping with Study 1 results, family discussion of organ donation was significantly higher at posttest.

Taken together, the results of Study 1 and Study 2 are encouraging. First, it is evident that a fairly low-cost Spanish-language mass media campaign using broadcast media can achieve considerable exposure, an outcome attained in the general population usually at considerable expense. Second, perceived religious barriers may be successfully addressed, and family discussion, a core feature of the donation process (Martinez et al., 2001; Marwick, 1991), may be facilitated via mass media. Of course, the lack of a no-intervention comparison group limits causal inferences, and no behavioral indicators of campaign impact are available—Arizona's donor registry did not exist at the time, and DMV registration was not an option. Nevertheless, the high exposure, combined with pre–post differences in beliefs targeted by the campaign ads, is suggestive of campaign impact.

In a final study (Alvaro et al., under review) in the series, we had an opportunity to replicate the campaign reported in Studies 1 and 2 with the important addition of a no-campaign comparison community. In this study, Las Vegas, Nevada, served as the intervention community, whereas Phoenix, Arizona, served as the no-campaign comparison site. Survey procedures were identical to those in the prior studies. As 3 years had passed since the end of the Phoenix intervention (Study 2), there was the possibility of a not entirely "clean" comparison site, but we believed that, if this was the case, any bias would work in a conservative direction—against finding significant differences between the intervention and comparison community. In another improvement over the prior studies, we were able to access behavioral outcome data in the form of hospital consent rates. The intervention consisted of a monthly rotation of our prior campaign ads and Spanish-language television and radio ads developed by the Coalition on Organ Donation (see Table 3.2). Media buys were identical for both sets of ads.

Table 3.2   Counterbalanced design for Las Vegas campaign

Month	Nov	Dec	Jan	Feb	Mar	Apr	May	Jun	Jul
Ads	B	D	C	D	B	C	D	C	B

Note: D = DNA ads. C = Donate Life ads. B = Both ads.

The results of the study are both enlightening and frustrating. First, call-tracking data showed no monthly variation—indicating no call impact due to ads from the two different campaigns; however, post-campaign aided and unaided-recall data revealed that ads created specifically for Arizona (Studies 1 and 2) were recalled at a higher rate than the Coalition ads. Overall exposure to the campaign was approximately 50%. Unfortunately, respondents in our comparison community also reported ad exposure around 50%. This is problematic considering that there was no campaign airing in Phoenix at that time.

Analyses using only those in the comparison site *not* reporting exposure reveal evidence for campaign impact on a number of variables: attitudes, intentions to discuss organ donation with loved ones, intentions to sign up as an organ donor, willingness to become a donor upon death, and willingness to donate a family member's organs upon his or her death. Support for campaign impact is perhaps most persuasively indicated by hospital consent data indicating consents for Hispanic rising from a pre-campaign level of 37% to a post-campaign rate of 50%. During the same time period, the percentage of actual donors of Hispanic ethnicity rose from 11% to 20%.

Taken together, this series of studies, combined with data from Frates and colleagues (2006), provides growing evidence for the positive impact of organ donation mass media campaigns on donation outcomes in Hispanic communities. What remains is unassailable evidence gathered from studies utilizing a functioning comparison or control group. The challenges we faced with our comparison community, in part, led us to embark on a current project where the same campaign is being replicated in the greater Los Angeles area with multiple intervention and control sites. Moreover, this current project will allow assessment of the relative impact of mass media and community outreach—major components coupled in most studies.

Mass Media Organ Donation Campaigns: Challenges and Considerations

Given the preceding review, a number of conclusions can be arrived at regarding the use of mass media campaigns to improve organ donation outcomes. First, a moderate number of campaigns have been implemented both in the United States and internationally. Second, considerable efforts have been made to reach minority audiences both disproportionately in need of organs and underrepresented in donor registration. Third, taken as a whole, this body of data strongly suggests that mass media campaigns may have a positive impact on organ donation outcomes such as beliefs, intentions, and perhaps even donor registration and/or family consent to donate. However, the evidence for the latter must be taken as merely suggestive and not anywhere close to definitive.

In that there is still much to be done in this area, we turn now to a discussion of broad issues and considerations affecting the use of mass media campaigns to improve organ donation outcomes. In this section, we draw on the lessons learned and examples set by the extant research. Our aim is to clarify what we believe to be important issues and provide some focus for future campaign designers and implementers.

Design Challenges

Although there have been considerable improvements in measurement and analytic approaches, evaluation designs have not kept pace with these improvements. One particularly important deficit is the general absence of control or comparison groups. Without such groups, secular trends in organ donation outcomes cannot be tracked—making the possibility of these trends strong rival hypotheses. Analyses that take into consideration measures of campaign exposure can go some way to compensating for the absence of a control or comparison group, but they are not enough. Another methodological deficit is overreliance on single intervention sites. The simultaneous implementation and evaluation of campaigns in multiple locations, with multiple control or comparison sites, would provide for more appropriate analyses taking into account the characteristics of each site (for an extended discussion of this issue, see Fischer, this volume). The design of our current study replicating our Hispanic campaign in the greater Los Angeles area is one of the few including multiple intervention and comparison sites.

Who Should Be Targeted by Mass Media Campaigns?

Audience considerations are indispensable to the success of mass media campaigns. Many of the studies reviewed in this chapter have focused on minority populations. We strongly encourage such interventions. Besides being an ethical approach to correct organ donation disparities, such a focus maximizes campaign expenditures and message impact. One of the greatest drawbacks of mass media campaigns is that they are expensive and, thus, difficult to sustain without considerable funding. The expense can be substantially limited by implementing campaigns via mass media outlets specifically geared to minority populations.

Programming and advertising on minority stations simply cost less than in the general market. Another argument in favor of minority media stations is that they have a considerable share of the target audience, whereas in the general market, with a nearly inexhaustible menu of programming options, the audience is more diffuse. For example, the Spanish-language Univision network consistently attains an 85% share of the U.S. Hispanic television market.

These factors have a considerable impact on campaign exposure as well as on attempts to ascertain such exposure given limited funding for survey samples. In short, it is often far easier to expose a minority audience to a particular message and to locate representative audience members who have been exposed to such messages. For example, as part of a recent project, we implemented a mass media campaign in the general market in order to raise awareness of local organ registration kiosks. We had a budget comparable to those for our prior Hispanic campaign studies but were only able to achieve aided-recall rates of 5%. This is far below recall rates of 40%+ obtained by the Hispanic campaigns.

In targeting a general audience, mass expenditure coupled with a focused message introducing a novel idea may result in meaningful exposure. For example, the campaign introducing Ohio's first-person consent registry was recalled by 38% of survey respondents (Downing & Jones, this volume). Alternatively, finding a niche within the general market could also prove efficient. One example may be a campaign targeting local sports fans via ads placed in broadcasts of local team events. Such targeted efforts may or may not be practical or desirable, but they would make efficient use of limited funds.

Assessing Audience Exposure to a Campaign

As just discussed, audience exposure is crucial in order to derive any benefit from even the best messages. Questions about how to best assess exposure are seemingly simple, yet they will elicit a fairly complex response if asked of mass media researchers. One industry standard for assessing audience exposure to a particular ad or program is the use of gross ratings points (GRPs). However, interpretation of GRPs is fraught with problems. For example, a GRP of 250 could be attained by a television ad airing either 10 times reaching 25% of a target audience or 100 times reaching 2.5% of that audience. Although GRPs are useful, they should be complemented by other measures of exposure.

Self-reported recall is one viable option. In fact, recall goes beyond exposure to reflect cognitive processing of a message—recalling a message indicates attention to that message and its storage in memory. However, this measure also requires careful scrutiny. First, one must distinguish between aided and unaided recall. For example, to assess the former, we (Alvaro et al., 2006) typically provide a brief description of a television ad, then ask respondents if they have seen it. In the case of unaided recall, respondents are usually asked if they have seen any television ads in a predetermined time period (i.e., the past 90 days). In comparing responses to these two measures, a familiar pattern emerges—unaided recall is higher than aided recall. Obviously, it is best to use both measures. However, if time is short, unaided-recall measures are the rule.

A second issue with self-reported recall is a tendency for respondents to over-report exposure. In aided-recall contexts, a common practice used to address this phenomenon is to assess self-reported exposure to a fake ad. Once can at least establish a base rate for the bias and include it in calculations of exposure. In our Study 3, 17% of survey respondents, after listening to a description of an ad that did not exist, answered in the affirmative when asked if they had seen the ad. One way to address this bias in unaided-recall contexts is to ask respondents reporting exposure to describe ads (see Siegel & Alvaro, 2006, for an example). However, this is a fairly difficult task and may result in considerable under-reporting. A second approach that should be considered with unaided recall is to include this measure in pre-campaign or comparison group surveys even when you know the ads have never been aired. This again allows for a base rate estimate that can be taken into account in exposure calculations. Again, using our Study 3 as an example, we discovered that 50% of respondents in the comparison site reported unaided recall of organ donation campaign ads in the past 6 months—despite the fact that no donation ads had run for a number of years.

Not All Messages Are the Same!

A message is not a message is not a message. Campaign effects are not maximized if messages are not derived from solid formative research and/or behavioral science theory. Moreover, intended outcomes may actually be harmed by bad messages (i.e., Burgoon, Alvaro, Grandpre, & Voloudakis, 2003). It is generally acknowledged that formative research is an essential component of any mass media campaign. Many organ donation campaign developers—especially more recently—conduct focus groups, interviews, or some other form of research to inform them as to audience responses to potential appeals. However, what is still rare is the systematic testing of multiple message types in order to determine relative message effects. Although definitive studies of mass media campaign impact are still required, efforts should also be made to ascertain which particular types of messages offer the best outcomes. Let us first acknowledge that we are as guilty of this as anyone when it comes to our community-based mass media campaign research. We, and many others, have conducted studies to assess the relative impact of varying message types in more controlled contexts. In fact, there is a small but growing body of research that investigates this very aspect of organ donation messages.

Smith and colleagues (Smith, Morrison, Kopfman, & Ford, 1994) have been pioneers in this area and have motivated other researchers to follow their lead.

Such research is very promising. For example, in our study on print messages featured on computer kiosks enabling registration on the Arizona Donor Registry (Siegel et al., 2008), we found considerable variation in registration due to the manipulation of specific message features. One approach for future campaign research is to, at minimum, conduct pilot research to assess relative message impact in a more controlled or less costly context, then use the data to inform message development for a larger mass media campaign. A second, and more ambitious, approach is to build multiple campaign message types into larger mass media campaigns targeting multiple sites. Of course, in both instances, message types selected for testing should be derived from theory (see Siegel, Alvaro, & Hohman, this volume; see also Fischer, this volume).

Conclusion

Although significant strides have been made in the study of mass media campaign impact on organ donation, considerable work remains to be completed. Definitive studies of mass media impact have yet to be undertaken, and more focused studies examining issues such as those outlined above should be encouraged and facilitated. A solid base has been built for future studies incorporating multiple intervention and comparison or control sites, targeting more narrowly defined audiences, using more sophisticated and sensitive measures of exposure and campaign recall, and assessing the impact of various message types on donation outcomes. The latter is especially pressing as it is increasingly evident that, even given equal exposure, not all message types result in equal outcomes (Siegel et al., 2008).

Moreover, almost all the studies reported herein operationalize mass media campaigns as a series of television and/or radio advertisements, leaving a number of potential media options largely unexamined. Would entertainment–education approaches work in this domain? How about radio call-in programs? Telethons? How effective is the placement of interviews and news stories focused on organ donation? How about dramatic programming? Documentaries? Furthermore, and perhaps most importantly, few studies have maximized the full potential inherent in theory-driven mass media interventions. Awareness and use of theories of mass media impact open entire new vistas on potential interventions as well as on novel approaches to the measurement of media impact. The studies reviewed in this chapter are pioneering efforts that have set a firm foundation upon which we can continue to fortify our knowledge about how mass media may best be used to improve organ donation outcomes. By taking stock of what is known, we can move on with renewed vigor and enthusiasm for the discoveries yet ahead.

Acknowledgments

The projects discussed in this manuscript were funded by grants from HRSA, Division of Transplantation grant (H39 OT 00021-01, R39OT01148). Sincere gratitudety Sara Pace Jones, Tim Brown, Stacy Underwood, and the rest of the Donor Network of Arizona for their collaboration and ongoing support. The opinions expressed herein are those of the authors and do not necessarily represent those of the funding agency.

References

Alvaro, E. M., Jones, S. P., Robles, A. S., & Siegel, J. T. (2005). Predictors of organ donation behavior among Hispanic Americans. *Progress in Transplantation, 15*, 149–156.

Alvaro, E. M., Jones, S. P., Robles, A. S., & Siegel, J. T. (2006). Hispanic organ donation: Impact of a Spanish-language organ donation campaign. *Journal of the National Medical Association, 98*, 1–8.

Alvaro, E. M., Siegel, J. T., Crano, W. D., & Pace Jones, S. (Under review). Replication and extension of a Spanish-language organ donation media campaign. *Journal of Health Communication.*

Aswad, S. (1991). The role of public education in cadaveric transplantation in Saudi Arabia. *Transplantation Proceedings, 23*, 2694–2696.

Bauer, R. A. (1964). The obstinate audience: The influence process from the point of view of social communication. *American Psychologist, 19*, 319–328.

Berelson, B., & Steiner, G. A. (1964). *Human behavior: An inventory of scientific findings.* New York: Harcourt, Brace & World.

Burgoon, M., Alvaro, E., Grandpre, J., & Voloudakis, M. (2003). Revisiting the theory of psychological reactance: Communicating threats to attitudinal freedom. In J. Dillard & M. Pfau (Eds.) *The handbook of persuasion* (pp. 213–232). Thousand Oaks, CA: Sage.

Callender, C. (1987). Organ donation in Blacks: A community approach. *Transplantation Proceedings, 19*, 1551–1554.

Callender, C. (2001). Obstacles to organ donation in ethnic minorities. *Pediatric Transplantation, 5*, 383–385.

Callender, C. Burston, B., Yeager, C., & Miles, P. (1997). A National Minority Transplant Program for Increasing Donation Rates. *Transplantation Proceedings, 29*, 1482–1483.

Cosse, T. J., & Weisenberger, T. M. (2000). Words versus actions about organ donation: A four-year tracking study of attitudes and self-reported behavior. *Journal of Business Research, 50*, 297–303.

Cosse, T. J., Weisenberger, T. M., & Taylor, G. J. (1997). Walking the walk: Behavior shifts to match attitude toward organ donation—Richmond, Virginia, 1994–1996. *Transplantation Proceedings, 29*, 3248.

Durkin, S., & Wakefield, M. (2006). Maximizing the impact of emotive antitobacco advertising: Effects of interpersonal discussion and program placement. *Social Marketing Quarterly, 3*, 3–14.

Frates, J., Bohrer, G. G., & Thomas, D. (2006). Promoting organ donation to Hispanics: The role of the media and medicine. *Journal of Health Communication, 11*, 683–698.

Gerbner, G. (1969). Toward "cultural indicators": The analysis of mass mediated public message systems. *AV Communication Review, 17*, 137–148.

Gerbner, G., Gross, L., Morgan, M., & Signorielli, N. (1980). The mainstreaming of America: Violence profile #11. *Journal of Communication, 30*, 10–29.

Gunther, A. C., Bolt, D., Borzekowski, D. L. G., Liebhart, J. L., & Dillard, J. P. (2006). Presumed influence on peer norms: How mass media indirectly affect adolescent smoking. *Journal of Communication, 56*, 52–68.

Hafstad, A., & Aaro, L. E. (1997). Activating interpersonal influence through provocative appeals: Evaluation of a mass media-based antismoking campaign targeting adolescents. *Health Communication, 9*, 253–272.

Kappel, D. F., Whitlock, M. E., Parks-Thomas, T. D., Hong, B. A., & Freedman, B. K. (1993). Increasing African American organ donation: The St. Louis experience. *Transplantation Proceedings, 25*, 2489–2490.

Klapper, T. (1960). *The effects of mass communication*. Glencoe, IL: Free Press.

Lauri, M. A., & Lauri, J. (2005). Social representations of organ donors and non-donors. *Journal of Community and Applied Social Psychology, 15*, 108–119.

Lazarsfeld, P. F., Berelson, B. R., & Gaudet, H. (1948). *The people's choice*. New York: Columbia University Press.

Martinez, J. M., Lopez J. S., Martin, A., Martin, M., Scandroglio, B., & Martin J. (2001). Organ donation and family decision-making within the Spanish donation system. *Social Science and Medicine, 53*, 405–421.

Marwick, C. (1991). Key to organ donation may be cultural awareness. *Journal of the American Medical Association, 265*, 176.

McCombs, M., & Shaw, D. (1972). The agenda-setting function of mass media. *Public Opinion Quarterly, 36*, 176–187.

McLoughlin, M. P., Chapman, J. R., Gordon, S. V., Ledwich, M., Macdonald, G., & Mochacsi, P. (1991). "Go on—say yes": A publicity campaign to increase commitment to organ donation on the driver's license in New South Wales. *Transplantation Proceedings, 23*, 2693.

McQuail, D. (1971). *Towards a sociology of mass communication*. London: Collier-Macmillan.

Morton, T., & Duck, J. (2001). Communication and health beliefs: Mass and interpersonal influences on perceptions of risk to self and others. *Communication Research, 28*, 602–626.

Noar, S. M. (2006). A 10-year retrospective of research in health mass media campaigns: Where do we go from here? *Journal of Health Communication, 11*, 21–42.

Persijn, G. G., & van Netter, A. R. (1997). Public education and organ donation. *Transplantation Proceedings, 29*, 1614–1617.

Sanner, M. A., Hedman, H., & Tufveson, G. (1995). Evaluation of an organ-donor-card campaign in Sweden. *Clinical Transplantation, 9*, 326–333.

Schramm, W. (1982). *Men, women, messages and media*. New York: Harper & Row.

Siegel, J. T., & Alvaro, E. M. (2006). An evaluation of Arizona's Youth Tobacco Access prevention media campaign. *American Journal of Preventive Medicine, 30*, 284–291.

Siegel, J. T., Alvaro, E., Pace-Jones, S., Crano, W. C., Lac, A., & Ting, S. (2008). A quasi-experimental investigation of message appeal variations on organ donor registration rates. *Health Psychology, 27,* 170–178.

Smith, S. W., Morrison, K., Kopfman, J. E., & Ford, L. A. (1994). The influence of prior thought and intent on the memorability and persuasiveness of organ donation message strategies. *Health Communication, 6,* 1–20.

Snyder, L. B. (2007). Meta-analyses of mediated health campaigns. In R. W. Preiss, B. M. Gayle, N. Burrell, M. Allen, & J. Bryant (Eds.), *Mass media effects research: Advances through meta-analysis* (pp. 327–344). Mahwah, NJ: Lawrence Erlbaum.

Wolf, J. S., Servino, E. M., & Nathan, H. N. (1997). National strategy to develop public acceptance of organ and tissue donation. *Transplantation Proceedings, 29,* 1477–1478.

4

The Effectiveness of the Donate Life—African American Campaign in Minneapolis–St. Paul

David M. Radosevich, Susan Mau Larson, Tiffany Scott, Clarence Jones, William Tendle, and Susan Gunderson

African Americans are disproportionately affected by kidney disease when compared to Whites. Although 35% of individuals on the kidney waiting list are African American, only 33% are designated as organ donors on their driver's license. This compares with a donor designation rate of approximately 60% for Whites. Whereas the percentage of African Americans designated as donors is unconfirmed, the donation authorization rate—that is, those donating organs—among African Americans remains lower than that of the overall population (Sheehy et al., 2003).

The LifeSource Donation Service Area (OSA) includes Minnesota, North Dakota, South Dakota, and three counties in western Wisconsin. In Region 7, for 2003, there were 30 African American transplant recipients compared with only six donors from the same population subgroup. At that time, there were 165 African Americans on the transplant wait list in the LifeSource region.

The Twin Cities of Minneapolis and St. Paul, Minnesota, comprise the largest metropolitan area within the LifeSource donation service area. African Americans make up 8.5% of the total population. In the past, the Twin Cities' African American community was close-knit; however, demographic shifts resulting from migration of new racial and ethnic groups and disruption of neighborhoods through urban development led to a change in the dynamic of the community. At present, opinion leaders describe the African American community as relatively small and not particularly close-knit. Its size relative to that of larger metropolitan areas, such as Washington, DC, and Atlanta, makes Minneapolis and St. Paul a particularly attractive locale in which to implement a media effort. The community can be quickly and effectively penetrated through a media campaign. The study reported herein evaluates the effectiveness of a multifaceted campaign to engage the African American community in the Twin Cities area to address these disparities and to learn ways to sustain a proportionate subgroup consent rate within the African American population. This was the first outreach activity by LifeSource involving the African American community.

Theoretical Basis for the Media Campaign

Research on organ donation decision making has drawn extensively on social influence theories. One predominant theory, the theory of reasoned action (TRA), was first proposed by Fishbein (Fishbein & Ajzen, 1975) as a model for understanding the relationship between an individual's attitudes, perceptions of others' attitudes, behavioral intentions, and actual behavior. The TRA has been widely applied in the study of health behaviors (Montano, Kasprzyk, & Taplin, 1997). Earlier studies have evaluated organ donation and the willingness to designate oneself as a donor using Fishbein's TRA (Fishbein & Ajzen). Several previous investigators have directly applied these models in their work (Horton & Horton, 1990a, 1990b; Morgan, 2006). The organ donation model (see Figure 4.1), influenced by the TRA and adapted from previous research (Horton & Horton, 1990a, 1990b; Morgan, 2006), is used as a guiding framework for this study. Following this model, individuals' attitude toward organ donation and registration as a donor is a consequence of their knowledge about organ donation and their personal values. The individual's attitudes affect the willingness or propensity to donate and undertake certain behaviors, such as signing a donor card, registering as a donor on a driver's license, and talking to family members about organ donation.

Subsequent research has confirmed certain facets of the model. For instance, investigators have found that knowledge about the need for organs in African

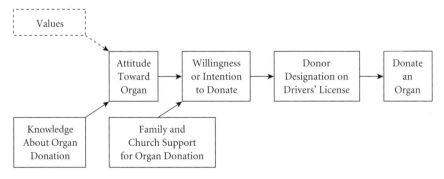

Figure 4.1   Conceptual model for the Donate Life—African American Campaign.

Americans and knowledge about transplantation were barriers to the donation of organs (Morgan, 2006; Plawecki, Freiberg, & Plawecki, 1989; Rubens, 1996; Siminoff & Arnold, 1999). Unfavorable attitudes toward organ donation logically follow from a poorly informed public. Thus, many previous media campaigns emphasized informing the public about the implications of organ donation and how to register as an organ donor.

Among African Americans, prevailing attitudes and beliefs about the allocation of solid organs are a source of bias. Siminoff and Arnold (1999) found that bias is strongly related to the individual's willingness to donate. This was manifested in a general distrust of the medical system and a belief that medical practitioners would not save their lives if they designated themselves as a potential organ donor (Siminoff & Arnold; Yuen et al., 1998). In addition to knowledge and attitudes, Morgan (2006) reported social norms as being of primary importance in decisions to donate.

Faith in God and how this impacts organ donation decision making in the African American community have comprised a focus of prior investigations (Davidson, 1991; Plawecki et al., 1989; Rubens, 1996; Spigner, Weaver, Cardenas, & Allen, 2002). In contrast to the position of the Roman Catholic Church, where Pope John Paul II formally promoted transplantation in his August 2000 address to the 18th International Congress of the Transplantation Society, African American churches, which are predominantly Protestant, do not actively promote organ donation. This partly reflects the heterogeneity of the churches in which African Americans are members.

We used the model illustrated in Figure 4.1 to guide the development and evaluation of a media-based campaign to increase organ donation designation among African Americans living in the Twin Cities. For example, the need for organs is explicitly addressed in the current media campaign with the goal of increasing knowledge. The conceptual model also served as a framework for our evaluation. Each box represents components that were included in the overall evaluation, excluding values that are signified in Figure 4.1 using the broken line. The intervention was referred to as the Donate Life—African American Campaign.

Methods

Goals and Objectives

The research evaluated the effectiveness of the Donate Life—African American Campaign and grassroots efforts to (a) inform the African American community about disparities in organ donation, and (b) increase the propensity to donate and the rate of donor designation. To this end, the evaluation asks,

1. Was there awareness of the media campaign (intervention fidelity)?
2. Was the media campaign associated with increased knowledge of organ donation and transplantation?
3. Was the media campaign associated with changes in organ donation attitudes?
4. Was the media campaign associated with changes in organ donation intentions?
5. Was the media campaign associated with changes in organ donation behavior?

The evaluation questions tap key components of the organ donation model, roughly following the causal path from exposure to the media campaign through intention to donate and organ donation behaviors such as donor designation and solid organ donor authorization. Authorization for organ donation has been poorly studied. It is assumed that donor designation will increase donor authorization by increasing discussions with family members about organ donation and designating directives toward donation prior to death.

Study Design

Before starting data collection, the evaluation was approved by the University of Minnesota Human Subjects Protection and Institutional Review. The evaluation used a pretest–posttest study design. Pretests were collected 6 months before the media campaign started. This period is referred to hereafter as the *precampaign period*, or *precampaign*. Posttests were collected one year later, which roughly corresponded to the end of the media campaign. This period is referred to hereafter as the *postcampaign period*, or *postcampaign*. Given logistical constraints, we used independent samples for both periods to assess changes in the variables of interest. Because it was not feasible to create a control group for the study, we used the grade of intensity of media exposure in lieu of a control group. The lack of a control group is a serious validity threat to our evaluation design. Unencumbered by budgetary and resource constraints, we would have selected separate and comparable media markets to serve as control conditions. Under this best-case scenario, separate media markets would permit a true test of the effects of the media campaign. As an acceptable alternative to no control community, we examine the intensity of media exposure in our design, treating this measure of exposure as a dose–response assessment. Based on this strategy, the intensity of media exposure is assumed to be directly related to the central constructs addressed in the theoretical model. The Donate Life—African American Campaign utilized mass media materials developed and implemented by the Coalition on Donation (now Donate Life America) in 2000. The media campaign was heavily based on extensive research examining individual motivation toward becoming organ donors. Donate Life—African American Campaign had five distinct components: (a) the media campaign, (b) a faith-based program, (c) high school outreach, (d) a volunteer program, and (e) grassroots community outreach.

The media campaign was by far the largest component and, as such, was the focus of our evaluation.

Media campaign materials included radio spots, television spots, brochures, and posters emphasizing the importance of organ donation and the number of African Americans needing organ transplants. Our intervention produced local print ads and press kits consistent with the design and messaging of the Donate Life America campaign with a focus on the importance of increasing the number of African American donors to ensure the best possible organ match for African American patients. The media campaign required a strategic effort to tie it directly with grass-roots outreach. For example, print advertisements ran in the African American newspaper, the *Minnesota Spokesman-Recorder*, the same week the newspaper presented high school scholarships and other similar occasions of high reader interest.

The effectiveness of the media buys was maximized by engaging in media relations efforts, hiring an African American public relations firm, and building effective relationships with influential media establishments in the Twin Cities. Media programming was strategically selected to reach the targeted population and complemented grassroots outreach efforts and events. Public relations efforts included media profiles of health care professionals, recipients, and donor families through interviews on two prominent local radio and TV stations.

Media Exposure

Questions asking individuals whether they had heard, read, or seen any information about organ donation during the past 6 months, and the frequency with which they recalled campaign efforts, served as measures of message exposure intensity. For the analysis, overall media exposure was quantified using individuals' exposure to media messages, the frequency of exposure to the Donate Life—African American Campaign, and the number of organ donation information sources. The latter construct was measured via a set of 14 true-false questions about different potential sources of information.

Outcomes

In order to determine campaign impact, the following outcomes were assessed via community surveys: (a) knowledge about organ donation, (b) attitudes and beliefs about organ donation, (c) willingness or intention to become an organ donor, and (d) self-reported driver's license donor designation. The donor authorization rate for the upper Midwest was used as a behavioral outcome using data provided by LifeSource, the local organ procurement organization.

Knowledge about organ donation
A 15-item, true-false index was developed to measure organ donation knowledge. Five of the items were drawn from those used in previous research (Gallup

Organization, 1993; Horton & Horton, 1990a, 1990b; Morgan & Miller, 2002). The remaining 10 questions, developed specifically for the project, were specific to either African Americans or messages from the current campaign. For the analysis, a knowledge index (the Knowledge About Organ Donation Scale) was constructed based on the number of correctly answered true-false questions. In testing for the reliability and validity of the Knowledge About Organ Donation Scale, we found varying levels of discrimination for the individual items, but strong support for the construct validity of our scale scores. Overall, African Americans with donor designation on their driver's license had statistically significantly (all tests are two-tailed) higher scores on their knowledge about organ donation than those without driver's license designation ($t = 4.26$, $DF = 455$, p value < 0.001) (with donor designation mean $= 11.93$, $SD = 2.93$; without donor designation mean $= 10.95$, $SD = 2.97$). The internal consistency coefficient ($\propto$) for binary data, an indirect measure of reliability, was 0.719 (Streiner & Norman, 2003).

Family and church support for organ donation

Religious and subjective norms were identified in earlier studies as playing critical roles in African American organ donation decision making (Morgan, 2006; Morgan, Miller, & Arasaratnam, 2003). To measure subjective norms, we used two single-item measures. Family support was assessed using a single yes-no question. Church support for organ donation was evaluated using a Likert-type scale with response choices ranging from *strongly agree* to *strongly disagree*. For the analyses, Likert-type questions were transformed to a 0–100-point scale with higher values indicating greater support for the attribute measured. In this case, higher values indicate greater support for the belief "My church supports organ donation."

Attitudes and beliefs about organ donation

Attitudes and beliefs about organ donation were measured using a four-item summative scale called the Attitudes and Beliefs About Organ Donation Scale. Individual items were derived from those developed by Horton and Horton (1990a, 1990b) and the Gallup Organization (1993). Several items were added to evaluate perceptions of (a) church support for organ donation, (b) prevailing attitudes about death, and (c) the fear of substandard medical care if the individual were dying and identified as an organ donor ($\propto = 0.65$). In comparing those with and without driver's license designation, we found significantly higher scores on the Attitudes and Beliefs About Organ Donation Scale for those with donor designation on their driver's license ($t = 2.64$; $DF = 458$; $p = 0.009$) (with donor designation mean $= 89.10$, $SD = 15.06$; without donor designation mean $= 77.97$, $SD = 18.60$).

Propensity to donate and driver's license designation

The willingness or intention to donate was measured using three items: (a) how often respondents thought about organ donation, (b) whether respondents would recommend donation to family or friends, and (c) their willingness to become a donor at the time of death. The Propensity to Donate Scale was constructed using the three items, with scores ranging from 0 to 100 and higher scores indicating a greater propensity to become an organ donor. The scale had an acceptable reliability for group comparisons ($\propto = 0.72$). The Propensity to Donate Scale significantly discriminated between respondents with (mean = 71.44; SD = 17.83) and without donor designation (mean = 44.60; SD = 21.59) on their driver's licenses (t statistic = 14.03; DF = 393; $p < 0.001$).

Authorization rates

For the most distal endpoint, LifeSource provided the principal researcher with the organ authorization rates for the donation service area according to race. Rates were reported quarterly for the years 2003 through mid-2007. Although the rates include the entire region (North Dakota, South Dakota, Minnesota, and western Wisconsin), African Americans live predominantly in the Twin Cities of Minneapolis and St. Paul. Thus, we are comfortable asserting that the authorization rates for African Americans reflect the local experience for the target of the media campaign.

Sampling and Data Collection Methods

Identifying the target population of eligible African Americans living in the Twin Cities was a major challenge for the evaluation. The Upper Midwest is unique in the sense that African Americans are not geographically segregated within a subset of zip code areas, but rather are geographically integrated across the Twin Cities. This is partly a consequence of in-migration of immigrant groups to the area leading to dispersion across the metropolitan area. Consequently, we created a sampling frame using three data sources with a high likelihood of including African American households. These sources were representative of the African American community and provided a reasonable coverage area. First, we used mailing lists from one of our community collaborators, Southside Community Health Services. This organization provides health and human services to a large proportion of African Americans within the Minneapolis area. Next, we used subscribers from the predominant African American newspaper in the metropolitan areas. This newspaper, the *Minnesota Spokesman-Recorder*, was the first African American newspaper in Minnesota and represents the community's voice in St. Paul and Minneapolis. Finally, we drew a sample from parishioners at each of the four churches nominally participating in the campaign. Because we were not granted access to names and addresses from the parish rosters, the mailings and implementation of the samples for the parishes were administered and carried out by each church. This contributed to a lack of standardization and inconsistency in the sampling strategy for the faith-based component of the sample frame.

Each of the two mailings consisted of a random sample of approximately 1,000 households. We oversampled from our list to accommodate for an anticipated low response rate from a single mailing. Non–African Americans among those responding also accounted for the perceived need to oversample. Data were collected using a 12-page survey that captured information about exposure to the media campaign, as well as outcomes and characteristics of the individual responding. A copy of the survey can be obtained from the corresponding author (D. Radosevich).

Statistical Analyses

Statistical analyses focused on looking at changes in outcomes between the premedia campaign and postmedia campaign for the outcomes specified in the model. Simple descriptive results are presented here, comparing *precampaign* and *postcampaign* values. Categorical values are compared using the chi-square tests for independence, whereas continuous values are compared using independent sample two-tailed *t*-tests. Components of the model were compared using bivariate correlation coefficients. All analyses were performed using Version 9.1 SAS™ for Windows.

Results

Sample Demographics

The demographic characteristics of African Americans responding to the two community surveys are presented in Table 4.1. In *precampaign*, 278 responded to the survey compared with 187 after the campaign. Compared with those responding after the campaign, *precampaign* respondents were slightly younger (49.9 years of age versus 53.3 years of age; $p = 0.017$) and less likely to be drawn from the *Minneapolis Spokesman-Recorder* (56.1% versus 70.1%; $p = 0.008$). The samples included several living donors and five organ transplant recipients. Otherwise, the characteristics were similar across the two samples with comparable experiences with organ donation and transplantation.

Media Campaign Exposure

Compared with the *precampaign* sample, the *postcampaign* sample was significantly more likely to have seen or heard information about donation and messages about the Donate Life Campaign. The postcampaign sample was also more likely to report sources of information about donation that were in accord with campaign emphasis (see Table 4.2). Conclusions regarding interpretation of

Table 4.1 Characteristics of African Americans responding to the community surveys, *precampaign* and *postcampaign*

Annotated Question	Precampaign (N = 278)		Postcampaign (N = 187)		P value
Age, mean ± standard error of mean	49.9 ± 0.95		53.3 ± 1.1		0.017
Gender					
Male	92	33.1%	63	33.9%	0.862
Female	186	66.9%	123	66.1%	
Marital status					
Married	111	39.9%	74	40.2%	0.809
Divorced	59	21.2%	38	20.7%	
Never married	65	23.4%	37	20.1%	
Other	43	15.5%	35	19.0%	
Education					
Elementary—some high school	8	2.9%	9	4.9%	0.118
High school graduate	33	11.9%	14	7.5%	
Some college	97	35.0%	56	30.1%	
College graduate	139	50.2%	107	57.5%	
Sample frame					
Minneapolis Spokesman-Recorder	150	56.1%	131	70.1%	0.008
Southside Community Health Services	39	14.0%	21	11.2%	
Participating Churches	83	29.9%	35	18.7%	
Experience with organ donation and transplantation					
Living donor	12	4.4%	4	2.2%	0.213
Organ recipient	2	0.7%	3	3.6%	0.359
Family member a deceased or living donor	28	10.3%	28	15.4%	0.106
Discussed organ donation with family	115	41.7%	86	46.5%	0.306
Family member received an organ	33	12.1%	25	13.7%	0.621
Ever donated blood	162	59.8%	100	54.4%	0.250
Family opposed to organ donation	20	7.5%	16	9.0%	0.558

responses to single-item questions about exposure to the Donate Life Campaign are ambiguous, because nearly one half (46.8%) of those responding before the media campaign began reported hearing or seeing messages about organ donation. Toward the end of the campaign, this percentage was increased to 82.3%. Although the differences in exposure were statistically significant ($p < 0.001$), self-

Table 4.2   Reported exposure to media messages about organ donation, precampaign and postcampaign

Annotated Question	Precampaign (N = 278)		Postcampaign (N = 187)		P value
Seen or heard information about donation	168	62.7%	141	75.4%	0.004
Message about Donate Life Campaign					
Very often	7	2.6%	27	14.5%	< 0.001
Fairly often	26	9.7%	40	21.5%	
A couple of times	64	24.0%	72	38.7%	
Once	28	10.5%	14	7.5%	
Never	142	53.2%	33	17.7%	
Source of information about donation					
Family member	82	32.4%	56	30.6%	0.688
Friend	80	31.8%	54	30.0%	0.699
Medical professional	49	19.8%	36	20.0%	0.967
Clergy or religious	16	6.5%	15	8.6%	0.424
Personal experience	47	19.0%	31	17.5%	0.692
Billboard or poster	87	35.2%	79	44.4%	0.056
General news on TV	140	55.1%	123	68.0%	0.007
Work or school	44	17.9%	31	17.9%	0.993
Minnesota Department of Motor Vehicles	74	29.7%	78	43.1%	0.004
Movie or TV show	117	47.0%	77	44.5%	0.615
Community activity	76	30.7%	79	44.1%	0.004
Internet or Web site	31	12.6%	23	13.0%	0.893
LifeSource	33	13.4%	48	27.0%	< 0.001
Local news	127	50.0%	119	66.1%	< 0.001
Media exposure		25.8%		32.5%	< 0.001

reports about the specifics of multimedia components should be interpreted with caution. Overall, it would appear that respondents experienced considerable exposure to media campaign messages regarding organ donation (62.7% *precampaign* versus 75.4% *postcampaign*; *p* = 0.004).

Between *precampaign* and *postcampaign*, the percentage of media-based sources about organ donation increased from 25.8% to 35.3% (*p* < 0.001). The largest differences occurred in the domains that were the focus of the overall Donate Life Campaign: billboards, posters, news, the Minnesota Department of Public Safety, and community activities. Most of these showed either a statistically significant increase or a strong increasing trend when compared to *precampaign* levels.

Knowledge About Organ Donation

As mentioned earlier, knowledge was measured using a combination of previously developed knowledge questions and items specific to our media campaign and the African American community. Table 4.3 gives an annotated version of the knowledge questions and a comparison of the *precampaign* and *postcampaign* responses. Statistically significant differences (two-tailed *t*-test) were found for increased knowledge about the number of African Americans waiting for transplant, the ability of organ donation to save lives, and the possibility of being a living donor. In comparing the *precampaign* sample with the *postcampaign* sample, we observed a significant increase in the number of correct responses to the knowledge items ($t = 3.21$; $DF = 460$; $p = 0.001$).

Table 4.3 Number and percentage of knowledge items about organ donation and transplantation answered correctly, and total number of knowledge items answered correctly, precampaign and postcampaign

Annotated Knowledge Questions	Precampaign (N = 278)		Postcampaign (N = 187)		P value
35% of African American waiting for transplant	211	75.9%	161	86.1%	0.007
Most African Americans willing to donate	240	86.3%	167	89.3%	0.341
Many African Americans are awaiting organs	236	84.9%	175	93.6%	0.004
10% of African Americans willing to donate	195	70.1%	143	76.5%	0.133
Being a donor saves lives	258	92.8%	185	98.9%	0.002
Being a donor costs money	235	84.5%	170	90.9%	0.044
Open casket not possible	249	89.6%	173	92.5%	0.282
Age, race, and medical conditions limit donation	131	47.1%	94	50.3%	0.506
Possible to be a living donor	224	80.6%	164	87.7%	0.043
Improve the lives of more than 50 people	192	69.1%	139	74.3%	0.219
Equal access for African Americans	113	40.7%	75	40.1%	0.907
Will receive best treatment if a donor	120	43.2%	88	47.1%	0.408
87,000 awaiting transplants	235	84.5%	162	86.6%	0.530
Family can decide on recipient	192	69.1%	140	74.9%	0.175
LifeSource manages organ donation in Minnesota	219	78.8%	158	84.5%	0.113
Knowledge about Organ Donation Scale*	10.9 ± 0.18		11.7 ± 0.16		0.001

* Values are mean ± standard error of mean.

Table 4.4   Family and church support for organ donation, attitude about organ donation, precampaign and postcampaign

	Precampaign (N = 278)		Postcampaign (N = 187)		P value
Family and church support for organ donation					
Family supports organ donation	258	92.8%	171	91.4%	0.558
Church supports organ donation*	80.1 ± 1.54		81.4 ± 1.88		0.605
Attitudes and beliefs about organ donation					
Strongly support the donation of organs*	84.4 ± 1.30		88.2 ± 1.55		0.059
Organ donation is an act of compassion*	90.2 ± 1.22		96.3 ± 1.11		0.019
Organ donors might receive inadequate care*	77.7 ± 1.92		83.9 ± 2.18		0.055
Worried organs might be recovered before death*	81.6 ± 1.77		86.9 ± 2.11		0.096
Attitude and beliefs about Organ Donation Scale*	83.6 ± 0.99		87.6 ± 1.17		0.010

* Values are mean ± standard error of mean.

Family and Church Support for Organ Donation

There was a precampaign perception of strong family and church support for organ donation (see Table 4.4). These already highly favorable perceptions were not influenced as a result of the campaign. No significant gains in these areas were reported from *precampaign* to *postcampaign*.

Attitudes and Beliefs About Organ Donation

Results (see Table 4.4) suggest a more favorable attitude toward organ donation among those responding to the postcampaign survey ($t = 2.57$; $DF = 458$; $p = 0.010$). The greatest improvement in attitude was noted for the item asking whether organ donation was an act of compassion—a message emphasized in the Donate Life Campaign. The score for this individual item improved from 90.2 to 96.3 between the *precampaign* and *postcampaign* surveys, respectively ($p = 0.019$).

Propensity to Donate and Donor Designation on Driver's License

Overall, the propensity to donate was comparable for the *precampaign* and *postcampaign* groups (see Table 4.5). Self-reported donor designation on one's driver's license showed a slight increase between the *precampaign* and *postcampaign*

Table 4.5   Propensity to donate and drivers' license designation, precampaign and postcampaign

	Precampaign (N = 278)	Postcampaign (N = 187)	P value
Propensity to donate			
Thought about donation	31.9 ± 1.9	35.0 ± 2.3	0.291
Recommends donation to family and friends	72.7 ± 1.5	70.9 ± 2.0	0.633
Likely to donate	59.2 ± 2.0	59.9 ± 2.6	0.832
Propensity to Donate Scale	53.9 ± 1.4	55.6 ± 1.8	0.446
Donor designation on driver's license	91 33.0%	73 40.1%	0.119

surveys. The increase of 7 percentage points was not statistically significant ($p = 0.119$).

Relationship Between Media Campaign Exposure and Outcomes

Results (see Table 4.6) are summarized for the *postcampaign* survey only because this group would have been exposed to the full campaign and its messaging. The intensity of exposure to the Donate Life Campaign had a direct, weak association with knowledge about donation ($r = 0.099, p = 0.179$), and family ($r = 0.129, p = 0.090$) and church support for organ donation ($r = 0.122; p = 0.101$). The campaign was significantly related to attitudes and beliefs about organ donation ($r = 0.176; p = 0.017$). Exposure to media messages was weakly associated with knowledge about organ donation ($r = 0.124; p = 0.092$) and significantly related to family support for organ donation ($r = 0.187; p = 0.013$). The propensity to donate was unrelated to any of the factors in our model, but was strongly related to donor designation on the driver's license.

Authorization Rates

Between 2003 and 2007, the authorization rate for the LifeSource donation service area increased for African Americans. Figure 4.2 shows the annual rates for four racial groups: *Whites, African Americans, Native Americans,* and *Other.* During the period roughly corresponding to the Donate Life—African American Campaign, authorization rates for African Americans increased for the LifeSource Donation Services Area (DSA) while the rates for Whites remained relatively stable over these years. Rates for the other racial groups also rose during the same time period; however, the increase in African American rates began a year earlier.

Table 4.6 Bivariate correlation coefficients for components of the Donate Life—African American Campaign conceptual model (respondents [$N = 187$] to the postcampaign survey only)

Exposure to Donate Life Campaign	Exposure to Media Messages	Knowledge about Organ Donation	Family Supports Organ Donation	Church Supports Organ Donation	Attitudes and Beliefs Toward Organ Donation	Propensity to Donate	Donor Designation on Drivers' License
1.000							
0.505	1.000						
< 0.001							
0.099	0.124	1.000					
0.179	0.092						
0.129	0.187	−0.029	1.000				
0.090	0.013	0.705					
0.122	0.074	0.096	0.209	1.000			
0.101	0.320	0.194	0.005				
0.176	0.008	0.256	0.211	0.338	1.000		
0.017	0.913	< 0.001	0.005	< 0.001			
0.074	0.044	0.059	0.120	−0.010	0.036	1.000	
0.317	0.550	0.424	0.110	0.888	0.642		
−0.006	0.001	0.137	0.020	0.038	0.285	0.205	1.000
0.940	0.993	0.065	0.794	0.611	< 0.001	0.006	

Note: Values are correlation coefficients and *p* values.

The timing of the media campaign, which is superimposed on the figure, suggests increasing authorization rates as a result of the program.

Discussion

This evaluation focused on the influence of a media campaign (Donate Life—African American Campaign). The evaluation sought to assess several aspects of the campaign. Strengths of this evaluation include an a priori theoretical framework and the number of measured outcomes, including authorization rates and campaign fidelity data.

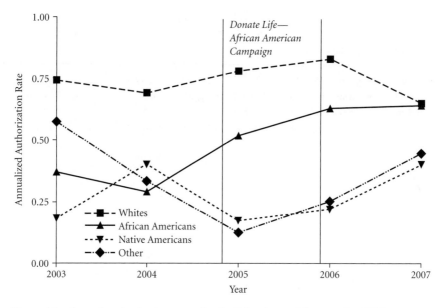

Figure 4.2   Annual authorization rates for the following racial categories: Whites, African Americans, Native Americans, and Other, 2003–2007.

The evaluation first assessed awareness of the campaign. In a comparison of the precampaign and postcampaign survey results, increased exposure to media campaign messages was reported. Although these efforts provide some assurance as to the dissemination of media content, they provide little guarantee as to exposure or receipt by the community targeted. Our experience suggests that in evaluating media efforts, it is critical to assess perceived media messages before the campaign begins. In the case of this current project, precampaign reports suggest dissemination of information about organ donation in the absence of a campaign. What cannot be ruled out are misreports of exposure to organ donation messages (see Alvaro & Siegel, this volume). Given the passive and subtle nature of media messages, it is important to incorporate preintervention measures into evaluations. These preintervention measures are critical in accounting for any systematic biases due to measurement or local history.

The evaluation next assessed whether the media campaign was associated with an increased knowledge of organ donation and transplantation. Pre- and postcampaign differences indicate statistically significant increases in the number of respondents aware of the need among the African American population. Pre- and postcampaign differences also indicate a reduction in the belief that organ donation costs money to the donor and an increase in the perceived life-saving properties of organ donation. The campaign appears to be less successful at persuading African Americans of equal access and the quality of care the donor will receive.

Changes in attitudes represent the next outcome of interest for the evaluation. From a TRA perspective, favorable changes in knowledge should correspond with more favorable attitudes. As suggested by the TRA framework, an increase in donor-favorable knowledge was indeed associated with more favorable donor attitudes. Causal directionality is not possible with the current design, but attitudes toward donation were more favorable postcampaign than precampaign; moreover, attitudes and knowledge were significantly correlated.

According to the organ donor model, favorable changes in attitudes will result in favorable changes in intentions. This did not occur. Attitudes changed; intentions did not. Equally surprising is the lack of correlation between propensity to donate and any other outcome measure including attitudes and norms. If the evaluation did not include behavioral measures, the lack of changes in intentions could have led to the conclusion that the campaign is incapable of changing donation behavior. This would have been unfortunate as pre- and post differences in behavior were indeed observed.

The final evaluation objective involved assessment of whether the campaign changed organ donation behavior. To be sure, the ultimate outcome for organ donor research is authorization rates. As mentioned, intention outcomes interpreted within the TRA framework give little reason for optimism—behavior is associated with intentions and intentions did not change. Surprisingly, the authorization rates for organ donation markedly increased among African Americans between 2004 and 2006. This period roughly corresponds to the timing of the 12-month Donate Life campaign. Given the lack of an appropriate control community, the results do not completely rule out alternative explanations such the effects of the Organ Donation Breakthrough Collaborative or other local programs implemented in the region's hospitals; however, there is no reason to believe that these other programs would not impact all population segments equally—again, results indicate an increase for African Americans that did not occur for other groups.

Considering the increase in authorization rates, it is unfortunate that increases cannot be more definitively attributed to the campaign. The evaluation faced a number of additional challenges that threaten the validity of final conclusions about the effects of the media campaign. Future investigators would benefit from our lessons learned and strategies we employed in their future studies. Overall, challenges fall into the two areas: (a) difficulties implementing studies in community settings, and (b) the outcomes necessary to answer questions about the campaign's effectiveness.

Difficulties Implementing Studies in Community Settings

Studies that take place in natural settings, such as geographic and ethnic communities, face unique challenges (Alvaro, Jones, Robles, & Siegel, 2006). As we pointed out earlier, within this setting it is impossible to fully control exposure to the intervention. Researchers in these real-life settings needs to be especially vigilant to conduct of the project and attentive to coordination and ongoing communication among partners. In the Donate Life campaign, we utilized regular meetings of a Community Advisory Council (CAC) to provide updates and communications with key constituents. Members of the CAC worked closely with media in the delivery of messaging to the African American community in the Twin Cities.

In controlled trials, local effects are accounted for through randomization of the intervention conditions and by having a control group. As mentioned earlier, resource constraints prevented us from having a control group in our observational study design. Absent a control, we cannot rule out the effects of local history. One of our principal endpoints, authorization rates, was potentially biased by local events. In the Twin Cities health care market, some hospitals were actively participating in the Organ Donation Breakthrough Collaborative to increase authorization rates and the number of organs per donor. Coupled with faith-based initiatives and other community outreach activities focused on organ donation, these nonmedia factors could represent the strongest antecedents for the effects observed—although, as previously noted, all else being equal, such activities should not differentially impact demographic groups.

All data collection faces certain validity threats that need to be considered in designing outcomes studies. Don Dillman (2006) called these sources of error: sampling, coverage, measurement, and nonresponse errors. Coverage error is a serious limitation of most studies examining health disparities. This derives from difficulties identifying the target population. Our previous work in the Twin Cities suggested African Americans were a geographically integrated community and, compared to other racial groups, not identifiable through their place of residence or surname. We chose to deal with this challenge by creating lists with a high likelihood of containing African American households. Even using this strategy, we found that nearly one half of the completed and returned surveys were from non–African Americans. In the Twin Cities, this is further confounded by the immigration of East Africans in recent years. This made it necessary to rule out recent immigrants from those who had a history of residence in the Twin Cities. This was accomplished by adding screening questions to the survey asking about recent immigration and country of origin.

Another source of error that should be highlighted concerns nonresponse. Our evaluation suffered from a lower than anticipated response rate because of our use of a single mailing. Dillman (2006) and other survey methodologists have advanced the use of the Tailored Design Method. Briefly, these involve multiple contacts and the use of incentives. Telephone interviews could provide higher completion rates; however, they impose restrictions on the type and number of questions asked of respondents. Tailored design methods applied to mail surveys yield higher response rates and results that are more representative of the population.

These approaches must be balanced against available resources and study goals. In our evaluation, we used community sponsorship to enhance the credibility and importance of the work.

Final Suggestions

Without precampaign measures of exposure, postcampaign results would have been met with false exhilaration at the thought of a 70% exposure rate. Without measures of authorization rates, the campaign would be considered incapable of changing donation behavior as a result of the outcomes related to intentions. Future evaluation efforts can benefit by implementing a cadre of measures assessing a host of variables of theoretical and evaluative import.

Relationships between variables are not what would be expected via TRA. Unfortunately, across the research in this area, outcome measures are not standardized. Accordingly, the lack of relationship between attitudes and intentions can be due to genuine issues with applying the theory to organ donation or difficulties with measurement instruments and procedures. The theory has a longer history than the items used in this evaluation, so the latter seems more likely. Further investigation of the properties of outcome measures is critical and needs to be in place before advancing research in this field. Potential clearinghouses for approved measures would be a positive force for advancing the field of media evaluation and organ donor registration.

Note

This research was supported in part by grant number 1 D71SP04139-01-00 from the Health Resources and Services Administration's Division of Transplantation (HRSA/DoT), U.S. Department of Health and Human Services. The contents of this publication are solely the responsibility of the authors and do not necessarily represent the views of HRSA/DoT.

References

Alvaro, E. M., Jones, S. P., Robles, A. S., & Siegel, J. T. (2006). Hispanic organ donation: Impact of a Spanish-language organ donation campaign. *Journal of the National Medical Association, 98*, 28–35.

Davidson, M. N. (1991). Attitudinal barriers to organ donation among Black Americans. *Transplantation Proceedings, 23*, 2531–2532.

Dillman, D. A. (2006). *Mail and Internet surveys: The Tailored Design Method, 2007 update with new internet, visual, and mixed-mode guide* (2nd ed.). New York: John Wiley.

Fishbein, M., & Ajzen, I. (1975). *Belief, attitude, intention and behavior: An introduction to theory and research*. Reading, MA: Addison-Wesley.

Gallup Organization. (1993). *The U.S. public's attitudes toward organ transplants/donation: 1996s*. Princeton, NJ: Author.

Horton, R. L., & Horton, P. J. (1990a). Knowledge regarding organ donation: Identifying and overcoming barriers to organ donation. *Social Science and Medicine, 31*, 791–800.

Horton, R. L., & Horton, P. J. (1990b). A model of willingness to become a potential organ donor. *Social Science and Medicine, 33*, 1037–1051.

Montano, D. E., Kasprzyk, D., & Taplin, S. H. (1997). The theory of reasoned action and the theory of planned behavior. In K. Glanz, F. M. Lewis, & B. K. Rimer (Eds.), *Health behavior and health education: Theory, research, and practice* (pp. 85–112). San Francisco: Jossey-Bass.

Morgan, S. E. (2006). Many facets of reluctance: African Americans and the decision (not) to donate organs. *Journal of the National Medical Association, 98*, 695–703.

Morgan, S. E., & Miller, J. K. (2002). Communicating about gifts of life: The effect of knowledge, attitudes, and altruism on behavior and behavioral intentions regarding organ donation. *Journal of Applied Communication Research, 30*, 163–176.

Morgan, S. E., Miller, J. K., & Arasaratnam, L. A. (2003). Similarities and differences between African Americans' and European Americans' attitudes, knowledge, and willingness to communicate about organ donation. *Journal of Applied Social Psychology, 33*, 693–692.

Plawecki, H. M., Freiberg, G., & Plawecki, J. A. (1989). Increasing organ donation in the Black community. *ANNA Journal, 16*, 321–324.

Rubens, A. J. (1996). Racial and ethnic differences in students' attitudes and behavior toward organ donation. *Journal of the National Medical Association, 88*, 417–422.

Sheehy, E., Conrad, S. L., Bringham, L. E., Luskin, R., Weber, P., Eaken, M., et al. (2003). Estimating the number of potential organ donors in the United States. *New England Journal of Medicine, 349*, 667–674.

Siminoff, L. A., & Arnold, R. (1999). Increasing organ donation in the African American community: Altruism in the face of an untrustworthy system. *Annals of Internal Medicine, 130*, 607–609.

Spigner, C., Weaver, M., Cardenas, V., & Allen, M. D. (2002). Organ donation and transplantation: Ethnic differences in knowledge and opinions among urban high school students. *Ethnicity and Health, 7*, 87–101.

Streiner, D. L., & Norman, G. R. (2003). *Health measurement scales: A practical guide to their development and use* (3rd ed.). Oxford: Oxford University Press.

Yuen, C. C., Burton, W., Chiraseveenuprapund, P., Elmore, E., Wong, S., Ozuah, P., et al. (1998). Attitudes and beliefs about organ donation among different racial groups. *Journal of the National Medical Association, 90*, 13–18.

5

Organ Donation and Transplantation

A New Tradition of Sharing for Alaska Natives

Margaret D. Allen and Barbara Stillwater

This chapter describes a 3-year (2000–2003) effort of a small but enthusiastic team to increase awareness about organ donation and transplantation among Alaska Natives. Largely centered on education at the individual, provider, and system levels, the team designed its approach so that the education methods were culturally sensitive and relevant to the values of Alaska Native peoples.

Alaska accounts for 17% of the landmass of the United States but contains only 0.2% of the U.S. population. Although 46 other states are more populous, Alaska has the highest percentage of Alaska Natives/American Indians of any of the states, at 18%, comprising nearly 125,000 persons.

Several issues impact both the need for organ transplantation and the availability of organs for donation among Alaska Natives. Both liver disease and diabetes occur disproportionately among Alaska Natives and American Indians. In 2002, chronic liver disease (CLD) accounted for 4.4% of all deaths among Alaska Native and American Indian people, four times higher than the percentage found in non-Hispanic American Whites and African Americans. Although age-adjusted CLD rates held steady from 1990 to 1998 among non-Hispanic Whites, and even declined among African Americans, rates have continued to increase among Alaska Native and American Indian people. Additionally, the prevalence of autoimmune hepatitis and primary biliary cirrhosis in Alaska Natives was found to be among the highest reported in the world. Although Alaska Natives have previously had relatively low rates of diabetes, it has recently become a significant emerging health problem. Notably, the percentage increase in age-adjusted diabetes prevalence among Alaska Natives between 1995 and 2000 was 33.5%, compared to only a 6.8% increase among the general Alaska population. Thus, it would be expected that the level of disease burden among Alaska Natives in both liver disease and diabetes could potentially translate into an escalating incidence of end-stage organ failure and a consequent increase in the need for transplants. Nationwide, over 800 Native Americans are currently on kidney transplant waiting lists, a figure that has doubled in less than a decade (U.S. Renal Data System, 2008).

There is potential for Alaska Native populations to contribute to organ donation as well. Injuries are the leading cause of death among Alaska Natives, accounting for 32% of all deaths in this population between 1999 and 2004. Unintentional injuries alone are the third leading cause of death among Alaska Natives, preceded only by cancer and heart disease. These high mortality rates due to injuries indicate a potential availability of organs that could be donated.

This program was developed to increase the awareness about both transplantation and donation among Alaska Native communities by producing and disseminating culturally appropriate educational materials across the State of Alaska.

Barriers and Challenges

The challenges in providing health care services for organ donation and transplantation within this population are significant. There are no organ transplant programs in Alaska, so patients must be listed on out-of-state program waiting lists. Furthermore, because of different frequencies of blood group and tissue antigens, Alaska Natives often wait longer for suitable organ matches, especially kidneys (U.S. Renal Data System, 2008). Across the country, Alaska Natives and American Indians have longer median waiting times for kidney transplants and are less likely than Caucasians to be transplanted (Narva, 2003; Organ Procurement and Transplantation Network, 2008a, 2008b; U.S. Renal Data System).

The geography of Alaska Native communities presents additional challenges. One half of the Alaska Native population and 25% of all Alaskans live in communities of fewer than 1,000 people, dispersed across a large rural area. Seventy-five percent of Alaskan communities are not connected by road to another community with a hospital, and most villages are located a considerable distance from Anchorage, the location of the Alaska Native Medical Center (ANMC), the only tertiary medical center serving Alaska Natives. Severe weather frequently limits air and marine travel, restricting access to preventive services and causing delays in obtaining health care. There is also limited access to ongoing health education. Rural communities are largely dependent on regional health facilities for health information. Collectively, these issues present a formidable logistical challenge of how best to get information on organ transplantation and donation out to Alaska Natives.

Health care in Alaska for Native populations is unique in several respects. Major medical hospitals and clinics serving Alaska Natives are regionalized, overseen by the 12 separate Alaska Native Corporations. Each regional Native medical center then supports a network of community health aides and practitioners (CHA/Ps), the majority of whom are Alaska Native, in villages that are accessible only by small aircraft. Although not physicians, the CHA/Ps provide the primary health care in rural Alaska, with radio and telemedicine contacts with physicians in often-distant regional medical centers. Tertiary care is centralized at the ANMC in Anchorage, which is designated as a Level II Trauma Center, serving all of the regional medical centers. All major trauma victims from across the state, comprising most of the potential organ donors, are airlifted to Anchorage. Similarly, patients being referred for evaluation as transplant recipients are also referred to specialists in Anchorage as the tertiary care center and, to a lesser extent, Fairbanks and Juneau.

In addition to this relatively recent system of western medicine, there is a long history of traditional healing practices that are deeply embedded into the multiple indigenous cultures of Alaska. Traditional medicine is still very much alive, with traditional healers being available for consultation and treatment in most Alaska Native medical centers. These cultural practices reflect a worldview that is quite different from that of western societies. Although there is diversity in the views across the 16 distinct Alaska Native cultural and language systems, there is also commonality. These include trust of tradition and inherited wisdom, respect for elders and teachers, honoring the family, sharing and cooperation, listening with respect, respect for the natural world, and transmission of oral history through storytelling (Alaska Initiative for Community Engagement, 2005; Barnhardt & Kawagley, 2005; Stephens, 2000). A unique challenge of this project was to provide a framework through which the new medical technology of organ transplantation might be not only viewed but also valued within the context of these Alaska Native traditions.

A final challenge was to ease the stress of decision making on individuals and families. The centralized health care system, although efficient, commonly puts the patient or accompanying family members in the position of being asked to make decisions about donation or transplantation without the extended family or friends available for consultation, that is, without the community support network. Furthermore, consents for organ donation or for listing for transplant are usually presented by non-Native health care providers. Prior to this project, no educational materials were available for patient study at the regional and tertiary care centers. An educational effort would require providing not only the needed educational materials at the centralized points of care but also general public education that could familiarize Alaska Natives with the subject matter and prompt family discussion outside of the crisis setting.

Project Objectives and Strategies

Given these challenges, we developed the following two objectives:

1. To disseminate information to Alaska Native communities through the existing CHA/P network and the public schools, while using the driver's licensing bureaus to target general public awareness for all Alaskans.

2. To provide specific information at the regional medical centers and tertiary care centers where individuals and families make health care decisions about organ donation and transplantation.

The project team to cover the state consisted of a project manager in Anchorage and a transplant physician in Seattle. The operational plan sought to leverage their efforts by (a) producing a video about organ donation and transplantation, (b) selecting centralized venues that could have statewide impact, and (c) implementing a "teach the teachers" model at the village and regional levels.

Due to limitations on resources, not every aspect of the program was evaluated. Within each intervention type, the nonevaluated aspects will be presented first, followed by the evaluated aspects.

Community Education

Several components of the program involved reaching out directly to the public using a variety of approaches, including display boards at health fairs, posters, handouts and fact sheets, informational brochures for the Division of Motor Vehicles (DMV), as well a video about organ donation and an accompanying resource book. The above were evaluated, and the results follow.

Display Board for Health Fairs

An interactive display board titled "Ours to Give" was developed with Alaska Health Fairs, Inc., as a means to disseminate general information about organ and tissue donation to Alaska Natives in their rural Alaskan villages. A health fair is the usual mechanism for providing health screenings and health education in rural Alaska. Typically, a CHA/P or community wellness advocate (CWA) will contact Alaska Health Fairs, Inc., and request assistance in planning a health fair for his or her village. Alaska Health Fairs, Inc., has been conducting health fairs in rural Alaska for over 20 years. A big event in small towns, attendance usually includes a majority, if not all, of the village residents. Because personnel from the associations that sponsor booths (e.g., the American Heart Association and American Diabetes Association) cannot travel to and staff each rural fair, Alaska Health Fairs, Inc., takes the traveling collection of booths throughout the state, using trained assistants to answer questions and set up displays. A prepared booth and display will be used for about 10 years, over time reaching almost all of the rural villages in the state. The organ and tissue donation display board took its first road trip in the spring of 2004 and was exhibited with the loop tape of the 3-minute version of the video. As of October 2008, the display board has taken 270 road trips to rural health fairs across Alaska.

Posters

The project in coordination with the Alaska Organ Procurement Organization (OPO)/Tissue Bank and with the Alaska Native Tribal Health Consortium developed and distributed a poster specifically for Alaska Native audiences. "Sharing—It's a Way of Life" shows the faces of six Alaska Native organ recipients and donors. Over 5,000 copies of the poster have been distributed to Alaska Native hospitals and health clinics and DMV offices in Alaska to date.

Handouts and Fact Sheets

Each of the 178 community health clinics in rural Alaska, as well as each of the Alaska Native regional hospitals and clinics, was supplied with both hard copies and CD copies of handouts and fact sheets on organ donation developed for Alaska Native families.

Informational Brochures for DMV Licensing Offices and DMV License Renewal Mailings

With no transplant programs in Alaska, the relevance of organ donation for Alaskan patients is often not recognized. We wrote and produced a brochure for the DMV offices that specifically features photos of transplant donors and recipients from Alaska (both Alaska Natives and non-Natives). Also, because most drivers' licenses in rural areas are renewed by mail, our project worked with the DMV and the OPO serving Alaska to have the brochure included in renewal mailings. In the first year, the Alaska OPO (Life Alaska, now affiliated with LifeCenter Northwest, headquartered in Seattle.) distributed 10,000 copies of the brochure statewide through the DMV offices.

A Video About Organ Donation and Transplantation for Alaska Native Audiences

The initial step taken was to meet with the health educators from all the Alaska Native tribal groups across the state, present them with the need for public education on this subject, and solicit their input on the best means to accomplish this. The consensus advice was that a video should be produced. Given the lack of transplant professionals in the state, it was evident that the presenters and discussants within the village schools and clinics would be nonmedical schoolteachers and community health aides. Showing a video would be more comfortable for them than giving a talk on a relatively unfamiliar health subject. They felt the stories of patients would also stimulate discussion among the audience more readily than a presentation of medical facts. Because storytelling is the traditional means of communicating information in Native communities, having the video consist of people telling their individual stories would put the unfamiliar transplant technology into a comfortable format.

An Alaska Native public health educator was chosen to be the video coproducer. A theme was sought that would echo across all of the different Alaska Native cultural groups and that would be recognized as being relevant to their lives. "Sharing" was chosen as a theme that would frame this new and seemingly foreign medical technology (transplantation) within the context of a strong Alaska Native tradition of sharing, one held in common by all tribal groups. Facts were presented and misconceptions addressed in the video through the personal stories so that all needed information would be delivered by the video. It was intended that the video could be viewed by a family at home or in a clinic or school without needing a knowledgeable commentator present. The goal of the video, *New Traditions of Sharing*, was to allow viewers to stand in the shoes of both the organ donor and recipient families and come to understand how these families made their own decisions on donation and transplantation—without marketing the viewer to sign up as an organ donor him or herself. Not only is this approach more respectful, but also it is more culturally appropriate to present or offer information rather than try to convince another person to take a particular action.

Supporting the culturally relevant peer model of learning (Barnhardt & Kawagley, 2005; Stephens, 2000), the featured transplant donors and recipients on the video were all Alaska Natives, the Alaskan physicians and hospital personnel were also Alaska Natives, and the video narrator was an Alaska Native talk show personality with a recognizable voice. The narrator was not visualized, so that each individual told his or her own story directly to the audience, without an intermediary, as would happen in a discussion among friends. People from different tribal affiliations, geographic locations, and medical centers from across the state were depicted to make it all-inclusive, and local music was added. The video was previewed at the Medical Center in Barrow, and refined following audience feedback. In addition to the 15-minute full-length video, a shorter 3-minute version was made into a loop tape designed for showing at health fairs and in clinic settings. Four 30-second public service announcements (PSAs) were produced for the DMV licensing bureaus and for television. Both the full-length video and the four PSAs verbalized the key message in four local Alaska Native languages, in addition to English, so that non-English speakers would get the essential information. Even though non-English-speaking viewers are likely to be older individuals, this recognized their important roles in family discussions and family decision making.

Video and PSA Distribution

Four hundred fifty-one copies of the full-length video *New Traditions of Sharing: Alaska Native Stories of Organ Donation and Transplantation* were distributed in

Alaska. A copy of the video was sent to each of the 178 rural village clinics staffed by CHA/Ps, accompanied by a resource handbook (see below) containing answers to common questions that might arise from viewers. Community members are able to see the video in the clinic or at a presentation, or borrow it from the clinic to take home for viewing. Other recipients of the video included CHA/Ps, health educators, public health nurses, kidney dialysis centers, nephrologists, and patients. Copies were given to the department managers of the critical and emergency care units at the ANMC. The ANMC, the tertiary care center for all Alaska Natives in Alaska, is where all critical Alaska Native trauma patients are transported and therefore the most likely location for potential organ donors to be identified. Prior to our video, there were no materials for families to read or view at the hospital when asked about organ donation after the death of a family member. The video and materials were also distributed to the regional Native medical centers across the state for families who may be considering tissue donation if a family member dies locally, as well as to the non-Native community hospitals in each of the three primary urban areas, Anchorage, Fairbanks, and Juneau. The full-length video has been shown multiple times on Anchorage television, as well as on rural satellite TV through the Alaska Rural Communication System (ARCS), which reaches even the smallest villages. It has also been incorporated into the in-house patient education program at the ANMC, which broadcasts over closed-circuit TV in patient rooms. The loop tapes of the shorter 3-minute video were distributed to the ANMC Primary Care Clinic to be shown at their monthly patient health fairs, and to Alaska Health Fairs, Inc., to be shown with our booth at village health fairs throughout rural Alaska.

The four 30-second VHS PSAs and the full-length video were distributed to the six DMV licensing offices in Alaska. Local radio networks are listened to extensively throughout rural Alaska. PSAs utilizing verbal segments from the video were developed by statewide radio stations KNBA and KHAR, both of which feature Alaska Native and American Indian programming and easy listening, respectively.

A Resource Handbook to Accompany the Video

A 51-page resource handbook on organ and tissue donation and organ transplantation was developed for CHA/Ps and health educators and sent to each of the 178 CHA/P clinics in the state. Because the CHA/Ps work in isolated rural environments, having access to information to answer questions that might arise from local patients and families was essential. The handbook contains the following topics: stories of Alaska Native organ donors and recipients for human interest; answers to commonly asked questions about organ and tissue donation; information and contacts for agencies involved in organ and tissue donation in Alaska; information about the process of referral for organ transplantation, and contact numbers for all regional transplant programs across the Northwest; information about kidney dialysis; and Web sites and contact information for local, regional, and national agencies involved in organ donation and transplantation. The entire first section of the resource book is dedicated to the individual stories of Alaska Native transplant recipients and donors from across the state, stories designed to stimulate interest and discussion about organ donation and transplantation. These stories not only are suitable for health care personnel but also can be read by patients, family members, or school students who come into the clinic with questions.

Included in the resource handbook was a CD of two PowerPoint slide shows, so that CHA/Ps, health educators, and school teachers would have a prepared presentation on organ and tissue donation and transplantation. Both presentations were developed for rural Alaska Native audiences: One slide show was designed for community and general public education, and the other was for middle and high school presentations. The CD format was selected because Alaska Native health clinics and village schools are equipped with computers, and computer-based presentations are commonplace in rural Alaska.

Every few months, health educators from the regional medical centers come out to a village to assist the local CHA/P in providing local health education, including assisting with health classes in the schools. Presentations and discussions on organ and tissue donation are now greatly facilitated because both the local CHA/P and the regional health educator have the same resources such as video and CD presentations that include school exercises, resource book, handouts, and information sheets.

Effectiveness of the Video Program

It is estimated that the video reached approximately 60% of the Alaska Native population. This estimate is based on audience viewing data compiled by the statewide rural TV network. It is further estimated that 25% of Alaska Natives living in Anchorage were exposed to the radio PSAs aired by an Anchorage-based Alaska Native radio station. In addition, approximately 650 persons per day viewed part or all of the video at the DMV offices in Anchorage and the six next largest DMV offices in Alaska.

Training Rural Health Care Providers and Health Educators on the Subject

Besides simply distributing educational materials, it was essential that the users themselves understand and feel comfortable about the subject matter so they could answer questions, lead discussions, and, most importantly, be equipped to find the answers to questions they could not answer. Three distinct groups of community rural health care providers and trainers received this training: health educators at the Alaska Native Medical Center; Alaska Health Fairs, Inc., wellness coordinators; and community health aides and practitioners.

Training Sessions for Health Educators at the Alaska Native Medical Center

Training sessions were held for the eight full-time health educators in the Patient Education Department in the Anchorage Native Primary Care Center of the ANMC. This department has the responsibility for providing health education to approximately 47,000 Alaska Natives residing in the south-central region of Alaska surrounding Anchorage, the largest city. ANMC is also the tertiary referral center for Native patients across the state. The presentation utilized the video, the PowerPoint slide show on organ donation and transplantation relative to Alaska Natives, and a question-and-answer session, with pre- and posttest evaluation. At the training session, plans were made to create a display board on donation for the Primary Care Center lobby and to load information about donation onto the health education computers for hands-on patient use.

Training Session for Alaska Health Fairs Wellness Coordinators

Alaska Health Fairs, Inc., holds regular training sessions in Anchorage that are attended by community wellness advocates (CWA) from all over Alaska. The function of the CWA is to both develop and facilitate community education events, including health fairs, for Alaska Natives residing in rural communities. An informal presentation was held for 28 CWAs at a training session for health fair staff so that the CWAs would be knowledgeable about the display board they would be showing at the fairs.

Training Session for Community Health Aides and Practitioners

A 3-hour presentation on organ donation and transplantation was developed for the CHA/P Forum in 2003. The forum, held every year in Anchorage, is the primary method by which CHA/Ps from all corners of the state obtain their mandatory continuing education in a concentrated week of learning, skill building, and recertification. It is very difficult to even get a slot on this agenda. However, because one third to one half of the CHA/Ps in the state attend each year on a rotating basis, this forum is the most efficient way to reach rural health practitioners from across the state with a single intervention.

The presentation was attended by 54 CHA/Ps (85% of whom were Alaska Native) in addition to the director and training staff of the statewide CHA/P office. The presenters and topics included a panel of seven Alaska Native organ donor families and transplant recipients from across the state, who shared their personal stories; a transplant surgeon from a transplant program in Washington State that serves Alaska, discussing organ donation and transplantation; the director of the LifeAlaska tissue bank, discussing tissue donation; and a local nephrology social worker, discussing renal dialysis. Pre- and posttests were used for evaluation. The resource handbook was handed out to all CHA/Ps at the forum and to CHA/P training program directors. Brochures on many health topics (heart disease prevention, diabetes, nutrition, and smoking cessation) were also supplied for CHA/Ps to take back home to their village clinics, reinforcing the message that learning about donation and transplantation should now be considered a standard part of general preventive health education. The CHA/P Training Office requested that the OPO and tissue bank provide a speaker and display table at subsequent CHA/P Forums. Every 2–3 years, all CHA/Ps in the state will be exposed or reexposed to this subject matter as part of the training course.

Effectiveness of the Community Health Aide/Practitioner Training Session

The effectiveness of the CHA/P training was measured by (a) changes in factual knowledge about organ donation and organ transplantation, (b) changes in willingness to become an organ donor, (c) changes in knowledge on how to access organ donation and transplantation resources, and (d) participant evaluations. Among the 54 participants, there was a significant increase ($p < 0.001$) in the mean scores on factual knowledge between the pretests and posttests with mean knowledge scores more than doubling. Furthermore, participants were significantly more likely to report that they intended to sign an organ donor card following the training ($p = 0.003$). The odds ratio for the posttest group to be *very likely* to sign an organ donor card relative to *unlikely* (reference group) was 10.25. The odds ratio for *somewhat likely* relative to *unlikely* was 3.55. Participants were significantly more aware of how and where to get information on organ and tissue donation following the intervention (post- vs. pre-odds ratio 10.41, $p < 0.001$), which is essential for educators in rural areas. On the evaluations handed in by the participants assessing the effectiveness, delivery, and relevance of the course, the overall score given to the training by the participants was 1,019 out of a possible 1,105 points, or 92% positive. Beyond just the point scores, some of the comments were as follows: "excellent," "I was very touched," "very helpful," "thanks for opening my eyes," and "we need to get this information out to the villages."

Developing Educational Curricula for the Schools

Educational curricula were created for Alaskan students. A program was created for Alaska Native student bodies, and then components were added for special subgroups including multicultural student bodies and rural schools.

For an Alaska Native Student Body

Our team developed and delivered a course on organ donation and transplantation for the high school students of Mt. Edgecombe High School (MEHS) in Sitka, Alaska. Each student was also given a resource handbook modified for students to take back to their respective communities. The student handbooks included not only basic information to reinforce the teaching session but also interesting stories about Alaskan patients and relevant newspaper articles to stimulate classroom discussion and highlight new developments in the field (e.g., islet transplants for diabetes, and living-related liver transplants). MEHS, the state-run high school for students across the state from villages too small and distant to have access to a local high school, has been a boarding school for Alaska Natives for more than 50 years and has a current student body of over 200 students. Because students are carefully selected for this special school, and because over 90% of graduates attend college, these students are set to become future leaders in Alaska Native communities. Thus, choosing this education venue was part of the leveraging strategy, not only educating the students in the classroom but also providing educational materials (that read like stories) that could be taken back to villages across the state. The students themselves, now more knowledgeable about facts versus misinformation, would be in a position to talk about the subject with family, friends, and community once back home. This program was so successful that both the MEHS school newspaper and even the Sitka town newspaper interviewed the presenters for news articles on the subject.

For a Multicultural Student Body

The local organ procurement agency has been providing presentations on organ donation to students in the Anchorage School District (ASD) for several years. The project manager observed several of these classroom sessions and worked together with the OPO to make the presentations more interactive. One of the areas with a new emphasis was talking about organ donation with other family members. In other parts of the country, including Seattle, it has been shown that people of color who intend to become organ donors are often reluctant to sign organ donor cards, due to a general distrust of the health care system. They prefer instead that the family carry out their wishes to donate if they die, making family discussions of utmost importance. The revised school presentation built role-playing and skill-building exercises into the PowerPoint show, which are intended to assist students when they approach their families to talk about organ donation.

For Rural Schools

A CD of this PowerPoint presentation for the schools was sent with the resource handbook to each CHA/P for the rural schools. In roadless rural Alaska, residents are less likely to get driver's licenses and therefore less likely to come into contact with organ donor cards, again giving further weight to family discussions on donation.

Effectiveness of School Presentations

Analyses were performed comparing the pre- to posttest results of the school program intervention at Mt. Edgecombe High School in Sitka, Alaska, in order to gauge program efficacy among an all–Alaska Native student body (as other school presentations had been to multicultural student bodies). Pre- and posttest questionnaires used in the Seattle public schools (Weaver, Spigner, Pineda, Rabun, & Allen, 2000) were modified for Alaskan students and approved by the Alaska Area Institutional Review Board. Sixty-three students, who represented all of the ninth and 10th graders at the school, participated.

Findings of Importance on the Baseline Study (Pretest)

1. Although only 21% of students reported that they had talked with their family about organ donation, those who did were significantly more likely to want to be an organ donor at baseline ($p = 0.0002$).
2. Although at baseline only 16% of students wanted to become organ donors after death, 77% indicated that they would be willing to be a *living* donor (kidney) if a family member needed an organ transplant. This suggests that living donation may be a more palatable option for Alaska Natives, although currently living donation is used uncommonly (Northwest Renal Network, 2007).
3. Compared to the small number of students who had decided to become organ donors at baseline (16%), 68% wanted to be able to receive an organ transplant themselves if they needed it.
4. Gender did not make a significant difference in opinions on donation in this sample, which is different from most studies conducted among both adults and youth in other communities.

Changes in Factual Knowledge

Knowledge scores on donation and transplantation increased significantly following the intervention ($p < 0.001$), with the mean percentage of correct answers increasing from 58% on the pretest to 95% on the posttest. The posttest answers on the factual questions demonstrated that misinformation and "urban myths" about organ donation had been corrected.

Changes in Opinions About Posthumous Organ Donation

Students were significantly more likely to consider becoming an organ donor ($p = 0.021$) after the intervention—there was a twofold increase in the percentage of students (38%) selecting the donation option. Of interest, this increase in willingness to donate occurred even though there were no differences from pre- to posttest on the major deterrents to organ donation, including fear of the surgical procedure, not having talked with one's family, and not wanting to think about one's own mortality. As expected in this young age group, the majority of students (50%) were still in the *undecided* group. Notably, only 13% had already made a decision not to be a donor. Widespread interest in receiving an organ transplant (if needed) was unchanged from pre- to post-test.

Summary

This public health awareness program was successful in reaching and educating a population that has not traditionally participated in organ donation or transplantation. Success was ascribed to several strategies: The primary messages, that of giving and sharing, are deeply embedded cultural values; the information was culturally relevant, and it was presented in ways that were culturally appropriate. Multiple channels were used for communicating to the community, including role models, storytelling, local health care providers, and visual and electronic media. Feedback from the targeted audiences was solicited at every step. With only a single program manager to cover a large geographical area, efforts were leveraged by producing a self-explanatory video and accompanying resource book for statewide distribution; by selecting centralized venues for courses and presentations that could have statewide impact; and by implementing a "teach the teachers" model at the village and regional levels.

Appendix 5.1   Suggestions for Delivering Organ Donation and Transplantation Information in Diverse Cultures

Listed below are some points of advice on conducting donation education that were given to this program by many community participants and local health educators. These points were heeded and incorporated into this public education program and subsequently used in the design and execution of other awareness and education campaigns in various ethnic minority communities in Washington State (Wong, Cárdenas, Shiu-Thornton, Spigner, & Allen, 2009). However, because alternate methods for producing, presenting, or delivering information on donation and transplantation were not investigated, it is not possible to determine whether other strategies might have been equally effective. These are therefore presented simply as points for consideration for future educational campaigns on sensitive health subjects in diverse communities.

1. To have relevance for community members, the health message should be presented within the appropriate social and cultural context. Decisions on organ donation not only are intellectual ones based on facts, but also incorporate considerations for family, social, cultural, and religious traditions. In designing and executing a program, take the time to understand your audience and put yourself in their shoes.
2. The most powerful message is a personal story, and the most powerful messenger is a patient or family member. Asking real people to tell their own story is much more effective than having health care professionals tell people what they should do. This is especially important when the patients and health care providers are from different cultural backgrounds.
3. Individuals like to be in full control of decision making on the sensitive issue of organ donation. Using a low-key approach to provide information so people can make their own decisions is more effective than trying to convince people that they should take a certain action. This is especially true if distrust of the health care system is an issue.
4. The choice about whether to sign up as an organ donor should be an informed one, no matter whether that decision is for or against donation. What the community want from the education are simply the tools to make an informed decision.
5. Do not presume that the audience will not want to know about organ donation. In fact, most people are interested in hearing about this subject matter, even if it is unfamiliar to them.
6. Making a decision about organ donation may be a process that evolves over time. Do not expect instant results.
7. Decisions about donation after a death affect a whole community, not just the donor family. Making this a positive experience and helping the family with follow-up affect a larger circle of people than one may first realize.
8. Do not reinvent the wheel. By searching out, engaging, and utilizing existing dissemination and communication networks and by using a "teach the teachers" strategy, small efforts can be greatly magnified.

Acknowledgements

This work was supported by grants R18AI40674 and R01AI37747 from the National Institute of Allergy and Infectious Disease, grant 5 H39OT00099-02-00, CFDA 93.134 from HRSA, and a grant from the Paul Allen Foundation.

References

Alaska Initiative for Community Engagement. (2005). *Traditional values of Alaska poster.* Retrieved October 20, 2008, from http://alaskaice.org/material.php?matID=310

Barnhardt, R., & Kawagley, A. O. (2005). Indigenous knowledge systems and Alaska native ways of knowing. *Anthropology & Education Quarterly, 36,* 8–23.

Narva, A. S. (2003). The spectrum of kidney disease in American Indians. *Kidney International, 83*(Suppl.), S3–S7.

Northwest Renal Network. (2007). *ESRD region 16: Annual report 2007.* Retrieved November 19, 2008, from http://www.nwrenalnetwork.org/AR/AR2007/AR2007Full.pdf

Organ Procurement and Transplantation Network. (2008a). *Data/view data: Results/regional data/region 6, Pacific Northwest.* Retrieved November 15, 2008, from http://www.optn.org

Organ Procurement and Transplantation Network. (2008b). *Data/view data results/national data.* Retrieved November 15, 2008, from http://www.optn.org

Stephens, S. (2000). *Handbook for culturally responsive science curriculum.* Fairbanks, AL: Native Knowledge Network.

U.S. Renal Data System. (2008). *USRDS annual data report 2008.* Retrieved November 19, 2008, from http://www.usrds.org/2008/ref/E_Transplantation_Process_08.pdf

Weaver, M., Spigner, C., Pineda, M., Rabun, K. G., & Allen, M. D. (2000). Knowledge and opinions about organ donation among urban high school students: Pilot test of a health education program. *Clinical Transplants, 14,* 292–303.

Wong, K. A., Cárdenas, V., Shiu-Thornton, S., Spigner, C., & Allen, M. D. (2009). How do communities want their information? Designing educational outreach on organ donation for Asian Americans. *Progress in Transplantation, 19*(1), 44–52.

6

First-Person Consent Ohio Donor Registry

The Influence of the First-Person Consent Registry on Increasing Organ Donation

Kimberly Downing and Linda Jones

The growth in statewide organ donor registries provides numerous research opportunities, such as opportunities for evaluation of how organ donation registration behavior is impacted by public education programs or state-level policy changes. By using registry data in the aggregate, with personally identified information removed, these data can provide information such as actual registration rates by geographic areas in the state, for example by county, metro area, or zip code. Geographic areas that may be particularly high or low in donation can be compared with other areas in the state or region. By comparing aggregate registration data with other information sources of an area, such as U.S. Census data, researchers can better understand possible demographic differences in low- and high-registration areas. In addition, this information can assist with targeting educational interventions to specific geographic and demographic areas. Although demographic information is limited in registry data sets, information such as registration rate by age group and by gender is available, and this can help researchers and practitioners understand which groups are registering to be organ donors and which groups are not. Furthermore, analyzing the aggregate data over time provides valuable information about the short-term and long-term impacts of a state law change or an educational campaign intervention.

Ohio's First-Person Consent Organ Donor Registry

In 2002, the State of Ohio changed state law to make the Ohio Organ Donor Registry a donor-designated registry, also referred to as a *first-person consent registry*. Ohio Senate Bill No. 188, known as The First Person Consent Ohio Donor Registry bill, took effect July 1, 2002 (Ohio General Assembly, 2000). Ohio became the sixth state in the United States to implement a first-person consent donor registry. The First Person Consent Ohio Donor Registry (hereafter, the 1stPCODR) makes the donor's own wishes to donate his or her organs upon death the only consent necessary for donation and recovery of medically suitable organs, tissues, and eyes. The donor's wishes are affirmed on the Ohio driver's license or state ID card as a legal document. Prior to July 2002, even if an individual indicated his or her wishes to donate on a driver's license, families were able to overrule these wishes and refuse to give consent for donation. This resulted in the loss of medically suitable organ donors. The 1stPCODR allowed individuals to make their decision to donate a legally binding directive. Public opinion research conducted in Ohio in 2001 found that prior to the implementation of the 1stPCODR, Ohio residents who had previously indicated their intent to donate organs on their driver's licenses thought that their wishes would be honored when, in fact, their wishes could have been overridden by their families (Downing, 2001). The State of Ohio's law change in 2002 gave Ohio adults the legal right to have their personal wishes for organ donation granted.

Historical Perspective of First-Person Consent and Donor Designation Implementation

The need to increase the number of solid-organ donors as well as the need for explicit language in state laws about donors' wishes and how those wishes would be recorded created the momentum for this law change in Ohio and similar changes in other states. To fully understand the importance of the changes in state laws, especially Ohio's, it is necessary to review the historical perspective of this issue.

The Uniform Anatomical Gift Act (UAGA) became a law in 1968, and within a decade it had been passed by all states. The UAGA provided for the legality of organ donation and defined the rights and responsibilities of the donor and the donee. The UAGA authorized persons 18 years of age or older to make an anatomical gift with such gift to take effect upon their death. The UAGA further provided that the gift could not be rescinded by another party without the donor's consent (U.S. Department of Health and Human Services [DHHS], 2003). Several provisions of the UAGA included requiring consent forms (such as a driver's license) and defining next of kin (e.g., who would sign the consent for donation).

Research indicated that potential organ donors were still not actually donating after the passage of the UAGA. In a retrospective medical chart review of potential organ donors, Gortmaker et al. (1996) found that in nearly one third of all cases, potential donors were neither identified nor was donation requested

from the family. The continuing need for organ donation and increased education was evident.

Despite the legislation, revisions, and amendments, families continued to
deny consent for organ donation of their loved ones (Lewin Group, 2002).
The reasons families often gave for denying consent included: they did not know
their loved one's wishes; they had never talked about donation; they were
uncomfortable with talking about death; and they made their decisions based on
their own beliefs, not the wishes of their loved ones. Furthermore, despite the
UAGA's adoption in all states, in practice, organ recovery organizations (ORO)
would refuse a donation if the family objected (DHHS, 2003; Wendler &
Dickert, 2001).

In the United States, the consent process is left to individual states within
the limitations of the federal National Organ Transplant Act of 1984 (Organ
Procurement and Transplantation Network, 1984). Each state's UAGA seeks to
streamline the process and standardize the rules among the various states, but
it still requires that the donor make an affirmative statement about his or her
willingness to be a donor.

More recently, as a way to increase organ donation, states began passing
legislation to require some form of donor designation to clarify that "the donor's
decision is paramount and should be respected at all costs" (Sokohl, 2002, p. 1).
Pennsylvania introduced and passed The Pennsylvania Act 102 in 1994
(Pennsylvania General Assembly, 1994), making it one of the first states to
explicitly state that the donor's wish was paramount. Sokohl noted that there were
four major components of the Pennsylvania law that had a dramatic effect on
donation rates in Pennsylvania: mandating that hospitals call the organ recovery
organizations on *all* deaths, setting up a donation registry through the Pennsylvania Division of Motor Vehicles, allowing licensed drivers to indicate their
consent for donation on their license, and strengthening the language to make
the donor's wish paramount and to ensure that consent of the next of kin was
not required (Sokohl; Pennsylvania General Assembly).

Between 2000 and 2004, six other states (including Ohio) began passing legislation in reference to first-person consent or donor designation (DHHS HRSA,
National Conference of State Legislatures and Council of State Governments, 2001).
The Ohio Donor Registry is a first-person consent registry that ensures that a
person's wish concerning organ and tissue donation is honored at the time of
death. The objectives of the registry are to provide organ recovery organizations
access to an individual's donation registration, to grant permission to act on that
registration as an advance directive declared by the individual, and to save lives
through increasing the number of organs available for transplantation. The Ohio
State Law section 2108.04 (F) (Ohio General Assembly, 2001) provides that a valid
declaration of an anatomical gift made prior to an individual's death prevails over
any contrary desires of the donor's family.

Statewide Registries for Organ Donors

Having a statewide registry is not synonymous with having first-person consent or designation legislation in the state. Statewide donor registries provide a mechanism for recording, storing, and retrieving an individual's wishes to be an organ donor, usually in an electronic database. According to the United Network of Organ Sharing (2008), in 2008 most states in the United States had developed donor registries, and many of these registries are affiliated with the state's motor vehicles agency. Affiliating with the motor vehicle agency provides state residents with a convenient opportunity to choose to be in the organ donor registry when obtaining or renewing their drivers' license (Siegel, Alvaro, & Jones, 2005).

The mechanism for the organ donor registration is left to individual states, thus, there are variations across the United States. Those states that do have statewide registries are housed at the motor vehicle agency, within the ORO, or in another organization.

Ohio as a Case Study of First-Person Consent Donor Registries

Ohio is an important state in studying the impact of first-person consent registries on organ donation for several reasons: Ohio was an early adopter of first-person consent registries, Ohio is the seventh largest state in the United States by population (U.S. Bureau of the Census, 2007), Ohio has approximately 8.7 million licensed drivers and identification cardholders in the state (Ohio Bureau of Motor Vehicles, 2007), and there are four Ohio Organ Recovery Organizations (OOROs) that have worked cooperatively on the implementation of the 1stPCODR and on statewide educational campaigns.

In conjunction with the establishment of the 1stPCODR in Ohio, a statewide educational campaign was implemented to promote the organ donor registry through television advertising, radio promotions, and public service announcements. This chapter summarizes a research project that was conducted to evaluate the impact of the 1stPCODR and the educational campaign. The research was funded by a 3-year grant awarded in 2002 from the Health Resources and Services Administration, Division of Transplantation (HRSA/DoT), U.S. Department of Health and Human Services.

Real World Issues With Implementation of the 1stPCODR

Although Ohio changed to a first-person consent donor registry in 2002, the state faced several issues in successfully implementing this new policy. First, there was a need to promote understanding of the policy change to the Ohio public and to inform the public that the organ donor registry was now a first-person consent registry. Professionals involved with organ donation (e.g., organ recovery organization staff, hospital staff, etc.) also needed to be informed about the change of the registry. The legal guardian of the 1stPCODR is the Ohio Bureau of Motor Vehicles (OBMV); thus, it was important to inform the OBMV administration and staff of the change in policy and provide new information at OBMV registrar locations. The promotion and education of the 1stPCODR was challenging for several reasons. First, there were various organizations involved. Ohio has four organ recovery organizations operating across the state. Ohio has three large media markets (Cleveland, Columbus, and Cincinnati) and several smaller media markets (e.g., Toledo and Dayton). Consequently, promotion of this policy change was potentially expensive and necessitated a collaborative effort with the different organizations across the state.

The second issue Ohio faced for a successful implementation of the 1stPCODR and its promotion was the need for data collection and tracking the impact of the policy change and the educational campaign. Again, a collaborative effort between the four organ recovery organizations and the OBMV was critical for a statewide evaluation of the impact of the policy change.

Third, there was a need to measure the impact and outcomes of the policy change and the influence of the educational campaign to inform Ohio residents about the 1stPCODR. This was important to our understanding of not only whether these efforts made a difference in people's attitudes and awareness of the registry, but also ultimately whether these efforts had an impact on registration behavior and actual organ donation.

A fourth issue was the need for collaboration among the multiple organizations involved with organ donation in Ohio. This was necessary to carry out a statewide educational campaign with a unified message, to gather donor registration data, and to gather actual deceased donor data for the entire state. Fortunately, a positive collaborative environment existed in Ohio in 2002 (Jones, Downing, & Holloway, 2006). The four OOROs had already worked together in establishing the need for the 1stPCODR and had taken the lead in supporting the 1stPCODR legislation. Three other organizations joined the OOROs[1] to form a statewide consortium for the research project. These organizations were the Ohio Department of Health, Second Chance Trust Fund (ODH/SCTF); the OBMV; and the University of Cincinnati. Although the number of organizations needed for conducting this project was large, such a group was necessary to implement a statewide educational campaign, to facilitate the data collection process, and to conduct the evaluation.

---

1.   The four organ recovery organizations in Ohio are Lifeline of Ohio (Columbus, Ohio), LifeBanc (Cleveland, Ohio), LifeCenter (Cincinnati, Ohio), and Life Connection (Dayton and Toledo, Ohio).

A fifth and related issue was funding and coordination of the educational campaign. The ODH/SCTF and the four OOROs served this role. The educational media campaign's design and implementation were managed by the Second Chance Trust Fund and the OOROs. This meant that the project's consortium members needed to have careful coordination and clear communication with each other.

Theoretical Basis for Research

The real-world issues addressed by this project are the need to inform Ohio residents about the 1stPCODR and to increase Ohio residents' willingness to become organ donors. The theoretical basis for the research draws from Horton and Horton's (1991) model developed to understand willingness to donate organs. This model has five major conceptual variables: values, factual knowledge regarding donation, attitudes, willingness to donate, and whether a person carried an organ donor card or requested one (Horton & Horton, 1991, p. 1039). For our research, we have labeled the last step in the model as *registered as organ donor*, because Ohio residents indicate their willingness by registering in the 1stPCODR.

Horton and Horton and other researchers noted that lack of knowledge about organ donation can influence attitudes about organ donation and willingness to be an organ donor (Horton & Horton, 1990, 1991; McIntyre et al., 1987, p. 331). In another article, Horton (1991) noted that there were misunderstandings about organ donation that may constitute major barriers to individuals who are considering registering to become potential organ donors. He stated that "the public is poorly informed about the process and implications of organ donation" (1991, p. 38). Horton and Horton (1991) also concluded that in order to increase favorable attitudes toward organ donation, the willingness to donate, and signing up to be an organ donor, marketing the concept of becoming a potential organ donor is needed. To do this, they suggested the following: Convey specific types of factual information to the public, and develop educational and persuasive messages that specifically relate to the act of becoming a potential organ donor (Horton & Horton, 1991, p. 1050).

The intent of our research project was not to revise or test a model. Instead, we used the willingness-to-donate model to guide the development and implementation of the educational intervention and guide our evaluation of the impact of the 1stPCODR and the educational campaign. The model and its related variations provide a theoretical basis for informing our research questions, developing educational interventions used in our project, and designing our research instruments, data analysis plan, and project evaluation.

Based on the previous research on willingness to donate, the project's educational interventions were developed to increase knowledge and awareness about organ donation and the 1stPCODR, increase favorable attitudes toward donation, increase the willingness to register as an organ donor, and increase organ donor registration in the 1stPCODR. Our research questions and survey instruments were guided by the following constructs in the theoretical models of willingness to donate: values, factual knowledge regarding donation, attitudes, willingness to donate (Horton & Horton, 1991, p. 1039), information exposure, and perceived social norms.

Research Design

The HRSA/DoT grant provided the opportunity to research the impact of the 1stPCODR and the influence of the educational campaign on organ donor registration as well as the impact of the registry and campaign on actual deceased donor rates. The two research questions were as follows:

1. Does the implementation of the 1stPCODR have a positive influence on organ donor registration rates and on actual deceased organ donor rates?
2. Do Ohio residents' attitudes and behavioral intentions concerning organ donation registration and the 1stPCODR positively change after the implementation of the 1stPCODR and an educational campaign?

Educational Interventions

Ohio's four OROs and the ODH/SCTF coordinated efforts and provided funding for two educational campaigns about organ donation and the 1stPCODR. The educational campaigns that took place during the 3-year grant period included a statewide marketing campaign at OBMV locations and a statewide media campaign. First, a statewide educational campaign at OBMV locations was implemented in July 2003. All OBMV registrar locations were provided with marketing materials (posters and brochures) informing Ohio residents about organ donation and joining the Ohio Donor Registry. This marketing campaign was designed to reach only Ohio residents who visited an OBMV location; this was not a mass marketed campaign to the Ohio general public.

Second, in 2005 a statewide educational campaign was implemented through a media mix of television advertising, radio promotions, public service announcements, billboards, posters, brochures, and a new state Web site, www.donatelifeohio.org. This campaign's purpose was to inform Ohio residents about organ donation and encourage them to join the Ohio Donor Registry. This campaign began in January 2005, with television spots that aired from January through April and repeated in October through December 2005 in Ohio's television markets. The other promotions (radio, print, billboards, bus benches, etc.) ran for a longer time period. The statewide media campaign has continued beyond the timeframe of the 3-year project with television spots airing again in 2006 and 2007. The coordinated statewide media campaign, also known as the "Hero" campaign, presented pictures of individuals of all ages, races, and ethnicities who represented registered organ donors. The campaign's tag line was "Be a hero. Be an organ and tissue donor. Join the Ohio Donor Registry. www.donatelifeohio.org."

Multiple Measures and Data Sources

To meet our research goals, we used a pre-post design to determine whether the implementation of the interventions (the 1stPCODR and educational campaigns) had an influence on attitudes and knowledge about organ donation, behavioral intent to donate and actual registration, and, ultimately, an increase in actual deceased organ donor rates. We relied on multiple data sources and multiple measures to accomplish our research goals. We used three separate cross-sectional surveys of Ohio adults conducted over a 5-year period, organ donor registry data from the OBMV over a 7-year period, and actual deceased donor data collected over a 7-year period. Furthermore, we measured individuals' actual registration in the 1stPCODR, not the signing of a donor card or of talking to a family member about organ donation decisions to show intention to be a donor. For the purposes of our research, "registering as an organ donor in the 1stPCODR" was the behavior we were measuring. Still, the willingness-to-donate model did guide our research hypotheses that increased knowledge and awareness as well as increased favorable attitudes would have a positive influence on willingness to donate and registration behavior.

Data *prior* to the implementation of the 1stPCODR was needed as well as data post implementation of the 1stPCODR to determine its impact. The following data sources were used for analysis: organ donor registry data 3 years prior to first-person consent from the OBMV (July 1999–June 2002) to compare with 4 years post implementation of the 1stPCODR (July 2002–June 2006);[2] deceased donor data from the four OOROs for 3 years prior to first-person consent and

2.   Most Ohio residents make their organ donation decisions during the driver's license renewal process. The driver's license renewal for Ohio residents is every 4 years. Although the HRSA grant proposal was designed to collect data for only 3 years, the grant consortium members agreed to collect and analyze the data for the additional year so that we could better assess the impact of 1stPCODR after all Ohio residents had the opportunity to renew their driver's license. The end of the fourth year of data collection for the OBMV and OORO data was June 30, 2006.

4 years post implementation of the 1stPCODR; and a 2001 statewide, cross-sectional survey of Ohio adults to assess attitudes, knowledge, and behavioral intent and willingness to donate prior to the implementation of the 1stPCODR. Additional surveys conducted in 2003 and 2005 measured attitudes, knowledge, behavioral intent to donate, awareness of the 1stPCODR, and the educational campaigns following the implementation of the 1stPCODR.

Research Methods and Results

The research relied on multiple data sources to address our research questions and goals. Using data triangulation, or the application and combination of several data sources to study the same phenomenon, granted us the opportunity to evaluate the impact of the 1stPCODR and the educational campaign on attitudes, behavior, and donation outcomes. The results presented here separately address the outcomes of each of the multiple data sources.

Organ Donor Registration Rates

Our goal was to determine whether there was an increase in the number and percentage of persons who consent to be organ donors on their driver's license after the 1stPCODR took effect in 2002. To accomplish this, we obtained OBMV registry data from July 1999 to June 2006. These data provided us with 3 years of registry data before the 1stPCODR took affect and 4 years post the 1stPCODR. Comparisons were made based on monthly registrations over a 7-year time frame. The outcome measure was behavior change, specifically whether or not there was an actual increase in organ donor registrations. OBMV data include the following variables: age, sex, whether a person was listed as a donor in the registry, and geographic location variables such as zip code and county. The registry data do not include other demographic variables such as race or educational attainment.

Based on the OBMV registry data, we found the statewide registration rates increased each year following the implementation of the 1stPCODR in July 2002 (Figure 6.1). Although the trend line shows an increase prior to the beginning of the registry in 2002, the increase in registration is greater following the implementation of the 1stPCODR. There has been an increase of approximately 4.3% in statewide organ donor registrations following the implementation of the 1stPCODR in 2002. This is compared to an increase of approximately 2.4% statewide in the 3 years prior to the 1stPCODR (1999 to 2002).[3] In July 2006, 4 years post

---

3.   The trend line shows seasonal fluctuations in registration data. Consistently, Quarter 3 (the winter quarter) shows a drop in registration across the trend line.

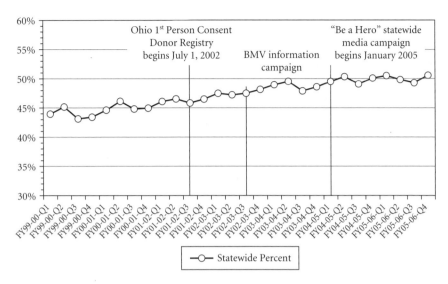

Figure 6.1   First-Person Consent Ohio Donor Registry, statewide donor registration data (presented quarterly).
Source: OBMV registration data, FY99–00 to FY05–06.

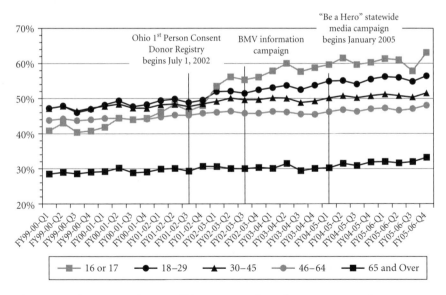

Figure 6.2   First-Person Consent Ohio Donor Registry, donor percentage by age (data presented quarterly).
Source: OBMV registration data, FY99–00 to FY05–06.

implementation of the 1stPCODR, approximately 51% of Ohio residents who were renewing or obtaining their driver's license indicated their wish to be an organ donor in the 1stPCODR. This is in contrast to the 44–46% statewide registration rate in the 3 years prior to the 1stPCODR.

Other findings from the OBMV registry data show that women continue to register at a higher rate than men (approximately 7 percentage points higher). This has been a consistent trend before and after implementation of the 1stPCODR. Although the trend line for both men and women in Ohio has increased post implementation of the 1stPCODR, the percentage difference between the two sexes remains similar to the pre-1stPCODR levels.

Age is an important demographic variable in organ donor registration. Younger Ohio residents are more likely than older adults to register in the 1stPCODR (Figure 6.2). Since the implementation of the 1stPCODR, youth (16–17 year olds) are more likely than any other age group to register to be an organ donor. This age group has had more than a 12 percentage point increase in registration since the beginning of the 1stPCODR in 2002. The young adult age group, those 18–29 years of age, also indicates an increase beyond the statewide trend. The young adult age group shows a 7 percentage point increase in registration since the beginning of the 1stPCODR. Registration rates for the oldest age group (65+) show little change over the 7 years of registration data. Although the campaign messages were targeted to the general Ohio adult population, these results indicate that implementation of the 1stPCODR and its educational campaign messages had more influence on the younger age groups than the older age groups in Ohio.

Actual Deceased Donor Rates

We also sought to determine whether an increase in the number and percentage of persons registering in the 1stPCODR resulted in an increase in actual deceased donor rates. To accomplish this, we used OORO data of deceased potential and actual organ donors. These data were matched with the OBMV registry data from July 1999 to June 2006 to determine whether the donor was listed as a registered donor. We compared OORO data before and after implementation of the 1stPCODR for the 7-year period. We expected that after implementation of 1stPCODR, we would find an increase in actual organ donations.

The OORO data results indicate that in the 4 years following the implementation of the 1stPCODR, the percentage and number of actual deceased donors increased compared to the 3 years prior to the implementation of the 1stPCODR.[4] By the

4.   It is important to note that the OBMV registry data and the OORO data are presented by fiscal year (July–June). These data are presented by fiscal year because the 1stPCODR began in July 2002, and for tracking before and after implementation, it was necessary to present the data in this manner.

end of the fourth year of the 1stPCODR in July 2006, all Ohio residents had the opportunity to register in the 1stPCODR. OORO data from the fourth year following 1stPCODR implementation show that 57% of potential deceased donors became actual donors compared to 48% the first year of the 1stPCODR and 44% 3 years prior to the implementation of the 1stPCODR. Also, by the fourth year post implementation of the 1stPCODR and after all Ohio residents had a chance to renew their driver's license and register for the first time in the 1stPCODR, 44% of the actual deceased donors in Ohio were registered as organ donors in the 1stPCODR compared to only 13% in the first year of the 1stPCODR.

Ohio Residens' Attitudes and Behavioral Intent Toward Organ Donation and 1stPCODR

Our research project monitored Ohio residents' attitudes, knowledge, and behavioral intentions concerning organ donation. We conducted three statewide cross-sectional surveys of Ohio adults. Each survey was a random digit-dial (RDD) telephone survey conducted with approximately 2,000 Ohio adults. The telephone interview was approximately 25 minutes in length (see Appendix 6.1, "Survey Methodology"). Surveys were conducted in 2001, one year prior to 1stPCODR implementation; in 2003, one year after the implementation of 1stPCODR; and in 2005, 3 years after the implementation of the 1stPCODR. The outcome measures were change in attitudes, knowledge, and behavioral intentions of Ohio adults. The three statewide surveys of Ohio adults provided data on attitudes, knowledge, and behavioral intentions concerning organ donation and the 1stPCODR.

First-Person Consent

Public support for the concept of first-person consent for organ donation has significantly increased since the 2001 survey. Comparing results from the 2001 survey to those of the 2005 survey, we find a significant difference in the proportion of Ohio residents who strongly agreed with the statement that the wishes of those listed in the registry should take precedence over the wishes of the individual's next of kin, $Z = 5.106$, $p < .05$. Table 6.1 presents these results.

The survey results also show a significant difference between the 2001 survey (81%) and the 2005 survey (87%) in Ohio residents' views that the wishes of individuals who have indicated that they want their organs donated *should* be carried out regardless of their family's feelings, $Z = 5.223$, $p < .05$. Table 6.2 presents these results.

Attitude Toward Organ Donation

Most Ohio adults surveyed had a positive attitude, either *very positive* or *somewhat positive*, toward the donation of organs for transplant. There was a

Table 6.1 Individuals' Wishes Should Take Precedence Over Next of Kin: Comparisons of Three Cross-Sectional Surveys

| | Percent of agreement | | |
	2001	2003	2005
Strongly Agree	47.6	52.4	55.8
Agree Somewhat	27.3	27.2	26.4
Disagree Somewhat	13.7	10.4	10.1
Strongly Disagree	7.9	7.1	6.2
Don't Know (Volunteered response)	3.5	2.9	1.5
(N)	2,114	2,062	2,006

Note: Z-test for difference in proportions, 2001 survey to 2005 survey: $Z = 5.106$, $p < .05$.
Note: Question wording, "Do you agree or disagree with this statement: The wishes of those listed in the registry should take precedence over the wishes of the individual's next-of-kin."

Table 6.2 Wishes Carried Out Regardless of Family's Feelings: Comparisons of Three Cross-Sectional Surveys

| | Percent | | |
	2001	2003	2005
Yes	81.1	80.7	87.4
No	12.4	14.1	9.9
Don't Know (Volunteered response)	6.5	5.2	2.7
(N)	2,118	2,067	2,033

Note: Z-test for Difference in proportions, 2001 survey to 2005 survey: $Z = 5.223$, $p < .05$.
Note: Question wording, "In your opinion, should the wishes of an individual who has indicated they want to donate their organs be carried out regardless of their family's feelings?"

significant difference in the proportion of Ohio residents who had a positive attitude toward organ donation in the 2001 survey (91%) compared with the 2005 survey (95%), $Z = 4.969$, $p < .05$.

Willingness to Donate

Willingness to become an organ donor is one measure of an individual's favorable opinion about organ donation. Respondents were asked a single yes or no question about whether they would want to have one or more of their organs donated to a patient in need of an organ transplant. Survey results over the three survey time periods show an increased trend in the willingness of Ohio residents to say they want to have their organs donated (75% in 2001, 77% in 2003, and 81% in 2005). There is a significant difference in the proportion of Ohio residents indicating that they are willing to donate their organs from the 2001 survey to the 2005 survey, $Z = 4.633$, $p < .05$.

Registered as an Organ Donor

Even though a large majority of Ohio adults say they are willing to be an organ donor, the percentage of those who have granted permission for organ donation on their driver's license is considerably smaller. The survey data show that the percentage of Ohio adults who say they have registered to be an organ donor has increased only slightly during the project time period (57% in 2003 and 59% in 2005),[5,6] though this is not a significant difference in the proportions of these two surveys, $Z = 1.274$, $p < .05$. Table 6.3 provides results to this question by sex, age, race, and educational attainment for each of the three surveys.

1stPCODR and Educational Campaign Intervention

A goal of the research project was to track the influence of the educational campaign on organ donor registrations and to measure awareness and attitudes about the educational campaign, the 1stPCODR, and organ donation. To accomplish this, we relied on the OBMV registry data to track registration before and after the educational campaign. The statewide surveys conducted in 2003 and 2005 also included questions to evaluate awareness and attitudes about the 1stPCODR and organ donation. The outcome measures included registration rate following the educational campaign, and awareness and favorable attitude levels about the 1stPCODR and organ donation.

The survey data and OBMV registry data were used to evaluate the influence of the educational campaign. The OBMV trend data, although useful in showing the increase in the registration rates over time, are less effective in evaluating the influence of the educational campaign statewide. Still, the OBMV trend data are useful in showing differences by age group, with greater increases in

5.   In the 2001 survey, 56.8% of Ohio adults indicated they were organ donors on their driver's license; however, these data were collected the year before the 1stPCODR was implemented.

6.   The percentage of registration in the survey data is inflated compared to the actual percentage of Ohio residents who have registered in the 1stPCODR. Currently, about 51% of Ohio residents have registered as an organ donor on their driver's license or state ID card. It is likely that some survey respondents (approximately 8–10%) think they are registered when they are not. This is an interesting finding and suggests further research, but it is beyond the scope of this research project.

Table 6.3 Register as an Organ Donor: Comparisons of Three Cross-Sectional Surveys

Registered as an organ donor: Driver's License	2001	2003	2005	Combined Files 2001–2005	
Yes, Driver's License	56.8	56.4	58.8	57.3	
No, have not granted permission	39.4	39.9	37.1	38.8	
Sex (% Yes)					$x^2 = 18.51, p < .000$
Male	61.3	57.1	62.5	60.3	
Female	52.7	55.8	55.4	54.6	
Age (% Yes)					$x^2 = 178.12, p < .000$
18–29	65.6	62.6	66.6	65.1	
30–45	63.0	62.2	65.3	63.5	
46–64	50.9	58.5	57.9	55.7	
65+	45.7	38.8	39.4	41.5	
Race (% Yes)					$x^2 = 179.01, p < .000$
Black	35.7	27.2	39.9	34.1	
White	59.2	60.2	61.3	60.2	
Education (% Yes)					$x^2 = 340.85, p < .000$
Less than High School	44.2	39.1	39.5	41.4	
High School Grad	53.4	51.0	52.5	52.3	
Some College	64.2	62.0	66.6	64.4	
College Grad	72.5	74.0	78.8	75.3	
Post College Grad	71.2	77.7	73.8	74.5	
(N)	2,117	2,066	2,039	6,230	

Note: Z-test for Difference in Proportions, 2001 survey to 2005 survey: Z value = 1.274, not significantly different at $p < .05$.

Note: Question wording, "Have you granted permission for organ donation on your driver's license, signed a donor card, or in some other way have you granted permission for organ donation?" (include those who say "yes, driver's license" and "yes, to both driver's license and donor card").

registrations among the younger age groups compared to older age groups following the implementation of the 1stPCODR and the educational campaign.

The survey data show a significant difference in the proportion of Ohio residents' recall of reading or hearing about the Ohio Organ Donor Registry (the 1stPCODR) from prior to the educational campaign in 2003 (17%) to after the educational campaign was implemented in early 2005 (38%), $Z = 15.036$, $p < .05$.

Although the OBMV registry data do not show a notable increase in the statewide percentages that can be accounted for by the educational campaigns, the statewide educational efforts regarding the 1stPCODR and organ donation in general have been important in informing the general public. During the time period of the educational campaigns, organ donor registration continued to increase, especially in the younger age groups. Furthermore, the increase in statewide registration post implementation of the 1stPCODR has been greater than the increase noted prior to the 1stPCODR implementation. The statewide educational campaign, along with positive statewide media coverage about the implementation of the registry, may have contributed to the continued increase in organ donor registration. The survey data show an increased awareness of the 1stPCODR following the statewide educational campaign.

Evaluation and Lessons Learned

This research project examined the influence of the 1stPCODR and an educational campaign to promote the 1stPCODR and organ donation. The results from the multiple data sources used in this research show an increase in organ donor registration and actual deceased donor rates following implementation of the 1stPCODR. The multiple data sources used to evaluate the influence of the 1stPCODR and the educational campaign proved to be beneficial. By using data triangulation, we were able to observe similar trends across all three data sources. The survey data indicated a positive change in attitudes, awareness, and reported behavior regarding organ donor registration. The OBMV registry data showed a steady increase in statewide organ donor registration over the same time period, with notable increases in the younger age groups. Although there was a noticeable trend in statewide registration prior to the 1stPCODR, the increase in registration was greater following the implementation of the 1stPCODR. Furthermore, actual organ donation, as measured by the OORO deceased donor data, increased following implementation of the 1stPCODR. Using these multiple data sources was critical in our evaluation of the impact of the state policy change and the promotion of the policy.

There were, however, limitations to each data source and with our design. The OBMV registry data were limited in the number of variables available for analysis. The OORO deceased donor data were limited in the number of cases for each year and the number of variables available for analysis. Although the survey data are rich and robust in the number of variables available for analysis, they provided a snapshot of only three points in time. Furthermore, we had little control over any external influences on the OBMV data and the survey data, such as national media coverage or entertainment media programs about organ donation.

Although we could not identify specific effects of the educational campaigns on organ donor registration, it did continue to increase during the time period of the campaigns. Along with positive statewide media coverage about the implementation of the registry, the statewide educational campaign may have contributed to the continued increase in organ donor registration, especially among the younger age groups.

We faced several challenges in this research, which are discussed below.

The Real World

This project involved a real-world situation. Ohio is a large state, with multiple OOROs and multiple media markets. Furthermore, the research project included a consortium of the four OOROs, the ODH/SCTF, the OBMV, and the University of Cincinnati that required coordination and ongoing communication. This challenge was met by regular updates through e-mail, phone, and face-to-face planning meetings.

In addition, the project necessitated working with multiple staff members at each OORO, including staff involved with data and information technology, public education, and media coordination. To successfully manage this challenge, each OORO's executive director was involved and informed about the involvement of his or her staff from the project's inception. Furthermore, there was energy and excitement in Ohio among consortium members about the 1stPCODR, and this project was effectively situated to tap into this collaborative energy.

Registry Data and Deceased Donor Data

The OBMV registry data and OORO deceased donor data for the 3 years prior to the 1stPCODR were critical in evaluating the influence of the policy change and educational campaign; however, this was one of the most difficult and time-consuming aspects of the project. For some organizations, this involved retrospective medical chart reviews. The OBMV had to develop data extraction protocols for historical data located in multiple databases.

Each organization successfully followed a research protocol to gather the data necessary to meet the research project's needs. Coordination and regular communication between the organizations' information technology staff led to the successful cooperation and high quality of the data gathering from the OOROs and the OBMV.

Limitation of Theory

Although theory guided our research design, as we noted earlier, the theory had its limitations. The willingness to donate model gave us insight into the possible variables that might have an influence on an individual's decision to donate his or her organs. Our research results, particularly from the survey data, found similar patterns that previous researchers noted (Horton & Horton, 1991; Morgan, Miller, & Arasaratnam, 2002). In a previously reported analysis of our survey data, we found that knowledge of organ donation and positive attitudes toward donation were associated with registering as an organ donor (Downing, Carrozza, & Jones, 2006).

Several questions remain about why some people register to donate and others do not. For instance, the difference between the age groups and their registration rates in the 1stPCODR is not easily explained. Adults in all age groups were exposed to the new state policy and had the opportunity to register in the 1stPCODR. Furthermore, the educational campaign was conducted throughout the state and targeted to a mass audience. Are there messages about organ donation that are more effective with the younger versus the older population? There may be specific information needs, messages about organ donation, and media strategies that are more effective with different age groups (Downing & Jones, 2008). What other influences, other than knowledge and information exposure, might be a factor in increasing registration rates? What external factors are having a positive influence on some adults to register as organ donors? Further examination of these issues is important to understand organ donor registration (see Alvaro & Siegel, this volume; Siegel et al., 2008).

Conclusion

The continuing critical need for organs for transplantation has led to changes in state laws as one way to increase the number of solid-organ donors. The development of first-person consent registries and statewide electronic registries has been a growing trend in the past decade as a way to increase the number of organ donors, to clarify state laws about the donor's wish to donate, and to easily record the donor's wishes.

The early adoption of first-person consent legislation in Ohio and the collaborative environment that existed in the state among the multiple OOROs and state government provided an opportunity to research the impact of the 1stPCODR policy change and educational campaign.

In conclusion, this research provides insight into the use of multiple data sources for understanding organ donor registration behavior. The research results indicate that there has been an increase in organ donor registration and actual deceased donor rates in Ohio since the implementation of the 1stPCODR. We know more about the impact of the 1stPCODR on organ donor registration and actual deceased donor rates than we did before this project took place. However, there is still more to learn and understand about the influences on individuals' decisions to register to be an organ donor. We will continue to explore this topic using the data sources we have already collected and through continuing projects to track organ donation in the 1stPCODR.

Appendix 6.1   Survey Methodology

Survey 1: 2001

Two thousand one hundred eighteen (2,118) randomly selected Ohio adults were interviewed for the survey. Interviews were conducted by telephone between January 11 and February 12, 2001, by centrally supervised interviewing staff at the University of Cincinnati, Institute for Policy Research. The sampling error for the survey is +/−2.1%. The survey used a RDD sample obtained from Survey Sampling, Inc.

Survey 2: 2003

Two thousand sixty-six (2,066) randomly selected Ohio adults were interviewed for the survey. Interviews were conducted by telephone between July 15 and August 28, 2003, by centrally supervised interviewing staff at the University of Cincinnati, Institute for Policy Research. The sampling error for the survey is +/−2.2%. The survey used a RDD sample obtained from Survey Sampling, Inc.

Survey 3: 2005

Two thousand thirty-nine (2,039) randomly selected Ohio adults were interviewed for the survey. Interviews were conducted by telephone between June 15 and July 21, 2005, by centrally supervised interviewing staff at the University of Cincinnati, Institute for Policy Research. The sampling error for the survey is +/−2.2%. The survey used a RDD sample obtained from Survey Sampling, Inc.

Acknowledgments

This research was supported in part by grant no. 6-H39-OT0009601-01 from the Health Resources and Services Administration's Division of Transplantation (HRSA/DoT), U.S. Department of Health and Human Services. The contents of this publication are solely the responsibility of the authors and do not necessarily represent the views of HRSA/DoT.

References

Downing, K. (2001). *Anatomical gift family survey, 2001* (Technical Report). Columbus: Ohio Department of Health/Second Chance Trust Fund.

Downing, K., Carrozza, M., & Jones, L. (2006, May). *Understanding the influence of facts, beliefs and myths on organ donation decisions.* Paper presented at the 61st Annual Conference, American Association for Public Opinion Research, Montreal, Quebec, Canada.

Downing, K., & Jones, L. (2008). Designing an educational strategy for increasing organ donor registration among older adults. *Progress in Transplantation, 18,* 290–296.

Gortmaker, S. L., Beasley, C. L., Brigham, L. E., Franz, H. G., Garrison, R. N., Lucas, B. A., et al. (1996). Organ donor potential and performance: Size and nature of the organ donor shortfall. *Critical Care Medicine, 24,* 432–439.

Horton, R. L. (1991). Marketing the concept of becoming a potential organ donor. *Journal of Health Care Marketing, 11,* 36–45.

Horton, R. L., & Horton, P. J. (1990). Knowledge regarding organ donation: Identifying and overcoming barriers to organ donation. *Social Science and Medicine, 31,* 791–800.

Horton, R. L., & Horton, P. J. (1991). A model of willingness to become a potential organ donor. *Social Science and Medicine, 33,* 1037–1051.

Jones, L., Downing, K., & Holloway, G. K. (2006, August). *Increasing organ and tissue donation through a state-wide collaboration.* Poster session presented at the 2006 NATCO Meeting, Chicago.

Lewin Group. (2002). *Proceedings from U.S. Department of Health and Human Services, Health Resources and Services Administration, Office of Special Programs, Division of Transplantation: Guidelines for donor registry development conference final report.* Retrieved October 11, 2008, from http://www.organdonor.gov/pdf/execsum.pdf

McIntyre, P., Barnett, M. A., Harris, R. J., Shanteau, J., Skowronski, J., & Klassen, M. (1987). Psychological factors influencing decisions to donate organs. In M. Wallendorf & P. Anderson (Eds.), *Advances in consumer research* (pp. 331–334), Provo, UT: Association for Consumer Research.

Morgan, S., Miller, J., & Arasaratnam, L. A. (2002). Signing cards, saving lives: An evaluation of the Worksite Organ Donation Promotion Project. *Communication Monographs, 69,* 253–273.

Ohio Bureau of Motor Vehicles. (2007). *2007 BMV facts & figures.* Retrieved October 14, 2008, from http://www.bmv.ohio.gov/media/2007_bmv_facts.htm

Ohio General Assembly. (2000). *An act to promote first person consent for the Ohio Donor Registry by amending Ohio Revised Code: Amended Substitute Senate Bill Number 188* (123rd General Assembly). Retrieved November 19, 2008, from http://www.legislature.state.oh.us/bills.cfm?ID=123_SB_188_

Ohio General Assembly. (2001). First Person Consent Donor Registry of 21 § Ohio Revised Code 2108.04(F). Retrieved May 25, 2009, from http://codes.ohio.gov/orc/2108

Organ Procurement and Transplantation Network. (N.d.). *National Organ Transplant Act of 1984.* Retrieved October 20, 2008, from http://www.optn.org/policiesandbylaws/nota.asp

Pennsylvania General Assembly. (1994). The *Pennsylvania Act 102 1994*, Amending Title 20 (Decedents, Estates, and Fiduciaries) of the Pennsylvania Consolidated Statues, (20 Pa. C.S.) 1994, Senate Bill 1662. Retrieved October 10, 2008, from http://www.legis.state.pa.us/CFDOCS/Legis/PN/Public/btCheck.cfm?txtType=PDF&sessYr=1993&sessInd=0&billBody=S&billTyp=B&billNbr=1662&pn=2566

Siegel, J. T., Alvaro, E., Crano, W. C., Lac, A., Ting, S., & Jones, S. P. (2008). A quasi-experimental investigation of message appeal variations on organ donor registration rates. *Health Psychology, 27*, 170–178.

Siegel, J. T., Alvaro, E. M., & Jones, S. P. (2005). Organ donor registration preferences among a Hispanic American population: Which modes of registration have the greatest promise? *Health Education and Behavior, 32*, 242–252.

Sokohl, K. (2002, September–October). First person consent: OPOs across the country are adapting to the change. *UNOS Update*, 1–3.

United Network of Organ Sharing. (N.d.). *UNOS online*. Retrieved October 14, 2008, from http://www.unos.org/inTheNews/factsheets.asp?fs=6

U.S. Bureau of the Census. (2007). *Annual estimates of the population for the United States, regions, states, and Puerto Rico: April 1, 2000 to July 1, 2007* (NST-EST2007-01). Retrieved October 14, 2008, from http://www.census.gov/popest/states/NST-ann-est.html

U.S. Department of Health and Human Services (DHHS), Health Resources and Services Administration, National Conference of State Legislatures, and Council of State Governments. (2001). *State strategies for organ and tissue donation: A resource guide for public officials*. Authors: L. Gilmore, T. Matthews, & V. A. McBride. Rockville, MD: DHHS.

U.S. Department of Health and Human Services (DHHS), Advisory Committee on Organ Transplantation. (2003). *Recommendations 19–28*. Retrieved October 14, 2008, from http://www.organdonor.gov/research/acotrecs19-28.htm

Wendler, D., & Dickert, N. (2001). The consent process for cadaveric organ procurement: How does it work? How can it be improved? *Journal of the American Medical Association, 285*, 329–333.

7

Improving Organ Donation in Chinese Communities in New York

Perspectives From Consortium Partners

Paul L. Hebert, Julia Rivera, Kelly Eng, Regina Lee, and Susan Seto-Yee

Chinese Americans make up 4.2% of the U.S. population (Barnes & Bennett, 2002) and are a growing sector of the New York City (NYC) population. They are of interest to organ donation researchers in that Asians comprise 6.7% of the kidney waiting list (males = 6.4%, females = 7.2%), and, to date, 2,916 Asians have died while waiting for a life-saving transplant. More locally, in 2004, the consent rate in New York City hospitals among people of Asian background was 20%, whereas the rate for the entire population was 49%. Clearly, there is a need to improve organ donation consent rates among this population. The New York Organ Donor Network partnered with the Mount Sinai School of Medicine and the Charles B. Wang Community Health Center—the latter a Chinese-founded and -administered organization with a renown track record in the provision of multiple services to the Asian community—to conduct a 3-year study to improve organ donation among Chinese Americans in New York City and to test the impact of integrated marketing campaigns.

The purpose of the study was to expand the pool of willing organ donors in Asian communities in New York City by focusing educational efforts on Chinese Americans in these communities traditionally isolated from donation campaigns by language and other cultural barriers. Our goal was to extend the reach of the New York State Organ Donor Registry to hard-to-reach Chinese communities in Manhattan, Brooklyn, and Queens.

The project had two specific but interrelated research objectives. The first was to assess the change, if any, in the number of Chinese Americans living in NYC choosing to join the New York State Organ and Tissue Donor Registry, or expressing a desire to become an organ donor at their death and communicating these wishes to family members. Second, by manipulating the timing and location of different outreach efforts in a quasi-experimental research design, we sought to assess the relative effectiveness of two traditional methods of communicating public education messages: grassroots community activities and paid media advertising.

To meet the project's aims, we followed a strategy consisting of three steps. We first identified the modifiable barriers to organ donation in the Chinese community through focus groups and a baseline survey. Second, we designed grassroots and media interventions to address those barriers. Third, we implemented the interventions and evaluated their impact using a quasi-experimental study design. Importantly, we took care to involve community members at each of these steps, so that the message of organ donation was truly designed, conducted, and evaluated by the community. This chapter provides a detailed overview of focus group results and emphasizes project lessons and implications.

Formative Research: Focus Groups

Our first task was to conduct focus groups to help identify major themes we were likely to encounter in the Chinese community. Our goals were to better understand organ donation attitudes, to identify key barriers to donation, and to elicit information and ideas about the best way to broach the topic of organ donation in the Chinese community. Due to limited research specifically on the Chinese community, and with the goal of exposing ourselves to any potential barriers, we expanded our search to include all Asian American populations. A review of the literature reveals that any intervention seeking to increase donation in Asian American communities will face challenges. The first issue is religious beliefs. Asian Americans have "a stronger concern about maintaining body integrity after death" than Caucasians do (Cheung, Alden, & Wheeler, 1998). In a questionnaire distributed by Lam and McCullough (2000), results suggest that spiritual beliefs, especially Confucianism, associate an intact body with respect for ancestors, which precludes organ donation. In focus groups conducted by Wheeler, O'Friel, and Cheung (1994), results found that the Japanese group felt the body should remain whole between death and cremation, the Filipino group felt that organ donation destroys the corpse and "interferes with God's work," and the Chinese group felt that you should be buried with everything in you. There is also concern about donating a family member's organs without explicit instructions to do so, and a feeling that "the body belongs to the inhabitor and the inhabitor alone could make the decision" to donate his or her organs (Wheeler et al., 1994; see also Yeung, Kong, & Lee, 2000). We were to discover considerable support for these findings in our own formative research.

The focus groups took place between December 20, 2003, and January 4, 2004. These late-year dates were necessary to avoid overlap with Chinese New Year celebrations beginning February 1, 2003, because speaking of death is not appropriate during the New Year celebrations. Three focus groups were conducted in order to account for the ethnic and socioeconomic diversity of the Chinese community in New York City. The first was conducted in Mandarin and took place at the Charles B. Wang Community Health Center in Flushing, Queens. The second and third groups were conducted in English and Cantonese, respectively, and took place in the Charles B. Wang Community Health Center offices in Chinatown, Manhattan, which is a somewhat older and more economically disadvantaged community than the Flushing community.

We recruited focus group participants using advertisements in local community newspapers. The focus groups consisted of between 9 and 12 participants, and were led by moderators recruited from the Chinese community who were experienced in conducting focus groups. Moderator guides instructed the focus group leaders to first elicit overall knowledge and attitudes toward organ donation; to then focus on specific barriers to donation, including religious and spiritual beliefs, superstitions in the Chinese community, and family issues; and finally to discuss appropriate ways of broaching the topic of organ donation so that people can make an informed choice. Notes of the focus groups were taken by a second moderator and translated to English for analysis. Participants were paid $25 for their time.

Focus Group Findings

Traditional Beliefs

Several important themes emerged from the group discussions. First, participants reported generally favorable attitudes toward organ transplantation. They saw it as a "good thing" that was not without risk but that generally helped save and extend lives. Organ donation, however, was a more complex issue because it impinged on several issues of considerable importance to the Chinese community—especially the importance of body integrity at one's death (Chan, Ng, Tse, & Cheung, 1990; Molzahn, Starzomski, McDonald, & O'Loughlin, 2005). Body integrity was important for two reasons. First, participants expressed the traditional belief that one's body is a gift from the ancestors, and, as such, it should not be desecrated either in life or in death. For example, one participant commented that, for this reason, offspring should not do "stupid" things to their bodies such as getting tattoos and/or body piercings. Being "buried whole" and not "cut up" was perceived as being more respectful to one's ancestors. Moreover, body integrity is an important issue for those who believe in reincarnation. One participant cited her mother's concern that if the mother donated her eyes and heart, she would become blind and heartless after death and "coming back" to the next life would not be possible.

Participants recognized these beliefs as emanating not from religious strictures, but from traditional beliefs or ancestor worship. One participant noted that Chinese people tend to believe in one of two religions, Buddhism and Protestantism, and that neither religion prohibits organ donation. He speculated that religious leaders would support organ donation because they encourage followers to "love others and sacrifice for other people." Nevertheless, traditional thinking, "old-fashioned mind," and ancestor worship made "death with no whole body" a taboo subject for many.

Another issue related to traditional thinking is the belief that talking about death and, therefore cadaveric organ donation, brings bad luck (Braun & Nichols, 1997). Focus group participants frequently acknowledged the widely held belief that talking about death can bring about one's death. One participant noted that thinking about death was so taboo to some Chinese that they do not write wills. Another participant related a story of a friend who was suspected to have cancer and angered her friends by showing them educational material about cancer. She also noted that some Cantonese speakers would never buy winter melons or mention the word for them because the pronunciation was similar to the word for death in Cantonese. This same participant also noted that her friends considered her participation in the focus group as a potential curse on her health. Clearly, the focus group members had less strongly held traditional beliefs than some in the Chinese community—a fact that should be noted in interpreting focus group findings.

Family

The most frequently cited barriers to cadaveric donation discussed in the focus group involved family. Due in part to traditional beliefs, families avoided discussions of organ donation (Braun & Nichols, 1997; Sze Wu, 2008), and some participants described uncomfortable encounters. One commented that although talking about organ donation was not difficult among her peers, she would not discuss it with her family. Prohibitions on discussing organ donation were especially salient during the Chinese New Year.

Much discussion regarding family issues was devoted to the effect of disagreements among family members on the organ donation consent process. The discord that these disagreements would cause was particularly worrisome. One participant commented that he would consent to donate his organs at his death only if no other family member opposed. There were extensive discussions about whose opinion in the family would be respected at the time of donation, and whether the family had the right to overrule an individual's stated consent. Participants in both the Cantonese- and Mandarin-speaking groups independently mentioned a case in the news in which a family had a dispute over whether the wishes of the deceased to donate his organs should be respected. One of these participants noted that, as a result of the dispute, the opportunity for donation was lost.

These family disputes are not limited to disagreements between generations. Three participants discussed disagreements regarding donation they had had with siblings or other family members closer in age. One said a male cousin prevented her from signing the back of her driver's license to signify her intention to donate, whereas another noted that her husband rejected the idea that she would become an organ donor at her death.

Distribution of Organs

In all focus groups, but especially the group conducted in English, equity was an important and frequently discussed concern. Participants wanted donated organs to go to people who truly needed them, and not just the rich or famous. Participants repeatedly mentioned the importance of knowing that procedures were in place such that organs were going to those who needed them most. However, there was much skepticism that organs were not going disproportionately to the most powerful. For example, a participant in the Cantonese speaking group said it was "99% true" that rich people or people from a higher social class have a better chance of getting an organ.

There was also some interest expressed in knowing who, in particular, the organs would go to. Potential donors would have different feelings about donation if they knew the donated organs would go to family members or some other deserving person. Two participants commented that they wanted organs to go to good people or young people, not "bad people," "criminals," "people who are selfish," or "a rich guy who could buy his organs."

Related to equity is the belief—or the willingness to believe—in a black market for organs. Participants were not sure if such a black market existed in the United States, but they could not discount the possibility that it existed in Third World countries in Asia, India, and Africa. This belief in the existence of a black market reinforces the concern that donated organs go mostly to the rich and powerful—a significant barrier to donation.

Discussions of a black market in Asia also highlighted how much information and news participants still received from China via Cantonese or Mandarin language newspapers. On 10 separate occasions, focus group participants reported on relevant news reports from Hong Kong or Taiwan. Often these were related to unfortunate stories of organ donation; however, participants also mentioned the popular Hong Kong singer Anita Mui, who died of cancer but expressed a desire to donate her organs. She was respected and admired for this decision.

Reaching the Chinese Community

Drawing on the case of Anita Mui and similar occurrences, participants often cited the need for personal testimonials to communicate the organ donation message to Chinese audiences. One participant suggested that simply spreading the word by the Internet or word of mouth that a person in the Chinese community needed a transplant would be an effective means of educating the community on the importance of organ donation. Others suggested obtaining testimonials from organ recipients and using these in outreach efforts.

Participants repeatedly emphasized the importance of information. According to one, "If people have no knowledge, they would definitely not donate." They noted that more information was needed on the procedures by which one becomes an organ donor as well as how the organs are distributed equitably. Lack of knowledge regarding organ donation made the issue more difficult to discuss with others. One person called for advertisement and promotion for organ donation, "so no one would laugh at you" for expressing a desire to donate.

Regarding message sources and channels, community organizations were most often discussed as the appropriate vehicle for delivering the information, and several participants suggested mass media advertising on Chinese radio. One participant said that a better mechanism was needed than the Department of Motor Vehicles (DMV) to declare intent because so few people in New York City own cars. Participants did not seem to be aware of alternatives to the DMV such as the New York Organ Donor Network, or the registry.

Formative Research: Baseline Survey

The focus groups helped to identify the important concerns about organ donation held by our target population, and the findings directly assisted development of a population-based survey that would serve both as a source of formative data as well as a baseline to assess intervention impact. We found or developed survey items to measure each of the major constructs that were brought up by focus group participants. Wherever possible, we selected survey items from previously published organ donation surveys. The survey was translated to Chinese and printed on two sides of a single sheet of paper.

Following pilot testing, we administered the in-person pencil-and-paper survey in late summer 2004. As with all steps of the campaign, the community was closely involved in the survey process. Paid volunteers were recruited from the community to collect questionnaires. These individuals went to city parks or other areas where people generally congregate in the three major Chinese communities in New York City to collect surveys. Three college students recruited from the community were paid to enter the survey data. Jason Wang, PhD, a health economist at Mount Sinai and a Chinese American, volunteered his help in designing the survey and coordinating the data entry. He later wrote favorably about the experience in a Chinese language periodical to which he frequently contributes— although this was not part of the campaign and the members of the team were unaware of his efforts. Coincidentally, his article appeared in the same issue as did an interview with Kelly Eng, the community organizer who led the grassroots campaign (see below).

We held some assumptions when we began this project. First, we assumed that few community members would be open to completing an organ donation survey due to their cultural beliefs (Boey, 2001; Lam & McCullough, 2000). As a result, we expected rather low survey response rates. However, our expectations were positively violated as the community outreach specialist and her volunteers were able to collect a great number of surveys. We met our goal of 400 surveys at baseline (as well as in subsequent postcampaign surveys at 1-year and 2-year follow-up).

We also assumed that community attitudes toward organ donation would be strongly negative (Molzahn et al., 2005). We were very surprised that, according to survey results, the majority of respondents recognized the benefits of organ donation and some respondents indicated their willingness to donate. Positive attitudes regarding organ donation are certainly a good sign, but we have a long way to go—especially given the considerable knowledge gap.

The results of the baseline survey were used to draw a more robust picture of the attitudes toward donation and the major barriers we would face. This informed the grassroots and media campaigns, as described below.

Interventions

The Grassroots Campaign

In addition to the selection of consortium partners, one of the most important decisions that we made was hiring the right person for the community outreach specialist position to promote the campaign. We hired Kelly Eng, a first-generation Chinese young woman, who was trilingual in English, Cantonese, and Mandarin and very familiar with the Chinatown community. She had extensive experience as a community advocate through her work with the Chinese American Planning Council and other community organizations in New York City. More importantly, she was passionate about the campaign goal of promoting more awareness and supporting organ donation among Chinese Americans.

During the project, Kelly worked tirelessly to recruit volunteers and conduct outreach. She was very visible in the community, bringing the campaign's message to many outreach events throughout Manhattan and Queens. She and her volunteers attended many local events (which usually took place on weekends), and she conducted many workshops on myths and facts of organ donation. She also made extensive efforts to reach out to the civic and religious leaders who were influential in shaping community opinions. Throughout these endeavors, she effectively used patient volunteers to tell the story of how they were able to receive a donated organ—the gift of life—due to someone's decision to donate. The messages were powerful and moving, and their stories were well publicized in the Chinese language media. Consortium members referred to the personal impact of this employee as the *Kelly Eng factor* to acknowledge hiring and staffing as important elements for the success of this project.

The Media Campaign

The media campaign was one of the most sophisticated social marketing campaigns launched in Chinatown in recent years. L3, a well-known agency with a strong track record for developing linguistically and culturally appropriate messages for the Chinese and Asian markets, served as the project's marketing and public relations agency. The campaign design and strategies were very strong, influenced by the personal interest of the agency's director, who, unbeknownst to the New York Organ Donor Network, was also the relative of an organ recipient.

Print advertising was the main channel for the dissemination of campaign messages. The ads were placed very prominently in several Cantonese and Mandarin language newspapers that are widely distributed in the tristate area. Besides the paid advertising, there was significant added value generated by L3's contacts among print and electronic media outlets—resulting in numerous radio, television, and print interviews as well as free airtime that extended the period of the campaign beyond the weeks paid for.

Evaluation

To evaluate the effects of the intervention, we took in-person surveys at places in Brooklyn, Queens, and Chinatown where Chinese people typically congregate. As shown in Table 7.1, we collected 634 baseline surveys before the campaign in 2004, and 500 surveys at the conclusion of the campaign in the summer of 2005. No grassroots campaigning took place in Brooklyn, so it is considered the control group for evaluating the effects of the grassroots campaign.

A History Effect

As is frequently realized in applied research, the best-designed studies can be derailed by circumstances completely outside of the researcher's control. As read by those perusing *CNN Money* on October 7, 2005, remember that Brooklyn was serving as the control group for this study: "A Brooklyn funeral home and a New Jersey company that harvests body parts from corpses are being investigated for their alleged roles in a body snatching ring that sold parts to companies specializing in medical grafts, sources close to the investigation said Friday." Essentially, a funeral home in Brooklyn was discovered to have been procuring tissue from

Table 7.1 Demographic characteristics of respondents to in-person surveys taken in 2004 and 2005

	2004		*2005*		
	Count	Percent	Count	Percent	*p*-value
Total	634		500		
Female	320	50.5	283	56.6	0.0510
Age					
18–30	169	26.7	163	32.6	0.0276
31–50	254	40.1	208	41.6	0.4953
50+	211	33.3	129	25.8	0.0010
Born in United States	13	2.1	15	3.0	0.8667
English Primary Language	34	5.4	45	9.0	0.4980

cadavers without obtaining the families' consent. The news was carried broadly on television, radio, and newspapers, and reported gruesome details of families discovering that their loved one's bones had been replaced by 2 × 4 planks. As described by the *Daily News* in 2008, when the indictment was official, "Michael Mastromarino—who earned millions of dollars through the ghoulish enterprise—agreed to the deal after lengthy negotiations with the Brooklyn district attorney's office. He will serve a minimum of 18 years in prison" (Sherman, 2008). News stories filled the airwaves throughout the country but particularly in the tristate area. Methods professors considering examples of historical threats to validity have one more to choose.

Intervention Results

Not surprising considering the scandal, the percentage of people who responded that they had no intention to donate their organs increased in each site, and increased significantly overall from 11% in 2004 to 21% in 2005 (see Figure 7.1). The number of people who responded *uncertain* decreased significantly from 64% at baseline to 53% in 2005. However, in logistic regressions, no statistically significant differences were found in the change in the odds of a negative response in either intervention site versus the Brooklyn control site. That is, negative responses toward intentions to donate increased roughly proportionately in each site between 2004 and 2005.

Stated intentions to donate increased in the intervention area of Chinatown, Manhattan, but not in Flushing, Queens, and it decreased substantially in Brooklyn, for a minimal overall change from 25% in 2004 to 26% in 2005. In a logistic regression that controlled for age, gender, primary language spoken, and years residing in the United States, the odds of saying an affirmative response increased 2.2-fold greater ($p = 0.040$) in Chinatown from 2004 to 2005 compared

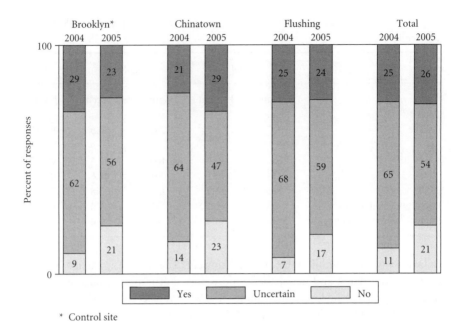

Figure 7.1   Responses to the survey question "I intend to donate my organs at my death", by year and intervention site.

to the change from 2004 to 2005 in the Brooklyn control site, although this was partly due to the decline in affirmative responses in Brooklyn between those years.

Again, these results need to be viewed in the light of the highly publicized funeral home scandal that occurred in Brooklyn during the course of the intervention. Given this, the fact that attitudes in the intervention sites did not decline as rapidly as they did in the Brooklyn control site could be interpreted as a minor success of the grassroots campaign.

The finding that the percentage of respondents who stated they were uncertain if they would donate their organs might also reflect a small step forward for efforts to help people in the Chinese community make informed choices regarding donation. Perhaps this finding reflects an increased willingness to talk about donation, even if it is only to admit to a surveyor that they are not interested in donating. Once people are willing to talk about organ donation, we may have the opportunity to dispel some myths or misconceptions that are barriers to donation.

Making the Most . . .

The coverage of the scandal dwarfed any efforts put forth as part of the campaign. Nevertheless, important information was gleaned from this project.

Generally, non-English speakers are at a disadvantage for obtaining and using correct health information. They do not understand the need for organ donation or know the number of people who are waiting for organs. Although one-on-one education is generally the most effective way to communicate sensitive information, this highly personal approach requires time and resources. Outreach efforts using media campaigns and distribution of literature are less labor intensive but may not yield the same results as one-on-one outreach. The New York Organ Donor Network has produced high-quality Chinese language brochures; however, placing materials in the right venue and encouraging the public's use of these materials remain challenging. There is an ongoing need to educate community members about the U.S. system for procuring and distributing organs (Ganikos, this volume). Many community members are not aware of the rules and safeguards to protect the integrity of organ donation in the United States (Molzahn et al., 2005).

Although the grassroots and media campaigns have been effective in promoting awareness, they have had less of an impact in turning awareness into action (see Alvaro & Siegel, this volume). Clearly, our project, the "strength" of the belief that organ donation saves lives, was not sufficient to translate beliefs into organ donation intentions. One significant barrier is that even without the scandal, community members are very reluctant to talk to their family members about donating for a variety of reasons—fear of bringing on bad luck, not wanting to upset parents, and so on (Braun & Nichols, 1997; Sze Wu, 2008). Poor intergenerational communication is unfortunately common within Chinese immigrant families. Many immigrant families in the United States struggle to negotiate differences in cultural practices resulting from different rates of acculturation between parents and children. Oftentimes, parents and children lack adequate communication and cultural awareness skills to discuss difficult issues such as death and dying.

Another challenge to improving organ donation consent rates in Chinese communities involves concerns with the medical establishment. The scandal did not help in this regard. Aside from the medical mistrust felt by community members, if physicians and nurses themselves have mixed feelings about organ donation upon death, they are less likely to support or educate their patients and the public about organ donation. Providers who are supportive of organ donation may also lack effective communication skills to broach complex clinical, moral, and ethical issues with their patients (Shih, Lin, Lin, & Lee, 1998a, 1998b).

Lessons Learned

We held some assumptions when we joined the campaign. First, we assumed that few community members would respond to the survey because of cultural beliefs. We assumed that the survey collection rate would be low. However, the community outreach specialist and her volunteers were able to collect a great number of surveys. We met our goal of 400 surveys at baseline, 1-year follow-up, and 2-year follow-up.

We also assumed that community attitudes toward organ donation would be strongly negative. We were very surprised that the majority of respondents recognized the benefits of organ donation, with some respondents indicating their willingness to donate. Positive attitudes regarding organ donation are a good sign, but we have a long way to go. The knowledge gap is significant. Even after the campaign.

Future Considerations and Replication

The current system of organ procurement relies solely on altruism to motivate donors. Fortunately, altruism appears to cut across boundaries of religious and ethnic groups. Organ donation education campaigns conducted in racial or ethnic communities might consider targeting messages to audiences that could be more responsive to moral appeals, such as church groups, civic associations, volunteer groups, giving circles, and the like. Educational campaigns targeting specific audiences might yield better results than community-wide campaigns aimed at a broader group.

Future campaigns to promote organ donation among Asian Americans must seek to increase knowledge about the organ donation process; debunk myths, especially regarding the inequitable procurement and distribution of donated organs; and promote communication among family members about organ donation. Having correct information and knowledge may lead to a willingness to donate. Also, it is important to work with community leaders and other influential groups to gain their support on organ donation. The importance of a culturally competent outreach worker with effective communication skills cannot be overstated. Lastly, the education and outreach campaign must be sustained over a longer period of time in order to yield results. As we have discovered, in the Chinese community, barriers to organ donation are deeply rooted in cultural and traditional beliefs. Sustained campaigns that provide accurate information and dispel myths will be required before open discussions and informed choices regarding organ donation will be common among this population.

Note

The research discussed in this article was funded by a U.S. Department of Health and Human Services grant (#R39 OT01213-01-00) awarded to Paul L. Hebert (PI). The opinions and interpretations expressed within are those of the researchers and not necessarily the funding agency.

References

Barnes, J. S., & Bennett, C. E. (2002, February). *The Asian population: 2000* (Census 2000 Brief). Washington, DC: U.S. Department of Commerce, U.S. Census Bureau.

Boey, K. W. (2001). A cross-validation study of nurses' attitudes and commitment to organ donation in Hong Kong. *International Journal of Nursing Studies, 39*, 95–104.

Braun, K. L., & Nichols, R. (1997). Death and dying in four Asian American samples: A descriptive study. *Death Studies, 21*, 327–359.

Chan, A. Y. T., Ng, W. D., Tse, M. H., & Cheung, R. (1990). Public attitudes toward kidney donation in Hong Kong. *Dialysis and Transplantation, 19*, 242–258.

Cheung, A. H. S., Alden, D. L., & Wheeler, M. S. (1998). Cultural attitudes of Asian-Americans toward death adversely impact organ donation. *Transplantation Proceedings, 30*, 3609–3610.

Lam, W. A., & McCullough, L. B. (2000). Influence of religious and spiritual values on the willingness of Chinese-Americans to donate organs for transplantation. *Clinical Transplantation, 14*, 449–456.

Molzahn, A. E., Starzomski, R., McDonald, M., & O'Loughlin, C. (2005). Chinese Canadian beliefs toward organ donation. *Qualitative Health Research, 15*, 82–98.

Sherman, W. (2008, January 16). Plea deal for body-snatch ring boss. *Daily News*. Retrieved June 4, 2009, from http://www.nydailynews.com/news/ny_crime/2008/01/16/2008-01-16_plea_deal_for_bodysnatch_ring_boss.html

Shih, F. J., Lin, M. H., Lin, H. Y., & Lee, C. J. (1998a). Profile of the ideal nursing image during the discharge-preparation transition: Chinese patients' perspective. *Dialysis and Transplantation, 27*, 269–312.

Shih, F. J., Lin, M. H., Lin, H. Y., & Lee, C. J. (1998b). The degree of recovery from kidney transplantation before discharge from the hospital: Chinese patients' perspective. *Transplantation Proceedings, 30*, 3639–3642.

Sze Wu, A. M. (2008). Discussion of posthumous organ donation in Chinese families. *Psychology, Health & Medicine, 13*, 48–54.

Wheeler, M. S., O'Friel, M., & Cheung, A. H. S. (1994). Cultural beliefs of Americans as barriers to organ donation. *Journal of Transplant Coordination, 4*, 146–150.

Yeung, I., Kong, S. H., & Lee, J. (2000). Attitude towards organ donation in Hong Kong. *Social Science & Medicine, 50*, 1643–1654.

8

Intervention Research With American Indian, Alaska Native, and First Nations Communities

An Organ and Tissue Donation Exemplar

Nancy L. Fahrenwald

Introduction

American Indian (AI) and Alaska Native (AN) peoples of the United States, and First Nations (FN) peoples of Canada, experience higher rates of many chronic health conditions when compared to the general population of both countries. Although the burden of specific issues differs by group, a shared reality is that rates of type 2 diabetes have reached epidemic levels. Research is needed to understand and address complex type 2 diabetes-related concerns, including efforts to resolve the disparity between need for renal transplantation and organ donation consent rates among AI, AN, and FN people. This chapter describes the need for social and behavioral research that works within the context of organ and tissue donation for Native communities. An essential approach to intervention studies that incorporate participatory research principles and build trusted partnerships with communities is described. The participatory framework is exemplified through application to behavioral research within the domain of intention to serve as an organ or tissue donor for Northern Plains AI tribes. Related future research needs for indigenous people of North America are articulated.

Aboriginal People of North America

In the United States and Canada, Aboriginal people are known by many names, for example, Native Americans, American Indians, and Alaska Natives of the United States, and First Nations indigenous people of Canada, including the Inuit, Métis, and North American Indians. These and other names are mere descriptors of diverse people from over 1,000 tribes and communities, each of which has a unique and important history and culture. It is the intent of this chapter to honor and respect the Aboriginal people of North America while choosing to use the names *American Indian, Alaska Native,* and *First Nations.* The major focus of the chapter is on AI tribes with exemplars from the literature that are particular to ANs and FNs.

According to the 2000 U.S. Census, those who identify as AI or AN constitute 1.5% of the population, or approximately 4.1 million people (U.S. Census Bureau, 2002). There are 569 federally recognized AI and AN tribes, plus an unknown number that are not federally recognized. The greatest concentrations of AIs and ANs are in the states of Alaska, Arizona, Montana, New Mexico, Oklahoma, and South Dakota (Centers for Disease Control and Prevention, 2008). In Canada, 3.3% of the total population, or nearly 1 million people, identified themselves as Aboriginal in 2001 (Statistics Canada, 2001). There are currently 614 FN communities (Indian and Northern Canada Affairs, n.d.), with the largest numbers of FNs living in the north and on the prairies, whereas the highest percentages are found in Nunavut, the Northwest Territories, and the Yukon (Natural Resources Canada, 2001). Tribal lands and FN communities are primarily located in rural areas. However, over the last 3 decades there has been a significant migration to urban communities where economic opportunities exist (Norrell, 2005). Approximately 56% of AIs and ANs and 40% of FNs live away from tribal lands (Baldwin et al., 2002; Tookenay, 1996).

Health Care

In the United States, tribes are sovereign entities that are entitled to health and educational services provided by the government if they are federally recognized (Centers for Disease Control and Prevention, 2008). Canada provides dedicated health and education programs for FN communities, yet the nature of Canada's socialized health system does not allow for a full comparison of the two systems (Indian and Northern Canada Affairs, n.d.).

The Indian Health Service (IHS) and the Alaska Native Tribal Health Consortium (ANTHC) are the federal organizations that serve the health needs of U.S. tribes. These health services are largely reservation based; thus urban dwellers have difficulty gaining care from the IHS, which devotes a very small percentage of its budget to urban programs (Zuckerman, Haley, Roubideaux, & Lillie-Blanton, 2004). Even for people with access to IHS or the ANTHC, the extent of services is limited to primary health care with limited specialty care offered only by the ANTHC. In order to meet demands for specialty health care services, tribes contract with outside organizations. The total funding for Contract Health Services (CHS) is determined by Congress. Access to specialty care is limited by these designated dollars. Individuals who need specialized care are placed on priority lists to receive only the most critically needed diagnostic tests or treatments. Individuals can wait on priority lists for months. After the waiting period, and only if monies are available, an individual is able to seek CHS (Commission on Civil Rights, 2003). The program provides compensation for one person's travel and accommodations at an authorized medical center. Obviously, the realities of the IHS and CHS include tremendous challenges to health care availability and accessibility.

Health Disparities

Geographic and economic factors play a part in health concerns for AI, AN, and FN people. The isolated locations of reservations and other Native communities are plagued by economic disadvantages that contribute to poor health status. Among these disadvantages, there are noted disparities in income, education, and employment. Native people of the United States have a much lower average annual income compared to Whites, which is exemplified by higher numbers of people living below the federally designated poverty level (33% among AIs and ANs, and 13% among Whites), as well as lower high school graduation rates. Rates of unemployment among AI and AN men are three times higher than the same rates for men of all races (U.S. Census Bureau, 1999). These socioeconomic differences certainly contribute to issues of access to prevention, early detection, and treatment of health-related issues, including chronic disease.

A particular chronic disease and its associated health consequences have prompted awareness of the need for organ donation. Type 2 diabetes is 3–8 times more prevalent in AIs, ANs, and FNs than in the general population (Lee et al., 1995; Population Reference Bureau, 1999). Evidence from the Strong Heart Study indicated that among Northern Plains AI tribes, 1 in 3 adults between the ages of 45 and 74 had type 2 diabetes (Population Reference Bureau). These excessive disease rates contribute to numerous secondary health issues, one of which is end-stage renal disease (ESRD). Type 2 diabetes is the most common cause of ESRD, which is an irreversible state of kidney impairment that requires hemodialysis or kidney transplantation to maintain life (Health Canada, 2007; Isaacs, 2004). Following the pattern of disparities in type 2 diabetes prevalence, ESRD among AIs and ANs is three times more prevalent than among Whites (Narva, 2003), and the age of onset is 6 years younger (Isaacs, 2004). These alarming statistics indicate a disproportionate burden of both type 2 diabetes and ESRD.

Considering a projected increase in type 2 diabetes, the geographic isolation of reservations, and the limited CHS funds available, the care of AI and AN people with ESRD is a challenge that will persist into the future. There is an undeniable need for renal transplantation, which is associated with lower total cost than ESRD management (Newman, Marfin, Eggers, & Helgerson, 1990). In addition to a cost savings, the outcomes of quality and length of life are greatly improved after transplantation versus prolonged dialysis (Evans et al., 1985; Port, Wolfe, Mauger, Berling, & Jiang, 1993).

Organ and Tissue Donation Among AIs, ANs, and FNs

Health-related decisions occur within a cultural context. Specific to organ and tissue donation, a study of Midwestern tribes reported that mistrust of the health care system deterred willingness to consent for cadaveric donation (Wolfe et al., 1999). In addition, there are potential concerns about the hastening of death in order to obtain organs for White people in need (Upper Midwest Organ Procurement Organization, 1995). Among Coast Salish FNs who were interviewed about their cultural beliefs, there was a lack of trust, a perceived misunderstanding of ways of life in Native communities, and tension between contemporary and traditional perspectives. Organ donation was summarized as something to avoid talking about, and a concern for transferring of one's spirit was raised along with a desire and need to help others (Scheper-Hughes, 2000). Some AIs and ANs believe the body should remain intact, a belief that conflicts with organ donation (Molzahn, Starzomski, McDonald, & O'Loughlin, 2004). Among Midwestern tribes, this belief was common for individuals who were unfavorable toward deceased donation, yet some of these participants were willing to donate a kidney to a relative (Blagg et al., 1992).

Rates of consent for cadaveric donation among AIs and ANs are lower than the rate for the general population (Danielson, LaPree, Odland, & Steffens, 1998; Molzahn et al., 2004). One published study conducted with Upper Midwestern Plains tribes reported a deceased donor consent rate of 39% for the AI population, compared to 66% for Whites and 34.6% for all minorities (Wolfe et al., 1999). This noted difference between need for kidney donation and low deceased donor consent rates among potential AI donors needs to be addressed. Higher numbers of Indian donors would increase the probability of better human leukocyte antigen matching and improve rates of graft survival. Genetic research indicates that among two Northern Plains tribes (i.e., Cheyenne River and Oglala Lakota), about 15% of people in need of a kidney can expect to find an exact match within their tribe. These intertribal donor compatibility rates are far better than the rates with differing population groups (Institute of Medicine, 2006).

Different from consent for deceased donation, willingness to serve as a living donor for a family member was favorably documented for members of four Midwestern tribes (Blagg et al., 1992). Among the Menominee, Ho-Chunk, Ojibway, and Sioux tribal members, 8 out of 10 were willing to be a living kidney donor for a family member. The IHS reported a similar finding that willingness to donate a kidney to a relative among AIs and ANs was the same as the willingness among Whites (Leffell et al., 2004). A survey completed in rural and urban AI communities indicated that residents learned about donation primarily from the television and newspapers, but one half of the participants also indicated that the radio, a friend, or a brochure was their information source. Knowledge of donation occurred within the context of diabetes. Thirty-nine percent of community members indicated that kidney disease was a major problem for their community, and 20% reported that they had a family member who experienced renal dialysis. Knowledge of transplantation as the most effective treatment for ESRD was noted by 71% of the people. Nearly one third of tribal members were willing to donate their organs, yet only 1 in 10 carried documentation of these intentions on a donor card or driver's license (Molzahn et al., 2004). There is an obvious gap between willingness to donate and documentation of those intentions through driver's license designation or through a donor registry.

Research With AI, AN, and FN Communities

A demand for kidney transplantation coupled with low donation consent rates among Native people comprise a health disparity. Efforts to narrow the gap cannot be based upon assumptions, pragmatism, or efforts known to facilitate related behavior change for different population groups. Culturally derived, theory-driven, and empirically tested approaches are needed; yet many AI, AN, and FN communities ask, "Why more research?" History bears the burden of responsibility for this question.

In the past, some health researchers lacked the cultural understanding and accountability needed to build long and trusting relationships with Native communities. Linda Tom-Orme described the characterization of these scientists as "helicopter researchers," who "descend upon the community" and then whisk themselves away without making a contribution to the health or quality of life of the people (Narva, 1996). Research of this type exploits communities and contributes to feelings of mistrust. In addition, there is a scrutiny of research among tribal leaders due to a perceived burden of too much data collection coupled with not enough change (Tom-Orme, 2006).

Historical treatment as subjects rather than as partners in research is a reality for AI, AN, and FN communities, and the solution of participation in the research process requires a long-term commitment to the community. It is through this long-term commitment that mutual respect and trust are built (Tom-Orme, 2006). Community-based participatory research (CBPR) is a collaborative approach to research that begins with a research topic of importance to the community. The aim of the approach is to combine knowledge and action for social change in efforts to improve health outcomes and reduce health disparities (Tom-Orme). All partners are equitably involved in the CBPR research process, and each partner recognizes the unique strengths of the others. The CBPR approach involves the community in both the conception and the conduction of a study.

Building relationships with Native communities requires a long-term commitment that is grounded in respect for the sovereignty of tribes and honors tribal rights to self-determination. Health research is not necessarily a top priority in Native communities, but health concerns are priorities. Bridging research interests with the understanding and resolution of real health issues is essential (Davis & Reid, 1999; Israel, Eng, Schulz, & Parke, 2005; Narva, 1996; Tom-Orme, 2006). A research agenda to increase solid-organ and tissue donation intent may seem remote from the everyday realities of other pressing health needs and limited health care resources. Yet, when framed within the context of community need, there is recognition of family and community members who receive renal dialysis due to type 2 diabetes and ESRD (Molzahn et al., 2004). Community members know the stories of their friends and family members who were fortunate enough to receive a donor kidney and how their health and outlook on life improved after the transplant. When organ donation is viewed as a community need and as a health disparity that communities can participate in resolving, there is a recognized benefit of the research.

Each tribe has a unique culture, history, and language. Generalizing research with one group to others is a contradiction of this reality. Researchers need to learn the worldview, history, and cultural traditions of each tribe. The process of working within the cultural context to conduct research in the domain of social and behavioral interventions to increase intention to donate organs and tissues is exemplified by research experiences with Northern Plains tribes.

Intervention Research With Northern Plains Tribes

There are two primary assumptions of the CBPR approach to research interventions that aim to improve health outcomes and reduce disparities. The first assumption is that strong interventions are informed by community insight and incorporate community theories of etiology and change into the scientific approach. The second assumption is that community participation is essential and that participation provides an added value to the approach toward improving health (Wallerstein & Duran, 2006). The scientific literature contains an increasing number of studies that purport to use a CBPR approach to intervention research, especially in efforts to reduce health disparities for disadvantaged populations. These studies vary greatly in the extent to which the community is a partner in research processes and outcomes. Models for the critique of the CBPR approach have emerged to facilitate the discernment of the quality of these studies (Viswanathan et al., 2004).

Community Engagement in a Colearning Dialogue

Community engagement embraces the notion that solutions to health concerns require the collective knowledge and wisdom of what works within the social norms and cultural beliefs of the target population. Engagement is ongoing, beginning long before a research proposal is written or a project is initiated. Engagement occurs when relationships are mutually beneficial and there is a sustained presence and commitment between the partners (Seifer, 2003).

The CBPR approach to research with Northern Plains tribes began with a colearning approach that engaged academic, organizational, and community partners. Colearning occurs when partners learn from each other, resulting in a stronger approach to problem identification and resolution (Wallerstein & Duran, 2006).

Initial dialogue occurred between tribal leaders, medicine men and women, as well as health providers who were invited to participate in conversation with board members from the South Dakota Lion's Eye Bank and Spirit of the North Tissue Services. Part of the Eye Bank's mission emphasizes community education about the importance of organ, eye, and tissue donation, and there was a recognized gap in the realization of this mission for the state's largest ethnic minority population, AIs. The Eye Bank receives notification of every death within the State of South Dakota and receives referrals for every consenting cadaveric donor. Patterns of referral for donation over a period of 10 years indicated flat and relatively nonexistent consent for cadaveric donation among NAs. The initial conversations with tribal members centered on the data. Tribal members offered their perspective on the data, provided insights into cultural beliefs and social norms that influence donation intent, and discussed approaches to resolving the problem. These early conversations led to the establishment of a community advisory council (CAC) that was charged to develop an intervention that could address the problem in a culturally acceptable way.

Community Advisory Council

Members of the CAC were recommended by participants in the initial tribal dialogue and by tribal leaders. The council included the organizational partner (i.e., the executive director of the Eye Bank and board members) and an academic partner. Efforts to conduct the council business were guided by cultural approaches to dialogue and engagement. The spiritual dimension of life was at the forefront of all conversations, which began with prayers for the community and for the people who were sick and who needed help. Tribal community insights and approaches to understanding the health phenomena of organ and tissue donation disparities were shared. These insights were integrated with data-driven information about donation consent and intent rates among NAs and contrasted with the demand for donation, especially kidney donation. Theoretical approaches to social and behavioral change were offered by the academic partner, and these conversations merged into an understanding that a cultural and theoretical approach to educational outreach was needed to allow community members to make an informed decision about serving as an organ or tissue donor (Fahrenwald & Stabnow, 2005).

The work of the CAC was the cornerstone of the research. Efforts of the CAC shaped the research questions, guided the cultural and theoretical basis of the intervention, selected outcome measures, facilitated the development and evaluation of intervention materials, and guided the testing of the intervention in local communities. Advisory council members realized that their personal beliefs about organ and tissue donation were not necessarily shared with community members, especially reservation-dwelling adults who embraced traditional values and beliefs. An exploratory study was needed to discover and represent at least some local knowledge and beliefs prior to planning an approach to the problem. Local knowledge was needed to inform the intervention efforts.

Application of Local Knowledge

Because there was little prior research related to organ and tissue donation among Northern Plains tribes, an ethnographic exploration was initiated in order to discover the sociocultural factors associated with organ and tissue donation among members of one tribe (Fahrenwald & Stabnow, 2005). A capacity-building approach was used to conduct this study. A tribal college nursing student who was interested in developing research skills was identified through a bridge to a baccalaureate degree initiative that was in place with the tribal college and the state university. The student learned qualitative research methods as part of a mentoring relationship with the university partner, then collected the data and participated in the analysis and sharing of the findings with the local and the scientific communities. This capacity-building process is essential to building the strengths of the community and is a principle of the CBPR approach.

There were five overall themes discovered from this ethnographic study that included reservation-dwelling adults. These themes were uncertain knowledge about donation, awareness of the diabetes crisis, transitioning of traditional beliefs with contemporary health issues, questioning of local health system competence to participate in organ and tissue donation, and suggested outreach efforts. Participants knew little about donation but had a basic understanding of donor–recipient compatibility. All participants were aware of the diabetes crisis in their community and the dire need for kidney donors. Participants voiced the need to reexamine traditional values, such as entering the spirit world with an intact body, because of the shortage of kidney donors. Yet, they were not confident about the local health system's ability to address traditional beliefs or to implement organ donation protocols. A need was identified for relevant community outreach using local communication networks including the family, media, and tribal leaders (Fahrenwald & Stabnow, 2005).

Participants suggested that outreach for organ and tissue donation was needed on the reservation and that such programs should show respect for traditional beliefs, present choice about donation in the cultural context, and tell the stories of tribal members affected by diabetes or donation while also promoting family conversations. Findings from this ethnographic exploration provided local know-ledge that informed the intervention research.

Investment of Community Members in the Research Processes and Products

Tribal organizations, including the tribal councils serving each reservation and the tribal chairman's health board serving the Aberdeen Area of the Indian Health Service, gave their approval for the intervention study in the form of formal resolutions. A tribal outreach coordinator who was selected by the CAC largely facilitated the intervention process.

The role of tribal outreach coordinator was not filled by the first person selected by the organizational and academic partners. These partners were focused on the energy and enthusiasm conveyed for the position by a younger candidate, who was a tribal member but did not reside on a reservation. The collective wisdom of the CAC was that the outreach coordinator needed to be a community-dwelling elder with a history of respected relationships within the tribe. The investment of the CAC in the selection of the outreach coordinator and the dedicated efforts of the outreach coordinator in seeking the necessary tribal approvals, and ultimately forging the relationships needed to deliver the intervention across four different reservations, facilitated the research process.

Intervention Development and Delivery Facilitation

The CAC named the intervention in local language, but recommended that it be promoted using the English translation. Wacip' unpi Wiconi—Sharing the Gift of Life—was designed to increase intention to serve as an organ or tissue donor among reservation-dwelling adults living on four Northern Plains reservations. The advisory council along with the outreach coordinator selected the methods of intervention delivery. They were face-to-face educational sessions delivered by the outreach coordinator to community members and groups in places of employment, gathering places, meetings of community groups, health fairs, health facilities, and church-based settings.

The intervention materials included an 8-minute narrated video that included the stories of tribal members who were organ donors and recipients, as well as people who were waiting for a donation. A brochure conveyed the stories of community member donors and recipients, an educational booklet provided contemporary education about donation, and both posters and radio messages were developed to raise awareness of donation. All materials were developed in collaboration with two AI-owned and -operated advertising firms.

Draft intervention materials were reviewed by the CAC, revised, then taken to reservation communities for evaluation prior to implementation. The final products blended the cultural perspectives with contemporary behavior change theory. The CAC chose the focus of educational strategies, which were derived from the oral tradition of storytelling. Listening to stories holds great value in passing on cultural values and traditions to subsequent generations. Another CAC choice was for the materials to exemplify and reflect the cultural value of generosity in contrast to predominant Western values of accumulated wealth and power. The approach to this recommendation was to access video footage of early tribes living communally and to narrate the introduction to the educational materials in such a way that reflected this tradition of generosity (Fahrenwald, Belitz, Keckler, & Sharma, 2007).

Both the video and print materials included visual images of local tribal members and their families. These participants consented to tell their story of receiving a donated organ or tissue, donating a kidney, waiting for a donor kidney, or making the decision to donate organs and tissues on behalf of a deceased family member. Traditional music and language were included in parts of the video, which was primarily developed for an English-language-speaking audience per the decision of the CAC. A local drumming group and a spiritual leader volunteered to share prayers on behalf of sick people, including those individuals waiting for a donated organ or tissue. The images, color, and messages included in the print materials were selected by the CAC.

Intervention messages were also grounded in a contemporary behavior change theory. The transtheoretical model (TTM) of behavior change has been around for 30 years (Prochaska, 1979) and has been applied to numerous health behaviors (Prochaska et al., 1994). The appeal of the TTM is that decision making is not conceived as a dichotomous, yes-or-no outcome, but rather as a nonlinear process of intention formation leading to action. The model was congruent with cultural notions of nonlinear processes in decision making and was selected primarily for this flexibility in exploring changes in intention to serve as an organ or tissue donor. The TTM integrates important constructs from diverse behavioral theories in order to facilitate progression from no intention to participate in organ and tissue donation (precontemplation stage), to intention formation (contemplation stage), to taking some steps to change such as signing a donor card (preparation stage), to both signing a donor card and sharing the decision with family members (action stage). The intervention messages were congruent with TTM constructs that would facilitate progress from no intention to serve as an organ or tissue donor to representation of donation intention by signing a donor card, registering as a donor through the driver's license registry, and, ultimately, talking with family members about the decision. Behavioral theorists validated message congruity with each behavior change construct and assured that at least three messages were present related to each construct.

Access to the settings where the intervention was delivered was facilitated by the outreach coordinator's relationship-building efforts with tribal leaders, elders, and health providers. Each reservation community was different, and the navigation of social structures and communication mechanisms within these communities was central to program delivery.

Selection of Outcome Measures

Representation of intention to serve as an organ or tissue donor and share the decision with family members was the primary outcome measured. The simple survey was modified from the original format, which was developed as a pre- and posttest measure for college students (Robbins et al., 2002). The tool was revised because the CAC did not agree that the original instrument was culturally acceptable, primarily due to the focus on timing of decision making (i.e., references to 30 days and 6 months). The modified instrument included three response options about timing of the decision to become an organ donor (Fahrenwald & Stabnow, 2005). The timelines of 6 months and 30 days were removed to simplify and apply the scale to the cultural context of time in the AI culture. Strong estimates of reliability and validity of this measure were established by pilot testing the instrument with reservation-dwelling adults.

Participants completed a stage of readiness for organ and tissue donation survey both before and after an educational session. When participants indicated a desire to sign a donor card or indicate donor designation on the state driver's license, forms were completed and the individuals were asked if they would consent to follow-up with family members after allowing for opportunity to share the decision. Verification of family conversation occurred over the phone and in person.

Summary of Findings

There were 1,580 adults who participated in the full intervention and for whom both pre- and postintervention data were available (Fahrenwald et al., 2007). Prior to the intervention, about 60% of these participants were not thinking about serving as an organ or tissue donor and the other 40% were thinking about it. After the intervention, nearly 10% of the 1,580 participants signed a donor card and informed their family, a conversation that was verified by the project outreach coordinator. Over 50% of all of the participants progressed in their intention to serve as an organ or tissue donor, whereas just over 40% remained unchanged in their intentions.

Results from this study were limited by the single-group design and a non-random sample. Favorable findings indicate that the intervention produced changes in decision making related to organ and tissue donation. An anecdotal finding was that younger participants were more likely to make the decision to become organ and tissue donors. Follow-up verification of a family conversation was challenging due to the large geographic area and the limitations of phone follow-up with reservation dwellers. Face-to-face conversation with family members was the preferable mode of follow-up.

Challenges of the Approach

Working with Native communities to develop culturally targeted and theory-based interventions, and ultimately testing those interventions using research methods and approaches that are congruent with community norms, takes time. Development of the intervention took nearly one year, time that was well invested in terms of process but not always within the expectations of funding agencies. Building relationships that led to the opportunity to collaborate on a project of this magnitude was a long-term process that was initiated over 2 years prior to intervention development.

Working with disadvantaged communities is an honor and a privilege, and pre-servation of trust is essential to ongoing collaboration. Payment for or acknow-ledgment of contributions of CAC members and community members who participate in the intervention development should be determined as part of a mutual conversation early in the process. Honoring the time and sharing of wis-dom by community members is essential. Mechanisms for payment are not always possible using traditional organizational structures such as direct deposit into bank accounts. Some of the reservations where this effort occurred do not have banking systems, and many residents do not have bank accounts.

Specific to the phenomenon of representation of donor intent in a registry is the reality of tribal sovereignty coupled with driver's license registries. Because a state driver's license is not needed for tribal members to drive within the reservation, representation of intention on such a license creates the need to con-sider alternative mechanisms, such as requesting a donor ID card from the state system or, at least, carrying a card that documents donation intent.

Delivery of community-based interventions in the Northern Plains reservation needs to consider the geography of the region. Harsh winter climates and large rural landmasses with limited resources are realities. Anticipating these challenges and planning for alternatives are essential to the research process.

Conclusion

Scientists have an opportunity and an obligation to participate in the remediation of health disparities. When working with AI, AN, and FN communities, our responsibility is to build trusted and long-term relationships as part of dedicated efforts to ameliorate factors that contribute to poor health or reduced quality of life. Additional community-based participatory research can strengthen our efforts to eliminate the disparity between need and availability of donated organs and tissues for AI, AN, and FN communities. Collaborative partnerships require flexibility in approach and openness to alternative viewpoints throughout the research process.

Acknowledgments

This study was supported by a research grant to the South Dakota Lion's Eye Bank and South Dakota State University from the U.S. Department of Health and Human Services, Health Resources and Services Administration, Division of Transplantation, R39 OT01211-01. The author would like to thank all of the people who participated in the development and evaluation of the intervention as well as the research team members; Christine Belitz, executive director of the South Dakota Lion's Eye Bank (SDLEB); and Arliss Keckler, outreach coordinator, SDLEB.

The opinions expressed in this chapter are those of the author and do not necessarily reflect the views of the Indian Health Service.

References

Baldwin, L. M., Grossman, D. C., Casey, S., Hollow, W., Sugarman, J. R., Freeman, W. L., et al. (2002). Prenatal and birth outcomes among rural and urban American Indians/Alaska Natives. *American Journal of Public Health*, *92*, 1491–1497.

Blagg, C. R., Helgerson, S. D., Warren, C. W., Keendenton, K., Seely, M., Peterson, L., et al. (1992). Awareness and attitudes of northwest Native Americans regarding organ donation and transplantation. *Clinical Transplantation*, *6*, 436–442.

Centers for Disease Control and Prevention. (2008). *American Indian and Alaska Native populations*. Office of Minority Health. Retrieved March 30, 2007, from http://www.cdc.gov/omh/Populations/AIAN/AIAN.htm

Commission on Civil Rights. (2003). *A quiet crisis: Federal funding and unmet needs in Indian country*. Retrieved March 30, 2007, from www.usccr.gov/pubs/na0703/na0731.pdf

Danielson, B. L., LaPree, A. J., Odland, M. D., & Steffens, E. K. (1998). Attitudes and beliefs concerning organ donation among Native Americans in the upper Midwest. *Journal of Transplant Coordination, 8,* 153–156.

Davis, S. M., & Reid, R. (1999). Practicing participatory research in American Indian communities. *American Journal of Clinical Nutrition, 69,* 755S–759S.

Evans, R. W., Manninen, D. L., Garrison, L. P., Jr., Hart, L. G., Blagg, C. R., Gutman, R. A., et al. (1985). The quality of life of patients with end-stage renal disease. *New England Journal of Medicine, 312,* 553–559.

Fahrenwald, N. L., Belitz, C., Keckler, A., & Sharma, M. (2007). Sharing the gift of life: An intervention to increase organ and tissue donation for American Indians. *Progress in Transplantation, 17,* 281–288.

Fahrenwald, N. L., & Stabnow, W. (2005). Sociocultural perspective on organ and tissue donation among reservation-dwelling American Indian adults. *Ethnicity & Health, 10,* 341–354.

Health Canada. (2007). *Diabetes among Aboriginal people in Canada: The evidence.* Retrieved March 30, 2007, from http://www.hc-sc.gc.ca/fnih-spni/alt_formats/ fnihb-dgspni/pdf/pubs/diabete/2001_evidence_faits_e.pdf

Indian and Northern Canada Affairs. (N.d.). *Frequently asked questions about Aboriginal peoples.* Retrieved March 30, 2007, from http://www.ainc-inac.gc.ca/pr/info/ info125_e.html

Institute of Medicine. (2006). *Organ donation: Opportunities for action, Committee on Increasing Rates of Organ Donation* (J. F. Childress & C. T. Liverman, Eds.). Washington, DC: National Academy of Sciences.

Isaacs, R. (2004). Ethical implications of ethnic disparities in chronic kidney disease and kidney transplantation. *Advances in Renal Replacement Therapy, 11,* 55–58.

Israel, B. A., Eng, E., Schulz, A. J., & Parke, E. A. (Eds.). (2005). *Methods in community-based participatory research for health.* San Francisco: Jossey-Bass.

Lee, E. T., Howard, B. V., Savage, P. J., Cowan, L. D., Fabsitz, R. R., Oopik, A. J., et al. (1995). Diabetes and impaired glucose tolerance in three American Indian populations aged 45–74 years: The Strong Heart Study. *Diabetes Care, 18,* 599–610.

Leffell, M. S., Fallin, M. D., Hildebrand, W. H., Cavett, J. W., Iglehart, B. A., & Zachary, A. A. (2004). HLA alleles and haplotypes among the Lakota Sioux: Report of the ASHI minority workshops, part III. *Human Immunology, 65,* 78–89.

Molzahn, A. E., Starzomski, R., McDonald, M., & O'Loughlin, C. (2004). Aboriginal beliefs about organ donation: Some Coast Salish viewpoints. *Canadian Journal of Nursing Research, 36,* 110–128.

Narva, A. S. (1996). ESRD in the American Indian population. *Nephrology News Issues, 10,* 28–30.

Narva, A. S. (2003). The spectrum of kidney disease in American Indians. *Kidney International Supplement, S,* 3–7.

Natural Resources Canada. (2001). *Percentage of Aboriginal population by Census division.* Retrieved March 30, 2007, from http://atlas.nrcan.gc.ca/site/english/maps/ peopleandsociety/population/aboriginalpopulation/abo_2001/pm_abpopcd_01/

Newman, J. M., Marfin, A. A., Eggers, P. W., & Helgerson, S. D. (1990). End state renal disease among Native Americans, 1983–86. *American Journal of Public Health, 80,* 318–319.

Norrell, B. (2005). Urban Indian summit mirrors population shift. *Indian Country Today, 24,* 36. Retrieved March 30, 2007, from http://indiancountry.com/content.cfm?id=1096410344

Population Reference Bureau. (1999). *Population bulletin.* Retrieved March 30, 2007, from http://www.prb.org/Publications/PopulationBulletins.aspx

Port, F. K., Wolfe, R. A., Mauger, E. A., Berling, D. P., & Jiang, K. (1993). Comparison of survival probabilities for dialysis patients vs cadaveric renal transplant recipients. *Journal of American Medical Association, 270,* 1339–1343.

Prochaska, J. O. (1979). *Systems of psychotherapy: a transtheoretical analysis.* Homewood, IL: Dorsey Press.

Prochaska, J. O., Velicer, W. F., Rossi, J. S., Goldstein, M. G., Marcus, B. H., Rakowski, W, et al. (1994). Stages of change and decisional balance for 12 problem behaviors. *Health Psychology, 13,* 39–46.

Robbins, M. L., Ganikos, M., Leino, E. M., Eastwood, A., Webster, L., & Bieterman, C. (2002). Stage-based intervention to increase intent for organ donation among college students. *Annals of Behavioral Medicine, 24,* S138.

Scheper-Hughes, N. (2000). The global traffic in human organs. *Current Anthropology, 41,* 191–224.

Seifer, S. (2003). Documenting and assessing community based scholarship: Resources for faculty. In M. Minkler & N. Wallerstein (Eds.), *Community based participatory research for health* (pp. 429–443). San Francisco: Jossey-Bass.

Statistics Canada. (2001). *Population reporting an Aboriginal identity, by mother tongue, by province and territory: 2001 Census.* Retrieved March 30, 2007, from http://www40.statcan.ca/l01/cst01/demo38a.htm?sdi=aboriginal/

Tom-Orme, L. (2006). Research and American Indian/Alaska Native health: A nursing perspective. *Journal of Transcultural Nursing, 17,* 261–265.

Tookenay, V. F. (1996). Improving the health status of Aboriginal people in Canada: New directions, new responsibilities. *Canadian Medical Association Journal, 155,* 1581–1583.

Upper Midwest Organ Procurement Organization. (1995). *Medical record review of 17 major donor hospitals in the region.* Minneapolis: LifeSources.

U.S. Census Bureau. (1999). *Statistical abstract of the United States: The national data book.* Washington, DC: U.S. Census Bureau.

U.S. Census Bureau. (2002). *The American Indian and Alaska Native population.* Washington, DC: US Census Bureau.

Viswanathan, M., Ammerman, A., Eng, E., Gartlehner, G., Lohr, K. N., Griffith, D., et al. (2004). *Community-based participatory research: Assessing the evidence* (Evidence report/technology assessment No. 99, prepared by RTI–University of North Carolina Evidence-Based Practice Center under Contract No. 290-02-0016; AHRQ Publication 04-E022-2). Rockville, MD: Agency for Healthcare Research and Quality.

Wallerstein, N. B., & Duran, B. (2006). Using community-based research to address health disparities. *Health Promotion Practice, 3,* 312–323.

Wolfe, R. A., Ashby, V. B., Milford, E. L., Ojo, A. O., Ettenger, R. E., Agodoa, L., et al. (1999). Comparison of mortality in all patients on dialysis, patients on dialysis awaiting transplantation, and recipients of a first cadaveric transplant. *New England Journal of Medicine, 341,* 1725–1730.

Zuckerman, S., Haley, J., Roubideaux, Y., & Lillie-Blanton, M. (2004). Health service access, use, and insurance coverage among American Indians/Alaska Natives and Whites: What role does the Indian Health Service play? *American Journal of Public Health, 94,* 53–59.

Part II

Organizational Interventions

9

Behavioral Research in Hospital Settings

The Family Communication Coordinator (FCC) Protocol and Research Applications in Organ Donation

Diane Dodd-McCue

Given the dynamic changes unfolding in the realm of organ donation and transplantation, 10 years is a very long time. In the United States, the past decade brought an increase in discussion, innovation, replication, funding, and evaluation of efforts aimed at increasing the number of organs available for transplantation. This period marked an even greater increase in the number of those awaiting transplantation. Regardless of the effectiveness of efforts to increase rates of organ donation through public awareness and donor registration, what unfolds in the hospital context ultimately determines whether donation and transplantation become a reality. Throughout this decade of change, the family communication coordinator (FCC) protocol was implemented, replicated, and refined, and new perspectives for its evaluation evolved. The FCC protocol is designed to improve the level of care provided to the donor family. This includes the promotion of uniform and consistent communication to families who lose a loved one.

This chapter begins with an introduction of the FCC protocol. Evaluation of the protocol required examination of theoretical frameworks and constructs rarely considered in the organ donation realm. These approaches are unique in that the focus is not on typical outcome measures such as donor conversion rates, but rather on what can be considered collateral outcomes feeding back into the system. The first approach, *role stress and work attitudes*, highlights the importance of any hospital intervention for the workers implementing the intervention. Data from previous studies are used to illustrate the importance of the construct and the effects of the FCC protocol on nurses. Next, stakeholder analysis and systems theory are proposed as potential approaches for assessing the impact of the FCC and other interventions on organization stakeholders and elements of the broader hospital system.

The Family Communication Coordinator Protocol

The FCC protocol is a hospital-based approach developed to improve organ donation effectiveness. The protocol was developed by drawing upon pastoral care (Tartaglia & Linyear, 2000) and organ procurement literature (Linyear & Tartaglia, 1999), and was first implemented in 1997 at an academic transplant center. Specifically, the FCC protocol—a multidisciplinary team approach—outlines a communication path to promote families' understanding of brain death and acceptance of loss, while also promoting a communication path among clinical staff and the organ procurement organization (OPO) coordinator (see Figure 9.1). Members of the team include a dedicated hospital chaplain, critical care nurses, other critical care medical staff, and OPO professionals.

The FCC protocol is implemented once the patient is identified as neurologically devastated by an accepted clinical measure: the Glasgow Coma Scale (GCS; GCS ≤ 4). Once a patient is identified by this clinical trigger, a designated FCC chaplain is assigned to the case and provides support to the patient's family throughout this medical event. Hospital chaplains are employed by the hospital as full-time employees on call to provide patients and their families with 24/7 spiritual support. The hospital chaplains' professional training includes extensive patient counseling; although they are also theologically trained and they represent a wide range of faith communities (including non-Christian), their emphasis is on *spiritual* care (in contrast to a religious orientation).

This came about via the Joint Commission. The Joint Commission, in its effort to strengthen the quality of care in U.S. health care institutions, established the standard of spiritual assessment for hospital patients; spiritual assessment is recommended to determine the impact of spirituality on care and services being provided (Joint Commission, 2009). Although the Joint Commission did not specify the qualifications required of those providing spiritual assessment or spiritual support, hospital chaplains frequently serve in this capacity. FCC chaplains, a specialized group of chaplains from within the larger pool of hospital chaplains, are specifically trained in the area of organ donation and transplantation and are responsible for responding to potential organ donation cases.

The FCC chaplains' role is critical in that if the medical case progresses to neurological death, the family is introduced to the OPO coordinator or to a designated OPO requestor only after two conditions are met: Brain death is determined, and the chaplain establishes family understanding of this grave prognosis. Historically, the amount of time FCC chaplains spend with patient families within the context of the FCC protocol can range from a few hours to several days, with chaplains establishing intense trust relationships with many families. Regardless of their donation decision, families receive the same level of support from chaplains.

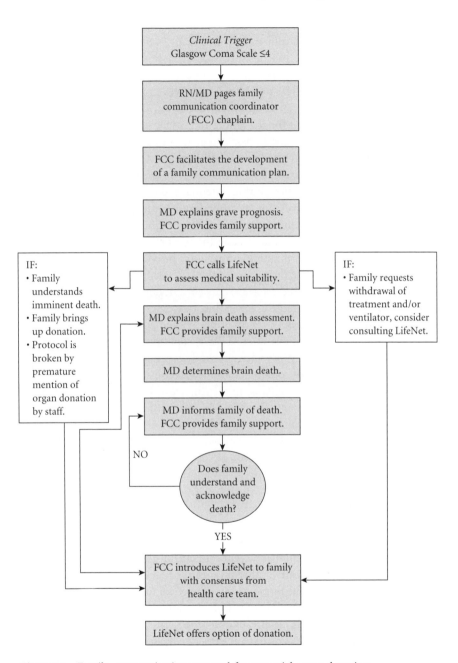

Figure 9.1   Family communication protocol for potential organ donation.

Returning to the FCC protocol, recognition of the specialized roles and coordination among different health care professionals as part of a multidisciplinary care team is critical to the protocol's success. During this medical event, the nursing and medical staff focus on the clinical needs of the patient, whereas the OPO coordinator evaluates medical suitability and serves as a clinical resource to the staff. Assuming the patient's neurological condition continues to deteriorate, the FCC chaplain is present for the family to provide spiritual care, to facilitate positive family interactions, and to help others in the care team translate medical status and procedures—such as brain death testing—to the family.

In short, the process outlined by the FCC protocol aims for consistent communication and interaction during potential organ donation cases (Tartaglia & Linyear, 2000). It achieves this by providing a clear definition of when the protocol is triggered, by defining specialized role responsibilities by members of a multidisciplinary team, by emphasizing the importance of monitoring family understanding, and by coordinating information provided to them.

An initial project assessed the impact of the FCC protocol on traditional organ donation outcomes: increased referrals, consents, organs available for transplantation, and organs transplanted. Favorable outcomes—as reflected by these traditional measures—led to tweaking and refinements as well as to Health Resources and Services Administration (HRSA) support (Grant No. CFDA 93.134, FY 2001) for replicating the protocol at a second academic teaching hospital served by the same OPO. Favorable outcomes also led to consideration of other aspects of the FCC protocol such as interest in the impact of the protocol on the organ donation process and how it influenced the relationships between participants in the process. Gains in consent rates will be short-lived if the FCC protocol leads to coworker friction and role frustration. In response, new perspectives for evaluating the FCC protocol surfaced.

New Perspectives

Conversion rates and referral ratios are the outcomes of interest for most hospital-based organ donation interventions during the past decade. Focusing exclusively on conversion rates and referral ratios reflects program effectiveness but offers few insights on the intra- and interpersonal influence on hospital staff. An effort to enhance organ donation can increase conversion rates; however, placing additional demands on already burdened critical care providers may in the long run lead to reduced conversion rates due to staff turnover and burnout.

Examining organizational outcomes beyond conversion rates is new ground for most organ donor researchers. Fortunately, there is no need to reinvent the wheel. Frameworks are well developed and established, particularly in organizational theory and organizational behavior, and are readily applicable to this

Table 9.1   The FCC protocol: Organizational theoretical perspectives

Theoretical Perspective	Level of Analysis	Reference	Related Measurements
Stakeholder analysis	Environment	Freeman (1984)	Descriptive
Systems theory	Team	Katz and Kahn (1966)	Descriptive
Role stress and work attitudes	Individual	Kahn et al. (1964) Locke (1976) Hackman and Oldham (1975) Rizzo et al. (1970) Mowday et al. (1979)	Job diagnostic survey Role questionnaire Organizational commitment questionnaire

context. These different perspectives and levels of analysis complement the organ donation environment—an environment characterized by multiple organizational systems and interactions among multiple stakeholders with potentially different views on what constitutes the desired emphasis or outcome.

Table 9.1 offers three unique perspectives that enriched our understanding and helped identify overlooked, underemphasized, or unintended consequences of the FCC protocol. The perspectives range from macro- to microtheoretical, and differ in terms of level of analysis. Some offer new avenues for future descriptive research, whereas others represent published empirical efforts. Although these illustrations focus on application of the FCC protocol, they are equally appropriate for gaining new insights on other health service activities. The individual as the level of analysis is discussed first.

Role Stress and Work Attitudes as the Level of Analysis

Potential organ donor cases pose a uniquely difficult situation for critical care nurses, who are often asked to provide both clinical care and emotional support. The demands of addressing the needs of families and also being responsible for providing patient care can result in increased and conflicting expectations. In addition, the timing and coordination of critical information, coupled with ongoing assessments of a grieving family's understanding of complex medical procedures, further complicate the role expectations of critical care nurses (Dodd-McCue, Tartaglia, Myer, Kuthy, & Faulkner, 2004). Nurses can face psychological turmoil as a result of frequent professional exposure to, and interactions with, patients and families following traumatic occurrences (Frazier et al., 2003; Price, 2004). Research suggests that over time, these demands leave caregivers susceptible to compassion fatigue and their responses may be similar to those of people with posttraumatic stress (Baxter, 2004). Accordingly, organizational efforts aimed at improving communication and coordination during potential organ donation situations must consider the impact on the critical care nurses involved in donation cases.

Fortunately, the role stress approach, originating in the organizational literature, provides a theoretical framework appropriate to understanding the impact of donation cases on critical care nurses. Arising from individuals' perceptions of their work context, role stress is a mature concept that has been used in various industry and organizational settings for over 4 decades (Kahn, Wolfe, Quinn, Smoke, & Rosenthall, 1964). Theoretically, role stress is composed of three distinct stressors: (a) role overload, the perceptions of excessive work responsibilities; (b) role ambiguity, the perception of vague or unclear responsibilities; and (c) role conflict, the perception of competing responsibilities. Locke (1976) demonstrated a link between role stress and overall job stress as well as a relationship between job stress and job satisfaction. Applied to the FCC protocol, the question is whether the protocol is associated with increased role stress for nurses. If the FCC protocol is associated with increased stress, satisfaction may decrease, turnover will increase, and patient care may decline as a result—a likely violation of "First do no harm."

Two different studies were conducted to assess the influence of the FCC protocol on role stress. The first was conducted at the hospital responsible for developing the protocol. This investigation consisted of a retrospective, non-experimental design, with observations of pre- and postprotocol perceptions (Dodd-McCue et al., 2004). Twelve items examining three aspects of role stressors (role ambiguity, conflict, and overload) revealed 12 significant relationships. The direction of the results would surprise anyone expecting the protocol to increase worker burden. Rather than increasing stress, the FCC protocol had the opposite effect: It reduced perceptions of role stress post intervention when compared to pre–FCC protocol intervention. Across all 12 items, large, significant and favorable differences emerged in the form of reductions in role ambiguity, conflict, and overload. Data triangulation was promoted through collection of complementary interview data as well as human resource data on retention and turnover (see Dodd-McCue et al., 2004). In-depth interviews were guided by specific open-ended questions relating to nurses' perceptions of their responsibilities during potential organ donation cases, and their perceptions of role stress, satisfaction, and commitment. The interview questions were generated and piloted with the assistance of critical care nurses, chaplains, and other health services professionals with experience in organ donation. All results point in the same direction. For example, critical care nurses touted the FCC protocol for its ability to allow nurses to focus on clinical tasks without concern that the families' needs are not being met.

Any methodological flaws in the first retrospective study (Dodd-McCue et al., 2004) were compensated via the 2-year longitudinal design of the second (Dodd-McCue, Tartaglia, Veazey, & Streetman, 2005). The same survey instrument and interview questions were used. In both cases, the sample included critical care nurses involved in potential organ donation cases and observations pre– and post–FCC protocol implementation. In both cases, those included in the sample received comparable FCC protocol and organ donation training. The results of both were surprisingly similar, positive, and practically as well as statistically significant.

As with the first study, the longitudinal effort indicates that the FCC protocol is associated with statistically significant reductions in role ambiguity and role conflict, as well as with improved job satisfaction and professional and organizational commitment (Dodd-McCue et al., 2005). As with the prior study, large and favorable significant differences emerged across all 12 variables. Interview data support the same picture that the FCC protocol leads to a reduction in role stressors among critical care nurses.

A third study, a cross-sectional study initiated in response to these findings, focused on the hospital chaplains involved in potential donation cases as FCCs (see Dodd-McCue & Tartaglia, 2005, for published findings). At the time of this study, only seven chaplains had been designated and worked as FCC chaplains. Although all participated in the study, the small sample size limits statistical analysis. However, the survey results suggest that the FCC chaplains associated the protocol with clarity of role direction, consistent and compatible role guidelines, and an adequate workload.

Together, these studies provide evidence that the FCC protocol positively, not negatively, impacts worker stress. Worker stress, a variable not typically considered in the organ donor literature, might account for variance previously unaccounted for when considering traditional organ donation outcomes. For example, results of the FCC protocol studies indicate an intervention can reduce stress of the hospital staff. Reduced stress has been associated with increased performance in a number of different contexts (Chatterjea, Bhattacharya, & Bhattacharyya, 1978). Interventions designed to ease the trauma to a person who has just lost a loved one may be effective either because they directly impact the patient or because they reduce worker stress and therefore lead to a better performing nurse or bring more ease to the patient with a more harmonious atmosphere.

On the flipside, if an intervention fails, one possibility is that it did not influence patient well-being. Another is that the intervention positively impacted patient well-being, or even influenced the patient's desire to donate a loved one's organs, but added such additional stress to the response team that gains were negated due to a more stress-filled environment and a less able critical care nurse as a result. Without explicitly examining variables on the individual level, such as worker stress, reasons for an intervention's success or failure will be unknown. If evaluation is limited to short-term assessments focused only on conversion rates, programs that lead to long-term consequences that affect the work environment (in this case, increased stress) may appear misleadingly effective. One possibility is that worker stress may moderate the relationship between interventions and changes in conversion rates.

In summary, going beyond traditional donation measures and assessing nontraditional outcomes such as role stress and work attitudes revealed protocol benefits that would have otherwise gone unnoticed. Role stress and work attitudes represent an individual-level analysis. Analyses on the team and environmental levels can be equally informative. Accordingly, two theoretical perspectives, one from each level of analysis, are briefly presented as potential new directions for organ donation inquiries.

Stakeholder Analysis and the Organ Donation Environment as the Level of Analysis

The premise of stakeholder analysis (Freeman, 1984) is that different parties have a stake or interest in a specific situation. What constitutes one party's desired outcome—how that party defines *effectiveness*—may vary or be in conflict with that of others, or the relative weight given different criteria may vary. Similarly, stakeholder analysis does not suggest that any perspective is patently flawed or flawless; it does suggest that a richer, more complex perspective encompasses the viewpoints of competing stakeholders.

Relative to the FCC protocol, stakeholders include, but are not limited to, potential donors, potential donor families, patients on transplant lists, critical care providers, chaplains, OPOs, hospitals, and health policy makers. Relative to the potential donor, effectiveness is the efficient delivery of clinically proficient care that respects the dignity of the individual. Potential donor families may view effectiveness in light of their perceptions of the emotional support they receive and their perceptions of the quality of care provided to a loved one. Patients on transplant lists evaluate effectiveness by whether needed organs are medically suitable and available for transplantation through a timely and equitable allocation system. Critical care providers, although attentive to the number of transplantable organs, also value resource or staffing adequacy and their level of moral distress when involved in organ donation cases. OPOs and policy makers define effectiveness in terms of quantitative outcomes based on the administrative goal of increasing the number of organs available for transplantation. Policy makers, although also interested in these quantitative outcomes, may more heavily weigh conversion rate as a means of program evaluation.

Thus, stakeholder analysis suggests recognizing different measures of effectiveness that are unique to specific stakeholders, and being sensitive to stakeholders' potentially conflicting interests. Efforts to recognize and address competing stakeholders' needs enhance mutual understanding and cooperation, and may lead to an overarching common goal to which different stakeholders are committed. Failing to recognize and address competing stakeholder needs can result in lack of understanding, conflict, and the creation of barriers that would impede commitment to a common goal.

In light of the FCC protocol, a stakeholder analysis can highlight the difficult balancing act played out during each potential donation case: ensuring that available organs are donated, recovered, and transplanted through an efficient process that assures the dignity of the donor, provides donor families with compassionate care, and ensures that health care providers have a working environment that supplies them with necessary clinical resources and emotional support. Evaluation based on a stakeholder approach can also ensure fuller understanding of different aspects of the donation process and expands opportunities for information exchange, which may eventually result in process improvements not initially identified. Evaluation based on the perspective of only one or some of these stakeholders provides only part of the picture: It increases the potential for conflict and dysfunctional processes and communication, leading to obstacles toward improvement.

Systems Theory and the Team as the Level of Analysis

Unlike stakeholder analysis, which emphasizes the diverse perspectives of effectiveness by key constituents in the organ donation process, systems theory emphasizes the differentiation and integration of different professionals in carrying out their roles within the organ donation process. The premise of systems theory is that organizations are systems of roles characterized by specific inputs, throughputs, and outputs, as well as interaction with other systems and their environment (Katz & Kahn, 1966, 1978).

Systems theory emphasizes the organic, fluid nature of different systems; the frequent interactions and exchanges between systems; and varying levels of interconnectedness that facilitate these exchanges. These exchanges involve information and resources, and these exchanges may vary in the extent to which they influence systems effectiveness. The interconnectedness of different systems during these exchanges may also vary from loose to tight linkages, and the interactions necessary to facilitate these exchanges may range from simple and unspecified to highly complex and intricately programmed. A systems theory interpretation of the organ donation process highlights the interaction of multiple systems comprised of specific roles with high levels of complexity and varying levels of system connectivity and interdependency.

Relative to the FCC protocol, a systems theory would seek to understand the workings of the multidisciplinary team involved in the organ donation process. This team is typically composed of a hospital chaplain dedicated to potential organ donation cases, critical care nurses, neurospecialists, physicians from different medical areas, and the donation coordinator. Once the protocol is put in motion, the FCC team members represent different organizational and professional systems. In organ donation cases, these different health services providers interface with a high degree of interconnectedness; each provides a unique competency and critical skill set, but the contributions of each provider often impact the ability of others in performing their roles. The nurse is focusing on patient care, but information about the specifics of the care being provided is necessary for neuro-specialists assessing neurological function. FCC chaplains are providing support to families but need information on clinical status and projected testing to provide more effective family care and better ensure family understanding of patient status. Both the clinical status of the patient, available from the medical staff, and family understanding of a grave prognosis, assessed by the chaplain, are needed by the donation coordinator to determine the appropriateness of initiating the donation discussion. Coordination among these different systems represented in the organ donation process is provided by compliance with the FCC protocol.

Conclusion

Traditional donation outcomes are used routinely to evaluate the effectiveness of protocols seeking to improve donation. The FCC protocol intervention is unique because it goes beyond these traditional donation outcomes to assess the impact of these changes on the work environment. Two different studies, both involving mixed-method approaches, indicate that the influence of the FCC protocol goes beyond improving traditional outcomes and affects the work environment itself. Knowledge of the specific influence of the FCC protocol from a work stress *perspective* provides evidence for program sustainability that goes beyond a typical focus on fiscal concerns. Considerations should include the influence of the intervention on the stress of those involved in the donation process.

The stakeholder analysis and systems theory approaches were proffered as potential frameworks for understanding the effect of organ donor interventions beyond traditional outcomes such as conversion rates. Researchers interested in understanding the direct and indirect influences of interventions must draw on theoretical approaches typically driving organ donation efforts—especially those involving levels of analysis beyond the individual. Both stakeholder analysis and systems theory differ in level of analysis; however, their use serves a common goal:

Both are valuable if researchers in the organ donation domain are interested in broadening the discourse regarding organ donation intervention impact.

On a practical level, the challenges associated with a project of this magnitude should not go unappreciated. Theoretically and empirically, the route traveled was marked by the input of a multidisciplinary research team, the cross-fertilization of different research traditions, and the application of existing theories and measures already well established and utilized in the organizational sciences. This investigation benefited from a unique opportunity to study the impact of the same intervention—the FCC protocol—in two different sites using different research designs. Equally important were the resources, freedom, and support provided by policy makers and administrators to pursue this secondary stream of inquiry.

At both intervention sites, the FCC protocol was implemented by organizational cultures that were supportive of organ donation. Utilization of the protocol at both hospitals was promoted by several factors: the endorsement of highly visible administrators, the availability of adequate resources, thoughtful attention to protocol development, thorough education and training, and a moderate to long-term perspective. At the clinical level, the key to the protocol's effectiveness was the nurturing and maintenance of open and candid communication within the multidisciplinary team as well as with members of critical stakeholder groups. Without such support, conducting such a multifaceted intervention would have been impossible. Other hospitals considering implementation of the FCC protocol could benefit from ensuring that these factors are present within their hospital environments. Researchers could also contribute to practice by pursuing studies that could lead to improved understanding of these contingencies and the extent to which they contribute to the success or failure of the FCC protocol.

In addition to enriching understanding of the phenomena associated with interventions like the FCC protocol, the studies emerging from this stream of research highlight the methodological challenges facing researchers. In the context of hospital-level interventions in the area of organ donation, research designs often are constrained by naturalistic settings and by any number of extraneous events limiting experimental control. Similarly, sample size is a function of the number of individuals who are involved in potential organ donation cases at the study hospital, and even within academic transplant centers this number may be limited, particularly within a single professional category. Thus, statistical power and effect size are negatively impacted. Although multisite studies offer the opportunity for increased sample sizes, this benefit may be offset by extraneous factors that threaten internal validity.

This experience emphasizes that, in the area of organ donation and probably in many other health services areas, researchers can partner with health care providers to improve processes and outcomes. Increased attention on the sustainability of the positive impact of processes and outcomes points to opportunities to move beyond commonsense arguments to more rigorous measures of long-term impacts. In pursuing applied research agendas in health care areas like organ donation, researchers do not have to reinvent the wheel. By encouraging novel and innovative ways of framing research questions, new and important opportunities for applying theoretical insights from other areas can be discovered.

Acknowledgments

This work was supported by grant CFDA 93.134, FY 2001 from the U.S. Department of Health and Human Services, Health Resources and Services Administration.

References

Baxter, A. (2004). Post-traumatic stress disorder and the intensive care unit patient: Implications for staff and advanced practice critical care nurses. *Dimensions of Critical Care Nursing, 23,* 145–150.

Chatterjea, R. G., Bhattacharya, R., & Bhattacharyya, A. K. (1978). Effects of induced stress on performance. *Journal of Psychological Research, 22,* 135–142.

Dodd-McCue, D., & Tartaglia, A. (2005). The role of "relatedness" in donation discussions with next of kin: An empirical study of the common wisdom. *Progress in Transplantation, 15,* 249–256.

Dodd-McCue, D., Tartaglia, A., Myer, K., Kuthy, S., & Faulkner, K. (2004). Unintended consequences: The impact of protocol change on critical care nurses' perceptions of stress. *Progress in Transplantation, 14,* 61–67.

Dodd-McCue, D., Tartaglia, A., Veazey, K., & Streetman, P. (2005). The impact of protocol on nurses' role stress: A longitudinal perspective. *Journal of Nursing Administration, 35,* 205–216.

Frazier, S. K., Moser, D. K., Daley, L. K., McKinley, S., Riegel, B., & Gavin, B. J. (2003). Critical care nurses' beliefs about and reported management of anxiety. *American Journal of Critical Care, 12,* 119–127.

Freeman, R. E. (1984). *Strategic management: A stakeholder approach.* London: Pitman.

Hackman, J., & Oldham, G. (1975). Development of the Job Diagnostic Survey. *Journal of Applied Psychology, 60,* 159–170.

Joint Commission. (2009). *Spiritual assessment.* Retrieved May 25, 2009, from http://www.jointcommission.org/AccreditationPrograms/LongTermCare/Standards/09_FAQ/PC/Spiritual_Assessment.htm

Kahn, R. L., Wolfe, D. M., Quinn, R. P., Smoke, J. D., & Rosenthall, R. S. (1964). *Organizational stress: Studies in role conflict and ambiguity.* New York: Wiley.

Katz, D., & Kahn, R. L. (1966). *The social psychology of organizations.* New York: Wiley.

Katz, D., & Kahn, R. L. (1978). *The social psychology of organizations* (2nd ed.). New York: Wiley.

Linyear, A., & Tartaglia, A. (1999). Family communication coordination: A program to increase organ donation. *Journal of Transplantation Coordination, 9,* 165–174.

Locke, E. (1976). The nature and causes of job satisfaction. In M. Dunnette (Ed.), *Handbook of industrial and organizational psychology* (pp. 397–422). Chicago: Rand McNally.

Mowday, R. T., Steers, R. M., & Porter, L. W. (1979). The measurement of organizational commitment. *Administrative Science Quarterly, 15,* 151–162.

Price, A. M. (2004). Intensive care nurses' experience of assessing and dealing with patients' psychological needs. *Nurse Critical Care, 3,* 134–142.

Rizzo, J. R., House, R. J., & Lirtzman, S. I. (1970). Role conflict and role ambiguity in complex organizations. *Administrative Science Quarterly, 15,* 151–162.

Tartaglia, A., & Linyear, A. (2000). Organ donation: A pastoral care model. *Journal of Pastoral Care, 54,* 277–287.

10

Design and Evaluation of Work Site Promotions of Organ Donation

Real-World Challenges and Strategies to Address Them

Michael T. Quinn, Jackie Gnepp,
G. Caleb Alexander, Diane Hollingsworth,
Kate Grubbs O'Connor, Willa Lang,
Joshua Klayman, and David Meltzer

The workplace is an important venue for promoting posthumous organ donation among healthy adults. Yet the design and evaluation of programs intended to promote organ donation at the work site carry special challenges. In this chapter, we discuss challenges we encountered in implementing and evaluating a workplace organ donation education program and strategies we used to overcome those challenges.

Public education efforts in the past decade have been highly successful in increasing awareness and acceptance of organ donation (Alvaro, Jones, Robles, & Siegel, 2006), but less successful in modifying organ donation intention (see Alvaro & Siegel, this volume). For example, national surveys on awareness, attitudes, and commitment to organ donation show that 90% of Americans are aware of the need for solid-organ and tissue donors and report being in favor of organ donation (Gallup Organization, 1993, 2005). Despite this high level of awareness and positive attitudes toward organ donation, only 52% of adults report having discussed their organ donation views with their family, whereas 42% report having made a personal decision about being an organ donor and a mere 28% report having made a behavioral commitment such as signing an organ donor card or enrolling in their state's organ donor registry (Guadagnoli et al., 1999). Thus, we chose to focus our research on increasing behavioral commitment to organ donation.

The workplace offers unparalleled access to adults in natural settings. The American workforce spends a significant proportion of their lives at the workplace and is typically willing to give of their time during these hours. The workplace provides a unique opportunity to study the impact of interventions among people of different racial, ethnic, and socioeconomic backgrounds (Bull, Gillette, Glasgow, & Estabrooks, 2003; Feldman, 1987; Lusk & Kerr, 1994; Thompson, Smith, & Bybee, 2005). Additional advantages to performing studies of health promotion in the workplace include the opportunity to study the impact of different work environments (Feldman, 1987), the influence of peer group support (Terborg, Hibbard, & Glasgow, 1995), and organizational work site changes that further intervention goals (Bull et al., 2003).

Reviews of work site health promotion research, however, report that these studies often use flawed designs or analyses that limit the usefulness of the findings (Conrad, Conrad, & Walcott-McQuigg, 1991). Threats to internal validity are exacerbated by the use of quasi-experimental designs, often employed after management raises objections to the random assignment of workers to intervention and control groups. Included among the threats to valid causal inference are selection bias (employees often volunteer to participate in programs and are not randomly assigned), differential attrition between intervention and control groups, effects related to the passage of time or intervening events, floor and ceiling effects, regression toward the mean when participants are selected based on extreme attitudes or beliefs, contamination of comparison groups when experimental and control groups interact socially, and reactivity such as rivalry among groups or interference by administrators (Conrad et al., 1991).

The value of research on workplace interventions may also be limited by incomplete information regarding external validity. In their review of work site health promotion studies in 11 leading journals, Bull et al. (2003) revealed that only a small minority of studies compared characteristics of their final sample to nonparticipants or to all eligible workers, whereas none compared characteristics of the participating work sites to other eligible work sites, and few reported the number of investigator-excluded participants or work sites. Such data are necessary if researchers are to discern how representative sampled participants and work sites are to larger workforce populations, informing how likely the findings are to generalize. Only a small minority of studies reported the extent to which the intervention was delivered as intended, none reported on the cost or time commitment required, and very few addressed long-term effects or program sustainability—all of which are critical to understanding how well the research might translate to practice (Bull et al., 2003).

The workplace holds tremendous potential for intervening in the lives of a large portion of the population. The challenge for researchers is to design work site interventions that are practical, efficacious, and capable of yielding valid outcome data. Flexibility and creativity in the design, delivery, and evaluation of these interventions may be required, but will pay ample dividends in cases where large numbers of people are impacted. The potential impact is high in the case of organ donation because each individual who commits to organ donation has the potential to save or improve the lives of many.

In carrying out research on work site promotions of organ donation, we faced challenges in everything from work site and subject recruitment to measurement and independent result verification. In this chapter, we describe the work site challenges we encountered, and ways in which we adapted the program and its evaluation to meet these challenges.

Methods

Intervention

We developed a behavior change intervention that had three aims: (a) to increase employees' intentions to be posthumous organ and tissue donors, (b) to increase their communication with family about their intentions, and (c) to increase family members' intentions to be posthumous organ and tissue donors. We grounded the intervention in the transtheoretical model (Prochaska, DiClemente, & Norcross, 1992). This model proposes that, in changing their behavior, individuals go through specific, sequential stages of precontemplation, contemplation, preparation, action, and maintenance. Specific processes, such as heightened awareness, social consciousness, and stimulus control, facilitate progress across stages, as does a cognitive weighing of the salient, perceived costs and benefits of engaging in the target behavior.

We designed our intervention to first raise awareness among employees by presenting relevant facts about organ donation. Next, we attempted to raise social consciousness through the personal testimonial of a transplant recipient. Following this, we highlighted personal benefits and refuted negative myths about organ donation through the testimonial of a donor family. Finally, we provided specific action strategies to help employees make a behavioral commitment to donate, inform their family of this commitment, and persuade family members to also make a behavioral commitment to become an organ donor.

Study Design

We designed our study as a randomized controlled trial with three treatment conditions: (a) a *basic* intervention, which had the goal of persuading participants to sign an organ donor card and to inform their families of their organ donation intention; (b) an *enhanced* intervention, which had the goal of persuading participants to sign an organ donor card and to then persuade family members to also sign organ donor cards; and (c) a *control* condition, which helped us to be more confident in drawing causal inferences about our interventions. We enrolled corporations with three or more relatively independent work sites (e.g., a food manufacturer with three separate production sites), and we randomized the work site as our unit of intervention. Quinn, Alexander, Hollingsworth O'Connor, and Meltzer (2006) provided additional information about the study design, intervention, and evaluation.

Work Site Recruitment

We developed specific work site recruitment criteria in order to accommodate our three-arm study design, ensure an adequate sample size, and facilitate recruitment and access to space. For example, we limited our corporations to those located within the State of Illinois, and we required a minimum of 30 employees per workplace site. An on-site contact, typically a representative from the human resources department, provided space and facilitated recruitment. Work sites with a likely favorable bias toward organ donation, such as hospitals, universities, and pharmaceutical companies, were excluded from recruitment. We also excluded work sites already participating in the Health Resources and Services Administration's ongoing Workplace Partnership for Life program.

We identified a sample of 21 corporations meeting our recruitment criteria. All had health and wellness programs, and routinely offered lunchtime educational seminars. In addition, all identified corporations had newsletters and e-mail, allowing subject recruitment efforts to reach most, if not all, employees.

Subject Recruitment

All participating corporations agreed to invite employees to a lunchtime "health education" seminar through company newsletters and e-mail circulation. This communication provided almost 100% exposure to work site employees and was sufficiently nonspecific to reduce the likelihood of any demand effect that might lead to a subject selection bias. That is, we were concerned that being invited to a specific organ donation program might lead participants to select themselves into or out of the program based solely on their preintervention views about organ donation, threatening the internal validity of the study.

Measures

To measure change in organ donation intention and communication of intention with one's family, participants were asked to complete a self-administered survey at baseline and one month post baseline. The survey included a measure of individuals' stage of organ donation intention, and a measure of individuals' stage of communicating organ donation intention with family, both of which were adapted from prior work (Prochaska et al., 1994). The survey also assessed respondents' knowledge of family members' organ donation intention by asking participants if their adult family members had signed an organ donor card.

Implementation Challenges

Recruitment

An unexpected work site recruitment challenge we encountered was that many corporations wanted an educational program for all their employees and voiced resistance to our plan to randomize some employees to an untreated control condition. We recognized that if we insisted on including an untreated control group, a number of corporations would fail to participate in the study, falling short of our recruitment goals; however, we felt as though controlling for selection bias through randomization was a key component to our research plan. Our solution to this challenge was to provide all employees with some educational program, with randomization to different educational offerings. A minimal-intensity educational intervention substituted for the planned control group. This minimal-intensity intervention was designed to approximate a community health fair. Research project staff set up tables at employee luncheon sessions with brochures and printed information about a range of health conditions (including hypertension, diabetes, and kidney disease) and were available to address specific questions posed by work site participants. Included in the brochures available to the minimal-intensity intervention participants was a full-color brochure developed by the National Kidney Foundation of Illinois specifically for this project. This brochure presented background information on the need for organ donation, offered brief testimonials of transplant recipients and organ donor families, dispelled common myths about organ donation, and provided an organ donor card.

We encountered an unexpected subject recruitment challenge when five enrolled corporations reported their concern that inviting employees to a "health education" seminar might be seen as misleading, and insisted that all their employees should be invited specifically to an "organ donation" presentation. Given our interest in retaining these work sites, we agreed for these five corporations to specify in their invitations that the seminar was about organ donation, with recognition that we were introducing several potential confounds (Campbell & Stanley, 1966). In an effort to rule out said confounds, recruitment differences across work sites were carefully tracked and tested for both baseline participant differences and Participant × Treatment interactions.

Measurement

We encountered several challenges to measurement. First, several corporations questioned our plans to survey participants, citing concerns about response burden to their employees and desire to ensure respondent confidentiality. To address concerns about response burden, we eliminated all but the most essential survey questions. Moreover, as an incentive for completing the surveys, participants were informed that all those who completed both surveys would be enrolled in a lottery and be eligible to win a gift certificate valued at $100. One lottery drawing was conducted at each work site. To address concerns about confidentiality, surveys were completed anonymously. The only identifiers survey respondents were asked to include were the last four digits of their home telephone number, which allowed for matching of pretest with posttest surveys while maintaining anonymity. This matched pretest–posttest design allowed us to assess changes in organ donation intention, communication with one's family about organ donation intention, and changes in family members' organ donation intention over the course of one month following the intervention. By agreeing to keep the surveys anonymous, we had to forgo the possibility of independently verifying donor intent via donor cards or registry.

Results

Corporation and Subject Recruitment

We recruited a total of 21 corporations meeting our inclusion criteria; however, about half ($n = 9$) of those recruited failed to complete the study. Four of the recruited corporations found they could not commit to the 45–60-minute intervention, and five corporations had personnel changes resulting in the loss of our on-site coordinators.

Across the remaining 12 corporations, a total of 754 employees in 40 work sites completed the baseline survey and attended one of the three interventions. Given that the total workforce across these 12 corporations was approximately 15,000, we were able to reach about 5% of the workforce. Of the 754 who provided baseline data and participated in the intervention, 495 (66%) returned one month later to complete a follow-up survey. Of the 495 participants retained in the study, the average age was 41 years, 75% were women, 56% were married, 71% were non-Hispanic whites, and 51% had at least a 4-year college degree. Subject retention rates across the 40 work sites ranged from 63% to 70% and did not differ significantly by treatment arm $(x^2 \; [df = 2; N = 754] = 3.001, p = 0.223)$. Subject retention also did not differ by age $(t \; [df = 752; N = 754] = 0.707, p = 0.480)$, marital status $(x^2 \; [df = 3; N = 754] = 3.226, p = 0.358)$, gender $(x^2 \; [df = 1; N = 754] = 3.628, p = 0.057)$, or baseline organ donor stage $(x^2 \; [df = 1; N = 754] = 3.315, p = 0.507)$. In logistic regression analysis, we found no differences across corporations in the percentage of participating employees who had, at baseline, signed an organ donor card ($p = 0.188$) or informed their families of their organ donation intentions ($p = 0.066$). We also found no differences across recruitment messages (i.e., invitation to a health education program vs. to an organ donation program) in baseline organ donation intention rate ($p = 0.279$).

Baseline and Follow-Up Measures

At baseline, 12% of study participants indicated that they had *not given any thought to being an organ donor* (precontemplation stage), 24% reported that they were *thinking about being an organ donor* (contemplation stage), 9% reported that they were *preparing to be an organ donor* (preparation stage), 18% reported that they had *signed an organ donor card but not informed their families* (action stage), and 37% reported that they had *signed an organ donor card and informed their families* (maintenance stage). Also at baseline, 20% of study participants indicated that they had *not given any thought to discussing with their family their views on being an organ donor* (precontemplation stage), 21% reported that they were *giving some thought about discussing with their family how they feel about organ donation* (contemplation stage), 9% reported that they were *preparing to talk with their family about how they feel about organ donation* (preparation stage), 23% reported that they had *talked with their family about how they feel about organ donation* (action stage), and 27% reported that they had *talked with their family about how they feel about organ donation, and about how family members feel about organ donation* (maintenance stage). Thus, at baseline, 55% (i.e., 18% + 37%) had already signed an organ donor card, and 50% (i.e., 23% + 27%) had already informed their families of their intentions. Baseline and follow-up stages of change for signing donor cards and communicating organ donation wishes to family, by treatment arm, were reported in Quinn et al. (2006).

Changes in organ donation intention, by intervention group, are shown in Table 10.1. Of the study participants who had not signed an organ donor card at baseline, 17% of control group subjects, 29% of the basic intervention group,

Table 10.1   Change in organ donation intention, by intervention group

	% No at Baseline[1]	Of No at Baseline, % Yes at Post-Tx[2]	p Value for Change[3]
Control ($n = 137$)	44	17	.454
Basic ($n = 172$)	50	29	.001
Enhanced ($n = 179$)	42	31	.022

[1] Percentage of respondents who reported at baseline that they had *not* signed an organ donor card.
[2] Percentage of respondents reporting at baseline that they had *not* signed an organ donor card who report at follow-up that they had signed an organ donor card.
[3] McNemar's test.

Table 10.2 Change in family notification of organ donation intention,
by intervention group

	% No *at Baseline*[1]	*Of* No *at Baseline,* % Yes *at Post-Tx*[2]	p *Value for Change*[3]
Control (*n* = 137)	53	44	.001
Basic (*n* = 172)	49	47	.001
Enhanced (*n* = 179)	47	39	.001

[1] Percentage of respondents who reported at baseline that they had *not* discussed their organ donation intention with their family.

[2] Percentage of respondents reporting at baseline that they had *not* discussed their organ donation intention with their family who report at follow-up that they had discussed their organ donation intention with their family.

[3] McNemar's test.

and 31% of the enhanced intervention group reported having signed an organ donor card at one-month follow-up. The change observed in the control group was not statistically significant, whereas the changes in the basic and enhanced intervention groups were statistically significant ($p < 0.001$ and $p < 0.002$, respectively). Changes in organ donation intention observed in the basic and enhanced intervention groups were significantly different from change observed in the control group ($p = 0.001$ and 0.048), whereas the basic and enhanced intervention groups were not statistically different from each other ($p = 0.825$). There was no significant change in organ donation attributable to recruitment message ($p = 0.386$), nor was there a significant recruitment message by treatment arm interaction ($p = 0.572$).

Table 10.2 depicts changes in family notification of organ donation intention stratified by intervention group. For example, of those study participants who at baseline had not informed their families of their organ donation intention, 44% of control group subjects, 47% of the basic intervention group, and 39% of the enhanced intervention group reported having had notified their families of their organ donation intention upon one-month follow-up. The changes observed in all three groups were statistically significant (all p values < 0.001), but there were no statistically significant between-group differences. Results indicated that participants from the basic intervention group and the enhanced intervention group were no more likely than participants from the control group to inform their families of their organ donation intention ($p = 0.685$ and 0.564, respectively).

Table 10.3 shows changes in family members' organ donation intention stratified by intervention group. As shown, the percentage of study participants' family members who were reported as having signed organ donor cards increased significantly in the control ($p = 0.016$), basic intervention ($p < 0.001$),

Table 10.3   Change in mean percentage of family members reported having signed organ donor cards, by intervention group

	% at Baseline[1]	% at Post-Tx[2]	p Value for Change[3]
Control (n = 137)	10	14	.016
Basic (n = 172)	9	17	.001
Enhanced (n = 179)	10	17	.001

[1] Mean percentage of respondents' family members who were reported at baseline as having signed organ donor cards.
[2] Mean percentage of respondents' family members who were reported at follow-up as having signed organ donor cards.
[3] Paired *t*-tests.

and enhanced intervention groups ($p < 0.001$). There were no significant differences between intervention groups in percentage of participants' family members who reported having signed organ donor cards ($p = 0.350$).

Discussion

We faced a number of challenges in planning and conducting our work site educational program to promote organ donation. These challenges, which threatened both internal and external validity, were encountered at each phase of the study, including intervention development, subject recruitment, work site randomization, and impact assessment. Although these challenges were not insurmountable, they required flexibility in program design and some clarity regarding what we considered to be minimally required study controls and measures, along with careful tracking of potential confounds.

Our theory-driven and behaviorally targeted work site intervention appeared effective in modifying individuals' organ donation intention. Over baseline, increases in organ donation intention in the basic and enhanced intervention groups were approximately 30%, whereas control group increases were only 17%. These data suggest that a relatively brief (i.e., approximately 45 minutes), multicomponent intervention that targets increased awareness, social consciousness, decisional balance, and action strategies can significantly impact organ donation intentions in corporate work site settings.

Of interest, our control condition was as effective as the basic and enhanced interventions in increasing family notification and third-party persuasion of family members to modify organ donation intention. In promoting family notification, the magnitude of change was substantial. Across all three conditions, an increase in family notification of organ donation intention was approximately

40%. This increase in family notification was greater than the observed increase in individuals' organ donation intentions, suggesting that some of the observed increase in family notification was related to individuals who were opposed to organ donation informing their families of their lack of intent. Of the 130 participants who reported at baseline and follow-up that they had not signed an organ donor card, 28% (*n* = 36) reported having communicated their views on organ donation to their families upon follow-up. These data suggest that even a relatively low-intensity intervention may be sufficient to prompt family communication about preexisting and salient donor intentions, but may not be sufficient to change those intentions.

The observed change in family members' organ donation intention, although statistically significant, was of a lesser magnitude. Across conditions, we observed an increase in family members' organ donation intention of only 14% to 17%. It is possible that a more intensive, and perhaps longer, intervention may be necessary to realize this family notification and third-party persuasion effect.

The fact that we did not observe an effect for different recruitment messages is somewhat puzzling. One might expect that individuals who respond to an invitation to a "presentation on organ donation" would be quite different from those who respond to an invitation to a "health education seminar," with the former group being more favorably biased toward organ donation, more likely to have already made a personal commitment to their organ donation intention, and, if not, more likely to respond favorably to the study interventions. However, no effect for different recruitment messages was observed. It may be that many of the study participants routinely attended their companies' lunch-and-learn seminars and that the particular content of the programs, or the content of the recruitment message, was not particularly salient. Alternatively, work sites that promised to recruit participants to a "health education seminar" may have actually informed many or all participants that the program was about organ donation. As a consequence, there may have been little to no difference in the actual recruitment messages.

Study Limitations

One limitation to this study was that we were not able to rule out a potential selection bias. Although our baseline sample of 745 was relatively large, this represented only 5% of the population of corporate employees at the sampled work sites. Because we were not able to obtain data pertaining to relevant characteristics of the employee population, we were not able to compare our sample with the broader population to rule out a selection bias. We did attempt to control for a selection bias associated with preconceptions about organ donation by inviting participants to a purposefully vaguely titled "health education seminar." When five of the 12 corporations insisted on including "organ donation" in their recruitment materials, there were no differences observed in participant characteristics or intervention effectiveness.

A second limitation to this study was that of a potential ceiling effect. At baseline, 52% of our study participants reported that they had already signed an organ donor card. This stands in contrast to national figures that suggest only about 30% have indicated their organ donation intention by signing an organ donor card or joining a donor registry (Guadagnoli et al., 1999). This high percentage of organ donation intention observed at baseline, which may be associated with sociodemographic characteristics of our sample, may have imposed a limit on the amount of change that might otherwise have been observed.

Conclusions

Work site interventions hold significant promise for broadly promoting individuals' commitment to organ donation, yet they also present unique challenges to the design, implementation, and evaluation of those programs. Understanding and anticipating challenges, flexibility, willingness to adapt, and creative tracking of potentially confounding factors are often necessary.

As described above, we faced a number of challenges in implementing this project. Many of these arose from the tension between a desire to use the most rigorous methods possible and our acknowledgment of the practical realities of conducting "real-world" research. These sorts of tensions are not unique to this type of project. For example, efforts to conduct community-based participatory research often require a similarly careful navigation of scientific rigor and fidelity to the principles of community participation in all phases of the research. In general, challenges that arise must be addressed on a case-by-case basis, and often there are creative ways to find a workable middle ground that does not unnecessarily compromise the analytic approach yet remains flexible in light of the unique workplace setting where the research takes place. There are no fixed rules in this regard, and clearly a one-size-fits-all approach does not suffice.

Future work site researchers will undoubtedly be confronted with similar challenges and will have to decide when to compromise scientific rigor for the sake of implementation and when to hold firm for the sake of knowledge creation. To assist researchers with this decision, we recommend they consider the following questions:

1. What impact will this challenge have on the ability to test the study hypotheses?
2. Can we adapt the research design to this challenge in a way that will still allow for a reasonable test of the study's hypotheses?
3. Why has this challenge arisen? What is the underlying cause to this challenge?
4. Are there other ways to address the underlying cause behind the challenge that will maintain the ability to test the study hypotheses?

5. What options exist for moving forward in a way that preserves both the scientific rigor and the practical value of the findings?

Certainly creativity and flexibility, along with a sound grasp of research design and methodology, are important skill sets in conducting work site research.

Acknowledgments

This work was supported by Grant Nos.1-H39-OT-00086-01 and R39-OT-03411-01-00 from the Health Resources and Services Administration (HRSA), Office of Special Programs, Division of Transplantation. Its contents are solely the responsibility of the authors and do not necessarily represent the official views of the HRSA.

References

Alvaro, E. M., Jones, S. P., Robles, A. S., & Siegel, J. T. (2006). Hispanic organ donation: Impact of a Spanish-language organ donation campaign. *Journal of the National Medical Association, 98,* 28–35.

Bull, S. S., Gillette, C., Glasgow, R. E., & Estabrooks, P. (2003). Work site health promotion research: To what extent can we generalize the results and what is needed to translate research to practice? *Health Education and Behavior, 30,* 537–549.

Campbell, D. T., & Stanley, J. C. (1966). *Experimental and quasi-experimental designs for research.* Boston: Houghton Mifflin.

Conrad, K. M., Conrad, K. J., & Walcott-McQuigg, J. (1991). Threats to internal validity in worksite health promotion: Common problems and possible solutions. *American Journal of Health Promotion, 6,* 112–122.

Feldman, R. H. L. (1987). Worksettings: New challenges for health education research. *Health Education Research, 2,* 1–3.

Gallup Organization. (1993). *The American public's attitudes toward organ donation and transplantation.* Princeton, NJ: Author.

Gallup Organization. (2005). *National survey of organ and tissue donation attitudes and behaviors.* Washington, DC: Author.

Guadagnoli, E., Christiansen, C. I., DeJong, W., McNamara, P., Beasley, C., Christiansen, E., et al. (1999). The public's willingness to discuss their preference for organ donation with family members. *Clinical Transplantation, 13,* 342–348.

Lusk, S. L., & Kerr, M. J. (1994). Conducting worksite research: Methodological issues and suggested approaches. *AAOHN Journal, 42,* 177–181.

Prochaska, J. O., DiClemente, C. C., & Norcross, J. C. (1992). In search of how people change. *American Psychologist, 47,* 1102–1114.

Prochaska, J. O., Velicer, W. F., Rossi, J. S., Goldstein, M. G., Marcus, B. H., Rakowski, W., et al. (1994). Stages of change and decisional balance for 12 problem behaviors. *Health Psychology, 13,* 39–46.

Quinn, M. T., Alexander, G. C., Hollingsworth, D., O'Connor, K. G., & Meltzer, D. (2006). Design and evaluation of a workplace intervention to promote organ donation. *Progress in Transplantation, 16,* 253–259.

Terborg, J. R., Hibbard, J., & Glasgow, R. E. (1995). Behavior change at the worksite: Does social support make a difference? *American Journal of Health Promotion, 10,* 125–131.

Thompson, S. E., Smith, B. A., & Bybee, R. F. (2005). Factors influencing participation in worksite wellness programs among minority and underserved populations. *Family and Community Health, 28,* 267–273.

11

Home Care Association of Louisiana (HCLA) Donate Life Workplace Partnership for Organ and Tissue Donation

Carolyn C. Johnson and Larry S. Webber

Introduction

This chapter describes the development, implementation, and evaluation of a Donate Life Workplace Partnership for the purpose of increasing intent to donate through participation in the Louisiana donor registry. The intent was to evaluate a model of a workplace partnership with a statewide professional organization, the Home Care Association of Louisiana (HCLA), as the "workplace" to determine the feasibility of integrating the program into the organization's infrastructure so that personnel and operating costs would not be significantly affected. With HCLA functioning as "program champion," *diffusion of innovation* is described as the blueprint for intervention activities. Formative research, process, and outcome evaluations are presented, as are the challenges and limitations that curtailed the intervention and influenced the outcome.

Problem Statement and Need

The need for organ and tissue transplants in the United States continues to far exceed the actual number of available donations. As of January 26, 2004, the Organ Procurement and Transplantation Network (OPTN) identified 89,112 registrations and 86,336 patients for transplants. From January to October 2003, a total of 21,366 transplants were performed, but, in one year alone (2002), more than 6,000 patients died while waiting. Of note is that kidney transplants accounted for almost two thirds of the need, a need that could be satisfied through living as well as cadaveric donors. As of October 2008, 100,151 wait list registrations have been identified, but there have been only 8,326 donors.

In 2004 in the State of Louisiana, 1,613 individuals (counted by single individual, although many were waiting for multiple transplants) were on the wait list, and 57% of those were African American. As of October 2008, the wait list in Louisiana includes 1,828 individuals, 63% of whom are African American. In South Carolina, a southern state with approximately the same population as Louisiana, the wait list includes 749 names, less than half the number identified in Louisiana. It should be noted that the population distribution in Louisiana is roughly two thirds Caucasian and one third African American. Yet the transplant need among African Americans was, and continues to be, disproportionately higher than that of Caucasians. It was anticipated that at least one third of the individuals targeted through the following described worksite program would be African American, a segment of the population in which a great need for organ and tissue donation exists but that is not highly represented among donors or individuals stating their intent to donate.

Legacy Organ and Tissue Donor Registry

A single organ procurement organization (OPO) serves the State of Louisiana. The Louisiana Organ Procurement Agency (LOPA) fully funds and administers the Legacy Organ and Tissue Donor Registry (hereafter, "Registry"). The Registry originated with an oral yes/no donation response at the Louisiana Office of Motor Vehicles (OMV). In its first 11 years, 225,000 individuals joined the Registry. In 1995, LOPA and the OMV began utilizing a donor registry form with a focus on increasing donor awareness activities throughout the state. Two years later in 1997, LOPA expanded registry accessibility to areas outside of the OMV offices to include public places, such as hospitals, community centers, and health fairs. LOPA made registration available on the Internet in 1999. In addition to the OMV, LOPA community presentations, and a Web site, in 2001 the Health Resources and Services Administration (HRSA) through the Division of Transplantation (DoT) funded a community-based kiosk program for additional registration opportunities. As of year end 2003, more than 1 million people had documented in the Registry their intent to donate, but this number represented less than 25% of the state population. Even this low proportion of registrants was believed to be inflated because of double entries resulting from different methods or name changes, as well as failure to delete individuals who have relocated or died. Because of privacy issues, LOPA has been unable to update the Registry, and therefore registration percentages would always be somewhat inflated. This is a common problem with most state registries.

Donate Life Workplace Partnership Programs

One method for increasing registrations in state donor registries is the Workplace Partnership for Life. The Workplace Partnership has been championed by the secretary of the U.S. Department of Health and Human Services (DHHS), and supported and promoted by the Division of Transplantation of the Health Resources and Services Administration. Through Workplace Partnerships, adults can be reached in a very personal way and within a common work culture, providing a mutually supportive environment in which to "vote yes . . . to donate the gift of life." Additionally, the workplace provides a great venue for utilizing diffusion of innovation principles to address organ and tissue donation. One problem that has surfaced relative to workplace partnerships is that an agency or corporation may register for and implement a program, but without incorporation into the particular work culture, it will not be sustained. When the Home Care Association of Louisiana (HCLA) decided to champion the Donate Life program, it was agreed that the main goal of the HCLA program was to test a model that could be adapted into the infrastructure of this or any kind of professional organization and be sustained over time, even with administrative turnover and economic uncertainty.

Home Care Association of Louisiana

The Home Care Association of Louisiana (HCLA) is a professional organization that serves all members of the home health care industry in Louisiana. A total of 220 home care agencies in Louisiana represents approximately 8,000–10,000 individuals who are nurses; nurse aides; administrative and billing personnel; physical, speech, and occupational therapists; and medical social workers. By year end 2003, 150 of these agencies were HCLA members and 10 ancillary organizations were associate members, representing an estimated total of 6,500–7,500 individuals. HCLA also serves the additional agencies and individuals that are not HCLA members, and these 8,000–10,000 individuals, both HCLA members and nonmembers, were the primary target population for the HCLA Workplace Partnership.

Membership in HCLA requires licensure for home health care work and payment of annual dues. Benefits to home care workers for membership in HCLA include discounted tuition for educational workshops, communications about updates in the industry through the Web site and e-mail, and the benefit of advocacy activities for legislation and policy on behalf of the home health industry. In recent years, HCLA has experienced continuous growth in its membership and a retention rate of almost 100%. HCLA provides communication, education, and advocacy to its members and nonmembers in the home care industry.

> *Communication*: HCLA internal communiqués with members and other state and national organizations within the industry are part of HCLA's daily activities. HCLA also views communicating with the public, the press, and other provider groups as key to their success as a trade association.
>
> *Education*: The home health industry has been inundated with congressional and regulatory change over the past 15 years. The magnitude of these changes has necessitated frequent seminars, workshops, and conferences to educate home care workers about these changes. HCLA holds various educational workshops each year in multiple venues around the state, as well as management, administrative, and billing workshops. HCLA also coordinates the educational content for the state and multistate conferences.
>
> *Advocacy*: HCLA provides monitoring, education, and guidance for the innumerable legislative and regulatory issues for home health care at both the state and federal levels. HCLA advocacy also involves working with fiscal intermediaries for Medicare, Medicaid, and sometimes managed care and private pay.

Within this framework of the HCLA professional organization and Louisiana home care industry, the Donate Life Workplace Partnership was adapted and implemented. The administrators of HCLA "felt strongly that the Home Care Association should be involved in promoting a cause that enhances our health care community and our industry's image." HCLA has demarcated six regions within the state—northwest (Shreveport), northeast (Monroe), southwest (Lafayette), southeast (New Orleans), central (Alexandria), and east (Baton Rouge)—with each region centralized around the major metropolitan city in the area. This regional separation allows HCLA to organize and cover the industry with needed educational, technical assistance, and advocacy activities. Meaningful for the Donate Life program was that HCLA as program champion has coverage across the entire state and not in just one location, whereas a single site workplace program would provide exposure only to those individuals who have contact with that single site.

Theoretical Guidance

The theory from which guidance was drawn for the proposed work was *diffusion of innovation* (Rogers, 1964), specifically because its principles are such a strong fit with the current work. The theoretical innovation is defined as "an idea, practice or object that is perceived as new by an individual or other unit of adoption."

Diffusion is viewed as "the process by which an innovation is communicated through certain channels over time among the members of a social system." The theory specifies that it is important that the focus of the program extend beyond adoption of the innovation, which is only one step in a multistage process. When the innovative program succeeds "in achieving a lasting and meaningful impact," then dissemination beyond the boundaries of the champion organization is where the greatest "reach" should be realized. Some of the theoretical attributes that have been identified as contributing to successful dissemination will be applied to the Donate Life Workplace Partnership and its dissemination:

1. relative advantage (will be better than what it replaced)
2. compatibility (fits the intended audience)
3. complexity (flexible and easy to implement)
4. time, commitment, and risk (minimal investment in time, and modest commitment and minimal risk)
5. trialability (a feasible enterprise)
6. observable and measurable
7. communicability (clearly understood).

The concept of program champion is not only important but also pivotal in the diffusion process, and HCLA will assume that role initially, but it was planned that multiple secondary program champions would be recruited and trained for greater "reach" throughout the state.

In the HCLA program, the "unit of adoption" was HCLA and the "social system" was the home care industry in Louisiana, with diffusion expected to take place within an expanded social system consisting of HCLA members and non-members. The home health care industry is a social system bound by a common philosophy and mission, regulated by both federal and state policies and legislation, and benefited by self-determined advocacy. The Donate Life Workplace Partnership would be an innovative component incorporated into the day-to-day activities of HCLA, the unit of adoption, for the purpose of increasing registrations of potential organ and tissue donors.

Key theoretical constructs utilized by HCLA were communication channels and diffusion context. The communication channels relevant to the program were varied, and, therefore, the collective "reach" of multiple channels was widespread. For example, presentations at regional HCLA technical assistance workshops and consistent reminders within the e-mail system and the HCLA Web site were used to maintain awareness of HCLA as the champion for the Donate Life program and encourage members to participate. Diffusion of innovation theory identifies five "adopter" categories that are similar to the stages of change but with the focus on the individual rather than on a staged process. In the HCLA program, however, three adopter categories were identified: workers in the industry already registered (i.e. workers who were already in the donor registry at the time the program was initiated), home health workers and community members who stated their intent to donate in response to the intervention by completing registration materials, and individuals who registered and provided evidence of family notification.

Beyond the adoption of this innovative program, diffusion would occur through dissemination into the community. A plan was therefore developed to recruit individuals within HCLA member agencies to bring the Donate Life message into the community. Theoretical attributes that have contributed to successful dissemination and were planned for use in the HCLA Donate Life Partnership were compatibility with the intended audience, ease of implementation, determining feasibility, minimal time and resource investment, communicability (the ability to be easily understood), and observable and measurable results.

Program Goal and Objectives

The overriding purpose of the proposed work was to increase the number of adults who are registered as organ and tissue donors in the State of Louisiana, and to obtain concomitant verification of family notification of intent to donate. The goals were to evaluate the feasibility and effectiveness of a Donate Life model for a Workplace Partnership program for the Home Care Association of Louisiana (HCLA). As the professional organization for the home care industry in Louisiana, HCLA would "promote . . . organ donor awareness and acceptance as a natural part of the end-of-life process." Through the use of diffusion of innovation theoretical principles, HCLA as program "champion" would engage in communication, education, motivation, and recruitment efforts with its membership, and advocate community activism beyond its membership to increase intent to donate demonstrated by registration in the Louisiana Legacy Organ and Tissue Donor Registry.

In summary, the purpose was to implement and evaluate a Donate Life Workplace Partnership *model* for donor registration that could be incorporated into the existing infrastructure of HCLA. Should this model be feasible and effective, then the model could be applied to other professional organizations without substantially increasing personnel or operating costs.

Intervention Objectives

The following were the specific intervention objectives for accomplishing the above purpose and goals:

1. Conduct formative research through focus groups in various HCLA regions around the state to inform the intervention regarding effective messaging

techniques, the most viable HCLA communication channels, and community venues that could be used for community recruitment for intent to donate.

2. Adapt Donate Life messages and presentation content to fit the HCLA target audience through information obtained from formative research.

3. Adapt Donate Life messages and presentations to a variety of communication channels (e.g., educational workshops, statewide conferences, multistate conferences, Web site, and e-mail).

4. Develop a network of HCLA volunteers to bring the Donate Life message into the community.

5. Continue implementation of the HCLA Donate Life Workplace partnership for a 2-year period.

Evaluation Objectives

In order to evaluate the feasibility of conducting a Workplace Partnership within a professional (or trade) organization, and to document the number of registrations achieved through program implementation, the following evaluation objectives were identified:

1. Develop and pilot test a survey for HCLA members that can be used for formative research.

2. Administer the survey with HCLA members to determine current donor registration status, knowledge, and beliefs and attitudes regarding organ and tissue donation.

3. Effect mechanisms through which donor registration and family notification can be measured (i.e. registration through a program-designated Web site and through registration cards).

4. Confirm validity of outcome data by developing a registry data feedback loop with LOPA by which donor registrations resulting from this program can be verified and potential contamination documented and controlled.

5. Conduct a postintervention survey similar to baseline to determine self-reported changes in beliefs and attitudes, registration status, community activities relative to intent to donate, and perceived impact on the organization, its members, and relevant communities.

6. Document process evaluation in terms of "reach, context, and fidelity."

Formative Research

Both quantitative and qualitative methods were used to obtain information for program development and evaluate receptivity to the HCLA Donate Life campaign. The focus groups were conducted early after funding, and the survey was implemented after attempts were made to identify the number of agencies within the state and the number of employees at each agency.

Formative Focus Groups

Seven focus groups were held with home health care agency executives and staff who represented large versus small and urban versus rural agencies in multiple locations throughout the state. There were a total of 33 participants who were predominantly female (79%), Caucasian (85%), and married (80%). Executives generally were better educated; had a broader knowledge of organ donation, wait lists, and organ assignment; and were more confident than staff about and willing to become community ambassadors for organ and tissue donation. One of the participants mentioned that she had been putting LOPA flyers into their agency's admit packets for quite a while. All participants agreed that organ donation was a natural way to prolong life, and several knew someone who had a transplant or had donated an organ (e.g., "My sister is having a liver transplant this week," and "My friend's sister had a liver and pancreas transplant 2 years ago, and she's doing great"). During this discussion, it was clear that the participants were completely in favor organ and tissue donation. They were smiling and talking about people's lives being saved, and there was no negative feedback. Some were a little concerned because of how their families would react, but stated that most people in the health care field would be in favor of organ and tissue donation as a way to save lives.

Participants thought that family discussions should occur early and that no one should change a person's decision to donate (e.g., "I would be really angry if anyone tried to change that"). Participants in every focus group expressed their anger at this idea and asked if the family could still change their decision if they registered and put it in their will or living will. This seemed to be a real concern, and they wanted to know more about this. Both groups believed that religion and common myths were barriers to becoming a donor (e.g., "I had a patient who needed a blood transfusion but wouldn't get it because it was against her religion"); however, they believed that myths could be overcome through an educational campaign. Many clinical questions surfaced that could be addressed in an educational campaign (e.g., kinds of organs recovered, age of donors and recipients, and practical issues such as open versus closed casket, brain death, surgical procedures, and other information about recipients). Suggestions were given concerning communication messages (e.g., "I think testimonials would be really effective, especially if they were by our own people"), methods, and incentives. They suggested a competition between agencies, and most strongly suggested having food at registration events along with incentives, such as lapel pins, pens, pencils, and so on. Potential community agency contacts were also identified, including law enforcement, fire departments, schools and universities, churches, and civic organizations. It was acknowledged that the cost of the focus groups was offset by the acquisition of useful formative data that assisted in the development of the intervention.

Formative Survey

A survey was developed by the consortium and pilot tested with graduate students at the Tulane School of Public Health and Tropical Medicine prior to field administration. Based on feedback from pilot testing, some questions were deleted, and wording changes were made in others. The resulting survey included three domains: demographic information; knowledge, attitudes, and beliefs; and family information about organ donation. The response format was a 5-point Likert-type scale, with response options ranging from *strongly disagree* (code = 1) to *strongly agree* (code = 5); the higher the score, the more positive the response.

A total of 781 home health care workers responded in 2005 to the survey. Information on gender or ethnicity was missing for 28 respondents, and they were excluded from most analyses. The sample sizes for Hispanics, American Indians, Asians, and Other racial and ethnic groups were very small; hence, these were grouped together as *Other* ethnicity for most analyses. Respondents included 40 (5.3%) Caucasian males, 498 (66.1%) Caucasian females, 9 (1.2%) African American males, 178 (23.6%) African American females, 9 (0.5%) Other males, and 24 (3.2%) Other females. Consistent with a priori expectations and the racial distribution for the state, the sample was approximately two thirds Caucasian and one third African American. It was also clear that the vast majority of respondents were female, which is consistent with the home care workforce. The mean age of the respondents was 42.2 years. Mean ages were similar for the various gender and racial and ethnic groups, ranging from 34.4 for Other males to 42.7 for Caucasian females.

Overall, the majority of respondents (about 64%) were married, and married status ranged from 25% for Other males to almost 72% for Caucasian females (Table 11.1). About 17% were single, 15.7% divorced or separated, and only about 3% widowed. The proportion of participants who were single was greater for African American females and Other females than for Caucasian females. The proportion divorced or separated was greatest for African American males, followed by Caucasian females and African American females.

Some 37.1% of the respondents had some college or training, with an additional 21% having an associate degree and 24.5% having a college degree (Table 11.1). Education level differed by gender and racial and ethnic group (Table 11.1). Among the Caucasian males, 55% had a college degree, perhaps indicating that a higher proportion of these respondents were owners or administrators for the home health

Table 11.1   Marital Status and Education of Participants by Ethnicity and Sex, HCLA Donate Life Baseline Survey, 2005

Demographic	Caucasian Males	Caucasian Females	African American Males	African American Females	Other Males	Other Females	Total
Marital status	n (%)	n (%)	n (%)	n (%)	n (%)	n (%)	n (%)
Married	27 (67.5)	358 (71.9)	6 (66.7)	81 (45.5)	1 (25.0)	10 (41.7)	483 (64.1)
Single	9 (22.5)	42 (8.4)	1 (11.1)	62 (34.8)	3 (75.0)	10 (41.7)	127 (16.9)
Divorced or separated	3 (7.5)	85 (17.1)	2 (22.2)	26 (14.6)	0 (0.0)	2 (8.3)	118 (15.7)
Widowed	1 (2.5)	13 (2.6)	0 (0.0)	9 (5.1)	0 (0.0)	2 (8.3)	25 (3.3)
Total	40 (100)	498 (100)	9 (100)	178 (100)	4 (100)	24 (100)	753 (100)
Education							
< High school	0 (0.0)	4 (0.8)	0 (0.0)	4 (2.3)	0 (0.0)	0 (0.0)	8 (1.1)
High school or GED	1 (2.5)	62 (12.4)	0 (0.0)	57 (32.0)	1 (25.0)	2 (8.3)	123 (16.3)
Some college or vocational training	6 (15.0)	169 (33.9)	6 (66.7)	85 (47.8)	0 (0.0)	14 (58.3)	280 (37.1)
Associate degree	11 (27.5)	128 (25.7)	1 (11.1)	12 (6.7)	1 (25.0)	5 (20.8)	158 (21.0)
College degree	22 (55.0)	136 (27.2)	2 (22.2)	20 (11.2)	2 (50.0)	3 (12.5)	185 (24.5)
Total	40 (100)	499 (100)	9 (100)	178 (100)	4 (100)	24 (100)	754 (100)

care agencies. Only 13.2% of the Caucasian females compared to 34.3% of the African American females had a high school degree or less.

Organ donation registration status differed by sex and racial or ethnic group (Table 11.2). For each racial or ethnic group, organ donation registration was higher for females than males. Among Caucasian respondents, 52.2% of the females compared to 42.5% of the males reported registration. Among African American respondents, 22.5% of the females compared to 22.2% of the males indicated registration. Among those in the Other racial or ethnic group, 41.7% of the females compared to 25% of the males indicated registration. About 5% of the respondents did not know if they were registered. So, more females than males and more Caucasians than African Americans indicated that they had already registered their intent to donate.

The formative survey consisted of 21 questions. As mentioned previously, a higher score indicated greater agreement with the question (*strongly agree* = 5; *strongly disagree* = 1). Two questions were reverse coded to the positive direction. Factor analysis of the formative survey produced three factors with items that loaded heavily onto those factors: (a) attitudes and beliefs about organ and tissue donation (9 items), (b) family discussion (4 items), and (c) beliefs about organ

Table 11.2   Organ Donation Registration Status of Participants by Ethnicity and Sex, HCLA Donate Life Baseline Survey, 2005

Registration	Caucasian Males	Caucasian Females	African American Males	African American Females	Other Males	Other Females	Total
	n (%)	n (%)	n (%)	n (%)	n (%)	n (%)	n (%)
Yes	17 (42.5)	260 (52.2)	2 (22.2)	40 (22.5)	1 (25.0)	10 (41.7)	330 (43.8)
No	20 (50.0)	212 (42.6)	5 (55.6)	132 (74.2)	3 (75.0)	13 (54.2)	385 (51.1)
Don't know	3 (7.5)	26 (5.2)	2 (22.2)	6 (3.4)	0 (0.0)	1 (4.2)	38 (5.0)
Total	40 (100)	498 (100)	9 (100)	178 (100)	4 (100)	24 (100)	753 (100)

recipients (2 items) (Table 11.3). Two behavior items hung together, but weakly, and the coefficient alpha was very poor; therefore, those two items, as well as the other four that did not load well on any factor, were eliminated from analysis. Inasmuch as the Other ethnic category included very small numbers of Asians, Latinos, and others, it was felt this category would be difficult to interpret; therefore, the analysis for the three factors included only African Americans and Caucasians. This resulted in a total of 620 respondents (Table 11.3).

The means for the attitudes and beliefs factor were at the high end of the range, indicating a high level of positive responses. An ethnic difference at the $p = 0.06$ level and an ethnic by gender interaction at the $p = 0.06$ level were observed. The interaction was a result of a difference in mean scores between African American males and females with the males scoring higher. This difference was not observed for Caucasians. There was a significant ethnic difference for the family discussion factor, indicating lower mean scores for African Americans than for Caucasians. The mean scores for beliefs about organ recipients were non-significant for gender or ethnicity.

In summary, the respondent sample was representative of the racial distribution of the state, but was highly skewed toward females and married individuals who were, on average, middle-aged. Although some gender and racial differences were observed in attitudes and beliefs, overall the indications were that the sample's attitudes and beliefs were very positive regarding organ donation and family discussion issues.

Although another survey had been planned near the end of the program, it was decided not to administer the second survey. One reason was the length of time required for multiple mailings to obtain less than 800 surveys. Although it was not possible to determine an actual response rate because of the absence of a well-defined denominator, the final rate should be low when considering the

Table 11.3   Means for Knowledge, Attitudes, and Beliefs, HCLA Donate Life Baseline
Survey, 2005

Domain

Attitudes and beliefs about organ and tissue donation[1] (9 questions; range 9–45)
Donation is a natural way to prolong life.
Donation is a good thing.
Donation is consistent with moral values and beliefs.
Would receive organ from a person of a different race.
Willing to donate organ to a person of a different race.
Trust doctors and hospitals to use organs as intended.
Doctors try just as hard to save my life whether or not I plan to be organ donor.
Donation is a safe, effective practice.
I support organ donation.
Cronbach's alpha coefficient = 0.89

Family discussion[2] (4 questions; range 4–20)
Important to discuss my wishes with family.
Comfortable talking to family about being donor.
Believe family would support my decision.
Already shared my decision with family.
Cronbach's alpha coefficient = 0.83.

Beliefs about organ recipients[3] (2 questions; range 2–10)
With equal need, a poor person has the same chance.
Most people who need a transplant get one.
Cronbach's alpha coefficient = 0.42

---

[1] Ethnicity, $F = 3.52$, $p = 0.061$; gender*ethnicity, $F = 3.44$, $p = 0.064$.
[2] Ethnicity, $F = 5.40$, $p = 0.021$.
[3] N.S.

estimated number of employees working in home care agencies around the state
that are members of HCLA. It was realized that a low response rate coupled with
the length of time involved made administration of a second survey infeasible.
Another reason for deciding not to administer a second survey was that overall
attitudes about organ and tissue donation were very positive among the respondent group. Although the responses obtained from this sample could not be
considered representative of the overall industry, they still provided indications
that the intervention did not have to focus on changing attitudes and beliefs; rather,
it should focus more on creating opportunities for the target group to declare
their intent to donate by registering in the Legacy Registry. If attitudes and beliefs

Overall Mean (SD) (N = 620)	Caucasian Males (n = 32)	Caucasian Females (n = 427)	African American Males (n = 9)	African American Females (n = 152)
37.8 (5.6)	38.5	38.5	39.4	35.5
16.8 (3.3)	16.8	17.4	16.1	15.2
4.8 (1.8)	4.8	4.8	4.0	4.9

did not require intervention and registrations would be documented through other means, then an additional survey administration was unnecessary.

The HCLA Donate Life Workplace Partnership Program

Table 11.4 contains a summary of the project activities for the HCLA Workplace Partnership Consortium. The main thrust of the partnership was to incorporate branding for Donate Life into the infrastructure of HCLA so that its members would become aware of HCLA's support for the Donate Life concept and its status

Table 11.4   HCLA Donate Life Workplace Intervention Activities by Consortium

Consortium Member	Consortium Roles and Responsibilities
HCLA	Present the Donate Life message at or during: • Educational workshops • State and multistate conferences • HCLA Web site • E-mail messages and newsletters • Office phone greeting • HCLA stationery
LOPA	• Provide incentives for registrations • Provide brochures and materials for the registry • Review information dissemination about organ and tissue donation • Check the Registry for repeat registrations
Tulane	• Conduct process evaluation through observation at presentations and monitoring other activities • Maintain statistical tables of registrations from the registration Web site and write reports • Coordinate meetings and conference calls • Mail cards to families for family notification

as program champion. Using diffusion of innovation as a guide, HCLA infiltrated its various communication channels with Donate Life messages. Domains covered in all messages were awareness, education, and encouragement to register.

The intervention was initially planned in two phases. The first phase would pivot around HCLA as the program champion, and a low-cost diffusion program would use all of the HCLA communication channels specifically for the purpose of encouraging registration among home health care employees, not clients of home care agencies. The second phase of the intervention would pivot around home health care industry volunteers as program champions who would diffuse the program into the community.

HCLA Communication Channels and Diffusion Context (Phase 1)

The communication channels that were operative within the HCLA system and were the main conduits for bringing the Donate Life program to HCLA member agencies were educational workshops, the HCLA Web site, e-mail messages, and state and multistate conferences. Additional branding was accomplished by adding the Donate Life logo to the HCLA stationery and adding "Donate Life" to the HCLA telephone greeting.

HCLA workshops and meetings
A Donate Life presentation was planned for all HCLA workshops and meetings throughout the state. The presentations ranged in length from 5 to 20 minutes. Presentation content included awareness and education through presentation of data and need, the sponsorship by HCLA and its partnering with LOPA and Tulane University, the rationale for involvement in this humanitarian effort by the home care people, and encouragement to complete "intent to donate" cards for registration, as well as a request for attendees to discuss donation with their families. The administrators of HCLA "feel strongly that the Home Care Association should be involved in promoting a cause that enhances our health care community and our industry's image." They indicated that championing such a humanitarian effort was well within the purview of an industry in which the main characteristic is caring. This result is a strong rationale for promoting and encouraging registration to donate among members of the industry.

A special Web site had been developed for registrations resulting from this program, and information about how to access this Web site in order to register was also included in the initial presentations. When it became clear that the Web site was not being used for registrations, the program relied solely on registration cards completed at workshops and other meetings. A graphic illustrating progress toward a goal for registrations was added to the official HCLA Web site, and this graphic was updated regularly with the latest number of registrations obtained.

State and multistate conferences
A booth for Donate Life materials, registration cards, and incentives such as pins, bracelets, and car ribbons was operated in the exhibit section of the annual HCLA statewide conference and the two multistate conferences each year. Texas, New Mexico, Oklahoma, and Louisiana participate in the Southwest Regional Conference, and the Gulf Coast Regional Conference involves Mississippi, Alabama, and Louisiana. Attendees at these multistate conferences included members of the home health care industry as well as individuals from ancillary organizations. The rationale for sponsorship of the Donate Life Partnership by the home health industry was a major focus at these conferences. Registrations obtained from states other than Louisiana were entered into the database as out-of-state registrations and forwarded to the national registry.

HCLA Web site
The Donate Life message and program information became a permanent component of the official HCLA Web site, which had a total of 658,000 hits in 2003. This Web site included a link to the special registration Web site, as well as other Web sites that could provide additional information about organ and

tissue donation. Testimonials were posted on the Web site periodically, as well as community happenings related to organ and tissue donation.

At the inception of the program, HCLA sent weekly e-mail messages to its members. It was planned that one "myth buster" about organ and tissue donation would be incorporated into the e-mail message each week. One example of a myth buster was "No religious organization opposes organ and tissue donation." Shortly after the program started, the e-mail messages were discontinued and their content was incorporated into the HCLA Web site. The myth busters continued to be included in this section of the Web site. A total of 25 unique myth busters were presented at the rate of one a week, and then they were rotated through the sequence over again.

Community Volunteers (Phase 2)

A second phase of the HCLA Donate Life program had been planned in which individuals from the home care industry would be recruited to conduct presentations on organ and tissue donation within their own communities at venues such as churches, schools, civic clubs, and so on. LOPA community educators would train these volunteers to bring the Donate Life message into the community and encourage registration for intent to donate with community members who were not within the home care industry.

Unfortunately, Hurricanes Katrina and Rita interfered with the implementation of the entire HCLA Donate Life program, but interfered most dramatically with the community volunteer phase of the program. It was at least 8 months before HCLA workshops were resumed after Hurricane Katrina, and almost a year before the priorities and mind-set of just about everyone in southern Louisiana returned to more everyday normal activities. As a result, the planned community volunteer phase of the partnership never really got started.

Unplanned Supplemental Activities

Two supplemental activities were initiated toward the end of the funding period to replace the community program component. These activities involved placing payroll stuffers in the payroll check envelopes of the larger agencies around the state, as well as LOPA community educators contacting home care agencies to set up meetings and encourage completion of registration cards. The first pilot trial of the payroll stuffers worked very well, and HCLA subsequently approached the Board of Trustees for its support in encouraging all of the statewide agencies to replicate this process. This activity is ongoing at this time. Initially the LOPA agency visits were infrequent, but currently LOPA is averaging four to five agency meetings a month. One barrier to these agency meetings was the fact that home care workers are more often in the field than in the office; however, whenever a meeting was well attended, the result was completed registration cards.

Evaluation

Process Evaluation

There are many methods for documenting the implementation of a program (i.e., conducting process evaluation); however, priorities for specific methods often need to be established based on need and resources. Process evaluation was one of the major responsibilities of the Tulane component of the consortium; therefore, resources relative to staff, time, and funding involved documenting the following process variables: (a) contextual factors, (b) reach, and (c) program fidelity.

Contextual factors

Contextual factors, those happenings that are beyond the control of the program but that could affect the implementation and outcome of the program, were documented by staff. All program activities and outcomes need to be considered within the context of these factors. Of course, for the HCLA Partnership, the largest negative contextual factor was the impact of Hurricanes Katrina and Rita. Another example of a documented contextual factor was the absence of the governor at the campaign kickoff in July 2005, an event she had committed to attend. As a result, the media dropped its interest, and the expected exposure did not take place.

Reach

Reach, or participation by the targeted audience, was recorded at every event and was also used as the denominator for registrations completed at those events. At small meetings and workshops, Tulane staff counted the number of attendees. At larger meetings such as regional conferences, official meeting registrations were counted. Participation ranged from a few attendees (skills-specific workshops) to several hundred (multistate conferences). The percent of registrations obtained ranged from 0% to nearly 50%. The highest registration rates were obtained over the first series of meetings and workshops throughout the first year of the program. After that, registration rates declined because attendance consisted mostly of repeat attendees.

Fidelity

The final process measure was fidelity, which answered the question about faithfulness of the program content to planned protocols. Staff monitored the HCLA Web site weekly for the Donate Life logo, testimonials, and announcements about the program. The newsletter, which was incorporated into the Web site, was monitored for the appearance of myth busters. Presentations at meetings and workshops were observed by Tulane staff to determine if presentations contained all of the essential elements. A checklist with key elements was prepared and reviewed as each element was presented. Initially, presentations at meetings and workshops were inconsistent, with key elements being omitted; however, over time with feedback from the process evaluator, the presentations improved dramatically.

Registrations

To date, almost 700 completed registrations have been obtained from individuals in the home health care industry through the efforts of the HCLA Donate Life Workplace Partnership. Although we did not have access to specific agency data, it is reasonable to assume that some of the registrations will have been from agencies that are members of HCLA, whereas others will have been from nonmember agencies. Through the feedback loop with LOPA, it was determined that approximately 18% of these registrations were repeat registrations. These had value, however, because family contact information had been obtained with the completed registration card, and the family was notified of their family member's decision through either e-mail or surface mail by the university in the name of LOPA. Sometimes, however, family contact information was not provided for any registration. This resulted in four categories of registrations obtained: (a) new registrations with family notification, (b) new registrations without family notification, (c) repeat registrations with family notification, and (d) repeat registrations without family notification. At the conclusion of the program in the spring of 2008, all registrations were categorized, and implications of the program relative to intent to donate were evaluated and will be discussed.

A Web site specifically designed for this program for the purpose of receiving and recording registrations was not successful; only two registrations were obtained through the Web site (some of the limitations of the Web site will be discussed later in the chapter). Almost all of the registrations recorded within the program were obtained through the workshops, meetings, and conferences described previously. Attendance at these events varied considerably, ranging from five (technical assistance workshop) to 170 (regional conference); attendance obviously depended on the kind and scope of the meeting. Registration rates were also variable, ranging from 0% (already registered or refusals) to 63%. Interestingly, the larger regional conferences, although providing the largest attendance, did not result in the highest registration rates. Smaller meetings and workshops with more personal interaction resulted in the highest registration rates.

The remainder of the registrations were obtained through the unplanned events described as implemented toward the end of the program: One involved face-to-face presentations, and the other involved payroll stuffers with registration cards.

Challenges and Resolutions

The greatest challenge to the implementation of the program was the impact of Hurricanes Katrina and Rita. On August 29, 2005, Hurricane Katrina hit south and southeastern Louisiana, and Hurricane Rita hit southwestern Louisiana on September 27, 2005. Everything changed. Hurricane Katrina was the worst natural disaster ever experienced on the U.S. mainland, and it totally devastated a major American city. New Orleans was inundated because of multiple levee breaches that brought the waters of Lake Pontchartrain into the city. An additional levee breach brought the waters of the Mississippi River into the lower 9th Ward of New Orleans. Evacuees crowded into other areas of Louisiana and into neighboring states. Tulane University closed its doors, and the Fall 2005 semester was cancelled. There was no access to offices or computers until the middle of December 2005. The mind-set of the entire State of Louisiana was focused on the tragedy, as well as the failures on the part of local, state, and federal governments to provide appropriate leadership or adequate support. All communications in the area had failed, and it was almost 2 months before even phone contact could be made with members of the HCLA Donate Life Consortium.

As soon as it was feasible, an emergency meeting was held at LOPA in the beginning of November 2005. The 10 HCLA workshops originally scheduled for the fall had been cancelled, and it was clear from all who attended this meeting that Hurricanes Katrina and Rita and all of the accompanying devastation, displacements, economic instability, and uncertainty were the priorities and had replaced all else. The first priority for Tulane University, LOPA, HCLA, and its member home care agencies and employees was to successfully maneuver through the aftermath of these storms. It was 8 months before the consortium could start functioning again, and almost a year before the psychological effects eased enough to return fully to the work of the HCLA Donate Life program.

In February 2006, the consortium renewed its dedication to the program, but knew that it would still be some months before the program would get back on track, not only because of the distraction to the principals involved but also because of the ravaged and depleted communities. In April 2006, the partnership began to function again, slowly workshops and meetings were rescheduled, and, in the midst of chaos, interest in the program was renewed. By September 2006, the consortium found it necessary to review its accomplishments in order to decide whether to continue or end the program. The decision was made to continue, and the consortium came together as a team with a common goal and started to move forward even more aggressively than it had prior to the storms. A lot of time had been lost; however, through a no-cost extension, the program remained functional until the spring of 2008.

Another unexpected challenge was the lengthy preparation period prior to kicking off the intervention. Eight months of preparation work included (a) the establishment of consortium relationships and roles through regularly scheduled conference calls and face-to-face meetings; (b) the collection of formative data through focus groups conducted with home health care workers and executives; (c) the collection of information about the home health care agency members of HCLA through mailed surveys; (d) the development, pilot testing, and implementation of mailed baseline surveys to home health care employees; and (e) the development and pilot testing of the HCLA registration Web site, which was our main outcome data source. This unexpected and lengthy preliminary work led to a campaign kickoff immediately prior to Hurricane Katrina, and so the intervention did not have a chance to begin before it was disrupted (as described above).

A third, unexpected challenge observed by the process evaluator was that participants in HCLA workshops in the northern part of the state were less receptive to the Donate Life message than participants in the southern part of the state. The northern HCLA regions include the cities of Shreveport, Monroe, and Alexandria. Even participation in the formative focus groups in these areas was low. Few HCLA workshops were conducted in this part of the state during the program period, and, because interest was generally low and intent-to-donate registrations were few, process evaluation for workshops in these areas was discontinued. It was simply not cost-effective.

A significant challenge was the observed reluctance to implement the community volunteer phase of this project. It has been difficult to ascertain the exact reasons for this, other than the changed physical, economic, and psychological landscape after Hurricanes Katrina and Rita, as well as concerns that volunteer activities would interfere with the target group's professional and work activities. The failure to implement this component of the intervention was unfortunate because the community component was needed for a true dissemination of innovation. Although the professional organization was initially the program champion within the home care industry, it was planned that positive-minded home health care volunteers would become champions within their communities to support and encourage intent to donate through participation in the statewide registry. In this way, the true strength of the dissemination of an innovative idea would have permeated all areas of the state. With the disinterest following Hurricanes Katrina and Rita, however, a true dissemination through multiple secondary champions did not have an opportunity to occur.

Staff turnover and staff unavailability for consortium members have been other challenges. Several HCLA staff who worked with the program resigned, and HCLA was without staff to help with this project until the beginning of 2007. For at least 3 months, no meetings or workshops were held. LOPA also has suffered from staff unavailability and turnover, including the leave of the principal investigator for LOPA in October 2007.

Ongoing technological problems have been experienced with the registration Web site, which was developed by an external technology firm for the purpose of documenting registrations. The Web site was designed for online registrations, but it quickly became apparent that the target audience was not registering on the Web site. The university, therefore, used the Web site mainly for data entry of completed registration cards, and as such, it became the main database for our primary outcome, number of registrations and family notification. Web site problems persisted throughout the program period.

One other challenge, mentioned previously, was that the attendance at workshops and meetings, although remaining at expected levels, comprised mostly repeat attendees. The purpose of the HCLA meetings and workshops is to keep the field apprised of new legislative and policy changes, to upgrade skills, and so on, and thus the same people attend new workshops for this purpose. This limited our contact pool and resulted in a decline in registrations obtained from these face-to-face contact opportunities.

There have certainly been more challenges than most in the implementation of this project. Our efforts are continuing in an effort to increase registrations to goal levels. The challenges we have had and the flexibility required to resolve these challenges have been a learning experience for us, and we believe this information will benefit the field of organ and tissue donation at large. Our goal has been and remains to determine the feasibility of a model that will work for a professional organization championing the Donate Life cause.

Lessons Learned

A major question to be answered by the HCLA Donate Life program was "Could a Donate Life Workplace Partnership, adapted for a professional organization such as HCLA, increase intent to donate among its members?" Clearly, the goal of simply "branding" the professional organization as champion of the Donate Life cause through its various methods of communication was insufficient. The program "dose" was too weak and benign. The expectation that such a "passive" intervention would motivate member agencies and their employees to initiate action on their own to seek registration—although low cost and requiring few resources—was untenable. Much more effective were the face-to-face encounters at workshops, regional meetings, and agency visits, with registration cards in hand offering the immediate and convenient opportunity for registration. Although the branding and messaging by HCLA has continued and will continue, the focus shifted to the most effective activities—any kind of face-to-face contact in which registration cards could be presented and completed.

An important lesson learned from this program is that adversity can be overcome. Although valuable time was lost, the resolve to continue and complete the program was stronger than ever. Quitting was always an option, but continuing was much more of a challenge and much more rewarding.

Practical Implications for the Field

Public Health Issue

It has been almost a decade since programs funded by the Division of Transplantation (DoT), Health Resources and Services Administration (HRSA), have successfully targeted a higher level of awareness and education about organ and tissue donation on a national scale. It may be that the majority of the lay population persists in the perception that the problem is a medical and clinical one. Although actual donation and transplantation are medical and clinical issues, it is our premise that awareness, knowledge, and motivation for intention to donate within the general population comprise a public health issue and need to be treated as such by public health professionals throughout the United States. To date, however, organ and tissue donation has not been mainstreamed into public health work. The American Public Health Association has no caucus or professional section devoted to organ and tissue donation. The same is true for many other health behavioral, educational, and social science organizations. Greater coverage of this issue needs to be achieved at a grassroots level and mainstreamed into the public health consciousness. Two methods of achieving this are feasible: regular presentations at professional health meetings, and Workplace Partnerships.

Donate Life Workplace Partnership for Professional Organizations

A Donate Life Workplace Partnership can be championed by a professional or trade organization. The concept is unique, but it can be done. The expectation that this adaptation can occur without the expenditure of any resources, however, is unrealistic. Partnering with the local organ procurement organization (OPO) can create a valuable alliance in which the professional organization champions the cause and provides access to the population, and the OPO can provide materials, educators, and opportunity for registration for intent to donate. With this kind of alliance, the Donate Life message can reach thousands of individuals at minimal expenditure of resources.

Acknowledgments

This program was supported by the Health Resources and Services Administration (HRSA) and the Department of Transplantation (DoT) through Grant No. 1 R39OT03409-01-00.

The authors would like to acknowledge the efforts of the Home Care Association of Louisiana (HCLA) in championing this effort and providing access to the target population for this study. A special and heartfelt "thank you" goes to Mr. Warren Hebert, RN, CHCE, CAE, the CEO of HCLA. He has been diligent, persevering, and committed to this humanitarian effort, even in the face of many trials and tribulations. Warren, thanks to you, your staff, and all of the good folks of Louisiana in the home health care industry, whose participation made this project possible.

No less of an acknowledgment should be awarded to the Louisiana Organ Procurement Agency (LOPA) for their role in this project. Of special note are Mr. Chris McCrory, MBA, director of development for LOPA for most of the program period; and Ms. Lana Stevens, LOPA community educator, both of whom have worked closely with Tulane University and HCLA and have been equally committed to this project.

Reference

Organ Procurement and Transplantation Network. (2004). [Home page]. Retrieved May 31, 2009, from http://www.optn.org

Rogers, Everett H. (1964). *Diffusion of Innovations*, Glencoe: Free Press.

12

Promoting Organ Donation Through College Student Campaigns

Thomas Hugh Feeley, Ashley E. Anker,
Donald E. Vincent, and Carla R. Williams

The national shortage of organs has attracted the attention of behavioral and social scientists over the past decade (e.g., Morgan & Miller, 2001; Siminoff, Gordon, Hewlett, & Robert, 2001; Smith, Kopfman, Massi Lindsey, Yoo, & Morrison, 2004). Advances in medical and clinical sciences have made organ and tissue donation a safe and popular health solution as evidenced by the approximately 100,000 individuals who now await a solid-organ donor (United Network for Organ Sharing, 2008). Recent research by Sheehy and colleagues (Sheehy et al., 2003) contends that increasing the number of individuals who *consent to donate* is the most promising solution to the critical shortage of donors. Data from organ procurement organizations (OPOs) indicate only 54% of eligible donors consent to donate, and 42% of those eligible actually become donors (Sheehy et al.). It is estimated that over 7,000 donors are lost yearly in the United States, and this number becomes more discouraging when you consider that one donor can provide tissue and up to eight organs to potential recipients.

The challenge for health care organizations and scholars is to identify effective interventions to increase awareness of the critical shortage of donors. An important direct outcome for any campaign is to increase the percentage of adults who notify next of kin of their donation intentions. Ideally, notification would occur through interpersonal communication with family regarding one's decision, but placement of one's name on state donor registries has also been found to assist families in making end-of-life donation decisions (Siminoff, Lawrence, & Arnold, 2003). Such actions are imperative to the success of transplantation medicine, as organ procurement professionals typically will not allow an organ donation to proceed without consent from next of kin, even if the eligible donor's intentions to donate are known (Wendler & Dickert, 2001). Even in states with first-person consent laws allowing individuals to legally document their donor status, families are still typically consulted about donation at the time of death (Institute of Medicine, 2006; Wendler & Dickert, 2001). Next of kin typically respect the wishes of the deceased (regardless of whether the wishes are for or against donation); however, too few families discuss donation (Siminoff et al., 2001).

Interventions and health education campaigns can benefit greatly from the wealth of recent research on the topic of organ donation. Scholars in education (Rubens, Oleckno, & Cisla, 1998), communication (Morgan, Miller, & Arasaratnam, 2002), social and preventive medicine (Tamburlin & Rice, 2002), and social psychology (Radecki & Jaccard, 1997; Shanteau & Harris, 1990) are studying organ donation from a number of vantage points. Results amassed from this literature converge on several findings: (a) Individuals self-report positive attitudes about the topic of organ donation, (b) approximately 50% of adults consider themselves registered or intended donors, and (c) differences exist in donation attitudes and intentions by race and education level. Motivated by such findings, the present chapter describes the development and evaluation of a college course designed to translate students' positive attitudes toward donation into behaviors (i.e., registration and communication of intentions to next of kin). It was proposed that the course would influence donation behaviors at two levels, impacting the donation behaviors of course participants themselves and those of individuals in the surrounding college community.

Active Learning: A Conceptual Model for Campaign Course Design

Overview and Effectiveness of Active Learning

The organ donation college course was developed under the premise that the course would be most effective if it included techniques designed to engage students in active learning processes. *Active learning* can be considered any pedagogical technique or activity that promotes learner-centered (as opposed to content-centered) instruction. Active learning techniques provide opportunities for students to do things and think independently about the things they are doing (Bonwell & Eison, 1991; Halonen, Brown-Anderson, & McKeachie, 2002). According to Kane (2004), active learners think on their own, think critically, take responsibility for what they learn, and organize and control their own learning. Broadly speaking, active learning is more likely to occur if students *do* things and are therefore less passive in their learning. For example, class projects, class exercises, and student discussion would be more active forms of learning, whereas listening to a lecture and watching a video would be more passive forms. Clearly, a student-generated, campus-wide campaign would lend itself to active learning activities.

Active learning has been encouraged for use with today's college students (Wilson, 2004), and the benefits of this approach have been well documented (Michael, 2006). Compared to passive course designs, active courses lead to greater student participation, more favorable course evaluations, and a stronger belief that the course content will be more applicable to future career choices (Clark, Nguyen, Bray, & Levine, 2008; Goldberg, Richburg, & Wood, 2006; Wingfield & Black, 2005).

Identification of *why* active learning may be effective has also begun. Michael (2006), for example, suggested that students engaged in active learning programs undergo meaningful learning by constantly expressing their understanding of course topics to others. Bonwell and Eison (1991) have suggested that active learning is important as it encourages student involvement with course material and class-room activities. Goldberg et al. (2006) commented on an active learning course that involved a service learning component (i.e., students are asked to partner with community organizations on a project) and suggested that such course designs are influential due to the fact that they require students to constantly reflect on how community experiences relate to their own life, resulting in the correction of previously held misconceptions.

Active Learning as a Persuasive Technique: Proposed Effects on the Student

In addition to the educational effects of active learning, research has also identified situations where active learning has resulted in suasory effects (Braun, Cheang, & Shigeta, 2005; Hillman & Martin, 2002; Strohmetz & Skleder, 1992). For example, college students who participated in a role-play or group dis-cussion activity regarding the stigmatization of minority groups were found to have less homophobic attitudes following participation, whereas students who received a lecture on discrimination and homophobia showed no such attitude change (Hillman & Martin, 2002). Based on these findings, it is suggested that the present organ donation course may result in positive attitude and behavior changes of enrolled students.

Three theories offer potential insight as to *why* students enrolled in the course may be persuaded to document their own donation intentions. First, students enrolled in the course are expected to gain increased literacy on the topic. In terms of health literacy in the context of organ and tissue donation (OTD), several studies have illustrated the additive effects of learning on individuals' behavioral intentions and actions related to OTD (Horton & Horton, 1990; Morgan et al., 2002). Thus, increased knowledge of donation and the correction of donation misperceptions could be expected to lead to increased donation intentions among course participants (Siegel, Alvaro, Crano, et al., 2008).

It is also suggested that the students' execution of an organ donation campaign will increase their own level of commitment to the cause of OTD. Cialdini (1993; Freedman & Fraser, 1966) termed this *commitment and consistency*, wherein individuals perform an action or commit to a cause and feel intrapersonal and social pressures to act consistently with the commitment. The literature also suggests that the more public the initial or early commitment, the more pressure to appear consistent later on (Deutsch & Gerard, 1955). In the current intervention, students will be actively and publicly campaigning to increase awareness and educate fellow students about organ and tissue donation. Thus, most of the students will display a public commitment to organ and tissue donation. Subsequent actions or reporting of attitudes or intentions inconsistent with donation might suggest a level of inconsistency in the student. Social psychologists have long understood inconsistency, or more specifically the drive to avoid it, as a strong motivational force in human behavior (Festinger, 1957; Heider, 1958).

Finally, participation in the campaign course may serve to persuade enrolled students by increasing their vested interest (Sivacek & Crano, 1982) and/or involvement in donation. Studies have documented that vested interest influences organ donor behavior (Siegel, Alvaro, Lac, et al., 2008). Students, unfortunately, exhibit low levels of vested interest in donation, and in particular lack the self-efficacy related to donating and express low levels of salience in relation to the topic (Anker, Feeley, & Kim, in press). Marshall and colleagues (Marshall, Reinhart, Feeley, Tutzauer, & Anker, 2008) reported students as having low to moderate levels of involvement in donation, suggesting that donation attitudes are most strongly tied to students' values (i.e., value-relevant involvement; Johnson & Eagly, 1989). The active learning components of the donation course may offer one method of increasing both involvement in and self-efficacy regarding donation. For example, Pearlman, Camberg, Wallace, Symons, and Finison (2002) trained adolescents to educate peers about HIV/AIDS and found that peer educators were more confident than the general public in providing education on the topic. In the donation course, students are asked to educate others in a similar manner, suggesting that their course preparations may instill the required self-efficacy for completing this task. Similarly, the presence of non-traditional learning activities in the donation course (e.g., visits from donor families or recipients) may be vivid activities for students, increasing their salience and involvement in donation and resulting in greater donation intent.

Active Learning as a Persuasive Technique: Proposed Effects on Others

In addition to persuading students enrolled in the course, it is suggested that donation course participants may influence their social and college campus networks to become donors through course communication campaigns (i.e., interpersonal and mass media activities). Active learning methods may also contribute to this effort, as students who value active learning tend to have higher levels of influencing motives (i.e., enjoy persuading others; Komarraju & Karau, 2008). Additionally, participation in active learning courses has been shown to result in greater social integration on college campuses (Braxton, Milem, & Sullivan, 2000). Donation course participants will thus represent a potentially motivated, educated, and integrated group who are ready to intervene within college populations. It is worth noting that defense evaluation (Radecki & Jaccard, 1999), or the evaluation of the act of telling someone about donation, may also play a role in students' communication efforts with others. Breitkopf (2006) suggested that beliefs that others will encourage one to reconsider a decision or feel unprepared to discuss a decision result in more negative attitudes toward communicating one's intentions. The active learning course may prepare students to overcome such barriers to communication by providing them with ample information and discussion about donation prior to their intervention in the college community.

Pilot Work on Active Learning in Organ Donation

A public relations (PR) course at the University at Albany (hereafter, UA) in the spring of 2002 provided the inspiration and pilot work for the project. A representative from the New York Alliance for Donation (www.alliancefordonation.org) approached the chair of the Communication Department at UA about using organ and tissue donation as a potential class project. The class adopted the campaign topic and a budget of $2,500, and carried out the campaign. Both empirical evidence (the class recruited over 500 new state organ registrants) and anecdotal reports from students (e.g., interest in the topic of OTD, and reported learning benefits from the project) generated a furor of pedagogical and research interest in the topic among faculty, the instructor, and professionals in OTD in the Albany, New York, area. Based on the successes of the initial course intervention, the present multicampus organ donation course intervention was constructed.

Multicampus Active Learning Organ Donation Course

Students taking upper-level public communication courses designed and implemented PR campaigns to increase organ and tissue awareness for university students. The student class sizes ranged from 25 to 35, and students were allowed to develop their own campaign messages and choose appropriate media, while understanding the limitations put upon them in terms of budget and time. Students in the PR courses volunteered for one or more work groups and undertook every facet of the campaign. Each of these work groups was charged with a different but indispensable function (e.g., print and radio advertising, public relations, and a web page). It is important to note that both classes and class instructors were given freedom to invent their own campaigns in order to meet identical predetermined campaign goals: (a) to increase knowledge and awareness of the critical shortage of donors nationally by dispelling myths surrounding donation and providing facts, and (b) to increase the number of students who declare their intentions to become a donor through the New York State Organ and Tissue Donor Registry (hereafter, the "Registry") and the number of students who communicate their intentions to next of kin.

Campaign course facets
The first facet of the intervention, the *pedagogy* facet, is to instruct the students in the course effectively in two content areas: PR campaign principles and background on OTD. For the first facet of the intervention, the students may be considered the primary persuasive target of the project. Borrowing from previous active learning strategies, the following course activities were undertaken: a class trip to the local OPO, guest speakers (e.g., researchers, OPO professionals, and donor parents), course discussions around recommended readings on the topic, and/or in-class exercises to promote active participation. Many of these activities have been suggested as good practice techniques to promote active learning (see Chickering, Gamson, & Barsi, 1989; see also Lubbers & Gorcyca, 1997). The 10–12 weeks of active learning activities before the campaign are critical to the project's success, as active participation, active discovery, and ultimately active learning on the part of the undergraduate students should reap more benefits than having program faculty provide a canned PR campaign for students to implement. Throughout the course, students were also exposed to principles and scholarship in public relations and public communication campaigns.

The second facet was concerned with the overall social marketing of organ donation to the campus community. The primary goal of the campaign was to inform students about OTD, and a secondary goal was to mobilize students with positive donation intentions to sign the state registry (and communicate these wishes to next of kin). Students used various media (e.g., radio, the Internet, campus TV, and print) to communicate the message and were warned that previous campaigns in OTD have produced mixed results (e.g., Cosse & Weinberger, 2000) due to general lack of knowledge and interest in the topic. Campaigns had to appeal to student audiences, engage and inform the audience, and ultimately encourage intended donors to formally declare their intentions through the New York State electronic OTD registry and communicate their intentions to family members.

Facet 3 of the intervention is considered the *interpersonal influence* facet of the campaign. Here we are interested in the following outcomes: (a) the number of new donor registrants who registered as the result of the interpersonal efforts of a campaign class student, and (b) the number of new donor registrants who informed their families of their decision.

Purpose

The purpose of the current study is to provide evaluative data for a 3-year, multicampus classroom intervention designed to promote organ and tissue donation. The data include findings over the 3 years and survey data from over 1,000 college students attending colleges or universities in New York State.

It should be noted that multiple campuses participated in the current grant-funded project; however, only two campuses were required to complete the extensive evaluation protocol (the University at Buffalo [UB] and UA), with the exception of tallying signed organ registration cards. Also, each course instructor was given complete independence in how the course was organized and how campaigns were executed. Only two requirements were asked of courses: (a) The instructor had to work with the local OPO, and (b) the campaign goal was to promote organ and tissue donation with the number of signed organ cards serving as the outcome variable of interest.

Method

The present chapter focuses on evaluating outcomes from students enrolled in the active learning organ donation courses at the UB and UA campuses during the Spring 2004–2006 semesters. To reiterate, all students were exposed to an active learning course in which students were asked to create their own organ donation campaigns for implementation across their campus. Evaluation of the course examined the effect of the course on enrolled students and the college community. There is a secondary interest in the influence of course participants who were asked to complete pre- and post-course surveys to evaluate the impact of the course. To evaluate the social network and social marketing effects of the campaign (i.e., the influence of students' interpersonal and mass-mediated communication efforts on others in their social and college campus networks), a cross section of randomly sampled students and individuals who signed the organ registry were asked to complete surveys.

Process and Impact Measures

Several measures were used to evaluate each facet of the classroom intervention. The Institutional Review Boards (IRBs) at UB and UA (2003–2006) approved all aspects of the study protocol where the data were collected.

> *Enrolled*: This refers to students who either reported signing the organ registry in the past (either through the Web site directly or when obtaining or renewing their driver's license) or completed an OTD registration card during the campaign.
>
> *Communication of intent*: This refers to whether students report communicating their donation intentions to their next of kin.
>
> *Knowledge and information*: Nine questions were used to test students' knowledge of facts and information surrounding the donation process. These

questions were in part taken from two previous studies on organ donation and college student samples (Feeley & Servoss, 2005; Horton & Horton, 1990). Overall knowledge was computed as the percentage of questions correct for each student. Two of the nine questions were changed from year 1 [Y1] to year 2 [Y2]. Also unique to year 1 and 2 is that students were asked on a single item, "How informed do you feel you are about organ donation?" Three answers were provided for this item: *not very informed, somewhat informed,* and *very informed.* In year 3 [Y3] of the project, the number of knowledge questions was reduced to six.

Experience: Two questions measured students' experience with organ donation. Specifically, students were asked if they knew a previous donor (living or deceased) or knew anyone who has received or is awaiting an organ or tissue donation.

Attitudes toward donation: A seven-item scale was used to measure attitudes, and students reported level of agreement for each of the seven items along a 4-point Likert-type scale of agreement, with 1 representing *completely disagree* and 4 representing *completely agree.* This 4-point scale of agreement was used also for intentions to donate and willingness to communicate scales. Scale items were taken from previous research in organ donation (Feeley & Servoss, 2005; Rubens et al., 1998; Smith et al., 2004). The final scale represents the average of the seven scale items with higher scores indicating a more positive attitude toward organ and tissue donation. These seven items were reduced to three items in year 3 of the project.[1] In Y3, the total range of attitude scores was 3 to 13 (two items had 4-point scales; one item had a 5-point scale).

Intentions to sign: The mean of four items measuring intentions to sign the registry was used, and students who reported signing were excluded from these analyses. One of the four items was negatively worded, and the scoring of this item was reversed for consistency; higher scores indicate a greater intent to become a signed donor.

Willingness to communicate (WTC): Willingness to communicate (WTC) about organ donation uses four items from a WTC scale employed by Smith et al. (2004) in a large university sample. One item was reverse scored, and higher scores indicate a greater willingness to communicate about donation.

Communicating about organ and tissue donation: Two single-item questions assessed if students have discussed organ donation in the past with friends,

1.   The motivation for changing the number of attitude items and the content of the questions was due to the observed ceiling effect in the data. That is, students were overwhelmingly reporting high attitudes (as most surveys of this nature yield; Feeley, 2007) and with little variation. Thus, the decision was made to develop a novel attitude measure based upon data from student interviews.

colleagues, or family members. One item specifically asked, "Have you had a conversation about organ donation with immediate family members?" and the second question later asked if students "have spoken to anybody in the last year about OTD?" The second item asked students to note, by checkmark, if they have spoken to their friends, family members, and/or boyfriend, girlfriend, or spouse about OTD.

Recognition of OTD media messages: To measure students' recognition of mass media messages and campaigns regarding OTD, students were asked, "Have you noticed any ads promoting organ and tissue donation?" Students who reported yes were then asked to check where they have noticed ads (TV, radio, billboards, print, and on campus).

Evaluation of Campaign Intervention Facets

Facet 1: Students in the course. To assess students' knowledge, attitudes, and behavior change related to organ donation, a survey was completed at the beginning and at the end of the semester in the spring of 2004, 2005, and 2006. The survey took an estimated 15 minutes to complete, and participation was voluntary—all students who were in class were given extra credit regardless of whether they chose to complete the survey. Students provided a unique three-digit code to allow for within-subjects data analysis.

Facet 2: Social marketing effects on college campuses. The number of students who signed the organ registry was used as a primary measure of campaign effects. A second measure of campaign effects was a random sample of 500 students at UA and UB at the end of each spring semester.[2] A $1.00 incentive was provided in each mailing, and each university's IRB approved the survey protocol.

Facet 3: Interpersonal influence. A sample of students who enrolled in the organ registry were asked to complete a short survey that asked five questions in the following areas: (a) what event prompted the student to sign; (b) why the student decided to sign; (c) if the student communicated his or her decision to sign with family, and, if not, if the student plans to notify family; and (d) if the research team may contact the student in the future via e-mail.

---

2.   For control purposes, a random sample of 500 students at two other campuses was conducted. In the spring of 2004 and 2005, students at the University of Massachusetts and Cleveland State University were surveyed; in the spring of 2006, students at Binghamton University (SUNY) and Stony Brook University (SUNY) were surveyed. As the University of Massachusetts and Cleveland State proved to be inappropriate control groups, due to higher baseline rates of donation behaviors, data are not presented here in the interest of space. Results on comparison campuses are available from the first author.

Results

Facet 1: Survey of Students in Communication Courses

Facet 1 examined the influence of the active learning organ donation course on students enrolled in the course. As no differences were identified across dependent variables based on college campus (i.e., UB or UA), results from both schools are collapsed. Table 12.1 provides a comprehensive overview of the improvements that course participants gained in knowledge, attitudes, and willingness to communicate about organ donation as a result of course participation.

Knowledge

> *Year 1.* Forty-eight students in 2004 (Y1) completed surveys at time 1, and
> 52 students at time 2, with 33 students completing surveys at both points
> in time. A within-subjects ANOVA for the 33 students who completed the
> knowledge quiz at both points in time for Y1 was statistically significant,
> $F(1, 32) = 49.66$, $p < .01$, $\eta^2 = .61$. Data also indicate that students self-
> reported being more informed about the topic of donation after taking the
> intervention course.

Table 12.1 Course participants' knowledge, attitudes, and willingness to communicate (WTC) about organ donation[a]

Measure	Range	Time 1 (M/SD)	Time 1 (N)	Time 2 (M/SD)	Time 2 (N)
Knowledge					
Year 1	0–9	6.00 (1.61)	48	8.39 (1.22)	52
Year 2	0–9	6.18 (1.48)	31	8.74 (0.60)	31
Year 3	0–9	3.58 (1.03)	38	4.48 (0.83)	42
Attitude					
Year 1	1–4	3.51 (0.42)	48	3.78 (0.34)	52
Year 2	1–4	3.39 (0.71)	31	3.88 (0.30)	31
Year 3	3–13	5.56 (2.08)	38	4.07 (1.56)	42
WTC					
Year 1	1–4	3.10 (0.77)	48	3.65 (0.61)	52
Year 2	1–4	2.91 (0.88)	31	3.77 (0.47)	31

Note: The WTC measure was not administered in year 3 of the study. In year 3, lower scores indicate more positive attitudes toward organ donation.

a. In the results section, repeated measures analyses included only data available from participants who completed both time 1 and time 2 measures. Tables, however, present data on all available participant responses.

Year 2. Knowledge scores increased significantly from time 1 to time 2, $F (1, 30) = 128.14$, $p < .01$, $\eta^2 = .81$.

Year 3. The number of knowledge questions was reduced to six items for Y3. This was done to shorten the survey while maintaining the knowledge items with the most variance in responses. Thirty-eight students completed surveys at the beginning of the semester, and 42 students at the end of the semester, and knowledge scores increased significantly, $F (1, 24) = 22.84$, $p < .001$, $\eta^2 = .48$.

Attitudes toward OTD and willingness to communicate

Year 1. Using within-subjects ANOVA, student attitudes were found to increase significantly from time 1 to time 2, $F (1, 27) = 10.62$, $p < .01$, $\eta^2 = .29$. Willingness to communicate about OTD also revealed an increase from time 1 to time 2, $F (1, 29) = 36.59$, $p < .01$, $\eta^2 = .57$.

Year 2. Use of a within-subjects ANOVA revealed a significant increase in attitudes from time 1 to time 2, $F (1, 33) = 11.73$, $p < .01$, $\eta^2 = .26$. Similarly, willingness to communicate improved from time 1 to time 2, $F (1, 33) = 29.76$, $p < .01$, $\eta^2 = .47$.

Year 3. For Y3, repeated-measures ANOVA identified that attitudes increased significantly from time 1 to time 2, $F (1, 25) = 8.82$, $p < .01$, $\eta^2 = .26$. Lower attitude scores for Y3 indicate more positive attitudes toward organ donation.[3]

Signing and communication about OTD

The data indicate a significant increase in the percentage of students who have communicated about OTD *in the last year.* Students' signing rates increased from time 1 to time 2: 25% to 75% in Y1, 13% to 66% in Y2, and 32% to 86% in Y3. The percentage of students who reported having a family conversation about OTD increased from the beginning to the end of the semester (Y1 [T1, T2]: 45%, 90%; Y2: 42%, 82%; Y3: 45%, 83%) (see Table 12.2).

Facet 2: Social Marketing Campus-Wide Effects

Enrollment in registry

The Spring 2004 campaign encouraged 641 students to sign the registry between the two intervention campuses—UA had 421 newly enrolled, and UB had 220. The Spring 2005 campaign influenced 866 students to sign the organ registry (UA 595, UB 271), and the Spring 2006 campaign had 702 new enrollees (UA 312, UB 390). Table 12.3 provides data on enrollment across both intervention and

---

3. All scales are available from the author. Please email thfeeley@buffalo.edu. See also www.alliancefordonation.org for more extensive report.

Table 12.2 Course participants' registration and communication with family

Measure	Time 1				Time 2			
	N	Yes	No	Unsure	N	Yes	No	Unsure
Signing								
Y1	48	12 (25%)	36 (75%)	—	52	39 (75%)	13 (25%)	—
Y2	31	4 (13%)	27 (87%)	—	31	20 (66%)	11 (34%)	—
Y3	38	12 (32%)	24 (63%)	2 (5%)	42	36 (86%)	3 (7%)	3 (7%)
Communication								
Y1	48	22 (45%)	26 (55%)	—	52	47 (90%)	5 (10%)	—
Y2	31	13 (42%)	18 (58%)	—	31	25 (82%)	6 (18%)	—
Y3	38	17 (45%)	18 (47%)	3 (8%)	42	34 (83%)	4 (10%)	3 (7%)

Note: Unsure was not utilized as a response category until year 3.

nonintervention project campuses. For the 3-year grant period, 3,868 students were newly enrolled in the New York State OTD electronic registry.

Campus-wide survey

A campus-wide survey was undertaken to measure the impact of the campaigns on the overall campus population of undergraduate students. Response rates ranged from 19% to 32% for the 3 years of data collection and may have been 10–15% lower in the absence of the $1.00 incentive provided for respondents (Hopkins & Gullickson, 1992). To sum up, the intervention campuses did not indicate greater attitudes, signing rates, or knowledge about OTD. The only significant difference had to do with the proportion of students at UB and UA recognizing on-campus campaigns promoting OTD (see Table 12.4).

Facet 3: Interpersonal influence

We proposed an interpersonal influence ripple effect, that is, students talking to salient others about donation. It was documented earlier that students in the campaign classes at UB and UA spoke to their circle of friends and family; however, it is unclear how these conversations influenced others to sign the registry or speak to family about their intentions. The current evaluation attempted to measure the interpersonal influence effect by having new student registrants report, via a short survey, the primary source of influence in their decision to sign the registry. A sample of signers ($n = 1,064$) was asked to complete a five-question survey upon turning in their organ donor registration card.

The survey instructs students to report what specific event, if any, prompted them to sign, and question 3 asked students why they decided to sign. Among

Table 12.3 Coded reasons why students chose to register in the organ registry

Category or Reason	Definition	Examples
Desire to help/ altruism ($\kappa = .91$) ($f = 555$, 56%)	Desire to help others, save lives, and do the right thing. Individual reports positive attitudes toward donation and/or ability to make difference to others through donation.	"I want to save lives." "Help other people." "It's a good thing to do."
Practicality ($\kappa = .88$) ($f = 123$, 13%)	Expresses donation as a practical and sensible alternative for organs.	"What good are organs when I'm dead?" "I don't need them."
Campaign influence ($\kappa = .82$) ($f = 59$, 6%)	Influence from presenters, messages, or students involved in class campaign.	"A guest speaker at the COM 464 ballroom event." "The class convinced me."
Intentions ($\kappa = .67$) ($f = 34$, 3%)	Previously intended to become donor and never realized by signing card or registry.	"I always had meant to." "I was not sure if I had signed up because it isn't on my license."
Personal experience ($\kappa = .83$) ($f = 27$, 3%)	Student cites personal experience with donation, such as relationship with donor or recipient.	"Knew someone who benefited from donation." "Cousin is awaiting a kidney."
Scientific advances ($\kappa = 1.00$) ($f = 2$, ??%)	Donation would benefit science or medical advances in future.	"Science/helps people." "Cure illnesses."
Miscellaneous/other ($\kappa = .85$) ($f = 79$, 8%)	Reasons other than those listed above.	"Greedy not to." "Girls!" "Why not?"

Note: κ = kappa (Cohen, 1960); f = frequency of category.

several responses to this question (i.e., what event prompted signing; Y1 only) was *another student*, and 26% ($n = 67$) checked this option. The reasons for signing were content analyzed along eight categories (see Table 12.4 for categories and reliability coefficients between coders), and overwhelmingly students reported altruism or a desire to help others as the main reason for signing (55%), followed by practicality (13%).

Students were next asked if their decision to sign was communicated to family members, and, if not, if the student plans to notify family in the near future. Forty-nine percent reported they notified their family of their decision to donate.

Table 12.4   Campus-wide effects: Signing and family communication rates

	University at Buffalo				University at Albany			
	Time 1		Time 2		Time 1		Time 2	
	n/% Yes	N	n/% Yes	N	n/% yes	N	n/% yes	N
Signing								
Y1	25 (20.7)	121	21 (22.6)	93	47 (26.4)	178	24 (25.5)	94
Y2	36 (27.3)	132	37 (34.6)	107	40 (28.8)	139	26 (25.5)	102
Y3	32 (22.5)	142	30 (24.0)	125	47 (33.3)	141	26 (25.5)	102
Aware								
Y1	12 (9.9)	121	18 (19.2)	94	12 (6.7)	179	20 (21.3)	94
Y2	13 (9.9)	132	21 (19.4)	108	12 (8.6)	139	18 (17.7)	102
Y3	21 (14.8)	142	37 (29.6)	125	13 (9.2)	141	16 (15.7)	102
Communication								
Y1	55 (45.5)	121	43 (45.7)	94	89 (50.0)	178	46 (48.9)	94
Y2	38 (28.8)	132	39 (36.1)	108	34 (24.5)	139	32 (31.4)	102
Y3	52 (36.6)	142	50 (40.0)	125	68 (47.9)	142	40 (39.6)	101

Note: Communication = Communication with family about donation. Aware = Awareness of on-campus donation campaigns. *n*/% yes = The number/percentage of students who completed the target behavior.

Of those students who have not ($n = 526$), 90% reported they plan to in the future. A final question asked students if the project team may contact them in the future via e-mail to follow up with a short survey. Five hundred twenty-seven students (52% of sample) left their e-mail addresses for future contact. A research assistant e-mailed these students over 4 months after the campaign (the Y3 e-mailing has not taken place yet); 90 e-mails came back undeliverable (most likely due to graduation from university). Forty-eight students (48/235, 20% response rate) completed the short survey, and 37 of these students (77%) reported that they have communicated to their family that they signed the registry.

Discussion

The current chapter provides evaluation data on a comprehensive and multifaceted project to promote organ and tissue donation on college campuses across New York State. Admittedly, the current project data are overwhelming, and interpreting the data is akin to sipping water out of a fire hydrant. The goal of the discussion is to distill the study data into several conclusions and finally provide recommendations for application of the college campus intervention, based upon the survey findings.

Conclusion #1: The Project Has a Profound Effect on Students Enrolled in the Campaign Course

The greatest effect of the project was unquestionably on the students who were enrolled in the campaign courses. Over the course of the semester (see Table 12.1), students reported demonstrable gains in knowledge, increases in positive attitudes toward donation, and greater intentions to become organ donors, if eligible (i.e., signing and family notification rates). Although the current project failed to provide process data on active learning, increases in student knowledge following course participation suggest that increasing students' literacy on a topic may be an important persuasive component to include in future active learning courses. Efforts are currently underway to explore how vested interest (Crano, 1995; Siegel, Alvaro, Lac, et al., 2008) and, specifically, self-efficacy may play a persuasive role in the context of active learning as well.

It is argued that students in the organ donor campaign course experienced positive organ donation outcomes due to the course's several active learning opportunities. Chickering and colleagues (1989) listed 10 practices that encourage active learning in the classroom, and at least six of these identified practices were present in one or both of the intervention classes: (a) conduct of the research project (execution of the project for an actual client), (b) field trips or volunteer activities (e.g., site visit to the local OPO), (c) student-initiated trips or activities (e.g., functions related to promotion of the topic), (d) role-playing and simulation in class (e.g., forming groups for discussion and brainstorming), (e) relating outside events to class and theories, and (f) student challenge of ideas and course materials. Such activities likely provided students not only with the necessary engagement with course material but also with opportunities to reflect on their learning experiences and apply them to their own lives.

Although the donation course clearly persuaded enrolled students in favor of donation, the data do not reveal *how much* active learning may need to occur to result in such effects. A recent medical school intervention on the topic of donation (Feeley, Tamburlin, & Vincent, 2008) that incorporated active learning components (i.e., guest lectures and group discussion with standardized patients) changed students' knowledge, self-efficacy, and family communication rates in a relatively short time frame (approximately one hour). Such results must be taken in context, however, as medical students are largely favorable toward donation (Essman & Thornton, 2006), potentially predisposing them to respond favorably to the intervention. Future research may want to consider how much active learning is necessary to make a topic involving and salient to audience members, or may aim to determine if the dose of active learning influences the persistence of persuasive outcomes.

Since the completion of the interventions at the University at Buffalo and the University at Albany, the active learning organ donation course has also been implemented in colleges in the New York City area to examine the persuasive effects of the course in colleges with large minority student populations. Data from two such campuses (SUNY Stony Brook and the City College of New York) indicate that although course participants were equally likely to communicate their donation intentions to family before and after course participation, they were significantly more likely to sign the registry following their participation in the course (Feeley, Anker, Watkins, Rivera, & Tag, under review). Such results suggest that the suasory effects of the campaign course are applicable and effective on campuses with diverse student populations as well.

Conclusion #2: The Interpersonal Channel of Communication Is a Successful Means for Promoting OTD With College Students

An anticipated side effect of course participants' hardened commitment to the topic of donation was their self-initiated discussion about the topic with family, friends, and peers. If equipped with a bit of information and inspiration from guest speakers, it appears students become advocates of the cause of donation. Data indicate that new enrollees report students as the primary influence on the decision to sign.

The current data and data recently meta-analyzed from over 20 studies on college students (Feeley, 2007) indicate that students are at a tipping point when it comes to organ donation. That is, if students are given an opportunity and reasonable motivation to do so, they are likely to sign the OTD registry (see Siegel & Alvaro, this volume, for a discussion of the importance of opportunity). By contrast, if students are not provided convenient access to join the registry and a rationale to do so, they will *not* sign the OTD registry (see Feeley & Servoss, 2005). Students in the current grant were significantly more persuasive and successful in informing students (and subsequently obtaining more signers) when the OTD promotional message was delivered face-to-face in the form of lectures or tabling (i.e., events where course participants sit at tables and provide students passing by with information about donation as well as a registration opportunity). The data collected from e-mailing previous signers provided empirical evidence for this conclusion. When asked, "What event prompted you to sign the OTD registry?" the modal response was "Another student in the campaign course." Other data in support of the impact of interpersonal communication include instructor reports to the principal investigator that indicated tabling to be by far the most successful campaign activity to obtain OTD signers.

As organ donation is only a moderately involving topic for students (Marshall et al., 2008), students passing by tabling events may be influenced through peripheral cues to persuasion (Petty, Cacioppo, & Goldman, 1981), stopping at tables based on factors such as free giveaways, exciting games, or friendly faces. Once at the table, however, students may be persuaded to declare their donation intentions. Along these lines, it may behoove students to deliver the donation message themselves rather than rely on a traditionally credible source (e.g., a physician) or well-known source (e.g., a celebrity). Student targets may respond more positively to fellow university students, as their university peers may be more likely to communicate the necessity and relevance of considering the topic of donation. A recent study (Vincent, 2006) examining student-generated family conversations about organ donation suggested that many parents became more favorable toward donation subsequent to a conversation with their son and daughter, providing support for the idea that interpersonal approaches may be effective in advocating for donation. Although heuristic cues to persuasion may catch students' attention on an uninvolving issue (i.e., donation), the information provided during interpersonal conversations and tabling events may offer students the motivation to actually declare their donation intentions. Moreover, the easy access to donor registration cards provided by such contexts enables students to immediately act upon their intentions (see Siegel & Alvaro, this volume).

Conclusion #3: The Campus-Wide Campaign Failed to Influence the Knowledge, Attitudes, and Signing Behavior of the General Population of Students

The campus-wide surveys over 3 years indicate no differences within the New York campuses with respect to the general population of students' sentiment toward OTD. In other words, unless students were directly involved with a campaign activity, they were not affected by the campaign. There may be two reasons why mediated campaigns were unsuccessful with college students. First, it may be that students do not pay attention to the ads, as OTD is not an involving topic for young adults. Second, the topic of donation may not readily lend itself to mass advertising, as the decision to donate is personal and can be closely related to one's core values.

Implications for Future Campaigns to Promote OTD in College Student Populations

OPOs and future public relations course instructors seeking to increase awareness through public campaigns should take note of the current study findings, especially those findings in relation to active learning and social influence effects. Giving students the opportunity to engage in and reflect upon vivid experiences related to donation (e.g., group activities, guest speakers, etc.) serves an educational, as well as persuasive, function. Although the exact mechanism through which this persuasion occurs (i.e., commitment and consistency, vested interest, and health literacy) is worthy of exploration, results suggest that active learning should continue to be implemented as a persuasive technique in the context of organ donation. OPOs seeking to intervene in college communities would do well to plan active learning activities, rather than rely on lectures to teach students about donation.

Active learning may also be credited with the noteworthy results related to social influence effects. As active learning has been shown to result in greater social integration on campus (Braxton et al., 2000), the technique may serve to explain why social influence was so effective in encouraging registration of donation intentions within the college population. Results suggest that students are best persuaded when they are engaged in one-on-one conversations about the topic of donation. In the current project, students using the Student Union and highly populated areas (e.g., areas of residence halls) for tabling met with great success in terms of engaging students to discuss and ultimately consider formally pledging their intentions to donate. Future campaigns that rely on mass media (e.g., radio, print, and billboards) may have to find a creative way to personalize the message in a way that will engage the college student.

Final Considerations

Some final considerations are worthy of mention. The most important component of the current project is providing students (who in turn educate the masses) with accurate and timely information about donation. Policies, practices, and sentiment change in the area of donation. For example, some states still do not have electronic registries, and some states and OPO jurisdictions have first-person consent. Thus, it is important that the instructor and his or her students are provided with timely and accurate information about donation and donation practices, understanding that donation knowledge is a moving target.

A second consideration is the necessary and important role of the OPO representative in executing the course. Students repeatedly discuss the value of the real-life anecdotes and narratives provided by OPO professionals themselves or by donor or recipient family members whose participation in the project was largely a function of the OPO representative.

Acknowledgments

This research was supported by a grant from the Human Resources Services Administration, Division of Transplantation, to the New York Alliance for Donation, Inc. (HRSA/ DoT #R39OT01205). The contents of this chapter are solely the responsibility of the authors and do not necessarily represent the views of HRSA/DoT. The authors acknowledge the ideas and work of Teresa Harrison, Anita Pomerantz, Deborah Silverman, Jonathan Pierce, Paul Denvir, and Lorraine Mara related to the current project.

References

Anker, A. E., Feeley, T. H., & Kim, H. (In press). Examining the attitude-behavior relationship in prosocial donation domains. *Journal of Applied Social Psychology.*

Bonwell, C. C., & Eison, J. A. (1991). *Active learning: Creating excitement in the classroom* (ASHE-ERIC Higher Education Rep. No. 1). Washington, DC: George Washington University, School of Education and Human Development.

Braun, K. L., Cheang, M., & Shigeta, D. (2005). Increasing knowledge, skills, and empathy among direct care workers in elder care: A preliminary study of an active-learning model. *The Gerontologist, 45,* 118–124.

Braxton, J. M., Milem, J. F., & Sullivan, A. S. (2000). The influence of active learning on the college student departure process: Toward a revision of Tinto's theory. *Journal of Higher Education, 71,* 569–590.

Breitkopf, C. R. (2006). Perceived consequences of communicating organ donation wishes: An analysis of beliefs about defending one's decision. *Psychology & Health, 21,* 481–497.

Chickering, A. W., Gamson, Z. F., & Barsi, L. M. (1989). *Faculty inventory for the 7 principles for good practice in undergraduate education.* Winona, MN: Seven Principles Resource Center, Winona State University.

Cialdini, R. B. (1993). *Influence: The psychology of persuasion.* New York: Morrow.

Clark, M. C., Nguyen, H. T., Bray, C., & Levine, R. E. (2008). Team-based learning in an undergraduate nursing course. *Journal of Nursing Education, 47,* 111–117.

Cosse, T., & Weinberger, T. (2000). Words versus actions about organ donation: A four-year tracking study of attitudes and self-reported behaviors. *Journal of Business Research, 50,* 297–303.

Crano, W. D. (1995). Attitude strength and vested interest. In R. E. Petty & J. A. Krosnick (Eds.), *Attitude strength: Antecedents and consequences* (pp. 131–158). Mahwah, NJ: Erlbaum.

Deutsch, M., & Gerard, H. B. (1955). A study of normative and information social influences upon individual judgment. *Journal of Abnormal and Social Psychology, 51,* 629–636.

Essman, C., & Thornton, J. (2006). Assessing medical student knowledge, attitudes, and behaviors regarding organ donation. *Transplantation Proceedings, 38,* 2745–2750.

Feeley, T. H. (2007). College students' knowledge, attitudes, and behaviors regarding organ donation: An integrated review of the literature. *Journal of Applied Social Psychology, 37,* 243–271.

Feeley, T. H., Anker, A. E., Watkins, B., Rivera, J., & Tag, N. (under review). A peer-to-peer campaign to promote organ donation among minority college students.

Feeley, T. H., & Servoss, T. J. (2005). Examining college student intentions to become organ donors. *Journal of Health Communication, 10,* 237–249.

Feeley, T. H., Tamburlin, J., & Vincent, D. E. (2008). An educational intervention on organ and tissue donation for first-year medical students. *Progress in Transplantation, 18,* 1–6.

Festinger, L. (1957). *A theory of cognitive dissonance.* Evanston, IL: Row Peterson.

Freedman, J. L., & Fraser, S. C. (1966). Compliance without pressure: The foot-in-the-door technique. *Journal of Personality and Social Psychology, 4*, 196–202.

Goldberg, L. R., Richburg, C. M., & Wood, L. A. (2006). Active learning through service learning. *Communication Disorders Quarterly, 27*, 131–145.

Halonen, J. S., Brown-Anderson, F., & McKeachie, W. J. (2002). Teaching thinking. In W. J. McKeachie (Ed.), *McKeachie's teaching tips: Strategies, research, and theory for college and university teachers* (11th ed., pp. 284–290). Boston: Houghton-Mifflin.

Heider, F. (1958). *The psychology of interpersonal relations.* New York: Wiley.

Hillman, J., & Martin, R. A. (2002). Lessons about gay and lesbian lives: A spaceship exercise. *Teaching of Psychology, 29*, 308–311.

Hopkins, K. D., & Gullickson, A. R. (1992). Response rates in survey research: A meta-analysis of the effects of monetary gratuities. *Journal of Experimental Education, 61*, 52–62.

Horton, R. L., & Horton, R. L. (1990). Knowledge regarding organ donation: Identifying and overcoming barriers to organ donation. *Social Science in Medicine, 31*, 791–800.

Institute of Medicine. (2006). *Organ donation: Opportunities for action.* Washington, DC: National Academies Press.

Johnson, B. T., & Eagly, A. H. (1989). Effects of involvement on persuasion: A meta-analysis. *Psychological Bulletin, 106*, 290–314.

Kane, L. (2004). Educators, learners and active learning methodologies. *International Journal of Lifelong Education, 23*, 275–286.

Komarraju, M., & Karau, S. J. (2008). Relationships between the perceived value of instructional techniques and academic motivation. *Journal of Instructional Psychology, 34*, 170–182.

Lubbers, C. A., & Gorcyca, D. A. (1997). Using active learning in public relations instructions: Demographic predictors of faculty use. *Public Relations Review, 23*, 67–80.

Marshall, H. M., Reinhart, A. M., Feeley, T. H., Tutzauer, F., & Anker, A. (2008). Comparing college students' value-, outcome-, and impression-relevant involvement in health-related issues. *Health Communication, 23*, 171–183.

Michael, J. (2006). Where's the evidence that active learning works? *Advances in Physiology Education, 30*, 159–167.

Morgan, S. E., & Miller, J. (2001). Beyond the organ donor card: The effect of knowledge, attitudes, and values on willingness to communicate about organ donation to family members. *Health Communication, 14*, 121–134.

Morgan, S. E., Miller, J., & Arasaratnam, L. A. (2002). Signing cards, saving lives: An evaluation of the Worksite Organ Donation Promotion Project. *Communication Monographs, 69*, 253–273.

Pearlman, D. N., Camberg, L., Wallace, L. J., Symons, P., & Finison, L. (2002). Tapping youth as agents for change: Evaluation of a peer leadership HIV/AIDS intervention. *Journal of Adolescent Health, 31*, 31–39.

Petty, R. E., Cacioppo, J. T., & Goldman, R. (1981). Personal involvement as a determinant of argument-based persuasion. *Journal of Personality and Social Psychology, 41*, 847–855.

Radecki, C. M., & Jaccard, J. (1997). Psychological aspects of organ donation: A critical review and synthesis of individual and next-of-kin donation decisions. *Health Psychology, 16*, 183–195.

Radecki, C. M., & Jaccard, J. (1999). Signing an organ donation letter: The prediction of behavior from behavioral intentions. *Journal of Applied Social Psychology, 29*, 1833–1853.

Rubens, A. J., Oleckno, W. A., & Cisla, J. R. (1998). Knowledge, attitudes, and behaviors of college students regarding organ/tissue donation and implications for increasing organ/tissue donors. *College Student Journal, 32*, 167–178.

Shanteau, J., & Harris, R. J. (1990). *Organ donation and transplantation: Psychological and behavioral factors.* Washington, DC: APA.

Sheehy, E., Conrad, S. L., Brigham, L. E., Luskin, R., Weber, P., Eakin, M., et al. (2003). Estimating the number of potential organ donors in the United States. *New England Journal of Medicine, 349*, 667–674.

Siegel, J. T., Alvaro, E. M., Crano, W. D., Lac, A., Ting, S., & Pace Jones, S. (2008). A quasi-experimental investigation of message appeal variations on organ donor registration rates. *Health Psychology, 27*, 170–178.

Siegel, J. T., Alvaro, E., Lac, A., Crano, W. D., & Alexander, S. (2008). Intentions of becoming a living organ donor among Hispanics: A theoretical approach exploring differences between living and non-living organ donation. *Journal of Health Communication, 13*, 80–99.

Siminoff, L., Gordon, N., Hewlett, J., & Robert, A. (2001). Factors influencing families' consent for donation of solid organs for transplantation. *JAMA, 286*, 71–77.

Siminoff, L. A., Lawrence, R. H., & Arnold, R. M. (2003). Comparison of black and white families' experiences and perceptions regarding organ donation requests. *Critical Care Medicine, 31*, 146–151.

Sivacek, J., & Crano, W. D. (1982). Vested interest as a moderator of attitude-behavior consistency. *Journal of Personality and Social Psychology, 43*, 210–221.

Smith, S. W., Kopfman, J. E., Massi Lindsey, L. L., Yoo, J., & Morrison, K. (2004). Encouraging family discussion on the decision to donate organs: The role of the willingness to communicate scale. *Journal of Health Communication, 16*(3), 333–346.

Strohmetz, D. B., & Skleder, A. A. (1992). The use of role-play in teaching research ethics: A validation study. *Teaching of Psychology, 19*, 106–108.

Tamburlin, J., & Rice, C. (2002). Exploring the use of the stages of change model to increase organ donations among African Americans. *Journal of Human Behavior in the Social Environment, 5*, 45–58.

United Network for Organ Sharing. (2008). *United network for organ sharing.* Retrieved September 27, 2008, from http://www.unos.org

Vincent, D. E. (2006). Exploring college students' family discussions about organ and tissue donation. *Communication Research Reports, 23*(4), 299–308.

Wendler, D., & Dickert, N. (2001). The consent process for cadaveric organ procurement. *JAMA, 285*, 329–333.

Wilson, M. E. (2004). Teaching, learning, and millennial students. *New Directions for Student Services, 106*, 59–71.

Wingfield, S. S., & Black, G. S. (2005). Active versus passive course designs: The impact on student outcomes. *Journal of Education for Business, 81*, 119–125.

13

Take Time to Talk

Improving Communication Between Recovery Professionals and Funeral Directors

Catherine Paykin, Gigi Politoski, and Linda Singleton-Driscoll

Background and Need

Leaders in both the organ recovery and funeral industries in the United States acknowledge that there have been "historically and potentially divisive issues" between them, and these issues have negatively impacted the recovery of donated organs and tissues (National Kidney Foundation [NKF], 2000a).

Professionals in organ and tissue procurement organizations privately expressed concerns that funeral directors were stifling donations. Funeral directors have expressed experiences of being belittled, disregarded, and left to deal with bereaved families who were unprepared for the disruption that donation caused in their funeral plans. Not only does this make for an unduly tense working relationship, but also it can create barriers to facilitating donation. Therefore, the NKF decided to apply for a HRSA grant to evaluate how better communication between the two groups (recovery organizations and the funeral industry) could improve people's intent to donate upon death, resulting in more organ and tissue donor recoveries. This chapter seeks to explain the depth of the discord that existed between the funeral industry and the recovery and transplant industries, and to measure steps taken to reduce the chasm and how they impacted people's intent to donate.

Differing Perspectives: Funeral Industry Professionals

Perhaps the naissance of this problem lies in the relative rarity of organ and tissue donation, the lack of experience both parties have in dealing with each other, and the lack of time spent learning about what each other does and how their different roles can support or negate each other. It is only since the early 1980s, when potent immunosuppressive drugs were introduced into medicine, that organ and tissue donation reached national prominence and led to extreme efforts to increase the number of organs donated. As the possibility of organs saving lives and preventing deaths was, and is, a life mission of medical professionals in the field, they often barreled ahead with plans to recover organs without thinking through, talking with, or understanding the nuances of how these recovery actions affected funeral procedures and the role of the funeral director. As the funeral director was not acknowledged as an important player in the transplant and donation world, this conversation was long in coming. By the time the conversation began, negative experiences and expectations had already developed. For example, when a person is pronounced dead and a funeral home is contacted, the funeral home staff may travel many miles to pick up the body, only to find that the body won't be ready for 8 or 10 hours because a recovery effort is being planned in the night when an operating room is available and the transplant team is arriving from another city. This left many funeral directors to sleep in their car, waiting uncomfortably away from home, and often not knowing when the body will be ready, what condition it will be in, or how the family is coping.

Though the cost to families should not be increased due to a donation, tissue donation may add more expenses for a funeral director. In addition, unless the hospital knows the details of the family's plan for viewing, it is possible that some types of funeral arrangements will need to be changed in the case of tissue donation. One example is a man who wanted to be buried in his Harley Davidson T-shirt, but due to tissue donation his bare arms could not be shown. The funeral director (not the hospital donation or transplant personnel) is left to explain and comfort the family, as well as to absorb (or explain) the increased costs of more complex burial techniques and the unexpected extra time spent waiting at the hospital. Also, the bereaved family often looks to the funeral director to provide explanations for what tissue and organ donation is, how it works, what is involved, and what the next steps will be—more work added to the director's job without easy access to answers to complex questions. The donation and transplant professionals, because they felt they are doing a larger "good" and because they believe in what they are doing, often belittled these inconveniences.

Differing Perspectives: Recovery and Transplant Professionals

From the view of the recovery and transplant professionals, the funeral directors were discouraging donation, providing misinformation and frightening information, and scaring families unnecessarily about how funerals would be in danger of not proceeding according to their loved one's wishes if organs or tissues were procured. Discussions about increased costs to the family, delays in the funeral timing, and other misinformation to frighten them from making a pro-donation decision were believed to happen in confidential talks between families and funeral directors. Recovery professionals accused funeral directors of being more concerned with their "bottom line" and their own comfort rather than the greater good of saving lives. Some funeral directors and crematories were even accused of being involved in illegal recoveries to line their own pockets.

Toward a Solution

With an ever-increasing demand for organ and tissue donation, it became apparent that this problem was not going to disappear. Recovery professionals and funeral directors recognized that to better meet their common goal of supporting grieving families (and to support organ and tissue donation), they needed to improve communication with each other and find ways to share and work collaboratively.

Although facilitating the process could be expected to prevent last-minute donation reversals, there was more at stake. The NKF knew that funeral directors could influence future donations as they often had long-term relationships with families that resulted in their taking care of the arrangements for multiple family members over time. They also had other opportunities to influence the public's views of organ and tissue donation. The NKF believed that if funeral directors encouraged donation, rather than discouraging it, the approximately 5,500 International Cemetery and Funeral Association (ICFA) members throughout the country could help increase the number of declarations to donate and the number of actual donations. The NKF thus sought to both improve communications between the two groups and make those in the funeral industry more informed and supportive of donation so that more encouraged it.

Research Design

Phase 1: Manuals and Guidelines

In June 2000, the NKF's National Donor Family Council convened a meeting between the National Funeral Directors Association (NFDA), the ICFA, and recovery agencies (the American Association of Tissue Banks [AATB], the Association of Organ Procurement Organizations [AOPO], and the Eye Bank Association of America [EBAA]) to begin discussions on how to facilitate the organ and tissue donation process and accommodate the specific requirements and preferences of a family for a funeral service. This led to the publication of the NKF's *Take Time to Talk* manual in 2000 (NKF, 2000b) and the adoption of *Best Practices* in 2001 (National Funeral Directors Association, 2001).

The *Best Practices* document was spearheaded by funeral directors and embalmers who had worked as organ donation professionals or as consultants to organ recovery organizations. It explains the importance of ongoing, steady relationships and communication between local recovery organizations and funeral homes, particularly when a donation was in progress, and regardless of whether or not there was a donation. The document carefully lays out expectations of both parties in order to allow both parties to achieve their desired outcomes: a funeral that fulfills the family's wishes and a successful organ recovery.

The *Best Practices* document also led the way to ongoing communication between the parties at times when a donation was not in progress. This allowed for less pressure in learning and relationship building. One outcome was the development of help lines and hotlines to help the two groups through difficult experiences. They also appointed each other to their respective boards (directors, advisory) and invited each other to attend educational sessions and knowledge-building programs so they could learn about each others' needs. Using the *Best Practices* document made it easier for the various professionals to begin discussing recovery specifics—such as at what intervals to make phone calls and provide reports to the waiting funeral directors, what body preparation materials would most likely be needed by the funeral directors, and the promise that the body would be treated with the utmost respect, even though the person was deceased. A paramount theme was using expert surgical cleanliness and respectful processes during the recovery.

Although the *Best Practices* document was an important step, the funeral directors and recovery agencies recognized that localities needed guidance on how to effectively implement these practices. Funeral directors and recovery professionals had built positive relationships, given talks, written message points, reviewed materials, and provided guidance for ideas on implementation.

Phase 2: IFCA Intervention Implementation

The NKF approached the professional organizations of the funeral and cemetery industries to partner on researching how to improve communications. This began with a series of focus groups conducted among ICFA and NFDA members (NKF, 2002) followed by in-depth telephone calls among experienced funeral directors (Southeastern Institute of Research, 2001). We conducted similar focus groups among recovery professionals where they identified potential barriers and generated ideas for implementation of the *Best Practices* document. Most of these discussions centered on the need for more communication, building relationships, and taking the time to learn about each others' work and needs.

With these ideas in hand, it was time to see whether local recovery and funeral professionals could be moved closer to the ideal of the *Best Practices* and of encouraging donation. Because most funeral directors and procurement professionals have limited time and budgets, the interventions tested in each area were those that did not require a great deal of resources. Further, a short intervention time frame was used to show what could be changed relatively quickly (within 6 months).

Rationale
We decided to focus our next phase on the members of the ICFA, at least in part because the NKF believed that people who worked in the funeral and cemetery industry were less afraid of talking with others about end-of-life decisions and would not mind educating the public about organ and tissue donation while preplanning their funerals. In much the same way, ICFA members provided the public with education (as a marketing technique) on Social Security, veterans' benefits, life insurance, power of attorney, and living wills. It was hoped that once they learned more about donation, it would lead to a better working relationship with organ and tissue donation professionals.

The members of the ICFA, mostly women, worked as preplanners, making a living selling burial plots, stones, and preplanned services to the well, healthy public. The general thinking in the transplant and donation field at the time was that the healthy well public was not educated about donation because it was too frightening for them to listen to donation appeals because death itself is too frightening to dwell on. The belief was that ICFA professionals were not afraid of talking about death and could educate the public while marketing their products. We believed this intervention would result in an intent to donate from the healthy public.

Intervention procedures
We worked with the ICFA to recruit a total of 100 preplanners (also called *counselors*) and funeral directors to participate in the study from nine geographic areas (Seattle; San Francisco; Ogden, Utah; Southern California; Denver; Indianapolis; Pittsburgh; Baltimore; and Miami). Eighty of them received a training booklet and an audio training tape educating them about donation and explaining how to include positive donation messages along with their usual messages about the helpfulness of Social Security, veterans' benefits, wills, and estate planning to potential clients. The training included information on how to set up a family discussion with the study participants' own family in order to practice what they had learned and gained from practical experience. The remaining 20 counselors, who served as a control group, were not given any training about organ and tissue donation. The counselors agreed to participate for one month—during that time, providing three clients a week with information about organ and tissue donation and a short survey for them to mail in about organ donation beliefs and intentions.

Two weeks after the visit, the NKF contacted the clients to see if they had discussed donation with their family or signed an organ donor card. A short structured telephone-based interview was used to gain an understanding of how the clients and counselors felt about the process. In terms of donation outcomes, we expected outcome ratios to be significantly higher for the treatment group at posttest than for the control group. We also expected a trend for the treatment group's ratios to steadily increase over time as compared to the control group's outcome ratios.

Challenges

The sample size was chosen to be large enough to accommodate one or more counselors quitting the study due to illness, job change, or unforeseen incidents. However, the dropout rate of counselors was much higher than we expected. We aimed to complete 12 different family visits per month for each of the 100 counselors. We yielded less. The ICFA, as a voluntary agency, could not mandate the reporting of data, even though the memorandums of understanding between the ICFA and NKF sought to minimize the risk of nonadherence to the study protocols.

Much to our surprise, the preplanners, though not afraid to talk about death with their potential clients, were afraid to talk about organ and tissue donation. From follow-up conversations with the preplanners and funeral directors who participated in the study, we uncovered the following reasons why: (a) It slowed them down—they were under such intense pressure to sell, meet quotas, and meet shareholder expectations for their employers that they wanted to keep the conversation focused on only what was absolutely necessary; (b) doubts still lingered that donation would lead to disappointment in funeral preparations, and they or their company would somehow be blamed; and (c) they had an uncomfortable feeling about the donation process, perhaps a fear of the deceased person's body being disrespected or dismembered, leading to what we labeled the *fear factor*.

This fear factor, coupled with no remuneration for completing the paperwork, and with anecdotal evidence that the counselors' employers were not always supportive of the efforts, resulted in relatively few counselors making more than a passing mention of donation. Even when they provided the survey to clients, it was often lost in a stack of paperwork, and their clients had little interest in completing the survey and mailing it back.

Phase 3: Funeral Director Intervention

The failure of the ICFA effort to yield measureable results showed us that we first needed to build trust. Thus, we reorganized the research effort to include both groups with the greatest need for a good working relationship—the local procurement organization and funeral directors. Moreover, unlike preplanners, funeral directors are less impacted by the need to meet quotas and make sales. We selected three pilot areas to test the impact of various grassroots efforts to build trust and improve the relationship between organ and tissue recovery professionals and funeral directors, change perceptions, and ultimately create more intentions to donate at the time of death among those who come in contact with funeral directors.

Setting

This study sought to mimic the situation faced by organ and tissue recovery professionals across the United States, one that is often fraught with limitations—of organs and tissues, of resources, and of perceived support from funeral directors. We felt that we needed to incorporate the reality of these all-too-common limitations in order to convincingly show other communities just how much is possible despite the limitations. Thus, we included small, rural areas as well as large, urban ones in this study.

The three pilot areas (clusters) were chosen based on their diversity. We included pilot areas located in the Northeast, the South, and the western half of the United States, with rural, urban, and suburban communities. The NKF contacted organ and tissue recovery professionals and funeral directors within Connecticut, Iowa, and North Carolina to explain the project and encourage their participation. The organ procurement organizations in these areas all had different resources, budgets, commitments, and staffing.

Interventions

To incorporate local sensibilities and make the project as "real world" as possible, local organ and tissue recovery professionals chose the actions they wanted to try. They started with a list of options (jointly developed by funeral and recovery professionals) such as providing information in a booklet or fact sheet, providing access to a knowledgeable professional from each side to help with problems or potential problems, and providing actual body preparation materials and instructions for complex recoveries. Recovery professionals were also encouraged to brainstorm to create additional options. Local efforts were supplemented by a letter and information packet mailed to funeral directors in all three pilot areas.

Interventions mainly consisted of the local procurement organization initiating a dialogue with funeral directors and providing them with information. John Carmon, past president of the NFDA, sent a personal letter to all participating funeral directors in all three geographic areas with a copy of the *Best Practices*, a camera-ready symbol for denoting an organ donor in newspaper obituaries and permanent memorials, and an article from *The Director* explaining the use of this symbol (Kroshus, 1997). Funeral directors also received a child's coloring book—the *Katie Coolican Story* (Carney, 1999)—explaining organ and tissue donation for children, along with information about other materials available on the subject.

The researchers encouraged personalization of the outreach to funeral directors in each geographic region to complement and reflect the staff expertise and available resources of the organ procurement organizations that are spearheading the effort. Each of the three areas implemented elements of the *Best Practices* documents in the way most comfortable for them. Finally, we kept the intervention period short: 2–5 months. Although we knew this was not sufficient to change donation rates, we wanted to see if it would be sufficient for changing attitudes and creating a foundation for a firmer, more trusting relationship between funeral directors and organ procurement organization professionals.

Procedures

We structured the study as a pre-post trial, with organ and tissue recovery professionals and funeral directors in these three areas sharing their perceptions before and after action was taken to improve communication. The preintervention survey assessed initial perceptions and attitudes of the funeral directors and recovery professionals. The postintervention survey was administered to the same people after the interventions in their area to measure any changes in attitudes and perceptions: (a) the perceived level of knowledge about the processes involved, (b) perceptions about communication (whether between funeral people and recovery people or as to its impact on the general public), or (c) attitudes toward organ and tissue donation itself (particularly among those in the funeral industry).

Interviewing for the pretreatment first wave took place in May–June 2002 for Iowa and Connecticut and during July 2002 for North Carolina. All posttreatment interviews occurred during September 2002. All participants were given the option to have a questionnaire mailed to them to complete and return by mail or fax. In keeping with promised anonymity, responses were stripped of any individual identifiers (such as the e-mail address). Completion of the questionnaire was considered the subject's consent to participate in the study. At least two reminders were sent to nonrespondents to encourage their participation. Despite these efforts, participation remained low (see Table 13.1). As a result, legitimate statistical analyses could not be conducted. Therefore, rather than report statistical findings, we will present study information in a case study format.

Table 13.1 Number responding out of number eligible

	Funeral Directors			Organ/Tissue			Study Total		
	Pre	Post	Both	Pre	Post	Both	Pre	Post	Both
Connecticut	10/29	5/26	5/26	11/12	7/11	7/11	21/41	12/37	12/37
Iowa	15/20	8/18	7/18	5/11	4/10	2/10	20/31	12/28	9/28
North Carolina	2/7	1/7	1/7	5/10	5/10	4/10	7/17	6/17	5/17
Total	27/56	14/51	13/51	21/33	16/31	13/31	48/89	30/82	26/82

Case Study 1: Connecticut

LifeChoice Donor Services, the OPO in Connecticut, has a service population of 2.1 million, and they perform approximately 100 tissue recoveries and 40–50 organ recoveries per year. For this project, John Carmon, a funeral director, past president of the NFDA, and local OPO employee, spearheaded outreach to local funeral employees. Highlighting his professional background, he included a personal note in the NKF educational packet sent to area funeral directors acknowledging both the inconveniences and benefits of organ and tissue donation for their industry. The note emphasized the informational and education opportunities (e.g., interactions with expert embalmers and funeral directors experienced in donation) available through the OPO, acknowledging deficits in donation expertise among funeral directors due to the few yearly donations they are involved in.

Other outreach efforts involved in-service sessions for funeral home employees and distribution of specialized materials to local funeral directors explaining what prosthetics have been used in the reconstruction, the role of the eye and tissue banks, organs and tissues taken, embalming tips and methods, and embalming procedures. Overall, the approach in Connecticut relies on the commitment and expertise of a core group of organ procurement organization employees and funeral directors to spearhead a consistent, ongoing outreach effort at the grassroots level.

Case Study 2: Iowa

In an approach similar to the one taken in Connecticut, in Iowa the local OPO allocated a staff member (Michelle Kelsey) dedicated to funeral directors: the funeral director liaison. The liaison's role was to develop positive relationships with funeral directors by educating them about donation and making sure they were included in the recovery process. A number of outreach efforts were undertaken to facilitate open communication between the OPO and the local funeral industry.

The liaison helped develop a funeral director advisory committee to advise the OPO about funeral director experiences statewide and brainstormed what could help make the process of donation work better for both parties as well as the families involved. The committee met during pre- and post-testing on a quarterly basis to solicit feedback on the donation process and recovery practices. The liaison also attended local funeral home district meetings and the Iowa Funeral Directors Association convention, and the OPO published articles in the state funeral director publication communiqué every quarter.

Other more personalized educational and outreach efforts included regular informational and educational visits with funeral directors, the delivery of donor family medals and family support kits to funeral employees, and the supervision of organ and tissue recoveries to ensure that funeral directors were included in important communications. According to Michelle, "Relationships with funeral directors were in large part nonexistent before 2000. We have found that communication is the key. One of the developments or improvements we made is an extensive follow-up program on any organ or tissue donation case that occurs" (Michele Kelsey, personal communication, 2008).

Challenges in Iowa included the sheer distances that organ procurement organization employees had to drive to meet with funeral directors individually and at functions. Inviting funeral directors to meetings, to sit on board of directors, and to trainings could be a logistical challenge and requires additional travel funds.

Case Study 3: North Carolina

Unlike in the other sites, the North Carolina OPO, LifeShare, did not designate a specific individual to lead the project. Educational visits with local funeral directors followed an introductory letter originating with the OPO coordinator, Alista Watkins. OPO staff visited 10 funeral homes to offer advice and support regarding organ and tissue donation, with the goal of developing a relationship based on trust and respect. The OPO is now expanding outreach by training recipients and donor families to conduct funeral visits—placing a face on the mission.

LifeShare and the funeral homes in their service area have each other's contact information handy and on mailing lists—thus enabling the OPO to contact funeral directors in a timely manner to inform them of family consent for donation while, in return, being informed of local activities in the funeral industry. LifeShare's mailing list for funeral homes became so up-to-date that when they mailed follow-up greeting cards to all area funeral homes, zero were returned, making this one of the most successful large-scale mailings they have conducted.

Study Limitations

Some limitations were accounted for by this study—brief interventions, few resources, and a small number of communities and participants—whereas others became evident as the study progressed. Because most of the interventions were initiated by organ and tissue professionals, they focused on making funeral directors more aware of the organ and tissue donation process. There was no comparable focus in these interventions on educating organ and tissue professionals about the funeral process. Still, the expanded dialogue may have made some realize that they did not know as much about the funeral process as they previously thought. It was hard to measure the impact of each individual intervention partly because they were so personal to the individual and the geographic area. We would suggest using standardized approaches in each geographical area.

Lessons Learned

The low response rate, particularly among funeral directors, reduced the sample size. For future research, engaging a larger number of funeral directors is warranted.

At the time of this study, the funeral industry was experiencing a structural and financial change. Independent funeral homes were being bought by large publicly held corporations and the traditional, independently owned, "mom-and-pop" industry was in certain instances being replaced by a corporate culture subject to influence by the financial climate of public companies on the stock exchange. Research conducted today may experience a different corporate culture: The industry has been consolidated and survived the adjustment period of conducting business a new way.

Both recovery professionals and funeral personnel believed that ongoing, honest communication between the two groups would greatly benefit the transplant community. The organ and tissue donation industry has seen a more consistent move toward having funeral directors on salary at OPOs, full- and part-time and as paid consultants.

Donor families in the NKF's National Donor Family Council, a "home for donor families," have reported that being able to have their loved ones donate has helped them in their grieving process. Funeral directors, who deal with family grief, are in a key position to recognize this value in the gift and encourage it, if they have reason to believe it is in the families' and their own best interest. Too many times, funeral directors do not see this positive side of donation, and this research aimed to show routes for changing this perception, with the goal of ultimately increasing donation. Donor families are apt to become ambassadors for organ and tissue donation when they have had a good experience donating. Future work with funeral directors may be aided by having donor family experiences shared with the funeral and cemetery personnel as well as the continued use of educational materials about the donation process.

At the study's inception, we had hoped to help recovery and funeral professionals recognize the need to communicate and form strong relationships in order to effectively sensitize and improve the donation process for the professionals involved in it as well as for donor families. This is a worthwhile goal. As long as the process of donation is fraught with professionals at odds, donor families will suffer. Ambassadors promoting the goodness of organ and tissue donation would be lost or, even worse, could become messengers spreading distrust and doubt to potential donors.

Conclusion

This study began in 1999. Though the landscape may have changed, today, 10 years later, engaging funeral directors in ongoing communication with recovery agencies is a low-cost way to facilitate organ and tissue donations. People doing research in this field will note that an increase in the quantity and quality of communication between the two groups can only enhance the operations and effectiveness of both groups. The information provided to funeral directors made them feel more knowledgeable. Although it might seem like a small matter, having organ and tissue professionals take the first step to establish a dialogue at the local level can make a difference. There is opportunity for even greater sharing of knowledge for increased understanding. For example, this study mainly focused on organ and tissue professionals educating those in the funeral services field about the donation process. Once the dialogue is begun, funeral directors may be willing to help educate organ and tissue professionals more about the funeral process.

Will this increase organ and tissue donation rates? We expect it will have a positive impact, though this remains to be proven. Removing disincentives for funeral directors by providing them with resources to assist them through particular cases would seem to be a commonsense way to facilitate the process of donation. These resources include on-call expertise for embalming, preparation questions, hands-on training opportunities, as well as instruments, materials, and fluids that may be more expensive or not readily available. The more families who view organ and tissue donation favorably, the more organ and tissue donation is viewed favorably among people who regularly counsel others about end-of-life issues. This, in turn, results in more fear being dissipated and more positive messages proclaimed about the action and experience of donation. The expectation is that this will develop into more opportunities for deceased donations.

Acknowledgments

This research was supported in part by grant # 1-H39-OT00005-01 from the Health Resources and Services Administration, Division of Transplantation (HRSA/DoT), U.S. Department of Health and Human Services. The contents of this chapter are solely the responsibility of the authors and do not necessarily represent the views of HRSA/DoT.

Grant partners: John C. Carmon, past president, National Funeral Directors Association; John H. Fitch, Jr., senior vice president, Advocacy Division, National Funeral Directors Association; P. Robert Rigney, Jr., CEO, American Association of Tissue Banks; Paul M. Schwab, executive director, Association of Organ Procurement Organizations; and Patricia Aiken-O'Neill, president/CEO, Eye Bank Association of America.

Special acknowledgments: HRSA HHS Grant Project Officer: Mary Ganikos, chief, Public and Professional Education Branch, Division of Transplantation; and, for pioneering efforts in communications: Kristen Lattimer, director of procurement, and Mark Lattimer, LFD, Funeral Service Coordinator, Lifebanc.

Advisory board members: Teresa Beigay, Division of Transplantation consultant; Joseph W. Budzinski, internal chief operating officer, International Cemetery and Funeral Association; Margaret B. Coolican, founder and past chair, National Donor Family Council; Barbara L. Crow, Eye Bank Association of America; Patricia L. Darrigan, American Association of Tissue Banks; Scott Hargett, recovery coordinator, Lifenet; Larry Hierholzer, executive director, Orange County Eye and Tissue Bank; Rusty Kelly, COO/ managing director, Eye Bank Association of America; Michelle Kelsey, development specialist, Iowa Donor Network; Ellen Kulik, chair, National Donor Family Council; Karl J. McCleary, assistant professor, Pennsylvania State University; Andrew Mullins, funeral director liaison, Life Connection of Ohio; Mary Schneider, director of quality assurance/ risk management, OneLegacy; Timothy J. Sartorius, director of Funeral Home Services, Oklahoma Organ Sharing Network; Shirley Brown-VanArsdale, National Funeral Directors Association; and Alista Watkins, organ recovery coordinator II, North American Transplant Coordinators Organization.

References

Carney, K. (1999). *Precious gifts: Katie Coolican's story—Barklay and Eve explain organ and tissue donation.* Wethersfield, CT: Dragonfly.

Kroshus, J. (1997). Embalming the vertebral body donor. *The Director, 69,* 30–34.

National Funeral Directors Association. (2001). *AATB-AOPO-NFDA joint initiative: AOPO update.* Retrieved January 4, 2009, from http://www.nfda.org/page.php?pID=203

National Kidney Foundation. (2000a). *Minutes of meeting: Transplant community and funeral directors meeting.* Retrieved January 10, 2009, from http://www.kidney.org

National Kidney Foundation. (2000b). Take time to talk: A family discussion guide about organ and tissue donation. Retrieved January 9, 2009, from http://www.kidney.org/ order/index.cfm/fuseaction/product.display/product_id/26/index.cfm

National Kidney Foundation. (2002). *Focus group at LifeBanc.* Retrieved January 6, 2009, from http://www.kidney.org

Southeastern Institute of Research, under the guidance of Chléire Consulting. (2001). *Focus group with funeral directors: 10/07/01.* Richmond, VA: Author.

14

The Challenges of Conducting and Evaluating Organ Donation Campaigns

Susan E. Morgan

Developing large-scale interventions to promote organ donation has obvious appeal; persuading large numbers of people through public campaigns to join organ donor registries provides the best chance of saving the lives of people waiting for life-saving transplants. Identifying appropriate target audiences, conducting the requisite formative research to pinpoint specific barriers that stand in the way (socially, psychologically, or physically) of donor registration, and then planning an effective campaign that utilizes effective messages and appropriate channels of dissemination can be a daunting, though exciting, challenge. However, the greatest, and probably least recognized and discussed, challenge is that of actual implementation. Experienced researchers often trade "war stories" at professional meetings and continue to learn how to navigate a variety of potential landmines, but those who are new to the field of organ donation promotion (or any other applied health issue) do not have the benefit of learning from these experiences. The challenges most frequently faced by researchers include the development of theory-based campaigns that take into account issues that are specific to the topic of organ donation itself. Additionally, there are challenges involved with working with community partner organizations, gaining and maintaining access to intervention sites, and maintaining intervention fidelity across sites and over time. A discussion of these challenges will be situated primarily within the context of worksite-based campaigns, though the recommendations that will be offered often can be generalized to many other types of interventions.

Organ Donation as a Targeted Behavior of Theory-Based Interventions

It is important to first consider the ways in which the promotion of organ donation differs from education about other health issues. Unlike smoking cessation, exercise, or injury prevention, becoming an organ donor does not benefit employees, at least not directly or tangibly. Most health campaigns result in the improvement of a person's health and, often, the avoidance of premature death. To become a (nonliving) organ donor, on the other hand, a person has to die. Not surprisingly, contemplation of one's own death is not likely to lead to a particularly comfortable cognitive state. Many people's instinctual avoidance of the topic of organ donation itself is an obstacle that researchers and practitioners must overcome when designing an effective worksite campaign. Appeals to employees to become an organ donor must emphasize other benefits, especially the satisfaction of saving the lives of others and perhaps even the spiritual or literal sense that donors survive death by "living on" through their recipients.

Unfortunately, we do not have well-developed theories of behavior change that allow us to plan successful interventions that take into account the probable reactions of people who will be asked to consider their own death (and the possibility of organ and/or tissue removal). The theories that are commonly used in health interventions presume a rational response to the persuasively framed information presented to them. As such, most theories are cognitively based and presume a linear, rational progression from (generally speaking across theories and models) knowledge, attitudes, and perceived social norms, to considerations of perceived benefits as well as the perceived barriers to becoming an organ donor, to the eventual decision to become a potential organ donor after death. The exact theoretical foundations of worksite interventions have varied considerably. Theories such as the theory of planned behavior, the theory of reasoned action (TRA), and the transtheoretical model (aka the "stages of change" approach) have predominated. However, theories that create a solid foundation for some types of health interventions may not be equally suited to other health issues. This appears to be the case with organ donation, where the transtheoretical model has not been used with much success in public communication campaigns to promote nonliving organ donation, whereas the theory of reasoned action and related models have proven to be far more useful as a guide for the development and evaluation of organ donation campaigns. However, it should be pointed out that even the theory of reasoned action, if not modified, is a poor predictor overall of the willingness to donate, even though TRA-based campaigns themselves have produced impressive behavior change.

By adding variables to existing models of individual behavior change, these theoretical approaches can be better tailored to the specific features of the issue of organ donation. Factors that appear to affect the willingness to donate include existential variables such as the perception that organ donors "survive" death, a concern about saving the lives of "bad" people, the fear that signing a donor card will tempt fate and possibly bring on premature death, and a general sense of disgust from the idea of putting the organs from one person into the body of another person (see Morgan, Harrison, Long, Afifi, & Stephenson, 2008; Morgan, Stephenson, Harrison, Afifi, & Long, 2008). Morgan and colleagues have added these variables to the theory of reasoned action to create a model tailored to organ donation, the organ donation model.

Translating Theory Into Practice

The operationalization of the variables described by the theory of reasoned action has taken the form of specific features of worksite organ donation campaigns. Formative research with both general and minority populations provided important information about the specific points of knowledge that were most predictive of the willingness to donate (Morgan, Harrison, Chewning, DiCorcia, & Davis, 2007; Morgan et al., under review). These include knowledge about the organ allocation system, understanding that potential donor status will not affect the quality of medical care in an emergency, knowledge that an organ donor can have an open-casket funeral, and knowledge that a black market does not exist in the United States (Morgan, 2006; Morgan & Cannon, 2003; Morgan, Miller, & Arasaratnam, 2003). Rather than overwhelm employees with unnecessary general information about organ donation, the worksite campaigns focused on providing details about these specific points of knowledge. Common strategies for distributing this information included cafeteria table tents, brochures (and universal donor cards) that reached every employee, paycheck stuffers, and e-mail and voice-mail blasts (Morgan, Miller, & Arasaratnam, 2002; Morgan et al., 2007, under review).

Organ donation worksite campaigns based on the theory of reasoned action also targeted perceptions of supportive social norms (Morgan et al., 2007). These campaigns prominently featured employees of organizations who had been touched by organ donation. Donors and recipients were featured on billboards on roads leading to an organization's building as well as full-color posters hung on bulletin boards. Their stories appeared in newsletter articles, which provided greater details about the employees' stories, and abbreviated versions of these stories were used as paycheck and mailbox stuffers. By emphasizing to employees that they all "knew" someone who had been affected by donation, the campaign sought to capitalize on the sense of affiliation that people often feel with their coworkers. Interpersonal discussions about their coworkers' experiences offered the opportunity to exchange personal thoughts and feelings about donation in the hopes that such discussions would elevate perceptions of social norms supporting organ donation. When this element of a worksite campaign was recently isolated and tested for its effectiveness, companies with employees personally touched by organ donation experienced greater increases in signed donor cards and/or donor registry forms. Also, the very fact that employees have crowded around an information table in a high-visibility, high-traffic area in the organization to sign up to become a donor becomes a form of social proof that may be quite powerful.

The organ donation model (Morgan, Stephenson, et al., 2008) has proved to be an important road map for navigating some aspects of the social psychology of individuals considering organ donation. Although superstitions about bringing on premature death by signing a donor card or a visceral-level disgust response at the idea of organ transplantation would be difficult at best to overcome through a worksite campaign, concerns about the deservingness of potential recipients are more easily addressed. By having transplant recipients help to staff information tables and by featuring a company's own employees in the campaign, most of whom were recipients, nondonors could establish a greater sense of connection with the sort of people who would be potential recipients of their own organs.

The development of theory-based campaigns is always a challenge, regardless of whether the decision-making process is rational or nonrational. This, however, is frequently not the biggest challenge faced by researchers.

Challenges of Working With Community Partner Organizations

Organ procurement organizations (OPOs) have been conducting public outreach and education for decades, and much like advertising professionals, OPO staff generally have a strong sense of what "works" and what "doesn't work" to effectively promote organ donation willingness. OPO professionals, like many people who work for nonprofit organizations, come from a wide variety of educational backgrounds and professional experiences. Although many people recognize the importance of evaluating their OPO's activities, few do so with any degree of validity relative to the standards set by social science.

After closing his office door, a manager who supervised outreach professionals told me that during their last outreach campaign at a major athletic event, 50 people signed organ donor cards. He asked me (sotto voce) if that was "good." I hardly knew where to begin to answer him without overwhelming him with research methodology concepts and terminology. This wasn't the first time (or the last) that I had been called upon to try to explain good campaign evaluation procedures. I probably spend as much time trying to persuade members of partner organizations, including managers of potential sites for our interventions, of the importance of conducting campaign activities in very particular ways because of the potential impact on evaluation procedures.

In my own experience, developing simplified ways of explaining key research concepts is critical. For example, one of the most frequent "helpful suggestions" by community partners or worksite managers is that the research team should collect pre- and posttest survey data by allowing people to stop by a centrally located information table to complete the survey if they are interested in doing so.

Explaining the concept of "random sampling" and "systematic bias" to a roomful of corporate executives debating whether to permit access for your project can involve a lot of ineffective fumbling if you are not prepared for this common question. Similarly, avoiding appearing difficult or ungrateful while explaining why being allowed to host only "lunch-and-learn" brown-bag lunches, which typically draw 10 to 30 employees even at the largest corporations, will not be worth your team's time could prove tricky unless you can quickly draw the analogy of "preaching to the choir"—clearly, these are not the people you are trying so hard to reach.

In working with any community partner organization, academic researchers must take great care not to imply that they know how to promote the targeted health behavior better than the professionals who work for the organization. This is especially true if the researcher has no experience in creating or implementing campaigns specific to the particular health issue. Although theories are valued for their capacity to generalize across areas of application, every health issue has its "ins and outs" that are important to learn. As a rule of thumb, an intense immersion in the health issue (by actually volunteering for outreach activities, for example) for at least 6 months is a good idea. Not only will your partner(s) be less likely to doubt your sincerity and dedication to the issue, but also the experiences you gain will help you avoid making foolish mistakes by using incorrect terminology, acronyms, and the like.

However, when you disagree with your community partners, ceding to their recommendations and preferences after you have worked with an issue for a number of years and have completed a number of successful interventions that have generated results surpassing the expectations of OPO professionals (which are based on their own considerable experiences) can prove to be difficult, especially when you are working under tight deadlines. There are no easy answers to this dilemma except to continually maintain dialogue until a mutual understanding has been reached. No partnership is free from conflict, and talking it through is the only viable alternative to quitting the project. Also, continually reminding your partner organization that you are on their side (and not simply chasing after data) because you share their goals for the organization is frequently helpful.

Another way of avoiding an "us-versus-them" mentality is to schedule frequent "whole-team" meetings focused on project progress and future tasks. Experience has demonstrated that weekly one-hour meetings are ideal, and need to be attended by everyone involved in the execution of project activities. These include the lead researcher, the principle liaison from the partner organization, any outreach specialists who help to staff events, volunteer coordinators who recruit and schedule volunteers for events, and any research assistants or coinvestigators involved in the project. Similarly, getting involved with your partner organization's activities by accepting a place on their advisory board (or, if invited, their board of directors) will help to keep your project a priority in the minds of upper management. This is important if you want to avoid your project being pushed down the list in relation to other competing activities and priorities for the organization. If you require staff hours, volunteers' time, and the cooperation of your community partner organization, maintaining a steady sense of connection is vital (though certainly no guarantee).

The deprioritization of your project by a community partner is a real danger. In addition to staying on their "radar" by volunteering for the organization and serving on advisory boards, if your project is (or will be) supported by grant funds, it is always a good idea to devote money toward paying some or all of an employee's salary. In this way, your demands on a community partner's employee's time can be fully justified, thus helping to protect your long-term outcomes. Although this might not help you to avoid a sense of divided loyalty on the part of the employee whose salary is coming (in part or wholly) from an outside project, it will allow you to remind the management of your partner organization of the multiple benefits of your project: Not only are you helping them fulfill their ultimate mission (in this case, to increase donation), but also you are covering the salary of the employee who is assigned to help achieve that mission.

Covering the entire salary of a part- or full-time employee is also desirable because of the deadlines that are built into projects, particularly those that receive external funding. Your community partners are unlikely to be accustomed to following a long sequence of successive deadlines within a single project; most nonprofit, health-focused organizations have a calendar of events that occur annually, but it is rare to work with a partner organization that understands that if your campaign billboards do not go up, say, by February, the methodology involved with the evaluation of the success of your campaign could be severely compromised. Being accountable to a federal or state funding agency (or even a private foundation) for the accomplishment of a long-term plan on time and on budget can be extremely stressful if your partner organization does not understand what is at stake. Providing everyone with a master timeline as well as a detailed, ongoing short-term timeline that include markers of the completion of important tasks can be extremely helpful in not only conveying the importance of meeting deadlines but also providing a sense of accomplishment once those deadlines have been met.

Challenges of Gaining and Maintaining Intervention Site Access

Getting your foot in the door of an organization to try to get access for campaigns or other interventions, whether your site is a school or a corporation, can itself be a daunting prospect. If the key management personnel who finally granted you access leave their position for another organization, maintaining access for your project can be an even bigger challenge, not simply because you are essentially starting over but also because a new authority figure may have his or her own (stated or unstated) priorities, one of which may be to distinguish him or herself from the "old administration."

My project teams have been most successful in maintaining access in these situations when we have previously identified members of the organization who have been personally affected by organ donation. Identifying the health issue with the organization itself generally circumvents the possibility that an individual's ego will interfere with the goal of implementing and evaluating a campaign. This was the case with the UPS campaign (see Morgan et al., 2002), where a middle manager, the husband of a young woman who saved several lives after becoming a donor after dying suddenly of a brain aneurysm, was a steady advocate of our proposed campaign throughout several changes in upper management. If UPS had not been our only site and had any other options been available to us, I am confident that we would have abandoned this project after our third or fourth meeting to try to salvage our access to their two large worksites. This one donor husband's advocacy and continual retelling of his story can be credited for saving this ultimately successful project.

Similarly, identifying your project as having been validated by other credible organizations can be invaluable. In the New Jersey Workplace Partnership for Life (Morgan et al., 2007), we were able to sign on Robert Wood Johnson Hospital and Johnson & Johnson's global headquarters for our first wave of campaigns that would ultimately include a total of 46 organizations. For both the University Worksite Organ Donation project and the New Jersey Workplace Partnership for Life, we began by seeking out people who were already affiliated or identified with the issue—whether they were a student health services coordinator who had a sister who had received a double transplant, or the vice president of a hospital currently serving on the board of directors of our community partner organization. Once large organizations that are admired by other organizations sign on to a large project, their "star power" or referent power as benchmark organizations makes it easier to convince new organizations to sign on. Perhaps it is not unlike the casting process for a major Hollywood picture. The production process may stall for months or years until a major film star signs on for a leading role. Then, quickly, other movie stars sign on to complete the cast of characters.

Nonetheless, when seeking access to a large number of sites, at some point it becomes necessary to cast a wider net, which inevitably involves cold calling. We selected organizations that were the largest employers in the state to ensure that we were taking advantage of the most significant asset of worksite campaigns: the ability to reach a large captive audience with our messages. We then developed a standardized script that was used with key gatekeepers to secure meetings that were hoped would lead to consent to conduct a campaign at the worksite. It should be noted that many of these meetings were conducted (or led) by our partner organization's employee, who worked solely for our grant project and who was a young, articulate heart transplant recipient. The power of messages that included accounts of her personal experience with the issue of organ and tissue donation cannot be overestimated. Although her personal accounts did not result in success at every attempt to secure access, there is no question that our rate of success was enhanced by our choice of source of our persuasive messages.

Another positive recruiting tool was our demonstrated ability to deliver on our promises. After the completion of one of our five cycles of campaigns, we generated high-quality reports of campaign results that provided data specific to each individual organization and how the organization compared to aggregated campaign results from all current and past organizations. Control site organizations, as promised, received campaign activities of their choice (though posttest surveys were not administered). Report materials, once identifiers were removed, were used to show potential new worksites what they could expect to receive after their campaign concluded. Moreover, a final report of the results of 3 years of campaigns for all 45 organizations was promised, along with key findings about the predictors of effective worksite campaigns so that organizations could make better informed choices about future worksite campaigns about other health issues.

Perhaps the most important lesson that was learned about the process of negotiating for site access is that we cannot assume that gatekeepers believe in the importance of our health issue and that they do not hold the same misconceptions about the issue as the general public. Despite ample evidence that highly educated (or otherwise high-socioeconomic-status) people are better informed about health issues in general and are more likely to be active in seeking out accurate health information, these advantages are merely relative. In other words, gatekeepers such as corporate managers may be statistically more likely to be better informed about some health issues, but their level of knowledge may not be meaningfully greater; moreover, any given individual will have his or her own prejudices about a specific issue that cannot be predicted before a researcher has a meeting to negotiate access. Thus, be prepared to both educate and persuade potential gatekeepers. Also, it is worth noting that framing your information about the issue as "Many of your employees may believe in X myth about Y" is much less of a threat to the ego of a gatekeeper than information that appears to be designed to educate gatekeepers themselves.

Maintaining Intervention Fidelity

The execution of a multisite intervention or campaign is a special challenge that requires a high degree of coordination among trusted partners. However, even with a single-site study, intervention fidelity is a particular challenge. Executing a campaign or other intervention according to your original plan (which ideally should, of course, be grounded in behavior change theory) is often fraught with unexpected roadblocks. It is vital that you choose to deal with unexpected problems in a way that will not compromise your goals or jeopardize your ability to conduct a valid evaluation of the success of your intervention.

If you have received external funding for your campaign, your funding proposal can serve as a "bible" for all staff members and community partners. In your regular staff meetings, it should be referred to frequently so all members are thoroughly familiar with the goals of your program. When problems arise, all possible courses of action should be evaluated in reference to the original proposal. Although solutions are rarely ideal, it is also true that some are less bad than others. Diligently keeping records of any compromises to your original blueprint for your intervention will allow you to account for possible variations in your evaluation findings. The biggest threats to a project are those you are not aware of; thus, it is imperative that all staff and volunteers feel comfortable telling you about any problems that have arisen in the course of the execution of your intervention. Problems cannot be solved if they are swept under the rug in the hopes that "the boss" doesn't find out about them.

A sense of "esprit de corps" is invaluable when it comes to maintaining intervention fidelity. When potential threats to fidelity arise, it is easy to panic and even resign oneself to a failed (or seriously compromised) intervention. The popular Bravo channel television show *Project Runway* has a design mentor, Tim Gunn. When novice designers flounder and despair over poor choices or their own bad luck, Gunn emphatically declares, "Make it work!" Fans of the show often marvel at just how often the designers do exactly that: Find creative solutions to impossible problems. A similar approach can be taken with health campaigns and interventions. For example, over the 4 years of the New Jersey Worksite Organ Donation Campaign, a handful of key worksites revoked our access, sometimes with very little notice after a great deal of preparation had already been done. In all but one case, sheer tenacity helped to reverse these organizations' decisions. Each case called for different specific strategies to get access reinstated, but pushing through, climbing over, or going around what seemed to be an impenetrable wall ultimately made the difference between success and failure.

Site access and personnel problems are not the only threats to intervention fidelity. A wolf in sheep's clothing can come in the form of a person or organization that tries to be helpful but whose assistance, if accepted, will compromise the ability to evaluate the success of your intervention. It is especially difficult to resist well-intentioned assistance when it comes in the form of "free money," not only because it will seem an outrageous refusal by the generous would-be benefactor but also because members of your own team will think that you are being foolish. (It is probably situations like this that cause some organ procurement organizations to complain that researchers "interfere" with their public outreach campaigns.) For example, a state representative who was the grateful recipient of an organ transplant wanted to support the cause of organ donation by purchasing a large amount of billboard space on heavily traveled roads and highways in his district. Unfortunately, his district was in an area that was assigned as a part of a "control" condition for the time period he proposed renting billboard space. The representative had a reputation for being bombastic, even aggressive, and project staff members were adamant that this was a man who could not be reasoned with once he set on a course of action, and that he would withdraw his generous offer of free publicity entirely if we refused to go along with his original plan. I convinced staff members to approach him, explain the situation, and offer a variety of alternatives that we brainstormed in advance. The result, not surprisingly, was complete cooperation and an avoidance of any compromises to our ability to evaluate the differences between intervention and control site activities.

Similarly, large "matching funds" from media outlets can create significant problems for intervention fidelity. Unless you are able to control the placement and timing of media spots, the result could be a compromised research design. One community partner was aghast that I was willing to give up $100,000 in donated media that would be aired in locations around the state (regardless of each city's assignment to media vs. control condition), but reconsidered once I pointed out that we were in the middle of a million-dollar federally funded project that would be rendered worthless if media spots were run in control sites. Not only is it important to honor a plan that you have set forth to a funding agency, but the wrong kind of "help" can compromise your ability to demonstrate the worth of principles that could positively influence the practices (and thus the effectiveness) of the entire OPO community.

Features of Successfully Implemented Organ Donation Campaigns

In spite of the many problems and challenges faced by health campaigns, including interventions targeting organ donation, there are some predictors of success (Morgan, 2005). Successful organ donation campaigns appear to have a number of shared features. First, the involvement of an experienced researcher (whether as the head of the team or as a co-director with a community partner representative) from the start of the planning process ensures that an intervention is developed that can be evaluated in a way that is valid from a social scientific perspective. Second, solid evaluation procedures must be in place. The ideal outcome measure is actual donor registration rates. However, well-designed pre- and posttest surveys on key measures of, for example, knowledge, attitudes, and self-reported behaviors can be done with control and intervention locations. It should be noted, of course, that random samples should be used and that the number of people sampled should be large enough to make valid statistical comparisons. These quantitative approaches can certainly be supplemented with the richer data that can be obtained through qualitative methods. Such data can provide valuable information about ways to improve campaign materials and intervention strategies for future campaigns.

Third, it appears from the literature that campaigns (especially worksite or university-based campaigns) that include interpersonal contact with trained staff and volunteers are more successful than interventions that deliver all messages via the mass media (radio, TV, billboards, posters, etc.; Morgan, 2005). It is important that staff and volunteers understand the actual barriers to the targeted behavior—in this case, donor registration—and know how to respond to key objections. It is common for OPO volunteers to be trained solely in ways to "share their story," an approach that can backfire if transplant recipients decide to lift up their shirts to show their scars from transplant surgery. ("Glorify organ donation, but please don't gore-ify it," one of our staff members used to plead before we implemented a retraining program for volunteers.) Related, outreach staff and volunteers should be demographically similar to the target population of the intervention, and messages should be delivered in the primary language of the population. Finally, "one-size-fits-all" campaigns should be avoided. The more specifically an intervention can be targeted to a single region or particular demographic, the more likely it will be successful.

In conclusion, conducting and evaluating successful campaigns and interventions to increase the rate of organ donor willingness or to improve health outcomes are fraught with a number of challenges. Clarity of purpose and maintaining a focus on shared ultimate goals can help overcome many of the challenges described in this chapter. Other challenges can be addressed through an effective, dynamic, and mutually respectful partnership between researchers and community partners. Both researchers and community partners must be willing to be open to learning what they do not know that may enhance the long-term effectiveness of both the intervention and the partner organization itself. Although this can take considerable time, patience, and trust in the good intentions of the other, the rewards and satisfactions come in the form of the possibility of many lives saved.

Acknowledgments

The research described in this chapter was supported by Grant Nos. 1H39OT00120, 1R39OT07652, and 1R39OT7652. The opinions expressed herein are those of the authors and do not necessarily represent those of the funding agency.

The author would like to thank the following coinvestigators and co–principal investigators for their work on the projects described in this chapter: Tyler R. Harrison, Michael T. Stephenson, Walid Afifi, Tom Reichert, Shawn Long, Eusebio Alvaro, Jenny Miller Jones, Tara Artesi, and Tom Cannon.

References

Morgan, S. E. (2005). *Report on the Division of Transplantation's grant program 1999–2004: Social and behavioral interventions to increase organ donation* (HRSA Contract OSP03780300). Washington, DC: Health Resource Services Administration. Retrieved May 22, 2009, from http://organdonor.gov/research/SBIIOD1999-2004/default.htm

Morgan, S. E. (2006). The many facets of reluctance: African-Americans and the decision (not) to donate organs. *Journal of the National Medical Association, 98*, 695–703.

Morgan, S. E., & Cannon, T. (2003) African Americans' knowledge about organ donation: Closing the gap with more effective persuasive message strategies. *Journal of the National Medical Association, 95*, 1066–1071.

Morgan, S. E., Harrison, T. R., Chewning, L. V., DiCorcia, M., & Davis, L. (2007, November). The Workplace Partnership for Life: The effectiveness of high- and low-intensity worksite campaigns to promote organ donation. Presented at the annual meeting of the National Communication Association, Chicago.

Morgan, S. E., Harrison, T. R., Long, S. D., Afifi, W. A., & Stephenson, M. T. (2008). In their own words: A multicultural qualitative study of the reasons why people will (not) donate organs. *Health Communication, 23*, 23–33.

Morgan, S. E., Miller, J., & Arasaratnam, L. A. (2002). Signing cards, saving lives: An evaluation of the Worksite Organ Donation Promotion Project. *Communication Monographs, 69*, 253–273.

Morgan, S. E., Miller, J., & Arasaratnam, L. A. (2003). Similarities and differences between African Americans' and European Americans' attitudes, knowledge, and willingness to communicate about organ donation. *Journal of Applied Social Psychology, 33*, 693–715.

Morgan, S. E., Stephenson, M. T., Afifi, W., Harrison, T. R., Long, S. D., & Chewning, L. V. (under review). The University Worksite Organ Donation Campaign: An evaluation of the impact of communication modalities on the willingness to donate. *Journal of Health Communication.*

Morgan, S. E., Stephenson, M. T., Harrison, T. R., Afifi, W. A., & Long, S. D. (2008). Facts versus "feelings": How rational is the decision to become an organ donor? *Journal of Health Psychology, 13*, 644–658.

Part III

Broad Perspectives and Future Directions

15

Community Organizations and Applied Research

Project Initiation, Implementation, and Dealing With Those Applied Researchers

Sara Pace Jones and David Bosch

In 1999, the U.S. Department of Health and Human Services, Health Resources and Services Administration's Division of Transplantation (HRSA/DoT) launched a grant program to improve research knowledge into behavioral and social science interventions that might lead to greater organ donation rates. This opportunity was seized by several Organ Procurement Organizations (OPOs) who had limited knowledge of research campaigns but a desire to increase both their abilities and budgets to do more. The initial grants required that OPOs team with researchers to expand the collective knowledge of what works and what does not work in terms of organ donation interventions. One of the unintended consequences of this connection was the opportunity to learn the differences, challenges, and opportunities that exist when researchers and community organizations are forced to work together.

Throughout this volume, you have heard from researchers and practitioners regarding a variety of projects and interventions. For some of you, reading about the trials and tribulations of applied research will motivate a desire to join the plight. For some, the thought may never enter your mind, but you might wonder what it would be like to do so. This chapter seeks to reduce the curiosity of the latter and offer advice for the former.

How Did This Whole Thing Get Started?

The projects discussed in this book have been carried out by communitybased nonprofit organizations—primarily federally designated (OPOs)—collaborating with social and behavioral science researchers. The primary functions of OPOs are clinical (recovering organs for transplant) and educational (educating the public about organ donation and transplantation) in nature.

As OPOs developed in the late 1970s and throughout the 1980s, the growing need for public awareness about donation became clear. Throughout the 1980s and 1990s, the developing shortage of organs for transplantation placed increasing pressure on OPOs, as well as other donation-related health organizations, to increase the number of donors. During this time, public "awareness" campaigns took many forms, including donor card drives, public service advertisements (PSAs) urging audiences to sign a donor card, and PSAs urging family discussion on the topic. Knowledge regarding national public attitudes about donation came from an initial Gallup survey (Gallup Organization, 1993), and the Coalition on Donation (now Donate Life America) utilized quantitative and qualitative research to develop its brand and campaign focus.

As with many not-for-profit organizations, funding for OPO marketing and promotional efforts has always been limited. In fact, there remain many people in the donation community who believe that the only legitimate role for the OPO is clinical: to provide as many organs for life-saving transplants as possible. Accordingly, early on, large-scale campaigns or interventions with solid measurement strategies were often beyond the reach and priority of OPOs in terms of budget and employee expertise. Measurement strategies often took the form of the number of materials distributed or the number of calls to the OPO. If promotional and marketing efforts were going to be taken to the next level, OPOs would have to be able to show a return on investment.

A Return on Investment

Grant funding is attractive to community organizations as a way to create new programs, try an idea, gain prestige in their field, increase revenue streams, increase programmatic activity, and generally contribute to the goals of the organization. At the end of any project, success is defined as a project that contributed to or advanced the organization's mission. In the case of an organ procurement organization, the overall goal is to save lives through organ donation. Because most transplantation involves nonliving donors, an individual cannot immediately save lives through organ donation. The challenge for the OPO is to somehow get an individual to commit in a meaningful way to being a donor sometime in the future. In the early days of the HRSA/DoT grant programs, this often involved family communication about donation. With the advent of donor registries in almost every U.S. state and registration acting as legal consent for donation, actual registration to be a donor has become the outcome measure of interest.

We have come to learn that although researchers evaluating the programs are also looking to achieve success and may like to help advance the mission of a cause or organization, the researchers' goals can be distinctly different from those of the community organization. In our experience, many of the researchers involved in social and behavioral interventions for organ donation have become committed to advancing knowledge and programs to improve donation rates, but they are also seeking grant projects as a way to advance science as well as to publish findings. In the first several years of the HRSA/DoT grants, an additional incentive for researcher involvement was the lack of published research on organ donation methodologies and programs. Although success of a project may be measured as increased donors by an organ procurement organization, success for the researcher is in a carefully constructed project, implemented flawlessly, that supports or disproves a theory.

Improving Collaboration With Researchers

In the initial grant project at Donor Network of Arizona (DNA; Grant # 1 H39 OT 00021-01, Sara Pace Jones, principal investigator [PI]), written entirely by the OPO with limited research input, every possible idea conceived or read about for Hispanic outreach was thrown into a 3-year grant proposal. DNA, including the first author of this chapter, had no idea about implementing interventions with the goal of figuring out what worked and what did not. In somewhat of a surprise, HRSA funded this proposal but required the development of a relationship with a researcher to assist in the development of the research design, including selection of outcomes measures. At first there was certainly hesitation. However, the result was a well-defined intervention that contributed significantly to the OPO's knowledge about barriers to donation within Arizona's Hispanic population, effective means of overcoming these barriers, and how to improve the organization's outcomes with this population (Alvaro, Pace Jones, Robles, & Siegel, 2005, 2006). This knowledge resulted in additional benefits through subsequent replication studies in surrounding states.

We have learned many lessons during the past decade of collaborating with researchers. Here, we present just a portion of those lessons in the hopes of increasing the likelihood of others meeting the same success as we feel we have.

Collaborate Early

Although collaboration on the initial project occurred after the grant proposal was written, we have learned that collaborating during the grant-writing process is a far superior approach. One advantage is the opportunity to communicate specifically about achievable objectives. Something that sounds great to a researcher may prove too difficult for a community organization with limited resources. For example, a project (Grant # 1 H39 OT 00118-01, Sara Pace Jones,

PI) designed in Arizona to test the ability of varied messages to get people to sign up on the Arizona Donor Registry (Siegel, Alvaro, & Pace Jones, 2005; Siegel et al., 2008) included a very specific requirement for changing posters throughout the state on a very tight, very prescribed schedule. Success for the intervention meant the schedule had to be perfectly adhered to. This kind of detail may be very tricky for community organization staff without building a paid staff member, or at least a partial paid staff member, into the proposal. Early collaboration allows researchers to explain their requirements and allows the community organization to explain their capabilities and understanding of the project.

It is also vital to make sure that everyone sees the project as beneficial. The researchers must feel as if their needs are being met, and the OPO must feel the same. Unlike driving a friend to the airport, a grant should not be entered into as a favor or begrudgingly. An applied research project requires a great deal of time and effort, and unless both enter with high hopes and expectations, it will be a long grant period. Being awarded a grant should be cause for celebration, not consternation. If both collaborators make sure to express their wants and needs early on and write the proposal accordingly, it will be a win–win situation. If it is not possible to write the proposal such that both sides will feel lucky to have been involved, the partnership should be reconsidered.

Educational Sessions and Frequent Communication

Once a grant project is funded, planning an educational session for all staff involved in the project can also lead to improved outcomes. In addition, future communication can be planned at this meeting to keep all parties on track. We have had experience with the ongoing communication being electronic and via telephone conference. Telephone conferences are particularly helpful in maintaining multisite communication and for catching challenges as they are happening. In a four-city program to test community forums (Grant #1 D71SP04141-01, Sara Pace Jones, PI), we found this extremely helpful in informing us which programs were progressing and where we needed to apply additional pressure or modify timing expectations. Frequent communication is a prerequisite for project success. Changes will occur, and adjustments will have to be made. If all parties are not involved when it comes time to adjust, aspects of the project that seem unimportant to one party might be dropped, much to the disappointment of the other.

Another way to get a project off to a great start, particularly if there are multiple partners, is to bring in an outside facilitator to team build. This approach was used successfully in the Arizona Donor Registry project (Grant # 1 H39 OT 00118-01, Sara Pace Jones, PI). This grant involved the collaboration of multiple organizations from throughout the State of Arizona to create a single donor registry for Arizona citizens. Buy-in by organizations beyond the OPO (e.g., the Hospital Association, transplant centers, and donation-related organizations such as the Kidney Foundation) was critical to a single registry effort. The group that put this effort together participated in several structured team-building exercises to build rapport. Such rapport can be critical to handling any difficulties that may lie ahead for a grant program.

This was actually tested with the same grant project when a new project coordinator was hired by the OPO. This new person came to a project meeting with the research team and, in an effort to show ownership and initiative, was critical of the project and suggested ways that the project should be improved for better outcomes in a somewhat less than positive manner. The existing rapport between the researchers allowed the possible rift that could have been created during this tense interchange to quickly be resolved. A level of trust already existed between the senior OPO personnel and the researchers. Everyone understood that the person could and would be coached and that improvement would take place.

Find Ways to Satisfy Everyone's Goals

Many researchers have a love for well-designed studies, and with good reason. If the study is not well designed, the success of the campaign will remain in doubt. Unfortunately, maintaining control over study design can be extremely difficult and time-consuming. Researchers and the OPO should communicate early and often about the design requirements and how design integrity can be maintained without siphoning all the grant's resources.

Researchers may need to be realistic about community organization staffing and their ability to keep up with strict program schedules considering their other duties. The project to initiate the Arizona Donor Registry included a stringent requirement to change messaging on the computer kiosks serving as registration portals. As mentioned above, the plan as outlined was to change the kiosk posters on an exact schedule in order to test which appeals were most successful at getting people to sign up. In order to be valid, the OPO needed to maintain a very specific schedule of kiosk delivery and poster changes. The OPO wanted to accompany the researchers' desire for a tight design but did not have the staff to do so. Working together, a plan was derived where undergraduate students would take responsibility for changing the posters and downloading the data. The researchers were happy to oversee the undergraduates, and the OPO was happy to have one less responsibility. This lessened the burden on the OPO and the tension for the researchers, resulting in a great project where the OPO learned a great deal and the research was valid.

Working Together

Be it personal or professional, different entities enter into relationships with their own background, motives, and goals. This is no difference in the relationship between a researcher and a community organization. Making a grant work and staying the course for a successful project require planning, communication, and ongoing attention!

Tips for Success

- Work together on the grant proposal to ensure that the work plan is feasible for both parties. A researcher alone should not craft a project that requires intricate attention to detail without input from the community organization about capabilities.
- Once a grant is funded, hold an education session for anyone who will be working on the grant. This session should focus on the following:
  ○ An overview of the project, including specific expectations of each organization
  ○ An overview of the community organization and how it works
  ○ An overview of the research team and organization, and how they work
- Plan routine communication to review progress and upcoming plans.
- Detail this communication so that each individual has access to the ongoing communication.
- Be bold, and discuss any concerns or questions as soon as you have them!
- Plan fun or social interaction to solidify rapport and build relationships.

Benefits

Although seeing a project through and then learning that it did not work at achieving the organization's goal may seem foreign to a community organization, it is not without benefit. A grant-funded project allows a community organization the opportunity to apply funds to try something that might provide greater benefits or outcomes. If it does work, they have a project that is proven to work, they have knowledge about why it works, and they can then justify sustaining funding for the project. If the project does not work, they save money that might have been spent on an ongoing project with limited return on investment. In addition, creating a culture that looks critically at programs and outcomes is very beneficial in terms of overall organizational outreach. The "grant culture" in fact may have helped move the OPO community along the route toward greater acceptance of donor registries and donor registry campaigns as opposed to the more generic "awareness of donation" campaigns of old. Doing more of what works and measuring both processes and outcomes are both good things. In addition, doing less of what does not work is a good thing!

Measurable outcomes provide a tremendous benefit to community organizations like those featured in this book that are engaged in public outreach and education. The ability to convincingly show that outreach projects work furthers the mission of an organization and can help make a case to possible funders and boards of directors about the importance of maintaining or increasing funding. Measurable outcomes have helped in a number of areas in our own OPO here in Arizona. At one time, we had very generic marketing materials available in English and translated into Spanish. We did not have a good rationale for providing anything else, although we had a growing Hispanic population. Through a grant project and research, we were able to determine that we needed specific materials for this population with specific messages and that we needed to cultivate the community with a specific liaison. All of this was tested with grant money, proved effective measurably in terms of actual consent for donation as well as donation attitudes, and continued as a sustained project funded by the organization after the grant ended.

Conclusion

Research opportunities bring researchers and staff from community organizations together for a common project. Although a funded grant may provide the opportunity to work on a specific project with defined objectives and plans, the goals and motivation for the community organization and the researcher may be different. Sometimes it might feel as if the two are from different planets! Understanding these differences and developing strategies and communication targeting the possible conflicts that can arise should make any project more successful, less stressful, and, yes, even fun. In fact, a good partnership between a community organization and a researcher can provide greater benefit to each and to the communities they serve. Researchers and community organizations may be from different planets, but they can work together, and through measurable project outcomes, published research, and theory advancement, they can benefit the individuals involved, science, and the mission.

Acknowledgments

The projects discussed in this chapter were funded by grants from HRSA/DoT grant (H39 OT 00021-01, R39OT01148) awarded to Sara Pace Jones, BA. The opinions expressed herein are those of the authors and do not necessarily represent those of the funding agency.

References

Alvaro, E. M., Pace Jones, S., Robles, A. S., & Siegel, J. T. (2005). Predictors of organ donation behavior among Hispanic Americans. *Progress in Transplantation, 15*(2), 149–156.

Alvaro, E. M., Pace Jones, S., Robles, A. S., & Siegel, J. T. (2006). Hispanic organ donation: Impact of a Spanish-language organ donation campaign. *Journal of the National Medical Association, 98*(1), 1–8.

Gallup Organization. (1993). *The American public's attitudes toward organ donation and transplantation.* Princeton, NJ: Gallup Organization.

Siegel, J. T., Alvaro, E. M., & Pace Jones, S. (2005). Organ donor registration preferences among a Hispanic American population: Which modes of registration have the greatest promise? *Health Education and Behavior, 32*, 242–252.

Siegel, J. T., Alvaro, E., Pace Jones, S., Crano, W. C., Lac, A., & Ting, S. (2008). A quasi-experimental investigation of message appeal variations on organ donor registration rates. *Health Psychology, 27*, 170–178.

16

Evaluating the Effects of Community-Based Health Interventions
Seeking Impact and Saving Lives via Organ and Tissue Donation Promotion Efforts

Robert L. Fischer

Introduction

The federal initiative to promote social and behavioral interventions to organ donation has had a specific emphasis on research since its inception in 1999. In each of its funding announcements, the Division of Transplantation (DoT) identified specific performance measures or outcomes that the applicant projects needed to address. In its most recent funding announcement, the DoT required projects to report on at least one specific performance measure according to the location of the project and whether it focuses on deceased donation or living donation. Deceased donation projects in jurisdictions where first-person consent is statutorily in effect must address either (a) increases in the number or rate of individuals who designate their consent to become donors, or (b) increases in rates of family consent for a deceased relative. For deceased donation projects in jurisdictions that do not have first-person consent, the first option is revised as increases in the number or rate of individuals who designate their intent to become organ donors as well as family notification of that decision. Projects that focus on living donation must report on the outcome of "increases in knowledge of opportunities for and the process, benefits, and risks of living donation" (U.S. Department of Health and Human Services, 2008, pp. 3–4).

From the beginning, the DoT's interest was not in simply documenting that an individual intervention was indeed effective; rather, the intent was to credibly assess program impact and create an evidence base for the field (Ganikos, this volume). The ability to identify a set of effective and replicable interventions that could be translated to new settings, populations, and contexts was the overall agenda. To accomplish this, the DoT needed to encourage the development of a range of interventions that would tap into populations where consent or donation rates were comparatively low. By extension, these interventions would need to be tailored to the characteristics of specific target populations in terms of their demographics, culture, geography, and the like. Across 10 years of funding awards, the DoT has delivered on its commitment to develop a diverse set of interventions. This chapter addresses how this diversity of programs impacts the evaluation of these interventions over time and what strategies have been used to advance our understanding of the effectiveness of such programs.

Interventions and Theory of Change

The broad set of interventions that have been developed in the organ donation arena have been framed around a number of underlying theories. The use of social psychological theories assists in the conception of the individual change process, and in the articulation of anticipated avenues of change. For evaluation purposes, the program theory provides direction as to how the intervention is expected to play out and suggests how data collection might best be mapped onto this process. Many bodies of theory relate to organ donation promotion, and individual programs can also draw on multiple theories. In this volume, Oskamp notes the role of three theories in the conception of program strategies in this arena—the transtheoretical model of change, the theory of reasoned action, and the elaboration likelihood model. These and other models such as social marketing theory (Kotler & Zaltman, 1971) and diffusion of innovations theory (Rogers, 1995) help one to understand operational delivery of the program. On a practical level, the use of a guiding theory can be helpful in the evaluation phase because the theory can provide a basis for selecting points of measurement and specific indicators for determining if a program is producing intended changes as anticipated. Furthermore, to the extent that individual studies are building an evidence base for the field, the testing of theory is essential to this developmental process (Lipsey, 1993). When an evaluation study seeks to test a theory and the results are not favorable, the challenge then becomes distinguishing between instances of theory failure and those of implementation failure (i.e., where the delivery of the intervention was poor or inconsistent such that it was not a good test of the theory).

On a macro level, organ donation promotion interventions can be envisioned as having a temporal aspect, that is, interceding in different parts of an individual's life course. One set of strategies is to target a general population from older adolescence through adulthood (see Figure 16.1). These strategies seek to impress upon individuals the importance of them committing to be an organ donor and informing their loved ones of this decision. For example, in Feeley, Anker, Uincent, & Williams' (this volume) study of a university-based project targeting college students, the key outcome was to have students enroll in the donor registry

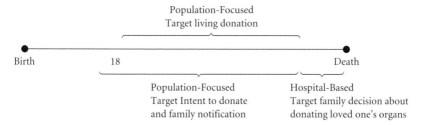

Figure 16.1 Organ donation program target timeline.

and to share this decision with their parents and family. As such, the main focus is educative, and the principal outcome is measured by the intent to donate when the opportunity presents itself. In addition, there may be a supplemental effect on individuals in regard to a decision they may need to make in regard to a loved one who is approaching death. Finally, these population-focused programs may also be targeted to persuading individuals to take action now in the form of becoming a living donor (Waterman & Rodrigue, this volume).

An additional category of programs targets only those individuals and families who are in fact faced with an immediate decision that relates to organ donation. These interventions necessarily occur in the context of hospitals and emergency departments, where there is often a short window for the decision to be made (Dodd-McCue, this volume). In this case, the primary outcome is, in fact, the consent to donate. These two categories of interventions carry with them a number of implications, as summarized in Table 16.1.

There are key differences between the two intervention categories in regard to factors such as the primary target, the relevant types of strategies, the likely maximal effect of an intervention, and challenges experienced in each approach. The scope and scale of these strategies as well as the contextual parameters dictate in large part the issues that arise in the research directed at assessing their effects.

Community-Based Intervention and Research

In planning and fielding organ donation promotion initiatives, program developers have needed to make two crucial decisions: where to locate the intervention in terms of setting, and how to deliver the intervention to the intended targets. These defining aspects have implications for our ability to document and assess the effects of the intervention. The choice of program delivery setting dictates the context for the collection of evaluation data. Hospital settings often offer the most control over program delivery and data collection, so for evaluation purposes, interventions in such settings have many strengths. Other community-based settings often take advantage of key contact points with target populations and as

Table 16.1   Comparison of intervention models in organ donation promotion

	Population-Focused Intent to Donate	Hospital-Based Consent to Donate
Focus	Reach broad cross section of population targets.	Reach individuals and families facing a donation decision.
Primary outcome domain	Future donation.	Current donation.
Targets	Potential donors and their families.	Donation candidates and their family members.
Types	DMV and donor registries; school and community-based educational interventions.	Alternate OPO approach strategies, staffing patterns, and defining brain death.
Maximal effect	Change in general attitude of population resulting in more favorable opinion toward donation.	Encourage individuals and families to consent in a real donation situation and honor their loved one's wishes.
Special considerations	Issues related to outreach to teens and ethnically diverse and disenfranchised communities.	Special sensitivity is required in working with families facing the death of a loved one.
Challenges	Weakness of outcome measures: signing a donor card as a proxy for attitude change, reliability of attitude measures, and family can override an individual's intent to donate. Barriers to consent, such as religious beliefs, and fear of the government and health care system.	Smaller candidate population: Eligibles are fewer than full potential donor population. Short window to influence family decision in a respectful way. Family declines despite loved one's expressed wishes to donate.

such may increase the odds of a positive outcome. At the same time, however, the setting may be less conducive to the collection of evaluation data (e.g., completing of study forms or surveys). For example, churches may be a good venue for program delivery and engagement but may be less conducive to the collection of evaluative data.

Similarly, the choice of delivery agent has implications for the evaluation. In general, the use of indigenous parties familiar with the delivery context may be the most effective in respect to connecting with the target audience. However, to ensure maximal control over the study and ensure fidelity of program delivery, an evaluation might prefer to use individuals external to the setting who are trained to deliver the program according to a specific protocol, or methods that rely more on technology than individual deliverers. Each aspect of this decision is now discussed.

Place-Based Strategies

Organ donation promotion initiatives have been taken to all manner of venues in order to tap into the potential for organ donors across a range of populations. The decision of intervention setting is informed by myriad factors, including the assessment of the potential donor pool reachable via the setting, the working theory of intervention, and the opportunities afforded by the local service land-scape and the partners engaged in the initiative. Any one project is often based on particular developments and situational advantages that present themselves to the organ donation and research community. For example, in Ohio the move to institute a first-person registry presented an opportunity to examine the effects of the educational outreach campaign and registry launch in partnership with the state's OPOs and Bureau of Motor Vehicles (Downing & Jones, this volume). Certainly, the specific formulation of projects heavily relates to the disciplinary training and institutional affiliation of the principal investigators and the team they assemble. In this sense, projects should and do maximize the assets and opportunities within the context from which they arise; the failure to do so dramatically lessens the probability of a project securing the necessary funding to proceed.

The Institute for Campaign Research and Evaluation (2005) reviewed the first 5 years of the Division of Transplantation's grant making and grouped the projects into eight categories: community outreach campaigns, campaigns with mass media, DMV-based campaigns, minority-focused campaigns, worksite campaigns, professional education, school-based interventions, and hospital-based interventions. For the present discussion the settings can be loosely classified into three categories, according to the frequency of engagement of the general populace with this setting. Table 16.2 presents a listing of settings along with an example of each type, including several that appear in the present volume.

Settings that might be classified as having a population with routine engagement with a target population include places of work, schools, and places of worship. Other settings might be seen as having more infrequent engagement with the population usually related to a specific life event or need. Hospital and DMV settings are classified as periodic and directly relevant, meaning that the discussion of organ donation might be reasonably expected in these contexts. In hospital settings where an individual or family is facing a serious health situation or decision related to a loved one, the topic of organ donation would likely be

Table 16.2 Settings for intervention

Level of Engagement in the General Population	Relevant Settings	Example Project(s)
Routine engagement	Worksites	Morgan (this volume), Quinn (this volume),
	Middle and high schools	Waldrop et al. (2004)
	Universities	Feeley et al. (this volume)
	Faith communities	Davis et al. (2005)
	Ethnic communities	Fahrenwald (this volume), Radosevich et al. (this volume)
Periodic engagement: direct relevance	Hospitals	Dodd-McCue (this volume)
	Division of Motor Vehicles	Downing and Jones (this volume)
Periodic engagement: indirect relevance	Funeral homes	Paykin et al. (this volume)
	Attorneys' offices	Tamburlin (2008)
	Cemeteries	Tamburlin (2008)
	Beauty salons and barbershops	National Kidney Foundation of Michigan (2008)
	Swap meets and flea markets	Donor Network of Arizona
	Web and social-networking sites	Merion et al. (2003)

anticipated to be raised with the family. Similarly, within the context of renewing a driver's license, it is standard practice for individuals to indicate their preference as to being identified as an organ donor. The salience of this topic in the DMV setting stems entirely from the bureaucratic reality that states record this information in donor registries and on the driver's license.

The third category of settings is those in which the population has infrequent engagement and there may be only indirect relevance to the topic of organ donation. Tamburlin (2008) described these as settings with a "gatekeeper," an individual with a relationship to the potential donor in which there is a special opportunity to capitalize on the interaction. The relevance dimension can vary substantially. For example, individuals who are engaged in preplanning at funeral homes, at cemeteries, and with attorneys (estate planning) are very much thinking ahead to the time of death. Broaching the topic of organ donation with these individuals may be completely consistent with their mind-set. Other settings, such as beauty salons and barber shops, are natural places where individuals gather and have conversations, but the topic of organ donation may have less direct relevance to the experience of customers in that venue. In these instances, there may be evidence of a general positive rapport between the staff and the client, but this may not translate into an advantage in engaging individuals on the topic of organ donation. This presents challenges in regard to evaluation in that variation in the delivery of the intervention may be accentuated by this client-specific reaction, resulting in measurement problems as to how the intervention actually was delivered. Similarly, with social-networking sites (e.g., MySpace), the electronic forum becomes another setting in which individuals inter- act around a wide range of topics, including decisions such as organ donation.

Program Delivery Variation

Organ donation promotion approaches have also varied substantially in respect to the delivery modality, that is, the vehicle for conveying the educational and behavioral content to the potential donor. The major categories of intervention type include media campaigns (radio, TV, and print), professional education and training, and technological applications. These three areas are discussed in turn. First, media campaigns directed at organ donation promotion have used all conventional media outlets to disseminate pro-donation messages. These have been directed to general populations in a media market, as well as niche populations in a specific geography, such as those defined by language or culture (Radosevich et al., this volume). Often these media campaign strategies have been multimodal and frequently include a grassroots outreach component as well. The evaluation of these approaches often includes cross-sectional surveys of residents in the target geography (akin to polling efforts) before and after the media campaign, and a time series examination of counts of donor registrations in relation to the timing of the campaign. In these instances, a major challenge for the evaluation is to integrate data from multiple sources to create a coherent summary of the outcomes. There may be only a tacit link between data collection at different levels (e.g., aggregate registration, community phone survey, and feedback data from community events), and this weakens the ability of the evaluation to attribute effects to the campaign itself.

Second, projects have used professional education and training to enhance the knowledge and pro-donation behavior of staff at hospitals (Dodd-McCue, this volume; Riker & White, 1995), as well as individuals who agree to serve as an advocate for organ donation with a specified population. These individuals might be fellow employees (Quinn, this volume), college students (Feeley et al., this volume), home care professionals (Johnson & Webber, this volume), or lay health advisors (Fahrenwald, this volume). Across these options, the training is tailored to the needs of the target audience as well as the context in which they will operate. In the evaluation of these efforts, there is a keen emphasis on the quality of the training received by these advocates and the degree of consistency in their approach techniques. Without good data on the character of the intervention delivery, it is more challenging to tease out the effect of specific advocates operating in specific settings, thus limiting the generalizability of findings.

Third, projects have used technological applications as the vehicle for delivering content. Though these might be seen as an extension of media campaigns, they offer some distinctive aspects as well. One type of approach has been the use of freestanding interactive kiosks that are placed at BMV locations, worksites, or other venues (Siegel, Alvaro, & Jones, 2005) and offer a range of information on organ donation as well as the ability to join the organ donor registry. An additional approach is via the use of Web-based applications as a method to deliver interactive educational intervention to a target population (Merion et al., 2003). With the advent of social networking sites as a regular sphere of interaction, it is not difficult to see application in this realm as well. Educational efforts that rely on a Web-based delivery mechanism present distinctive challenges in regard to evaluation. For example, this includes being able to ensure that intended targets have access to the Web site materials that comparison targets (i.e., control group) do not. Beyond access, the ability to measure exposure to content in regard to frequency, duration, and sequence is often quite important. These are aspects that often are easily handled within a Web site environment by establishing unique login identifications and password protection, and monitoring of logins and page views by individual users. The challenge for evaluation may relate more to the extraction of meaningful data from these systems and linking it to other data about program delivery (e.g., if the program includes a direct contact with individuals as well).

Issues in the Evaluation of Organ Donation Promotion

As organ donation promotion initiatives took on greater importance, and interest in their results grew, so too did the emphasis on evaluation of these interventions, as has been the case in the broader human service sector (Fischer, 2001). Early on, this led to a specific interest in devoting attention and resources to understanding the evaluation of these organ donation initiatives (U.S. Department of Health and Human Services, 1998). Though the field of medicine has a long history of research on therapeutic interventions, this expertise translated only in part to the task of examining the donation promotion efforts. These programs drew extensively on the broader social and behavioral field, so it was reasonable to look to this broader domain for guidance on the evaluation of these undertakings. By attracting expertise from the disciplines of psychology, education, social work, nursing, sociology, and the like, organ donation promotion efforts have been examined using a multidisciplinary set of perspectives. This has been beneficial given the variety of challenges facing the evaluation of such initiatives. An overview of these challenges will be discussed.

Selection of Design

As with applied research in any setting, the credibility of the ultimate evaluation findings is derived from the rigor of the evaluation design as well as the nature of the data collected. Though the field of medicine is the bastion of the randomized clinical trial, regarded by many as the "gold standard" for assessing program impact, the applicability of this design is limited within the organ donation promotion domain. Often due to the variability of the community settings in which the interventions are delivered, evaluation designs using randomization at the level of the individual have been used only in specific instances (Rodrigue, Cornell, Kaplan, & Howard, 2008). More frequently, the randomized designs have been at the group level (e.g., random assignment of classes of students) or the site level (e.g., random assignment of work sites). In addition, the field has numerous examples of quasi-experimental designs, which have used matched comparison groups or sites to generate an estimate of treatment effect (e.g., Quinn, this volume). These have also taken the more elaborate form of cross-over designs and counterbalanced designs that aim to control for bias in particular combinations of treatment and target groups (Siegel et al., 2008). A final set of studies has used cohort designs and time series approaches, and these have proven particularly valuable in detecting system-level changes over time in indicators such as consent rates, registrations, and the like.

Over time, the sophistication of the designs in use in the organ donation promotion literature has improved markedly. There are now high-quality examples of a number of different evaluation designs available, many of which are described in this volume. Examples of such designs include place-based designs that are multisite with strong matching and latent variables, intervention studies with assignment to groups based on randomization or a near equivalent, time series designs for cases of time-specific policy change, and cross-sectional community data for large-scale initiatives.

Data Planning

Beyond the evaluation design, another major factor influencing this research is the selection of data sources and methods to address the research questions. A first consideration is the scope and timing of the data collection. Conventionally, evaluation studies will collect both process data and outcome data as part of the overall study. Process data will allow for examination of the delivery of the intervention itself, and the extent to which it was implemented according to plan. Process data capture the degree to which individual targets received specific components of the intervention as intended (e.g., a brief orientation, home-based educational sessions, and supporting materials); at a minimum, this would include dates and timing of interactions as well as delivery of essential program content. To the extent that a program is well implemented, it offers a sound test of the underlying theoretical model; this allows for a judgment of whether poor outcomes might be a reflection of a theory failure or merely a failure of program implementation (Rossi, Lipsey, & Freeman, 2007). If a program is poorly implemented and the outcome data are not favorable, it will be impossible to discern whether the negative results were due to the poor implementation or a fundamentally unworkable program concept and theory. Outcome data relate directly to the measurement of the knowledge, attitude, or behavior of interest, most centrally intent to donate, consent to donate, and organ procurement. Taken together, measures of process and outcome allow the evaluation to examine subgroup effects as well as dose–effect relationships, such as whether individuals who were exposed to a more intensive intervention, however defined, showed more direct or larger effects on the outcome measure.

Associated with the discussion of the nature of the data is the decision related to timing of data collection. The default approach in most instances is some variation of a paired pre- and postintervention data collection. This provides the opportunity to measure the change in the outcome concurrent with the intervention and, coupled with an untreated comparison group, a more direct measurement of the net program effect. The duration of data collection and the length of follow-up for evaluation can be the subject of some debate. For hospital-based interventions where a donation decision is imminent, the data collection need only extend to that decision event. For educational interventions where the outcome is an individual's intent to donate coupled with the individual notifying his or her family of this desire, the duration of follow-up can be unclear. If the finite goal is to secure a registration on the state organ donor registry and verify that the individual spoke to his or her family about the decision, the evaluation might reasonably extend a matter of weeks or months. Some projects have sought to remove the individual from the notification process by having his or her registration generate a postcard to a designated family member informing them of the individual's decision. This, however, raises concerns about whether such procedures can ensure that the family actually receives the information and understands the implications of the individual's decision, and/or whether a depersonalized notification is appropriate when dealing with a personal decision such as this. When organ donation is considered part of an ongoing behavior that must be sustained or maintained, the evaluation could be seen extending out over a period of years. Under this conception, the idea of a simple time-specific family notification may not adequately assess the desired change.

A final area of discussion relates to the nature of the data sources and specific indicators to be employed in the evaluation. Indicators such as numbers of families consenting to have a loved one's organ donated, and actual numbers of organs procured, would be seen as concrete measures that have a high degree of accuracy and reliability. If the outcome of the intervention is best understood as an affirmative donation decision, then these measures are most central to documenting programmatic success. Such measures link most directly to hospital-based interventions where the records of the hospital and/or organ procurement organization would be available for the purposes of the evaluation. In these cases, routine records could supply the best data available on program outcome. Additionally, living donation initiatives can also be effectively assessed using these measures as one indicator. Though measures of the donation decision and numbers of organs have the benefit of being concrete and easily understood, the reality is that these indicators are not relevant to many organ donation promotion efforts.

For the evaluation of the broader set of community-based interventions, a wide range of other data sources become relevant. Here the outcome is the individual's decision to become an organ donor, and depending on the laws in the individual's state of residence, this intent may or may not be seen as binding. Chief among the relevant data sources is the state organ donor registry, which routinely retains information on individuals and their decision as to whether they want to be an organ donor. The form and function of these registries vary by state, and can be populated with registrations generated through the DMV, through a registry Web site, and via a paper-based process. Registration data can be powerful for tracking increases in registrations resulting from an intervention, but there can be challenges to doing this. In the era of many states moving to first-person consent registries, an individual's consent to be an organ donor and appear in the registry takes the form of a legal commitment. This reality has greatly lessened the need to verify that an individual has notified the family of his or her wishes. The challenges of using registry data are often of a mundane variety. These include instances such as (a) a registry does not collect race and ethnicity data on registrants, making it difficult to measure changes in registrations from a specific race or ethnicity targeted with intervention; (b) a registry maintains data at specific geographic levels (e.g., zip codes) but not at the exact level targeted with an intervention (e.g., a set of neighborhoods); and (c) there is a lack of reliable mechanisms for linking intervention target population with data in the registry (e.g., employees at a worksite or members at a church).

A final class of data for evaluation purposes comes from informant surveys and/or interviews. These self-report data can address participant knowledge and attitude changes specific to an intervention but usually have limitations associated with respondent bias. Such bias could lead to an overreporting of favorable outcomes in an effort to appear more altruistic and/or reflect what may be a valued societal perspective. Despite such limitations, these data from participants are inherently valuable and possess a recognized level of face validity. No other party can effectively represent the perspective of these participants in regard to their experience of the particular intervention. As such, participant data are a critical component of any evaluation approach. The effective integration of participant data is best accomplished by reviewing instruments already developed and used by researchers in the field. The projects described in this volume, for example, have led to the development of many high-quality instruments, and the DoT has begun collecting these measures for reference by others. These instruments can offer a way to build on existing research and may also provide reference data from a relevant population as a benchmark for a new project. The validity and reliability of any new survey or instrument will be enhanced through pilot testing of the instrument and method with members of the target population. New instruments may include subscales developed by other researchers integrated with items specifically related to the new project's content and objectives.

Evaluation Issues

In addition to the issues already addressed, there are a few additional matters of specific note in the evaluation of organ donation promotion efforts. First, issues of sample size are a major concern for these studies. As is the case in many other domains, the required sample size to support a particular study is often underestimated. The ability to ensure sufficient statistical design power to find an effect is a critical component to our studies. An additional element, however, is that sampling methods often dictate the degree of generalizability of the findings from an individual study. In the organ donation promotion field, with attention to intervention replication, care must be taken to lessen the threat of selection bias issues in the samples used in studies. A common instance of concern is when the participants in the intervention have volunteered for the program but the comparison group is identified from a passive population. In this case, if the participant population shows a greater increase in intent to donate, we will be unclear regarding what portion of the difference is due to the intervention and what portion is due to some predisposition of these individuals, as evidenced by their volunteering. Evaluation designs are strengthened if they (a) target populations that meaningfully represent broader populations of interest for intervention, and (b) ensure the comparability of groups used in the design to allow for the detection of true program effects. Second, increasingly studies in this arena are drawing on nested design approaches, wherein the intervention targets exist in naturally occurring units (e.g., classrooms and worksites), and these are, in fact, the unit of analysis. Such designs require a more elaborate analytic approach, such as hierarchical linear modeling, to disentangle the multilevel effects, and can limit the types of subgroup analyses that can be conducted. Third, the issue of human participant protection and consent must be consistently raised. Though the risk of harm associated with participation in educational or media interventions is often quite minimal, the principle of human participant protection requires that all risks must be assessed. The notion of informed consent, along with privacy and confidentiality concerns, are dimensions of the evaluation work that must be explicitly dealt with. A subcategory of interventions that seek to solicit registrations or intent to donate from minors in their mid- to late teens must also deal with the matter of the consent process for minors. This usually requires that a guardian provide informed consent for the minor to participate in the study, and the minor must offer affirmative assent for his or her participation as well. Last, a final consideration is the broad movement underway in the area of organ donation. This evolution or secular trend means that in the absence of specific interventions, there is a general shift toward organ donation and efforts encouraging organ donation. Over time, we observe increased donation behavior and more positive attitudes toward organ donation reflective of a broad societal movement in this regard. For example, the Breakthrough Collaborative is an initiative that is identifying and promoting the adoption of best practices in the organ donation field (Marks et al., 2006; Shafer et al., 2006; U.S. Department of Health and Human Services, 2003). In this context, an individual study must consider how this general trend may be impacting the groups under study—both the intervention group and the comparison group—so as to not underestimate or overestimate the effect of the new intervention. If the evaluation design results in truly comparable groups, then the general trend will impact the intervention and comparison groups equally, and the estimate of the treatment effect will not be biased. If, however, the comparison population is taken from an unserved area or setting, special attention must be given to assessing whether this secular trend has resulted in some enhancement to the usual approaches used for organ donation promotion in that setting. This is especially true in multisite and multisetting evaluation approaches and will require the evaluator to actively explore the experiences of individuals in the comparison settings.

Conclusions

The research on organ donation promotion efforts has seen dramatic growth and enhancement over the last decade. The quality of the evaluations that have been conducted has increased markedly, and these have contributed to a substantial expansion in the evidence base in this domain. Based on the current state of the field, three observations are merited as to next steps in advancing the field. First, there should be continued promotion of the use of more rigorous evaluation methods. This includes the use of experimental and quasi-experimental designs but also more use of systematic and multimethod designs. Approaches that have been shown to be particularly appropriate in this arena include group-based random assignment, matched site designs with counterbalanced intervention strategies, and time series designs. Multimethod efforts enhance the opportunities for canceling out shortcomings associated with individual data methods and sources, and increase the odds of identifying unintended effects. So, an evaluation design that integrates information from a comparison of two sites using time series registry data, cross-sectional community survey data, and key informant interviews will necessarily be more reliable than a design that uses only one of these data strategies. Second, the field should examine cross-setting learning to assess how the value of the experiences to date can be leveraged to maximize impacts. So, for example, to what extent can we integrate findings from worksites, schools, and churches to develop more powerful intervention strategies? Finally, the field should seek to further expand collaborative work between evaluators and organ donation professionals. This volume certainly is evidence of hopeful movement in this regard, but much more can be done. The experience to date suggests that the best intervention and evaluation approaches are informed by an interdisciplinary approach that draws on the expertise of both these constituencies.

References

Davis, K., Holtzman, S., Durand, R., Decker, P., Zucha, B., & Atkins, L. (2005). Leading the flock: Organ donation feelings, beliefs, and intentions among African American clergy and community residents. *Progress in Transplantation, 15*, 211–216.

Feeley, T. H. (2007). College students' knowledge, attitudes, and behaviors regarding organ donation: An integrated review of the literature. *Journal of Applied Social Psychology, 37*, 243–271.

Fischer, R. L. (2001). The sea change in nonprofit human services: A critical assessment of outcomes measurement. *Families in Society, 82*, 561–568.

Institute for Campaign Research and Evaluation. (2005, January). Report on the Division of Transplantation's grant program 1999–2004: Social and behavioral interventions to increase organ donation. Salt Lake City, UT: Author.

Kotler, P., & Zaltman, G. (1971). Social marketing: An approach to planned social change. *Journal of Marketing, 35*, 3–12.

Lipsey, M. W. (1993). What can you build with thousands of bricks? Musings on the cumulation of knowledge in program evaluation. *New Directions for Evaluation, 76*, 7–24.

Marks, W. H., Wagner, D., Pearson, T. C., Orlowski, J. P., Nelson, P. W., McGowan, J. J., et al. (2006). Organ donation and utilization, 1995–2004: Entering the collaborative era. *American Journal of Transplantation, 6*, 1101–1110.

Merion, R. M., Vinokur, A. D., Couper, M. P., Jones, E. G., Dong, Y, Warren, J., et al. (2003). A Web-based intervention to promote organ donor registry participation and family notification. *Transplantation, 75*, 1175–1179.

National Kidney Foundation of Michigan. (2008). *Healthy hair starts with a healthy body.* Retrieved December 1, 2008, from http://www.kidney.org/site/306/hairstylists.cfm?ch=306

Riker, R. R., & White, B. W. (1995). The effect of physician education on the rates of donation request and tissue donation. *Transplantation, 59*(6), 880–884.

Rodrigue, J. R., Cornell, D. L., Kaplan, B., & Howard, R. J. (2008). A randomized trial of a home-based educational approach to increase live donor kidney transplantation: Effects in blacks and whites. *American Journal of Kidney Diseases, 51,* 663–670.

Rogers, E. M. (1995). *Diffusion of innovations* (4th ed.). New York: Free Press.

Rossi, P. H., Lipsey, M. W., & Freeman, H. E. (2007). *Evaluation: A systematic approach* (7th ed.). Thousand Oaks, CA: Sage.

Shafer, T. J., Wagner, D., Chessare, J., Zampiello, F. A., McBride, V., & Perdue, J. (2006). Organ Donation Breakthrough Collaborative: Increasing organ donation through system redesign. *Critical Care Nurse, 26,* 33–48.

Siegel, J. T., Alvaro, E. M., Crano, W. D., Lac, A., Ting, S., & Jones, S. P. (2008). A quasi-experimental investigation of message appeal variations on organ donation rates. *Health Psychology, 27,* 170–178.

Siegel, J. T., Alvaro, E. M., & Jones, S. P. (2005). Organ donor registration preferences among Hispanic populations: Which modes of registration have the greatest promise? *Health Education and Behavior, 32,* 242–252.

Tamburlin, J. (2008, May). Strategies to increase organ donation rates: Use of "gate keepers" to deliver the message and foster action. Presentation at the Working Group in Organ Donor Intervention and Methodology, Washington University in St. Louis School of Medicine, St. Louis, MO.

U.S. Department of Health and Human Services. (1998). *Conference report—increasing organ donation and transplantation: The challenge of evaluation.* Washington, DC: Assistant Secretary for Planning and Evaluation, prepared by the Lewin Group.

U.S. Department of Health and Human Services. (2003, September). *The Organ Donation Breakthrough Collaborative: Best practices final report.* Washington, DC: Health Resources and Service Administration.

U.S. Department of Health and Human Services. (2008, December 3). *Social and behavioral interventions to increase organ and tissue donation, FY 2009 program announcement* (HRSA-09-189). Washington, DC: Health Resources and Services Administration.

Waldrop, D. P., Tamburlin, J. A., Thompson, S. J., & Simon, M. (2004). Life and death decisions: Using school-based health education to facilitate family discussion about organ and tissue donation. *Death Studies, 28,* 643–657.

17

The Value of Qualitative Studies of Interpersonal Conversations About Health Topics

A Study of Family Discussions of Organ Donation and Illustrations

Anita Pomerantz

Introduction

Interpersonal discussions about sensitive health topics provide people with new information, help them to decide which courses of action to take, and promote behavioral change. Because of their importance, public campaigns often encourage people to engage in such discussions. However discussions of sensitive health-related topics involve challenges, and, as a result, they are often avoided or end up being unproductive and dissatisfying. Research studies are needed that will enable people to overcome the obstacles to, and manage the challenges of, discussing sensitive health-related topics.

I argue that qualitative studies of interpersonal health discussions are well suited for discovering the reasons that people have for avoiding sensitive health topics, for identifying the challenges that occur during such discussions, and for offering resources that can enable people to overcome the obstacles and handle the challenges that occur during discussions of sensitive health-related topics.

Organ donation is one such sensitive topic. Given that family discussion is a variable of considerable theoretical and practical import in the organ donation domain, detailed examination of such discussions is warranted. Qualitative methods are highly relevant to, yet woefully underutilized in, organ donation research. Whereas quantitative approaches would be concerned with uncovering or confirming the role of family discussion as an outcome or predictor variable, qualitative methods are more amenable to the detailed study of participants' perceptions and interpretations of family discussions and the ways in which family members express their concerns and deal with each others' concerns.

The overall goal of this chapter is to argue for and demonstrate the value of using qualitative methods for conducting studies of interpersonal discussions of health-related topics. There are three sections that, together, build the argument and demonstration.

In the first section, I argue for the importance of studying interpersonal discussions about sensitive health-related topics. Although interpersonal discussions about health play a significant role in changing people's knowledge, attitudes, and/or behaviors, such discussions often either are avoided or are managed in less than optimal ways. The kinds of studies that shed light on the nature of the difficulties involved in conducting such discussions and that offer solutions to those difficulties should be useful in facilitating health-related interpersonal discussions.

The next section provides an introduction to qualitative methods in general and conversation analysis in particular, and explains why they are appropriate choices for studying interpersonal discussions of health-related topics. Attention is given to the types of research questions appropriately answered by qualitative studies, the types of data sought by qualitative researchers, and analytic guidelines.

The third section provides an illustration of the uses of qualitative methods by reporting on a conversation analytic study of family discussions of organ and tissue donation. The study identified the practices that family members use to handle various challenges to discussing organ and tissue donation with family members.

The concluding part of the chapter discusses some of the strengths and limitations of qualitative methods for studying interpersonal discussions of sensitive health topics.

Importance of Studying Discussions About Health-Related Topics

A Basic Reason That People Discuss Health-Related Topics Within Their Social Networks

A study that sheds light on why people treat others in their social network as credible sources of information and why they are influenced by them was conducted by Rutenberg and Watkins (1997). Using household surveys and in-depth interviews, the researchers examined the role of informal social interaction in influencing the use of contraceptives in rural Kenya. They asked the following question: If nurses give good information about family planning, why do women go and talk with other women who have no official training in providing health services? Rutenberg and Watkins found that the women who were ambivalent about family planning supplemented the providers' instructions with the experiences of women whose bodies and circumstances were similar to their own. In other words, they sought the views of social network people because they identified with them and hence could trust that their experiences would be relevant to their own circumstances.

Functions Served by Interpersonal Discussions About Health Topics

When people seek information, interpret information, make decisions, and take action related to their health, they often turn to, and/or are influenced by, those in their social networks. A growing number of studies have shown that discussions about health topics within social networks matter to people and influence the actions that they take.

In an ethnographic study of women in a mothers and toddlers' playgroup, Tardy and Hale (1998) studied the types of health information that were exchanged in discussions with friends and family members and the sense of impact that the discussions had upon the participants' health care decisions. Based on observations and interviews, they found that women not only followed their friends' prescriptions and advice, but also purposefully solicited that assistance. There were several areas in which this influence was observed. Based on interview responses, Tardy and Hale found that the women's discussions about healthy foods impacted their choices for the foods they served family members at home. They found that women often followed the recommendations of people who had experience with similar medical conditions in their social network regarding whether or not a visit to the doctor or to the emergency room was necessary. They also found that the women followed up on the recommendations regarding health care providers given by those in the social network, and they used the information they received on how to navigate the health care system for services.

Although interpersonal discussions of health may serve as an important source of information about health matters, not all people rely on interpersonal networks as primary sources of information. Based on an analysis of 1999 HealthStyles data, Dutta-Bergman (2004) found that individuals who are health oriented seek health information from different primary channels than individuals who are not health oriented. They found that individuals who are health conscious, have strong health beliefs, and have a commitment to healthy activities use active communication channels such as interpersonal communication, print readership, and Internet communication as primary health information sources. On the other hand, individuals who were not health oriented choose passive consumption channels such as television and radio as their primary health information sources.

Mass media health campaigns are a primary means through which public health organizations attempt to raise a population's awareness about health risks and motivate them to change unhealthy behaviors. A body of research indicates that interpersonal discussions work synergistically with mass media campaigns (see Alvaro & Siegel, this volume).

Campaigns that utilize mass media alone generally can be effective in raising awareness and increasing knowledge; however, depending on the area of health behaviors, they may have only partial success in bringing about behavioral changes (Flora, 2001). Researchers have argued that interpersonal conversations may work to augment the effectiveness of mass media campaigns.

Interpersonal communication can effectively propagate campaign information (Valente & Saba, 1998), thus greatly increasing the reach of the campaign. Furthermore, although the mass media can serve to increase awareness about health issues, interpersonal discussions are instrumental in persuading people to make requisite behavior modifications (Johnson & Meischke, 1993; Rimal, Flora, & Schooler, 1999; Rogers, 1996).

In their analysis of data from the Stanford Five-City Project, Rimal et al. (1999) found that exposure to campaign materials was a significant predictor of inter-personal communication about health. They also found that changes in overall health orientation were predicted by interpersonal communication. They suggested that in addition to the exchange of information, conversations can keep the campaign health issue salient in people's minds, which should increase the likelihood that that issue will be prominent in the community's agenda. Also, they suggested that conversations about health can serve to change community norms, and normative changes can further influence behaviors.

In another study that used the cross-sectional and longitudinal data from the Stanford Five-City Project, Rimal and Flora (1998) found that household members were influenced not only by the campaign materials but also by each other in changing and maintaining health behaviors. They suggested that public health campaigns can be made more effective if they conceptualize both children and adults as potential sources of influence. Although they documented the reciprocal influences of family members, they argued that we need further research on the dynamics of the processes of influence—especially as many concepts such as gatekeeping have been driven by top-down models reflecting traditional concerns regarding family structure.

In sum, it has become well recognized that campaigns provide information, messages, and images that can stimulate discussions among social networks. These discussions provide an important source of disseminating the health information, and they can further influence people to change their behaviors. Discussions among family members and friendship networks often involve mutual influence.

Problematic Aspects of Interpersonal Discussions of Health Topics

Although it is true that people often turn to others in their social networks to acquire and interpret information and to get input on health-related decisions facing them, it also is true that people often find it difficult to have certain kinds of discussions within their social networks. One source of difficulty is the sensitive nature of the health topic. Rogers (1996) enumerated some of the sensitive or taboo health topics in the following statement: "Many preventive health campaigns must address highly sensitive or taboo topics, such as sex, disease, and death that are difficult to discuss freely. It is clear that achieving preventive health behavior change is a particularly difficult communication activity" (p. 19).

To say that a particular health topic is a sensitive one is really just the starting point. Studies are needed to investigate the nature of the sensitivities, and then to explore whether they can be mitigated or overcome. One study that explored the nature of the sensitivities of discussing condom use with family members and friends was conducted by Bull, Cohen, Ortiz, and Evans (2002), who conducted 12 focus groups, totaling 89 women ages 14 to 25, with the aim of eliciting parti-cipant knowledge, attitudes, practices, and behavior toward male and female condom use. Among other concerns and sensitivities, they found that the women anticipated that such a discussion would lead to unwanted questions and neg-ative inferences and attributions. To illustrate that concern, they included the following quotations from women in the focus groups: "A lot of questions come with it that I don't want, like why do you want to use these? How many people have you slept with? Who have you slept with?" and "And then if anyone sees me with them they're going [to] think you're doing it" (Bull et al., 2002, p. 482).

Another deterrent to having discussions on health-related topics, and a source of difficulty during such discussions, was anticipating unfavorable reactions by others in the social network. When people anticipate that others in their social networks have contrary views to their own, they tend to shy away from discussing their views and revealing their perspectives. Morgan, Miller, and Arasaratnam (2002) have proposed that perceived social norms regarding resistance to organ donation discus-sions may be a crucial barrier influencing willingness to hold such conversations.

The Quality of Interpersonal Discussions Matters

Several quantitative studies have shown that the quality of interpersonal dis-cussions of health topics bears on their effectiveness. The aspects of the quality of discussions that have been of interest generally center on how responsive the family member or friend is perceived to have been. The concept of responsive-ness includes such factors as the degree to which the family member or friend is seen to be open, is perceived to have understood the other's position, and is comfortable in the discussion.

It is not the case that simply having interpersonal discussions on sensitive health topics necessarily will result in the desired benefits. What matters is how those conversations are conducted and perceived. In the following two studies involving parental communication with adolescents about sexual conduct, the positive benefits of discussions held only when the communication was perceived to be positive.

Based on a quantitative analysis of 372 interviews, Whitaker, Miller, May, and Levin (1999) found that parent–teenager discussions about sexuality and sexual risk were associated with an increased likelihood of teenager–partner discussions about sexual risk and of teenagers' condom use, but only if teenagers perceived their parents as open, skilled, and comfortable in having those discussions. Based on a quantitative analysis of 530 interviews, Fasula and Miller (2006) found that in conversations about sex between African American and Hispanic adolescents and their mothers, when the mothers' communication was perceived as displaying openness, comfort, and understanding, they had a buffering effect on the negative effects of sexually active peers. The findings for both of these studies suggest that quality matters—that not any kind of discussion about sensitive health topics will be beneficial. The two studies mentioned above were large interview studies designed to determine the effects of the quality of family discussions on the conduct of the adolescents. The survey data collected and the statistical analyses performed were appropriate to answering the types of research questions the researchers posed. However, the research questions that motivate qualitative studies and the data that qualitative researchers collect are of a different sort. Qualitative researchers would be inclined to investigate the nature, texture, and subtleties of the perceptions of the family discussions and/or nature of the discursive practices and moves associated with those perceptions. In other words, instead of making claims about causes and effects, qualitative researchers tend to study the participants' perceptions and understandings, their discursive practices, and the processes at work. To do that, qualitative researchers require the types of data that allow them to investigate phenomena of interest to them. The next section contains a discussion of some methods used by qualitative researchers in studying interpersonal discussions of health topics.

Qualitative Methods

Although the label *qualitative research* subsumes a variety of methods of collecting and analyzing empirical materials, researchers doing qualitative research generally share some common assumptions and interests. Denzin and Lincoln (1994) offered an initial, generic definition of qualitative research:

> Qualitative research is multimethod in focus, involving an interpretive, naturalistic approach to its subject matter. This means that qualitative researchers study things in their natural settings, attempting to make sense of, or interpret, phenomena in terms of the meanings people bring to them. Qualitative research involves the studied use and collection of a variety of empirical materials—case study, personal experience, introspective, life story, interview, observational, historical, interactional, and visual texts—that describe routine and problematic moments and meanings in individuals' lives. Accordingly, qualitative researchers deploy a wide range of interconnected methods, hoping always to get a better fix on the subject matter at hand. (p. 2)

As can be gleaned from the quoted statement above, qualitative researchers make choices about the types of research questions they will answer, the data that are appropriate for their studies, and how to investigate and substantiate their claims. Below, I sketch out some interests, assumptions, and principles that are associated with the use of qualitative methods.

Types of Research Questions

Using experimental or quasi-experimental methods, quantitative researchers generally study the causes or factors that influence specific outcomes. Using qualitative methods, researchers generally study the participants' perceptions and interpretations, and their methods of performing and interpreting actions and activities. Rather than *why* questions, qualitative researchers often ask *what* and *how* questions, such as "What are the concerns, perspectives, interpretations, discursive practices, and social processes within this group?" or "How do members of the group manage specific types of problems and perform certain rituals?"

Types of Data

Qualitative researchers generally are committed to collecting data that are naturalistic and rich in nature.

Naturalistic data

Rather than using laboratory studies, qualitative researchers prefer to study the participants' meanings and sense-making procedures in "their natural setting," that is, in the settings in which the participants engage in the activities that are of interest. Natural settings for organ donation research may include hospitals as donation requests are being made and homes where family members discuss their organ donation beliefs. As with any research choice, there is a trade-off involved with this type of data. The loss is that in relying on data from natural settings, the qualitative researcher cannot control variables and hence cannot make strong claims about the factors that bring about certain effects. The gain involves environmental validity, that is, qualitative researchers can have more confidence that the phenomenon they observe indeed represents the phenomenon of interest.

Rich data

The ability to do qualitative research depends chiefly on the richness of the data collected. To gain an understanding of the nuances and subtleties of informants' attitudes and perspectives, qualitative researchers collect in-depth interview or focus group data over survey data. To gain an understanding of how the participants perform roles, rituals, or activities, qualitative researchers would seek to obtain as rich a record of the performances as possible, by using camcorders, audio-recording devices, and field notes.

Analytic Claims

There are several guidelines that many qualitative researchers follow for developing and substantiating analytic claims. The following four items were drawn from a message sent by Jane Hood on the Qualitative Research for the Human Sciences electronic list (qualrs-l@listserv.uga.edu) on April 18, 2007.

1. Stay close to one's data while analyzing it. Develop codes and themes from the data rather than imposing preconceived codes and themes.
2. Use constant comparison to arrive at claims about the common features of, and the differences between, cases. Constant comparisons allow one to see the common and distinct features of the phenomenon.
3. Be fully accountable to one's data when reporting findings. Always talk about negative cases. When faced with disconfirming instances, modify one's analytic claim and/or account for the exception.
4. Commit to having analytic claims assessed with reference to empirical evidence. Provide sufficient data to others so that they can determine for themselves whether or not the claims have been adequately supported.

Conversation Analysis (CA)

As an illustration of the uses and value of qualitative research to study interpersonal discussions of health topics, the next section contains a report on a conversation analytic study of family discussions of organ and tissue donation. For those unacquainted with conversation analysis, I introduce key aspects of the approach in this section.

Key concepts and assumptions of conversation analysis

The central aim of CA is to provide a systematic account of the ways in which talk in interaction is constructed and understood by the participants. Two key concepts of conversation analysis are conversational actions and practices.

Conversational actions

Conversation analysts view people in interaction as, first and foremost, performing conversational actions with one another. People employ words and gestures in the service of such conversational actions as greeting each other, making and responding to inquiries, making and responding to invitations and requests, issuing complaints, offering disagreements, and so on. The action that words and gestures are recognized to enact (that is, the meaning of the conduct) is dependent upon the context of its production in two senses: the type of occasion (who is inter-acting with whom, where, and when) and the local interactional context (what was just said, and what responses are anticipated).

Actions generally are understood to be parts of sequences of actions. For ex-ample, when one person issues an invitation to another, it becomes relevant for the other person to perform a responding action (for example, to accept or reject the invitation). The way an action is performed affects what the conditionally relevant next actions are. For example, if someone directly asks you to be my living kidney donor, it is conditionally relevant for you to either comply with, or decline to comply with, the request. However, if someone indirectly asks you by telling you that my doctor believes a living kidney donation is my best bet for long-term functioning and survival, that way of performing the action creates a sequential context in which it is relevant for you to show a response to the news about living kidney donation. In this sequential environment, you would have the option of offering to be tested to be a donor, where making an offer is a very dif-ferent sort of conversational action than complying or not complying with a request.

Practices

Conversation analysts view the orderliness of interactional conduct as a product of people using shared practices, or methods, to perform and understand con-versational actions. CA's goal is to explicate the shared practices that interactants use to produce and recognize their own and other people's conduct (Pomerantz & Fehr, 1997). For example, if community educators hope to find out whether or not someone has registered as an organ donor on a state registry but are hesitant to ask, they may use the practice of "fishing for information" in which they report their limited access to a situation, giving the other person the oppor-tunity to offer a fuller account (Pomerantz, 1980).

Types of data preferred by conversation analysts

In a previous section, it was argued that qualitative researchers seek data that are "natural" and "rich." The same qualities of data are the ones valued by conver-sation analysts as well.

Natural interaction

For conversation analysts, the best data consist of interactions in which people do the activities they would be doing in that situation anyway, with as little interference from the researcher as possible. Conversation analysts study all types of interaction, including discussions between friends, interactions between health care providers and patients, talk between coworkers, interactions in team meetings, and interviews with politicians on the media. Ideally, in these situ-ations, the researcher has obtained permission to study it without having set up the situation itself.

A potential dilemma exists for conversation analysts who seek natural inter-actions on particular topics or with particular activities. In such situations, conversation analysts juggle the two goals of wanting natural data on the one hand while needing particular types of data on the other hand. Typically, conversation analysts would structure the occasions only enough to secure the needed data so that the naturalness of the data is compromised as little as possible.

Rich data

Conversation analysts require audiotaped or videotaped recordings of the inter-action and fine-grained transcripts of the interaction. They require recordings because certain features of the interaction are not recoverable without such recordings. Neither researchers' memories nor their field notes can be relied on to recover such things as where hesitations occur, what participants start to say and then abandon, and how the voice changes when people are talking in over-lap. Also, recordings allow for replaying the interaction, which is important for both transcribing and developing analyses.

Although recordings are essential to capture the details of interaction, conversation analysts are mindful to consider whether and how the recording device's pres-ence affects the observed conduct. Self-conscious participants can alter some kinds of behavior but not other kinds.

Analytic Framework

Pomerantz and Fehr (1997) offered a set of tasks that were intended to guide people in developing their analyses. Some of the tasks are as follows:

1. For the segments of interaction that are of analytic interest, characterize the conversational actions that were performed. Notice the relationship between the actions and whether the actions performed were the ones that were made relevant by the prior turns.
2. Analyze the practices used to accomplish the conversational actions of inter-est. To do this, consider the consequences of the alternative ways of performing the action for what should happen next, and consider how the participants' roles and relationships bear on the way the action is performed. Also con-sider how the specific terms and the timing and taking of turns provide for certain understandings.
3. Analyze practices as solutions to challenges. When people interact, they often are faced with multiple goals, constraints, concerns, and/or sensitivities. Although an examination of interaction cannot directly reveal the goals and concerns experienced by the participants, the participants' conduct, their selec-tion of specific practices, can be seen as solutions to a set of goals and concerns. For example, given that someone uses the practice of "fishing for information"

rather than asking directly for a piece of information, the use of that practice may reflect the speaker's goal of wanting the information while also being concerned about the appropriateness of directly asking that person for it.

Case Study: Dynamics of Family Discussion

From 2003 to 2006, a multicampus classroom intervention to promote organ and tissue donation was conducted on college campuses in New York State. On each of the college campuses participating in the study, the students in the intervention courses designed, implemented, and evaluated campaigns that were aimed at raising awareness of the need for organ and tissue donations, increasing the number of people who signed the donor registry, and raising awareness about the importance of family notification. Research on the effects of the intervention was supported by a grant from the Human Resources Services Administration, Division of Transplantation (HRS/DoT). Summary data on the effects of the classroom interventions are presented in Feeley, Anker, Vincent, & Williams (this volume).

As a part of the classroom intervention project, we conducted a qualitative study on the dynamics of family discussions (Pomerantz & Denvir, 2007). For the purpose of illustrating the uses of qualitative research to study interpersonal discussions of sensitive health topics, below I present a brief description of the methods and findings of the study.

Research Questions

Based on previous research findings as well as our in-depth interviews of the students in the intervention courses, we identified several issues that represented challenges for, or deterrents to, discussing organ donation with one's family (Morgan & Miller, 2002; Morgan et al., 2002; Pomerantz & Denvir, 2007; Smith, Kopfman, Lindsey, Yoo, & Morrison, 2004). Three of the challenges are (a) difficulty in knowing how to comfortably raise the topic of donation, (b) concern with appearing morbid and with violating family taboos about talking about death, and (c) uncertainty about whether family members will oppose or be critical of students' perspective on donation. As we were interested in identifying the practices that were used to deal with the specific challenges and dilemmas, we developed the following research questions:

RQ1:   What practices did the participants use to comfortably raise the topic of donation?

RQ2:   What practices did the participants use to discuss donation while also dealing with the likelihood that a family member viewed such discussions as morbid?

RQ3:   What practices did the participants use to inform family members of their perspectives while also minimizing the likelihood of engendering their critical reactions?

Data Collection

The data for this project consisted of audio recordings of family discussions about organ and tissue donation. The family discussions were initiated by students who were enrolled in communication campaign courses. The students recorded one or more of their own conversations with family members. During the pilot study at University 1 in the spring of 2003 and the federally funded study at University 1 and University 2 in spring 2004–2006, we collected 57 tapes from 47 of the 180 students who were registered for the intervention courses.

Because the students read articles on donation throughout the semester and had designed and executed a campaign on organ donation, the family discussions involved one or more participants who had considerable exposure to both the facts and concerns about donation.

Data Preparation and Analysis

All family discussions were fully transcribed. We employed open coding of the transcripts and tapes in order to generate some initial themes of interest. Once themes began to emerge, we produced collections of all data extracts that were relevant for each theme. These collections then provided a basis for fleshing out and refining the themes of interest. For example, one collection contains instances in which any of the participants announced their perspectives and/or decision regarding donating their organs and tissue, another collection contains instances in which opposition or resistance was expressed, and another collection contained instances in which participants responded to family members' concerns of receiving less than optimal care if known to be on the donor registry.

Findings

RQ1: What Practices Did the Participants Use to Comfortably Raise the Topic of Donation?

The two most commonly used practices for raising the topic of donation were *updating* and *topical pivots*. Both of these practices make raising the potentially sensitive topic of organ and tissue donation part of the flow of the conversation, and hence would feel like a more natural way to raise the topic of donation.

Updating

People in interpersonal relationships routinely update each other on the events and activities that have taken place in their lives since the time of their last contact (Drew & Chilton, 2000). By reciprocally engaging in this activity, people maintain a sense of keeping in touch. The fact that updating is a normal, routine activity allows it to be comfortably used to raise the topic of organ and tissue donation.

The students in the intervention courses planned and implemented donation campaigns; hence, they had donation-related events and activities on which they could report as updates since the time of their last contact. Students frequently initiated discussions of donation by first reporting course-related experiences. As is usual with updating, these reports occurred near the beginning of interactions. As exemplified in the transcript below, students sometimes progressed from updating to soliciting family members' perspectives or announcing their own perspective. Numbers in parentheses in the transcript represent time in seconds (e.g., .05 = ¹/₂ second).

Updating [UA04 S12 T1]

STUDENT: So (1.2) I'm taking a class this semester (0.5) where we uh (1.2) create a campaign for organ and tissue donation
FATHER: Okay
           (0.2)
STUDENT: And (1.2) we (just) (0.5) put everything together and (0.7) present we like (.) our audience is the student population and (0.7) we actually ge- have a grant (.) that funds us from the Center for Donation and Transplant so (like) an actual campaign that we implement
           (3.0)
STUDENT: So how do you feel about organ and tissue donation?

In this discussion, the student initiated the topic of donation with a report about the class she was taking, after which she solicited her father's perspective on donation. Because updating is a customary activity for family members, it is a more comfortable way to raise the topic than starting with a solicitation of the family member's perspective on donation.

Topical pivots

Studies of the ways in which topics are introduced and developed in discussions have shown that people introduce new topics either as disjunctive from the prior topics or in a step-wise approach (Jefferson, 1984). In using a step-wise approach, a participant can gradually move either from a more sensitive to a less sensitive topic or from a less sensitive to a more sensitive topic.

Some students in our study used a step-wise approach to introduce the sensitive topic of donation in family discussions. They used a somewhat less sensitive topic as a pivot or jumping-off point to then move to the topic of donation. In the following instance, the student first inquired about whether her father had a will, then she asked about his comfort level with discussing topics related to death, and then moved on to asking him about donation.

Topical Pivot [UA04 S06 T2]

STUDENT: Do you have a will, Dad?
FATHER: Do I have a will, no. ( ).
STUDENT: What?
FATHER: I should really make one out.
STUDENT: It doesn't bother you thinking about that kind of stuff?
FATHER: ( ).
STUDENT: Well, once you sell this house what do you have left to leave us besides
( ) ((laughs))?
FATHER: ( ).
STUDENT: Do you ever think about. (0.2) organ donation?

Raising a topic that is less sensitive than organ donation but close enough thematically to allow a natural shift to organ donation itself would be a more comfortable way of initiating an interpersonal discussion of donation. This type of sequence also allows a participant to take a reading of the other person's receptivity to discussing the sensitive topic.

RQ2: What Practices Did the Participants Use to Discuss Donation While Also Dealing With the Likelihood That a Family Member Viewed Such Discussions as Morbid?

The primary practice that students used to head off unwanted reactions and offer a counterinterpretation of the upcoming discussion of donation was the use of disclaimers (Hewitt & Stokes, 1975). Hewitt and Stokes (1975) defined a *disclaimer* as an interactional tactic used by actors faced with upcoming acts that threaten to disrupt emergent meanings or discredit situational identities. The function to disclaimers is to define, in advance of their occurring, problematic events in a manner that reduces their salience. It functions to preserve the alignment between the interacting parties in the face of disruptive lines of conduct.

In the following discussion, the student put forward the idea that the mother would view a discussion of donation as morbid. In putting out the idea first, the student was able to get a reaction from the mother (in this case, a confirmation) and then continue on to present the case for why it would be important anyway to discuss it.

Disclaimer UA06 S07 p1

STUDENT: . . . how do you feel about, like if ((pause)) but they're not, they're really no good to anybody once like you're gone. I know that the thought is like morbid and like really sad—

MOTHER: That's really true.

STUDENT: —but if, if my eyes or, or whatever they wanna take, would help someone

In this case, the student was able to anticipate her mother's reactions to the idea of discussing donation ("I know that the thought is like morbid and like really sad—"). In anticipating her mother's negative reactions with the use of the disclaimer, the student displayed sensitivity to her mother's feelings and, in the light of that displayed sensitivity, continued on with an argument in favor of donation. Recognizing the family member's concern is part of building a state of mutual receptivity to hearing each other's perspectives.

RQ3: What Practices Did the Participants Use to Inform Family Members of Their Perspectives While Also Minimizing the Likelihood of Engendering Their Critical Reactions?

In notifying family members of their intention to donate, students generally were acutely sensitive to the perspectives of their family members. Often students would elicit family members' perspectives prior to announcing their own perspectives to members of their family. When students put forward their perspectives first, they often did so cautiously and/or framed their perspectives to be in at least partial alignment with those of other family members.

Two practices that students used to put forward a perspective while minimizing the likelihood of family members' critical reactions are weakly stating a perspective and describing their own conversion.

Weakly stating a perspective

By weakly stating a perspective on donation, a participant provides the family member the opportunity to react to the weak version. Depending on the family member's reaction, the participant then can shape his or her perspective with reference to the family member's perspective or even withhold his or her perspective if it is unaligned with those of the family members. This is analogous to a person testing the water before fully immersing him or herself.

Below we illustrate two formats that students used to test the water by weakly stating their perspectives. One format involves casting one's perspectives as in process, tentative, or not firmly held. This can be seen most vividly in the following instance, in which the student initially formulated her perspective using a weak version and then corrected it to a stronger version. Earlier in this discussion, the student and her brother discussed donation. At that point, she elicited a favorable perspective from him on donation. After discussing various other topics, the student returned to the topic of donation to announce her perspective.

Casting perspective as tentative to test the water (UA04 S08 T3)

STUDENT: So back to this organ tissue donation, 'cause I'm thinkin' about um, registering. Well, I'm registered so—
BROTHER: So you did?
STUDENT: Yeah,

The student initially told her brother that she was "thinkin' about um, registering." By casting her state of decision making as still in process, the student provides her brother with the opportunity to state a negative view without criticizing her decision. However, in this instance, the student offered a second version in which she announced that she already was registered. The fact that the student started with a weaker version points to the functionality of casting one's perspective as not firmly held, especially in the context in which a participant is uncertain about family members' reactions. The weak version is consistent with the observation that students often formed their announcements to convey that they still were in the process of thinking about donation, or that the decision they announced was only tentative rather than definite.

Another format that students used to test the water by weakly stating their perspective was to put forward one's perspective as a hypothetical case. In the following instance, the student had not gone on record with any perspective on donation up until this point.

Using a hypothetical statement to test the water (UA04 S09 T1)

STUDENT: What'd you say if I said I think I wanna do it?
MOTHER: Well, I think it would be, I think it's a good thing

Using a hypothetical case, the student solicited his mother's reaction to the imagined situation of his saying that he thinks he wants to donate his organs. As is done in HIV counseling (Perakyla & Vehvilainen, 2003) the use of hypothetical situations allows the participants to explore various issues without going on record with assertions of fact or with commitments. With this form of testing the water, a participant can check out a family member's sympathies before committing to a perspective on donation.

Describe one's own conversion: I used to feel as you do until . . .
If a student is in the position of presenting a perspective that is contrary to other family members' perspectives, the student may produce a narrative in which the differences are in some ways lessened and through which they can see themselves

in partial alignment with one another. One way to accomplish partial alignment and the lessening of difference is by reporting on one's conversion. In these narratives, the students claim that they held the family members' perspective until recently, when they were exposed to new information or experiences. The inference that can be drawn is that the student still would be aligned with the family members' perspectives except for the recently acquired information or experience. Two illustrations of this type of narrative are presented below.

Describe Conversion, #1 (UB06 S03)

STUDENT: . . . So I, I mean I kinda felt the same way you guys do I think about it, until I went and spoke to these people and like, went on a tour of their, you know, units and everything. And then I, I always kinda was interested in doing it but now I feel like completely comfortable with it, and not just because they like convinced me. They didn't do any convincing, you know what I mean? Like I think they really need, like they need a PR campaign to let people know that they're not out there selling people's ( ) ((laughs)).

Describe Conversion, #2 (UA06 S07)

MOTHER: . . . now, I cannot. Maybe in 3 years I may change my mind. That's how I am.
STUDENT: It's interesting 'cause like the more I like thought about it and the more I was exposed to it, you know, twice a week for a whole semester, I thought like—
MOTHER: Now you wanna do it.
STUDENT: Now I want to because, but like you said, you're beyond it hurting for, you know, you know, you're at a point where they cover it up like they, you can't even tell anything is gone, you know. They replace everything and like what-not.
MOTHER: And do ( ).
STUDENT: Yeah. And so I mean— ((pause)).
MOTHER: You really have to give a lot of thought to it. It's not at the spur of the moment like
STUDENT: Yeah.
MOTHER: —you're filling out an application.

In framing their current perspectives as a change from their previous reservations and concerns based on information and experiences acquired through the course, the students provided their family members with a way to see the past commonality with the students even as they describe the different perspectives. Perhaps positioning their current perspectives as having developed from ones that were shared with their family members functions both to maintain relational solidarity between the family members and to promote greater receptivity to contrary perspectives.

Discussion

As described in the discussion of social scientific research methods, quantitative and qualitative research provide us with different types of knowledge. For example, most of the research to date on family notification is quantitative and determines associations between measures of willingness to communicate with a variety of theory-based predictors, such as particular attitudes, degree of knowledge, and dispositional factors. Some qualitative studies of naturalistic family conversations focus on understandings, perceptions, and experiences of the participants. These studies are particularly well suited to explore the reasons that people shy away from certain discussions, even when they know that they should engage in them. Other qualitative studies of naturalistic family discussions focus on the practices that the participants use in carrying out the discussions. These studies provide a set of potential resources for handling the challenges that occur when engaging in discussions about sensitive topics.

In the course of our qualitative studies of family discussions on donation, we became increasingly convinced that family discussion research must take into consideration the complex relational and communicative dynamics that occur in families. One feature of families is that family members are interdependent on one another, are aware of a history with one another, generally project a future relationship with one another, and usually have some concern with the quality of the family relationships. Family members usually are concerned with knowing the degree to which their views on important matters coincide with the views of other family members. Also it is important to remember that family discussions on salient topics often extend over a series of conversations and across time. Qualitative longitudinal studies are needed to examine what happens in such discussions over time.

Additionally, families are organized around roles such as parent and child, and these roles may have important implications for how discussions proceed. For example, when students attempted to inform or persuade their family members, they did so in ways that avoided appearing superior or domineering. Given broad cultural notions about the parent–child relationship, it is not clear whether parents would approach their children with the same concern or if the parent role would permit a more authoritative voice on such matters. Qualitative studies that attend to these kinds of subtleties conceptualize the family as an interdependent collective, with complex roles, and with preexisting relational histories and investments in their future relationships.

Acknowledgments

The research project on the dynamics of family discussions of organ and tissue donation was supported by a grant from the Human Resources Services Administration, Division of Transplantation (HRSA/DoT; grant #R39OT01205). The contents of this chapter are solely the responsibility of the author and do not necessarily reflect the views of HRSA/DoT. The research project was done collaboratively with Paul Denvir, who served as my research assistant for the duration of the grant period. The author acknowledges the ideas and work of Teresa Harrison, Carla Williams, Tom Feeley, Don Vincent, Jonathan Pierce, and Deborah Silverman.

References

Bull, S. S., Cohen, J., Ortiz, C., & Evans, T. (2002). The POWER campaign for promotion of female and male condoms: Audience research and campaign development. *Health Communication, 14*, 475–491.

Denzin, N. K., & Lincoln, Y. (1994). *Handbook of qualitative research.* Thousand Oaks, CA: Sage.

Drew, P., & Chilton, K. (2000). Calling just to keep in touch: Regular and habitualised telephone calls as an environment for small talk. In J. Coupland (Ed.), *Small talk* (pp. 137–162). Harlow, UK: Pearson Education.

Dutta-Bergman, M. J. (2004). Primary sources of health information: Comparisons in the domain of health attitudes, health cognitions, and health behaviors. *Health Communication, 16*, 273–288.

Fasula, A. M., & Miller, K. S. (2006). African-American and Hispanic adolescents' intentions to delay first intercourse: Parental communication as a buffer for sexually active peers. *Adolescent Health, 38*, 193–200.

Flora, J. A. (2001). The Stanford Community Studies: Campaigns to reduce cardiovascular disease. In R. E. Rice & C. K. Atkins (Eds.), *Public communication campaigns* (pp. 193–213). Newbury Park, CA: Sage.

Hewitt, J. P., & Stokes, R. (1975). Disclaimers. *American Sociological Review, 40*, 1–11.

Hood, J. (2007, April 18). [Listserv message.]. Qualitative Research for the Human Sciences electronic list. Retrieved April 18, 2007, from qualrs-l@listserv.uga.edu

Jefferson, G. (1984). On stepwise transition from talk about a trouble to inappropriately next-positioned matters. In J. M. Atkinson & J. C. Heritage (Eds.), *Structures of social action: Studies of conversation analysis.* Cambridge: Cambridge University Press.

Johnson, J. D., & Meischke, H. (1993). A comprehensive model of cancer-related information seeking applied to magazines. *Human Communications Research, 19*, 343–367.

Morgan, S. E., & Miller, J. K. (2002). Beyond the organ donor card: The effect of knowledge, attitudes, and values on willingness to communicate about organ donation to family members. *Health Communication, 14*, 121–134.

Morgan, S. E., Miller, J. K., & Arasaratnam, L. (2002). Signing cards, saving lives: An evaluation of the worksite organ donation promotion project. *Communication Monographs*, *69*, 253–273.

Perakyla, A., & Vehvilainen, S. (2003). Conversation analysis and the professional stocks of interactional knowledge. *Discourse and Society*, *14*, 727–750.

Pomerantz, A. (1980). Telling my side: Limited access as a fishing device. *Sociological Inquiry*, *50*, 186–198.

Pomerantz, A., & Denvir, P. (2007). *Final report on research project: Dynamics of family discussions* (Final Report on HRSA Grant No. R39OT01205-02-00). Washington, DC: Health Resources and Services Administration (HRSA), Office of Special Programs, Division of Transplantation.

Pomerantz, A., & Fehr, B. J. (1997). Conversation analysis: An approach to the study of social action as sense making practices. In T. A. van Dijk (Ed.), *Discourse as social interaction* (pp. 64–91). London: Sage.

Rimal, R. N., & Flora, J. A. (1998). Bidirectional familial influences in dietary behavior: Test of a model of campaign influences. *Human Communication Research*, *24*, 610–637.

Rimal, R. N., Flora, J. A., & Schooler, C. (1999). Achieving improvements in overall health orientation: Effects of campaign exposure, information seeking, and health media use. *Communication Research*, *26*, 322–348.

Rogers, E. M. (1996). Up-to-date report. *Journal of Health Communication*, *1*, 15–23.

Rutenberg, N., & Watkins, S. C. (1997). The buzz outside the clinics: Conversations and contraception in Nyanza Province, Kenya. *Studies of Family Planning*, *28*, 290–307.

Smith, S. W., Kopfman, J. E., Lindsey, L. L. M., Yoo, J., & Morrison, K. (2004). Encouraging family discussion on the decision to donate organs: The role of the willingness to communicate scale. *Health Communication*, *16*, 333–346.

Tardy, R. W., & Hale, C. L. (1998). Bonding and cracking: The role of informal, interpersonal networks in health care decision making. *Health Communication*, *10*, 151–173.

Valente, T. W., & Saba, W. P. (1998). Mass media and interpersonal influence in a reproductive health communication campaign in Bolivia. *Communication Research*, *25*, 96–124.

Whitaker, D. J., Miller, K. S., May, D. C., & Levin, M. L. (1999). Teenage partners' communication about sexual risk and condom use: The importance of parent–teenager discussions. *Family Planning Perspective*, *31*, 117–121.

18

Ethically and Effectively Advancing Living Donation

How Should It Be Done?

Amy D. Waterman and James R. Rodrigue

For the 500,000 patients with end-stage renal disease (ESRD) in the United States (U.S. Renal Data System, 2009), the possibility of a kidney transplant brings with it tremendous hope. Compared with remaining on dialysis, most patients who receive kidney transplants have better long-term survival (Bartlett et al., 1998) and improved quality of life (Christensen, Holman, Turner, & Slaughter, 1989; Neipp et al., 2006). However, with estimates that by 2015 there will be over 100,000 new ESRD patients yearly (Gilbertson et al., 2005), increasing the number of kidneys available for transplant is critical.

Increases in deceased organ donation are certainly being realized with the U.S. Department of Health and Human Services' Breakthrough Collaborative (Burdick et al., 2006; Shafer et al., 2006). However, these increases still will not meet the projected need for transplantable kidneys (Sheehy et al., 2003; Sung et al., 2008). Living donor kidney transplantation (LDKT), where a family member, friend, or another altruistic person donates a kidney while he or she is still alive, is another possibility for increasing the donor pool. In comparison to deceased donor kidney transplantation, LDKT can occur before the patient is in full kidney failure, thus preempting the need for dialysis (Tarantino, 2000). Kidneys from living donors also yield better graft survival, lower rates of acute rejection, and improved patient survival (United Network for Organ Sharing, 2009) compared with deceased donor kidneys. Living donation has been occurring since 1954, with over 90,000 individuals having become living donors in the United States (United Network for Organ Sharing, 2009).

In light of the increasing prevalence of chronic kidney disease, the known benefits of transplantation over dialysis, and the long waiting times for deceased donor transplantation, LDKT has become an increasingly important option for patients to consider. So, why, then, hasn't LDKT been actively promoted as a treatment of choice for more kidney patients? First, ethical debate about whether LDKT should be conducted at all and the difficulty of conducting interventions involving both living donors and recipients have slowed progress. Second, recommendations from successful interventions promoting LDKT are rare. Therefore, this chapter will outline the debate surrounding living donation, current approaches to promote LDKT, and a theoretical framework to guide future LDKT efforts.

The Living Donation Ethical Debate

Living donation has been ethically debated since its inception (Hilhorst, Kranenburg, & Busschbach, 2006). The government, the medical community, and potential donors and recipients are all committed to the idea that no harm should befall a healthy living donor (Vastag, 2003).

Over the last 40 years, extensive research has been conducted to explore living donors' transplant experiences and to learn whether donors have been harmed in any way. Multiple studies have shown that donors do not regret donating (Burroughs, Waterman, & Hong, 2003; Fehrman-Ekholm et al., 2000; Jordan et al., 2004; Waterman, Stanley, et al., 2006) and actually report receiving benefits like increased self-worth (Fellner, 1976), improved relationships with their recipients (Burroughs et al., 2003), and improved life satisfaction post donation (Franklin & Crombie, 2003; Jacobs & Thomas, 2003; Johnson et al., 1999; Karrfelt, Berg, Lindblad, & Tyden, 1998; Waterman et al., 2004). However, other studies, primarily of donors who received open nephrectomies, also show that living donors have a 0.03% risk of death due to donating (Najarian, Chavers, McHugh, & Matas, 1992), have a 5 mm Hg increase in blood pressure within 5 to 10 years after donation over that anticipated with normal aging (Boudville et al., 2006), and may incur transportation or lodging costs or lose wages while they recover from donation (Clarke, Klarenbach, Vlaicu, Yang, & Garg, 2006; Klarenbach, Garg, & Vlaicu, 2006). Finally, of the over 90,000 individuals who have become living donors since the 1980s, at least 56 living donors have been wait-listed for a deceased donor transplant because they have lost their remaining kidney (Ellison, McBride, Taranto, Delmonico, & Kauffman, 2002).

Due to these findings, the medical establishment has taken many steps to improve clinical practice and ensure quality care for living donors. To ensure unbiased care, most transplant centers have coordinators or living donor advocates who evaluate only potential living donors (Abecassis et al., 2000; Olbrisch, Benedict, Haller, & Levenson, 2001). A group of health care professionals and ethicists comprising the Living Donor Consensus Group developed recommendations that outline what information should be communicated with donors about transplant (Abecassis et al., 2000; McQuarrie & Gordon, 2003). Brochures informing potential living donors about what risks they might face (Joint Commission on Accreditation of Healthcare Organizations, 2009) and addressing common questions and fears about living donation (National Kidney Foundation, 2009; Waterman & Duhig, 2002) are available from transplant centers, governmental agencies, and kidney organizations. Finally, laparoscopic and mininephrectomy surgical techniques have been developed to reduce the size of the donor's incision, postdonation pain, and recovery time (Andersen et al., 2006; Schweitzer et al., 2000; Shenoy, Lowell, Ramachandran, & Jendrisak, 2002).

Living donation research will and should always continue in this area. Ethical issues like transplant tourism and patient solicitation of living donors through billboards and Web sites (Rodrigue, Antonellis, Mandelbrot, & Hanto, 2008; Steinbrook, 2005; Stephan, Barbari, & Younan, 2007) continue to arise. However, in view of the organ shortage, most U.S. transplant centers have active living donor transplant programs and continue to conduct over 6,000 living donor transplants each year (United Network for Organ Sharing, 2009).

Advancing LDKT: Current Approaches

Due to the great need for transplantable kidneys (Burrows, 2004; Lyon, 1998), the government, health care professionals, and researchers have begun to examine the effectiveness of interventions to promote LDKT awareness, including, but not limited to, (a) increasing access to paired donation and nondirected donation programs, (b) providing reimbursement for costs associated with being a living donor, and (c) improving the delivery and quality of LDKT educational programs. These first efforts reveal possible avenues for increasing LDKT awareness and overcoming barriers to living donation.

Paired Donation and Nondirected Donation Programs

To increase LDKTs, alternative living donation programs have been developed to utilize (a) living donors who had previously been ruled out for their recipients, and (b) living donors without potential recipients. One third of evaluated living donors are estimated to be ruled out due to blood type or antibody incompatibility with their intended recipients (Segev, Gentry, Warren, Reeb, & Montgomery, 2005). Paired donation, where an incompatible donor donates to another recipient so that his or her intended recipient will receive a kidney from another living donor (i.e., paired donation) or the deceased donor pool (i.e., list paired donation), is an innovative alternative to increasing LDKTs (Gentry, Segev, & Montgomery, 2005). In one study of 174 ruled-out potential donors, a significant proportion reported interest in participating in paired donation (68%) and list paired donation (38%), should these programs be available in their area (Waterman, Stanley, et al., 2006).

To date, 398 paired donations and 207 list paired donations have occurred (United Network for Organ Sharing, 2009). The development of the Paired Donation Network in Ohio, as one example, resulted in a 4% increase in the number of LDKTs in the state in its first 2 years. Johns Hopkins has conducted a triple kidney paired donation, where three recipients simultaneously received kidneys from previously incompatible donors (Montgomery et al., 2008).

The New England Organ Bank (2009) has performed 38 list paired donations from 2000 through 2008. However, paired donation programs are not available in every area; one survey of U.S. kidney transplant programs found that only 49% participate in a paired donation program and 29% participate in a list donation program (Rodrigue, Pavlakis, et al., 2007). In 2008, a national Kidney Paired Donation pilot program was approved by the United Network for Organ Sharing (UNOS; Waterman, Stanley, et al., 2006) to increase access to paired donation.

Nondirected donation programs function similarly to blood donation programs, where charitable individuals anonymously donate a kidney to a patient listed on the transplant waiting list. Research has shown that spiritual beliefs and empathy for those needing transplants are key motivations for nondirected donors (Henderson et al., 2003; Jendrisak et al., 2006; Mueller, Case, & Hook, 2008).

Although over 500 nondirected donations have occurred to date (United Network for Organ Sharing, 2009), no universal allocation policy exists, and only 61% of transplant programs currently allow nondirected or stranger donors (Rodrigue, Pavlakis, et al., 2007; Segev & Montgomery, 2008). Because there are relatively few studies on this select group of donors, more research is needed to better explicate the psychological risks and benefits of their donation experiences.

In summary, paired and nondirected donation programs allow more recipients to receive the health benefits of living donor kidneys (Daar, Salahudeen, Pingle, & Woods, 1990; Jacobs, Roman, Garvey, Kahn, & Matas, 2004; Ross et al., 1997; Ross & Woodle, 2000; Spital, 2000) and are more cost-effective than patients remaining on dialysis or undergoing desensitization protocols (Segev, Gentry, Melancon, & Montgomery, 2005; Smith et al., 2000). Because trends are being reported where Caucasians are more likely to participate in nondirected donation with other ethnic groups (Segev & Montgomery, 2008), attention needs to be paid to ensure that these types of programs are available for and benefit all ethnic and socioeconomic groups. Whether these programs can be successfully established nationally and whether sufficient patients enroll to significantly increase LKDT rates are still unknown.

Reimbursement of Living Donation Expenses for Eligible Donors

Research has shown that over 80% of the general public is supportive of financial incentives like reimbursement for medical costs and paid leave for LDKT, with African Americans more supportive of financial incentives than Caucasians

(Boulware, Troll, Wang, & Powe, 2006). In 2007, the National Living Donor
Assistance Center (NLDAC) was established to assist individuals who could not
afford the travel and subsistence expenses associated with becoming living
donors. For potential living donors who meet specific financial eligibility criteria, the NLDAC provides up to $6,000 in reimbursement for the costs of donor
evaluation, surgery, and follow-up, including hotel, travel, and meal expenses.
Currently, over 100 transplant centers have filed NLDAC applications on behalf
of prospective living donors who are donating directly or through paired donation, with over 200 individuals receiving funds (Katrina Crist, NLDAC, personal
communication, October 1, 2008). With 40% of applicants reporting that they
would be unable to afford donation expenses without NLDAC financial support,
this is an important initiative for overcoming financial disincentives to living
donation. However, because NLDAC does not provide reimbursement for lost
wages associated with donation surgery, some interested individuals still may be
prevented from donating due to financial considerations.

Improved Transplant Center Educational Delivery

Another approach to increasing awareness of LDKT is to improve the delivery
and quality of LDKT education for transplant candidates and potential living donors.
Transplant centers traditionally provide education through unstructured discussions with health professionals at routine clinic visits and through general access
to brochures and videos. This type of LDKT education is cost-effective, can naturally be integrated into patient care, and reaches motivated patients who are actively
deciding what type of transplant to pursue.

However, there are several reasons why clinic-based education may not
adequately address issues associated with LDKT. First, current clinic-based education, which often takes less than 20 minutes at one visit, may not provide enough
time to discuss the evaluation and surgery of both recipients and living donors,
common fears about living donation and its risks, and how to find a living donor
(Waterman, Barrett, & Stanley, 2008; Waterman, Stanley, et al., 2006). Patients
who have not had a chance to discuss their questions and concerns with
providers are less likely to consider LDKT as a medical option. Second, this
education can be presented only to the patient and any individuals who accompany him or her to the transplant clinic. The patient must then be relied upon
to disseminate information about living donation to family members, relatives,
and friends.

Unfortunately, research has shown that patients turn down offers from potential living donors due to fear and misinformation. One study found that 20%
of wait-listed patients had turned down a potential living donor's offer to be
evaluated (Martinez-Alarcon et al., 2005). Many studies have shown that
patients also feel very uncomfortable talking about living donation with their friends

and family (Pradel, Limcangco, Mullins, & Bartlett, 2003; Pradel, Mullins, & Bartlett, 2003; Waterman, Stanley, et al., 2006; Zimmerman, Albert, Llewellyn-Thomas, & Hawker, 2006). Non-Caucasians and patients without a college education are significantly less likely to talk to their family and friends about living donation than other groups (Rodrigue, Cornell, Kaplan, & Howard, 2008a). Many parents also refuse to consider having their children be living donors for them (Gordon, 2001b). The numbers of patients who rule out LDKT as a possibility and of potential donors who are unaware or turned away by their recipients are potentially very high.

Successful LDKT educational interventions in transplant centers are few and far between. Several transplant centers have increased LDKT rates by offering formal family education programs and targeting African Americans (Foster et al., 2002; Schweitzer et al., 1997). Rodrigue and colleagues (Rodrigue, Cornell, Lin, Kaplan, & Howard, 2007) conducted a randomized controlled trial of an educational program where health professionals discussed LDKT with prospective recipients and their family and friends in their homes. Compared with traditional clinic-based education, significantly more patients in the home-based education condition had living donor inquiries, evaluations, and LDKTs (Rodrigue, Cornell, et al., 2007). In exploring why this program worked, compared to patients educated in the clinic, patients who participated in the home-based educational program had an opportunity for family decision making and LDKT discussion in an informal setting in the presence of knowledgeable health professionals. The program also educated family members and friends who might not have come to the clinic, and allowed questions or concerns to be addressed. African Americans, particularly, were more likely to pursue LDKT after this home-based education strategy (Rodrigue, Cornell, Kaplan, & Howard, 2008b).

Improved Education for Dialysis Center Patients

Another venue for educating patients about LDKT is at the dialysis center. Over 350,000 patients in the United States are on some form of dialysis (U.S. Renal Data System, 2009). Many transplant-eligible dialysis patients, some with living donor volunteers, may never have presented to the transplant center for evaluation (Alexander & Sehgal, 2001). African Americans, the poor, women, and patients at for-profit dialysis centers are less likely to be referred for and present for transplant (Alexander & Sehgal, 1998; Garg, Frick, Diener-West, & Powe, 1999). Dialysis patients' knowledge about LDKT has been shown to be poor; one study found that 78% of surveyed dialysis patients reported no or incomplete knowledge about transplant (Vianello, Palminteri, Brunello, Calconi, & Maresca, 2000).

Compared with education provided at the transplant center, educating patients about transplant in dialysis centers has a different set of advantages and disadvantages. Because kidney patients are at dialysis centers weekly or monthly for their dialysis care, dialysis educators have multiple opportunities for transplant conversations, often over many years. Providers can introduce the topic of transplant and LDKT when patients are most healthy and interested in learning about it.

However, transplant education at dialysis centers also may be problematic. Because many patients never have presented for transplant evaluation, conversations may have to focus on simple messages recommending transplant evaluation versus providing in-depth education about LDKT. Discussions with potential living donors also may be difficult at this location, because many centers prohibit family members from being present during dialysis. In addition, dialysis providers may not have had extensive transplant training or may have concerns about the value of transplant or LDKT versus dialysis (Consesa et al., 2005). They may have insufficient time to administer transplant education or may work in dialysis centers unsupportive of extensive transplant discussion (Beasley, Hull, & Rosenthal, 1997). Education programs for dialysis health professionals may reduce inaccurate information about transplant being disseminated to patients (Maiorano & Schena, 2008; Murray, Conrad, & Bayley, 1999) and help professionals assist patients in making informed transplant choices.

Several educational randomized controlled trials are being conducted in Missouri and Maryland to learn whether improved dialysis center education increases pursuit of transplant and LDKT. Transplant-eligible patients in these studies watch videos sharing transplant stories of living donors and recipients, receive educational brochures, and have conversations with health professionals about transplant. Consistent with the transtheoretical model of behavioral change (DiClemente et al., 1991; Prochaska, DiClemente, & Norcross, 1992), interventions are tailored based on how ready a patient is to pursue LDKT. For example, a patient who is not yet considering living donation may receive only general education about the advantages of living donation over remaining on dialysis, whereas a patient with an interested living donor might be given detailed information about what the transplant surgery entails. Research has found that, compared to their baseline attitudes about living donation, African Americans, younger patients, and patients who have spent less time on dialysis have been shown to be significantly more willing to pursue living donation one week after this type of LDKT educational intervention (Pradel, Suwannaprom, Mullins, Sadler, & Bartlett, 2008).

Improved Community Education About Preemptive Transplantation

Educating patients about LKDT before starting dialysis also might enable some patients to bypass dialysis altogether (Hayes & Waterman, 2008). Only 2.5% of all ESRD patients get transplants prior to starting dialysis—a treatment option called *preemptive living donor transplantation* (PLDT; Abecassis et al., 2008). Patients who get a PLDT before they start dialysis avoid the possibility of health complications due to dialysis, have the highest graft success, and have the lowest mortality rates (Abou Ayache et al., 2005; Grochowiecki et al., 2006; Mange, Joffe, & Feldman, 2001; Simforoosh et al., 2003). Patients generally get a PLDT from a living donor, because a patient has to be in full kidney failure before he or she can be listed on the deceased donor waiting list. Unfortunately, most potential kidney recipients do not have the opportunity to learn about and consider PLDT because of inadequate early renal care or insufficient education about transplant during the early stages of their kidney disease. Patients who are racial minorities or have Medicare as a primary insurance payer (Kasiske et al., 2002) are more likely to present to physicians in full kidney failure and have to begin dialysis immediately (Ismail, Neyra, & Hakim, 1998; Kahn, 1994). For these and other reasons, a health disparity exists between patients who get living donor transplants before dialysis and those who do not. Patients presenting for PLDT are currently more likely to be Caucasian, have health insurance, and have a college degree (Butkus, Dottes, Meydrech, & Barber, 2001).

One difficulty of PLDT is locating and educating eligible patients before they reach ESRD and their kidneys stop functioning. Partnerships with kidney organizations that work with patients in early stages of kidney disease and with community nephrologists' or primary care physicians' offices may be helpful in educating more patients and their families about PLDT. Several randomized controlled trials are being conducted nationally working with community partners to promote PLDT.

What Is Next? A Theoretical Framework for LDKT

As researchers consider where to go next, what theoretical framework should guide our LDKT interventions? Based on our clinical experience and research findings, we propose a social-ecological framework in which to develop, implement, and evaluate programs to promote LDKT (reprinted with permission from James R. Rodrigue; see Figure 18.1). This model proposes that patients' decision making about LDKT is influenced by multiple systems, including their personal values, their core family, their extended social network, the health care system at large, and their community or culture. Each system, represented graphically as a series of concentric rings, represents a type of influence, with the rings closest to the patient indicating systems in which the patient most directly interacts (e.g., family). What successful interventions highlight is the need to promote LDKT both at the individual level and within other systems in which the patient is embedded.

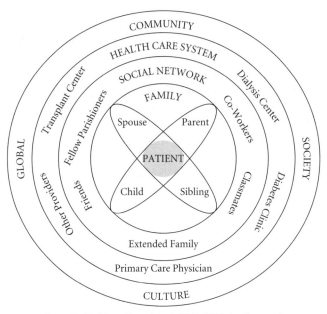

Figure 18.1   Social-ecological transplant model.

Patient Level

At the core of the social-ecological model are patient-level factors—how patients think, feel, and make decisions about their illness. Research has shown that these factors have important implications for how willing patients are to consider living donation. For example, patients not pursuing LDKT have been shown to lack knowledge about the benefits of living donation; have concerns about involving and possibly risking a living donor's health, the surgical pain, and the possibility of kidney rejection (Gordon, 2001a; Pradel, Limcangco, et al., 2003; Schweitzer, Seidel-Wiesel, Verres, & Wiesel, 2003; Waterman, Schenk, et al., 2006); and be unsure how to ask someone to be a living donor for them (Lunsford et al., 2006; Pradel, Mullins, et al., 2003; Waterman, Stanley, et al., 2006). The influence of these factors varies based on the patients' intellectual functioning, disease progression, family environment, and relationship with health care professionals. It is important for new living donation interventions to consider all patient elements because they play an important role in how proactive patients will be in discussing LDKT with others.

Family and Social Network

For many reasons, the involvement of a patient's family and social network is crucial to the success of a living donor transplant. At the most basic level, the needed kidney is most often donated by a family member or friend of the patient. Many renal patients never ask a family member or friend to be a potential living donor because the prospective donor volunteers first. The prospective donor and the recipient, therefore, jointly make the living donation decision, complete their transplant evaluation, and undergo surgery together. From a systems perspective, because renal disease also affects other people with whom the patient has a close emotional relationship, transplantation can improve both the patient's quality of life and their families' lives as a whole.

Therefore, education about living donation must reach both prospective donors and their recipients. Many family members of renal patients are unaware that they could be kidney donors while they are alive. Many potential living donors and ESRD patients begin learning about LDKT at home by using the Internet (Seto et al., 2007). With the variability in accuracy of health information on the Internet (Berland et al., 2001), LDKT information must be easily available through common search engines, written for individuals with low health literacy, and comprehensively cover all treatment options and their risks and benefits (Abecassis et al., 2000; Delmonico, 2005; Moody et al., 2007). Because some patients and potential donors may not have Internet access, dissemination of print versions of this information through health organizations reaching potential living donors must also occur.

Health Care System

Health care professionals managing the care of renal patients include primary care providers, community-based nephrologists, dialysis nurses and staff, diabetes clinic staff, social workers and psychologists, and transplant center nurses, nephrologists, and surgeons. These professionals have varying access to patients and their donors, and patient care agendas that can make coordination of patient care and transplant education difficult (Table 18.1). When choosing health professionals and organizations for LDKT education interventions, it will be important to consider at what point in patients' disease progression and treatment they meet. For example, organizations like the National Kidney Foundation may reach more patients newer to kidney disease, whereas transplant social workers may be the right group to educate motivated patients about how to ask living donors to donate. Finally, Medicare's partnership in supporting discussion of transplant in dialysis centers is particularly critical, because for-profit dialysis centers have been shown to be less likely to refer patients for transplant than not-for-profit dialysis centers, possibly because of the loss of dialysis revenue (Garg et al., 1999).

Table 18.1 Living Donation Education Opportunities for the Health
Professional Community

	Donor and Recipient Access	Primary Focus and Education Opportunity
Primary care physicians and community nephrologists	Patients with newer diagnoses of kidney failure and their family members	• Primary focus is on medical care of kidney patients. • General education about dialysis and transplant treatment options provided.
Dialysis health professionals	Dialysis patients both eligible and ineligible for transplant	• Primary focus is on medical care of dialysis patients. • Referral for transplant and general transplant education provided.
Transplant coordinators and nephrologists	Patients and potential living donors presenting for transplant evaluation, and family members of patients	• Primary focus is on evaluation of recipients and donors for possible transplant or donation. • Detailed education about living and deceased donation provided.
Transplant surgeons	Recipients and their matching living donors, and family members of patients	• Primary focus is on successful organ retrieval. • Detailed education about surgery and recovery for recipients and donors provided.
National and regional kidney organizations (e.g., the National Kidney Foundation and the United Network for Organ Sharing)	Patients with kidney disease, potential and actual living donors, and family members of patients	• Primary focus is on educating kidney patients and families about dialysis and transplant options. • Brochures, videos, and community education opportunities about treatment options provided.
Researchers studying clinical issues regarding kidney disease	Patients with kidney disease, potential and actual kidney recipients and living donors, and the public	• Primary focus is on studying research issues and testing interventions to increase deceased and living donation. • Transplant education and intervention may be a research focus for some.
Governmental agencies (i.e., the Health Resources and Services Administration and the National Institute of Diabetes and Digestive and Kidney Diseases)	Indirect kidney patient and donor access through health care professionals and researchers	• Primary focus is on providing grant funds to allow research and interventions to be conducted. • Some transplant education materials developed using grant funds.
Medicare	Patients with kidney disease	• Primary focus is to provide health care and insurance for patients in renal failure. • Some transplant education materials are available, especially about financial issues involved with kidney disease.

Community and Culture

Finally, community and cultural factors, such as race and socioeconomic status, are significant factors that affect the willingness of patients and others to pursue LDKT (Alvaro et al., 2008). In the past, Caucasians have donated 68–70% of the living donor kidneys (United Network for Organ Sharing, 2009). Research has shown that African Americans and individuals of other ethnic groups are less likely to pursue living donation (Prasad, 2007) or be living donors than Caucasians, possibly due to distrust of the medical establishment (Boulware et al., 2002), fear about organ distribution inequity (Frates & Garcia Bohrer, 2002; McNamara et al., 1999; Verble & Worth, 2003), lack of awareness about living donation (Landolt et al., 2001; Siegel, Alvaro, Lac, Crano, & Dominick, 2008), or cultural decision-making differences (Perez et al., 1988). The lower incidence of living donation is especially troubling when looking at the disproportionate number of African American and Hispanic renal patients waiting for kidneys who suffer from diabetes, hypertension, and kidney disease (U.S. Renal Data System, 2009).

Living donation educational interventions must give careful consideration to cultural influences—both historical and current—to be most effective. Culturally and ethnically tailored transplant education has been developed and piloted with Hispanics (Alvaro et al., 2008) and American Indians (Thomas, 2002). Education materials must be made available in Spanish and other languages.

Societal and Global Factors

Societal and global factors like the growing demand for kidney transplants, changes in the kidney allocation system, and advances in transplant surgical techniques may affect health professionals' and patients' attitudes about LDKT. As the shortage of organs increases, transplant programs have become more willing to accept unrelated—and even solicited—living donors using expanded medical and sociodemographic criteria than in years past. The U.S. government continues to explore whether to develop new policies, educational programs, and laws to promote living donation. Finally, with general public confusion about LDKT (Boulware et al., 2002, 2005), a consistent, balanced message about the opportunity of living donation needs to be developed to educate U.S. consumers about this treatment option using print, radio, and television.

Research Excellence and Partnership to Increase LDKT

As researchers and educators continue to promote LDKT, the importance of creating interventions and educational materials grounded in established behavioral theory, developing valid survey instruments, and accurately measuring changes

Table 18.2   Overall Recommendations for Promoting LDKT

Improve quality of education about living donation.	Promote advantages of LDKT over remaining on dialysis or getting on the waiting list.
	Apply established behavioral change theories to the design of educational materials and interventions.
	Utilize past LDKT research and intervention findings in design of educational campaigns.
	Publish successful LDKT educational campaign materials for use by researchers and educators.
Provide LDKT education to patients and living donors prior to transplant evaluation.	Educate patients and prospective donors earlier through the following:
	• LDKT education from community kidney organizations
	• Education about preemptive living donor transplantation at primary care physicians' or community nephrologists' offices
	• LDKT education at dialysis centers
	• LDKT media campaigns.
Increase access to donor exchange programs for all patients.	Provide patient and living donor access to donor exchange and nondirected donation programs in all states.
	Develop and disseminate educational materials about donor exchange programs to patients.
Address LDKT educational needs of patients and donors who are ethnic minorities.	Continue to conduct research to understand what barriers to LDKT emerge for patients and their donors who are ethnic minorities.
	Design tailored educational materials based on what is learned.
Improve measurement of living donation interventions.	Develop and validate surveys for measuring LDKT and donation knowledge, attitudes, and barriers.
	Develop a national data repository capturing physical and psychological outcomes of being a living donor for communicating living donor risk statistics.

in LDKT cannot be understated (Table 18.2). Educational interventions to promote LDKT should be grounded in the transtheoretical model of behavioral change (Prochaska & DiClemente, 1983), the health belief model (Janz & Becker, 1984), or other models of communication, motivation, or behavioral change. Although survey instruments on transplant knowledge (Devins et al., 1990), dialysis patient quality of life (Wu et al., 2001), satisfaction with renal treatment (Barendse, Speight, & Bradley, 2005), and donors' expectations for donating (Rodrigue, Guenther et al., 2008) have been published, validated surveys measuring prospective recipients' and living donors' LDKT attitudes and behaviors still need to be developed. Finally, rather than relying only on patient self-report, which may be biased due to social desirability, objective sources of data provided by transplant centers, Medicare and UNOS databases, or patient claims data should be used to confirm that an increase in LDKT actually occurred.

In closing, the promotion of LDKT is still in its infancy. Standing on a strong theoretical and research foundation, in partnership with health professionals and agencies serving kidney recipients and donors, an improvement in LDKT awareness and education is certainly possible. However, our ongoing research and education efforts must keep pace with clinical judgments, and we must systematically monitor the long-term outcomes of living donation.

Acknowledgments

This research was supported by grant # D71HS04318 from the Health Resources and Services Administration, Healthcare Systems Bureau, Division of Transplantation. The contents do not necessarily represent official views of the Health Resources and Services Administration.

References

Abecassis, M., Adams, M., Adams, P., Arnold, R. M., Atkins, C. R., Barr, M. L., et al. (2000). Consensus statement on the live organ donor. *Journal of the American Medical Association, 284*, 2919–2926.

Abecassis, M., Bartlett, S. T., Collins, A. J., Davis, C. L., Delmonico, F. L., Friedewald, J. J., et al. (2008). Kidney Transplantation as Primary Therapy for End-Stage Renal Disease: A National Kidney Foundation/Kidney Disease Outcomes Quality Initiative (NKF/ KDOQITM) Conference. Clinical Journal of the American Society of Nephrology.

Abou Ayache, R., Bridoux, F., Pessione, F., Thierry, A., Belmouaz, M., Leroy, F., et al. (2005). Preemptive renal transplantation in adults. *Transplant Proceedings, 37*, 2817–2818.

Alexander, G. C., & Sehgal, A. R. (1998). Barriers to cadaveric renal transplantation among blacks, women, and the poor. *Journal of the American Medical Association, 280*, 1148–1152.

Alexander, G. C., & Sehgal, A. R. (2001). Why hemodialysis patients fail to complete the transplantation process. *American Journal of Kidney Disease, 37*, 321–328.

Alvaro, E. M., Siegel, J. T., Turcotte, D., Lisha, N., Crano W. D., & Dominick, S. A. (2008). Hispanic living kidney donation: A qualitative examination of barriers and opportunities. *Progress in Transplantation, 18*, 243–250.

Andersen, M. H., Mathisen, L., Oyen, O., Edwin, B., Digernes, R., Kvarstein, G., et al. (2006). Postoperative pain and convalescence in living kidney donors—laparoscopic versus open donor nephrectomy: A randomized study. *American Journal of Transplantation*, 6, 1438–1443.

Barendse, S. M., Speight, J., & Bradley, C. (2005). The Renal Treatment Satisfaction Questionnaire (RTSQ): A measure of satisfaction with treatment for chronic kidney failure. *American Journal of Kidney Disease*, 45, 572–579.

Bartlett, S. T., Farney, A. C., Jarrell, B. E., Philosophe, B., Colonna, J. O., Wiland, A., et al. (1998). Kidney transplantation at the University of Maryland. *Clinical Transplantation*, 177–185.

Beasley, C. L., Hull, A. R., & Rosenthal, J. T. (1997). Living kidney donation: A survey of professional attitudes and practices. *American Journal of Kidney Disease*, 30, 549–557.

Berland, G. K., Elliott, M. N., Morales, L. S., Algazy, J. I., Kravitz, R. L., Broder, M. S., et al. (2001). Health information on the Internet: Accessibility, quality, and readability in English and Spanish. *Journal of the American Medical Association*, 285, 2612–2621.

Boudville, N., Prasad, G. V., Knoll, G., Muirhead, N., Thiessen-Philbrook, H., Yang, R. C., et al. (2006). Meta-analysis: Risk for hypertension in living kidney donors. *Annals of Internal Medicine*, 145, 185–196.

Boulware, L. E., Ratner, L. E., Sosa, J. A., Tu, A. H., Nagula, S., Simpkins, C. E., et al. (2002). The general public's concerns about clinical risk in live kidney donation. *American Journal of Transplantation*, 2, 186–193.

Boulware, L. E., Ratner, L. E., Troll, M. U., Chaudron, A., Yeung, E., Chen, S., et al. (2005). Attitudes, psychology, and risk taking of potential live kidney donors: Strangers, relatives, and the general public. *American Journal of Transplantation*, 5, 1671–1680.

Boulware, L. E., Troll, M. U., Wang, N. Y., & Powe, N. R. (2006). The general public's attitudes regarding incentives for living and deceased organ donation: A national study of different income and racial/ethnic groups. Unpublished Abstract. Johns Hopkins.

Burdick, J., Wagner, D., McBride, V., O'Connor, K., Rosendale, J., & D'Alessandro, A. (2006, July 15). The organ donation breakthrough collaborative: Achieving systematic increases in organ donation and transplantation. Paper presented at the Transplantation, Boston.

Burroughs, T. E., Waterman, A. D., & Hong, B. A. (2003). One organ donation, three perspectives: Experiences of donors, recipients, and third parties with living kidney donation. *Progress in Transplantations*, 13, 142–150.

Burrows, L. (2004). Selling organs for transplantation. *Mt. Sinai Journal of Medicine, 71*, 251–254.

Butkus, D. E., Dottes, A. L., Meydrech, E. F., & Barber, W. H. (2001). Effect of poverty and other socioeconomic variables on renal allograft survival. *Transplantation, 72*, 261–266.

Christensen, A., Holman, J., Turner, C., & Slaughter, J. (1989). Quality of life in end-stage renal disease: Influence of renal transplantation. *Clinical Transplantation, 3*, 46–53.

Clarke, K. S., Klarenbach, S., Vlaicu, S., Yang, R. C., & Garg, A. X. (2006). The direct and indirect economic costs incurred by living kidney donors: A systematic review. *Nephrology Dialysis Transplantation, 21*, 1952–1960.

Conesa, C., Rios, A., Ramirez, P., Sanchez, J., Sanchez, E., Rodriguez, M. M., et al. (2005). Attitude of primary care nurses toward living kidney donation. *Transplant Proceedings, 37*, 3626–3630.

Daar, A. S., Salahudeen, A. K., Pingle, A., & Woods, H. F. (1990). Ethics and commerce in live donor renal transplantation: Classification of the issues. *Transplant Proceedings, 22*, 922–924.

Delmonico, F. (2005). A Report of the Amsterdam forum on the care of the live kidney donor: Data and medical guidelines. *Transplantation, 79*, S53–S66.

Devins, G. M., Binik, Y. M., Mandin, H., Letourneau, P. K., Hollomby, D. J., Barre, P. E., et al. (1990). The Kidney Disease Questionnaire: A test for measuring patient knowledge about end-stage renal disease. *Journal of Clinical Epidemiology, 43*, 297–307.

DiClemente, C. C., Prochaska, J. O., Fairhurst, S. K., Velicer, W. F., Velasquez, M. M., & Rossi, J. S. (1991). The process of smoking cessation: An analysis of precontemplation, contemplation, and preparation stages of change. *Journal of Consultation Clinical Psychology, 59*, 295–304.

Ellison, M. D., McBride, M. A., Taranto, S. E., Delmonico, F. L., & Kauffman, H. M. (2002). Living kidney donors in need of kidney transplants: A report from the organ procurement and transplantation network. *Transplantation, 74*, 1349–1351.

Fehrman-Ekholm, I., Brink, B., Ericsson, C., Elinder, C. G., Duner, F., & Lundgren, G. (2000). Kidney donors don't regret: Follow-up of 370 donors in Stockholm since 1964. *Transplantation, 69*, 2067–2071.

Fellner, C. (1976). Renal transplantation and the living donor. Decision and consequences. *Psychotherapy and Psychosomatics, 27*, 139–143.

Foster, C. E., III, Philosophe, B., Schweitzer, E. J., Colonna, J. O., Farney, A. C., Jarrell, B., et al. (2002). A decade of experience with renal transplantation in African-Americans. *Annals of Surgery, 236*, 794–804; discussion 804–805.

Franklin, P. M., & Crombie, A. K. (2003). Live related renal transplantation: Psychological, social, and cultural issues. *Transplantation, 76*, 1247–1252.

Frates, J., & Garcia Bohrer, G. (2002). Hispanic perceptions of organ donation. *Progress in Transplantation, 12*, 169–175.

Garg, P. P., Frick, K. D., Diener-West, M., & Powe, N. R. (1999). Effect of the ownership of dialysis facilities on patients' survival and referral for transplantation. *New England Journal of Medicine, 341*, 1653–1660.

Gentry, S. E., Segev, D. L., & Montgomery, R. A. (2005). A comparison of populations served by kidney paired donation and list paired donation. *American Journal of Transplantation, 5*, 1914–1921.

Gilbertson, D. T., Liu, J., Xue, J. L., Louis, T. A., Solid, C. A., Ebben, J. P., et al. (2005). Projecting the number of patients with end-stage renal disease in the United States to the year 2015. *Journal of American Society for Nephrology, 16*, 3736–3741.

Gordon, E. J. (2001a). Patients' decisions for treatment of end-stage renal disease and their implications for access to transplantation. *Society for the Science of Medicine, 53*, 971–987.

Gordon, E. J. (2001b). "They don't have to suffer for me": Why dialysis patients refuse offers of living donor kidneys. *Medical Anthropology Quarterly, 15*, 245–267.

Grochowiecki, T., Szmidt, J., Galazka, Z., Nazarewski, S., Madej, K., Meszaros, J., et al. (2006). Comparison of 1-year patient and graft survival rates between preemptive and dialysed simultaneous pancreas and kidney transplant recipients. *Transplant Proceedings*, *38*, 261–262.

Hayes, R., & Waterman, A. D. (2008). Improving preemptive transplant education to increase living donation rates: Reaching patients earlier in their disease adjustment process. *Progress in Transplantation*, *14*, 251–256.

Henderson, A. J., Landolt, M. A., McDonald, M. F., Barrable, W. M., Soos, J. G., Gourlay, W., et al. (2003). The living anonymous kidney donor: Lunatic or saint? *American Journal of Transplantation*, *3*, 203–213.

Hilhorst, M. T., Kranenburg, L. W., & Busschbach, J. J. (2006). Should health care professionals encourage living kidney donation? *Medical Health Care Philosophy*, *10*, 81–90.

Ismail, N., Neyra, R., & Hakim, R. (1998). The medical and economical advantages of early referral of chronic renal failure patients to renal specialists. *Nephrology Dialysis and Transplantation*, *13*, 246–250.

Jacobs, C. L., Roman, D., Garvey, C., Kahn, J., & Matas, A. J. (2004). Twenty-two nondirected kidney donors: An update on a single center's experience. *American Journal of Transplantation*, *4*, 1110–1116.

Jacobs, C. L., & Thomas, C. (2003). Reducing transplant evaluation costs by early identification of unsuitable patients. *Progress in Transplantation*, *13*, 130–136.

Janz, N., & Becker, M. (1984). The health belief model: A decade later. *Health Education Quarterly*, *11*, 1–47.

Jendrisak, M. D., Hong, B., Shenoy, S., Lowell, J., Desai, N., Chapman, W., et al. (2006). Altruistic living donors: Evaluation for nondirected kidney or liver donation. *American Journal of Transplantation*, *6*, 115–120.

Johnson, E. M., Anderson, J. K., Jacobs, C., Suh, G., Humar, A., Suhr, B. D., et al. (1999). Long-term follow-up of living kidney donors: Quality of life after donation. *Transplantation*, *67*, 717–721.

Joint Commission on Accreditation of Healthcare Organizations. (2009). *Information for living organ donors*. Retrieved January 16, 2009, from http://www.jointcommission.org/NR/rdonlyres/E036E7A9-C7FE-446C-8084-11565B540409/0/speakup_donor_brochure.pdf

Jordan, J., Sann, U., Janton, A., Gossmann, J., Kramer, W., Kachel, H. G., et al. (2004). Living kidney donors' long-term psychological status and health behavior after nephrectomy: A retrospective study. *Journal of Nephrology*, *17*, 728–735.

Kahn, L. D. (1994). Career development strategies for minorities. *Health Care Executives*, *9*, 40–41.

Karrfelt, H. M., Berg, U. B., Lindblad, F. I., & Tyden, G. E. (1998). To be or not to be a living donor: Questionnaire to parents of children who have undergone renal transplantation. *Transplantation*, *65*, 915–918.

Kasiske, B. L., Snyder, J. J., Matas, A. J., Ellison, M. D., Gill, J. S., & Kausz, A. T. (2002). Preemptive kidney transplantation: The advantage and the advantaged. *Journal for the American Society for Nephrology*, *13*, 1358–1364.

Klarenbach, S., Garg, A. X., & Vlaicu, S. (2006). Living organ donors face financial barriers: A national reimbursement policy is needed. *The Canadian Medical Association Journal*, *174*, 797–798.

Landolt, M. A., Henderson, A. J., Barrable, W. M., Greenwood, S. D., McDonald, M. F., Soos, J. G., et al. (2001). Living anonymous kidney donation: What does the public think? *Transplantation, 71,* 1690–1696.

Lunsford, S. L., Simpson, K. S., Chavin, K. D., Menching, K. J., Miles, L. G., Shilling, L. M., et al. (2006). Racial disparities in living kidney donation: Is there a lack of willing donors or an excess of medically unsuitable candidates? *Transplantation, 82,* 876–881.

Lyon, S. (1998). Organ donation and kidney sales. *Lancet, 352*(9126), 484.

Maiorano, A., & Schena, F. P. (2008). The dynamics of kidney donation: Viewpoints from the donor, the recipients, and the transplant team. *Kidney International, 73,* 1108–1110.

Mange, K. C., Joffe, M. M., & Feldman, H. I. (2001). Effect of the use or nonuse of long-term dialysis on the subsequent survival of renal transplants from living donors. *New England Journal of Medicine, 344,* 726–731.

Martinez-Alarcon, L., Rios, A., Conesa, C., Alcaraz, J., Gonzalez, M. J., Montoya, M., et al. (2005). Attitude toward living related donation of patients on the waiting list for a deceased donor solid organ transplant. *Transplant Proceedings, 37,* 3614–3617.

McNamara, P., Guadagnoli, E., Evanisko, M. J., Beasley, C., Santiago-Delpin, E. A., Callender, C. O., et al. (1999). Correlates of support for organ donation among three ethnic groups. *Clinical Transplantation, 13,* 45–50.

McQuarrie, B., & Gordon, D. (2003). Separate, dedicated care teams for living organ donors. *Progress in Transplantation, 13,* 90–93.

Montgomery, R. A., Katznelson, S., Bry, W. I., Zachary, A. A., Houp, J., Hiller, J. M., et al. (2008). Successful three-way kidney paired donation with cross-country live donor allograft transport. *American Journal of Transplantation, 8,* 2163–2168.

Moody, E. M., Clemens, K. K., Storsley, L., Waterman, A., Parikh, C. R., & Garg, A. X. (2007). Improving on-line information for potential living kidney donors. *Kidney International, 71,* 1062–1070.

Mueller, P. S., Case, E. J., & Hook, C. C. (2008). Responding to offers of altruistic living unrelated kidney donation by group associations: An ethical analysis. *Transplantation Review, 22,* 200–205.

Murray, L. R., Conrad, N. E., & Bayley, E. W. (1999). Perceptions of kidney transplant by persons with end stage renal disease. *American Nephrology Nurses' Association Journal, 26,* 479–483, 500; discussion 484.

Najarian, J. S., Chavers, B. M., McHugh, L. E., & Matas, A. J. (1992). 20 years or more of follow-up of living kidney donors. *Lancet, 340,* 807–810.

National Kidney Foundation. (2009). Kidney transplant. In National Kidney Foundation (Ed.), *Chronic kidney disease.* New York: Author.

Neipp, M., Karavul, B., Jackobs, S., Meyer zu Vilsendorf, A., Richter, N., Becker, T., et al. (2006). Quality of life in adult transplant recipients more than 15 years after kidney transplantation. *Transplantation, 81,* 1640–1644.

New England Organ Bank. (N.d.). [Home page]. Retrieved June 4, 2009, from http://www.nepke.org

Olbrisch, M. E., Benedict, S. M., Haller, D. L., & Levenson, J. L. (2001). Psychosocial assessment of living organ donors: Clinical and ethical considerations. *Progress in Transplantation, 11,* 40–49.

Perez, L. M., Schulman, B., Davis, F., Olson, L., Tellis, V. A., & Matas, A. J. (1988). Organ donation in three major American cities with large Latino and black populations. *Transplantation*, *46*, 553–557.

Pradel, F. G., Limcangco, M. R., Mullins, C. D., & Bartlett, S. T. (2003). Patients' attitudes about living donor transplantation and living donor nephrectomy. *American Journal of Kidney Disease*, *41*, 849–858.

Pradel, F. G., Mullins, C. D., & Bartlett, S. T. (2003). Exploring donors' and recipients' attitudes about living donor kidney transplantation. *Progress in Transplantation*, *13*, 203–210.

Pradel, F. G., Suwannaprom, P., Mullins, C., Sadler, J., & Bartlett, S. (2008). Short-term impact of an educational program promoting live donor kidney transplantation in dialysis centers. *Progress in Transplantation*, *14*, 263–272.

Prasad, G. V. (2007). Renal transplantation for ethnic minorities in Canada: Inequity in access and outcomes? *Kidney International*, *72*, 390–392.

Prochaska, J. O., & DiClemente, C. C. (1983). Stages and processes of self-change of smoking: Toward an integrative model of change. *Journal of Consultant Clinical Psychology*, *51*, 390–395.

Prochaska, J. O., DiClemente, C. C., & Norcross, J. C. (1992). In search of how people change: Applications to addictive behaviors. *American Psychologist*, *47*, 1102–1114.

Rodrigue, J. R., Antonellis, T., Mandelbrot, D. A., & Hanto, D. W. (2008). Web-based requests for living organ donors: Who are the solicitors? *Clinical Transplantation*, *22*, 749–753.

Rodrigue, J. R., Cornell, D. L., Kaplan, B., & Howard, R. J. (2008a). Patients' willingness to talk to others about living kidney donation. *Progress in Transplant*, *18*, 25–31.

Rodrigue, J. R., Cornell, D. L., Kaplan, B., & Howard, R. J. (2008b). A randomized trial of a home-based educational approach to increase live donor kidney transplantation: Effects in blacks and whites. *American Journal of Kidney Disease*, *51*, 663–670.

Rodrigue, J. R., Cornell, D. L., Lin, J. K., Kaplan, B., & Howard, R. J. (2007). Increasing live donor kidney transplantation: A randomized controlled trial of a home-based educational intervention. *American Journal of Transplantation*, *7*, 394–401.

Rodrigue, J. R., Guenther, R., Kaplan, B., Mandelbrot, D. A., Pavlakis, M., & Howard, R. J. (2008). Measuring the expectations of kidney donors: Initial psychometric properties of the Living Donation Expectancies Questionnaire. *Transplantation*, *85*, 1230–1234.

Rodrigue, J. R., Pavlakis, M., Danovitch, G. M., Johnson, S. R., Karp, S. J., Khwaja, K., et al. (2007). Evaluating living kidney donors: Relationship types, psychosocial criteria, and consent processes at US transplant programs. *American Journal of Transplantation*, *7*, 2326–2332.

Ross, L. F., Rubin, D. T., Siegler, M., Josephson, M. A., Thistlethwaite, J. R., Jr., & Woodle, E. S. (1997). Ethics of a paired-kidney-exchange program. *New England Journal of Medicine*, *336*, 1752–1755.

Ross, L. F., & Woodle, E. S. (2000). Ethical issues in increasing living kidney donations by expanding kidney paired exchange programs. *Transplantation*, *69*, 1539–1543.

Schweitzer, E. J., Wilson, J., Jacobs, S., Machan, C. H., Philosophe, B., Farney, A., et al. (2000). Increased rates of donation with laparoscopic donor nephrectomy. *Annals of Surgery*, *232*, 392–400.

Schweitzer, E. J., Yoon, S., Hart, J., Anderson, L., Barnes, R., Evans, D., et al. (1997). Increased living donor volunteer rates with a formal recipient family education program. *American Journal of Kidney Disease, 29,* 739–745.

Schweitzer, J., Seidel-Wiesel, M., Verres, R., & Wiesel, M. (2003). Psychological consultation before living kidney donation: Finding out and handling problem cases. *Transplantation, 76,* 1464–1470.

Segev, D. L., Gentry, S. E., Melancon, J. K., & Montgomery, R. A. (2005). Characterization of waiting times in a simulation of kidney paired donation. *American Journal of Transplantation, 5,* 2448–2455.

Segev, D. L., Gentry, S. E., Warren, D. S., Reeb, B., & Montgomery, R. A. (2005). Kidney paired donation and optimizing the use of live donor organs. *Journal of the American Medical Association, 293,* 1883–1890.

Segev, D. L., & Montgomery, R. A. (2008). Regional and racial disparities in the use of live non-directed kidney donors. *American Journal of Transplantation, 8,* 1051–1055.

Seto, E., Cafazzo, J. A., Rizo, C., Bonert, M., Fong, E., & Chan, C. T. (2007). Internet use by end-stage renal disease patients. *Hemodial International, 11,* 328–332.

Shafer, T. J., Wagner, D., Chessare, J., Zampiello, F. A., McBride, V., & Perdue, J. (2006). Organ donation breakthrough collaborative: Increasing organ donation through system redesign. *Critical Care Nurse, 26,* 33–48.

Sheehy, E., Conrad, S. L., Brigham, L. E., Luskin, R., Weber, P., Eakin, M., et al. (2003). Estimating the number of potential organ donors in the United States. *New England Journal of Medicine, 349,* 667–674.

Shenoy, S., Lowell, J. A., Ramachandran, V., & Jendrisak, M. (2002). The ideal living donor nephrectomy "mini-nephrectomy" through a posterior transcostal approach. *Journal for the American College of Surgeons, 194,* 240–246.

Siegel, J. T., Alvaro, E. M., Lac, A., Crano, W. D., & Dominick, A. (2008). Intentions of becoming a living organ donor among Hispanics: A theory-based approach exploring differences between living and nonliving organ donation. *Journal of Health Communication, 13,* 80–99.

Simforoosh, N., Basiri, A., Pourrezagholi, F., Einolahi, B., Firouzan, A., Moghaddam, M. M., et al. (2003). Is preemptive renal transplantation preferred? *Transplant Proceedings, 35,* 2598–2601.

Smith, C. R., Woodward, R. S., Cohen, D. S., Singer, G. G., Brennan, D. C., Lowell, J. A., et al. (2000). Cadaveric versus living donor kidney transplantation: A Medicare payment analysis. *Transplantation, 69,* 311–314.

Spital, A. (2000). Evolution of attitudes at U.S. transplant centers toward kidney donation by friends and altruistic strangers. *Transplantation, 69,* 1728–1731.

Steinbrook, R. (2005). Public solicitation of organ donors. *New England Journal of Medicine, 353,* 441–444.

Stephan, A., Barbari, A., & Younan, F. (2007). Ethical aspects of organ donation activities. *Experimental and Clinical Transplantation, 5,* 633–637.

Sung, R. S., Galloway, J., Tuttle-Newhall, J. E., Mone, T., Laeng, R., Freise, C. E., et al. (2008). Organ donation and utilization in the United States, 1997–2006. *American Journal of Transplantation, 8,* 922–934.

Tarantino, A. (2000). Why should we implement living donation in renal transplantation? *Clinical Nephrology, 53*, 55–63.

Thomas, C. (2002). Development of a culturally sensitive, locality-based program to increase kidney donation. *Advances in Renal Replacement Therapy, 9*, 54–56.

United Network for Organ Sharing. (2009). *Living donation: An overview.* Retrieved January 16, 2009, from www.unos.org

U.S. Renal Data System. (2009). [Home page]. Retrieved June 4, 2009, from www.usrds.org

Vastag, B. (2003). Living-donor transplants reexamined: Experts cite growing concerns about safety of donors. *Journal of the American Medical Association, 290*, 181–182.

Verble, M., & Worth, J. (2003). Cultural sensitivity in the donation discussion. *Progress in Transplantation, 13*, 33–37.

Vianello, A., Palminteri, G., Brunello, A., Calconi, G., & Maresca, M. C. (2000). Attitudes and knowledge about transplantation in dialyzed patients requesting a cadaveric kidney graft. *Clinical Nephrology, 53*(Suppl.), 64–66.

Waterman, A., & Duhig, S. (2002). *The living gift: Education about living kidney donation.* Columbia: Missouri Kidney Program & International Transplant Nursing Society.

Waterman, A. D., Barrett, A. C., & Stanley, S. L. (2008). Optimal transplant education for recipients to increase pursuit of living donation. *Progress in Transplantation, 18*, 55–62.

Waterman, A. D., Covelli, T., Caisley, L., Zerega, W., Schnitzler, M., Adams, D., et al. (2004). Potential living kidney donors' health education use and comfort with donation. *Progress in Transplantation, 14*, 233–240.

Waterman, A. D., Schenk, E. A., Barrett, A. C., Waterman, B. M., Rodrigue, J. R., Woodle, E. S., et al. (2006). Incompatible kidney donor candidates' willingness to participate in donor-exchange and non-directed donation. *American Journal of Transplantation, 6*, 1631–1638.

Waterman, A. D., Stanley, S. L., Covelli, T., Hazel, E., Hong, B. A., & Brennan, D. C. (2006). Living donation decision making: Recipients' concerns and educational needs. *Progress in Transplantation, 16*, 17–23.

Wu, A. W., Fink, N. E., Cagney, K. A., Bass, E. B., Rubin, H. R., Meyer, K. B., et al. (2001). Developing a health-related quality-of-life measure for end-stage renal disease: The CHOICE Health Experience Questionnaire. *American Journal of Kidney Disease, 37*, 11–21.

Zimmerman, D., Albert, S., Llewellyn-Thomas, H., & Hawker, G. A. (2006). The influence of socio-demographic factors, treatment perceptions and attitudes to living donation on willingness to consider living kidney donor among kidney transplant candidates. *Nephrology Dialysis and Transplantation, 21*, 2569–2575.

19

A Dawning Recognition of Factors for Increasing Donor Registration

The IIFF Model

Jason T. Siegel, Eusebio M. Alvaro, and Zachary P. Hohman

Considering the low percentage of Americans who are registered as organ donors, it can appear that the majority of the U.S. population is against the practice. This is not the case (Gallup Organization, 1993, 2005–2006). Up to 85% of those surveyed support organ donation, and 90% agree that organ donation allows something positive to come out of a person's death (Gallup Organization, 1993, 2005–2006). The latest Gallup poll on organ donation (2005–2006) indicates that 95.4% of a representative sample of 2,000 Americans supports the donation of organs for transplantation. From a social psychological perspective, the small percentage of individuals registering to be organ donors is an issue of attitude–behavior consistency—an issue social psychology has been wrestling with for decades (see Crano, this volume). There are a multitude of reasons as to why attitudes and behaviors might not match (Crano & Prislin, 2008). Figuring out why positive attitudes toward donation are not necessarily associated with donor registration behavior could result in thousands of lives being saved.

The information presented herein represents an attempt to disentangle the mystery as to why positive attitudes toward donation do not necessarily result in registrations. We will soon describe several efforts, only feasible with the collaboration of the Donor Network of Arizona (DNAZ), which occasionally resulted in success, and sometimes not. Regardless, a piece of the puzzle was always revealed—or, at the very least, something perceived to be a piece of some puzzle under the bamboozlement of the moment.

Theory of Planned Behavior (TPB)

The TPB guided our thoughts throughout this research endeavor (Ajzen & Fishbein, 1980; Fishbein & Ajzen, 1975). The theory offers an elegant explanation for the lack of attitude-behavioral consistency found in regard to donor registration: Attitudes are not the only determinant of behavior. The TPB proposes behavior is determined by an individual's intent to perform that behavior, of which attitude is only one of three predictors. Intention is a construct referring to an individual's plan to engage in a specific behavior (in this case, registering to become an organ donor). Intentions are impacted by attitudes as well as subjective norms and perceived behavioral control.

An attitude towards a behavior, such as registering to be an organ donor, reflects the extent to which engaging in the behavior is positively or negatively valued. Important for the realm of donation is the proposition that one's attitude towards a behavior is the result of *activated* behavioral beliefs. A person may believe that registering as a donor will save lives, but if this belief is not activated it will unlikely influence attitudes and therefore unlikely influence behavior. Subjective norms, a second determinant of intentions, refer to the individual's beliefs that referent others think they should engage in the behavior and how motivated the individual is to comply with the inclinations of these others. The third predictor of intentions is perceived behavioral control (PBC). In general, PBC refers to one's ability to enact a recommended behavior. Ajzen (1991) defined the construct as follows: "Perceived behavioral control refers to people's perception of the ease or difficulty in performing the behavior of interest" (p. 183). Several researchers have argued that perceived control and perceived difficulty are two different constructs (Trafimow, Sheeran, Conner, & Finlay, 2002; Yzer, Hennessy, & Fishbein, 2004). Ajzen (2002) acknowledged that PBC could be a composite of perceived control and perceived difficulty. In the context of organ donation, perceived difficulty refers to individuals' perceptions of their ability to perform the act of registering as an organ donor. Perceived control refers to individuals' perceptions that they can become an organ donor. If someone believes they are too old for their organs to be useful, and do not register as a result, this is a problem of perceived control.

Because attitudes toward donation are generally positive (e.g., Gallup Organization, 1993, 2005–2006), TPB would indicate that the lack of attitude–behavior consistency is due to problematic subjective norms or a lack of PBC. We began by considering if a lack of PBC could be responsible for the relatively low registration rates. PBC offered a simple logic for why many people with positive attitudes were not donors: They did not know how (perceived difficulty), and/or they perceived they would not become donors even if they registered (perceived control). Either instance could reflect a lack of perceived PBC, leading to a reduction in donor registrations. If people do not know how to register and/or do not perceive themselves as eligible, short of intervention, registration is unlikely regardless of one's desire to be a donor. While considering different methods for assessing PBC's role in organ donation attitude-behavior discrepancy, and means of intervening, opportunity knocked.

An Opportunity for Assessing Donor Registration Behavior Under Maximum PBC

DNAZ, an organization with which we had previously partnered (Alvaro, Jones, Robles, & Siegel, 2005, 2006) and with which we have collaborated many times since (e.g., Siegel, Alvaro, & Jones, 2005; Siegel, Alvaro, Pace-Jones, et al., 2008), was planning on launching a state registry offering potential donors a virtual location for recording donor intent. Unlike previous registration mechanisms, such as placing a sticker on one's license, indicating donor intent via the registry is legally binding—technically, the family cannot override the deceased's intent (Ganikos, this volume). In Arizona, computer kiosks were being considered as a mechanism for increasing access and drawing attention to the online registry. Although kiosks had been previously used to inform individuals about organ donation, DNAZ had its sight set on registration kiosks—ATM-like machines where individuals can register in a single step. At that time, standard practice for registration Web sites required the individual to not only print out and sign a donor card, but also mail the card.

From a theoretical perspective, these registration kiosks offered a means of examining donor registration behavior when the perceived difficulty aspect of PBC is not an issue. If attitude–behavior consistency is hampered by a perceived inability to go through the registration process, providing kiosks that make it clear registration is a click away should increase attitude–behavior synchronicity. If people holding positive attitudes toward donation were given an easy means for registration in the form of the kiosk—barring viciously negative subjective norms—behavioral expression of pro-donation attitudes via registration should follow.

We again partnered with DNAZ and responded to a call for proposals from the Health Resource Services Administration, Division of Transplantation. To our distinct pleasure, reviewers saw merit in our proposal.

Focus Groups

The first phase of the grant involved conducting focus groups to explore potential donors' thoughts concerning registration kiosks. Six focus groups were conducted ($n = 42$). The selection criteria for participation were (a) positive attitudes toward donation, and (b) nondonor status. Restricting participation was not a passive-aggressive attempt to punish those holding negative attitudes; rather, it was a step in the direction of focusing donor campaigns on the 70% or so of the population who are in favor of donation but have yet to register as donors—*passive positives*. Persuading individuals with negative attitudes toward donation to register is a different task than motivating those already holding positive attitudes. We perceived the kiosks as being best suited for the latter.

The focus groups were conducted in Tucson and Phoenix, Arizona. Participants were first asked to discuss their views on donation. In the very first group, as expected, everyone expressed positive attitudes; unexpectedly, a barrage of questions about donation rained down on the moderator. Questions about registration and eligibility, confidentiality and doctors' greed, cost and immigration issues—all were put forth with nearly every angle covered. "I am in favor of organ donation, but . . . (insert question)" was a common phrase. Throughout the focus group session, for every question asked of the participants, participants asked nearly a dozen of the moderators. After a nearly 2-hour discussion that saw a plethora of questions being answered, something unexpected occurred: requests for donor cards from several participants.

The postgroup requests for donor registration cards became of prime interest and motivated a small adjustment for the remaining groups. Initially, we planned on each group receiving a posttest questionnaire to allow participants to voice comments and/or ask remaining questions. An item was added to the postgroup survey: "If there was an organ donor registration kiosk in the room, would you register?"

Five additional groups were conducted. Across groups, approximately 50% indicated a willingness to register. The participants had their whole lives to register; they did not. However, at the end of one focus group, 50% were willing. Interpreted through TPB, and with PBC on our minds, we theorized that the extensive question-and-answer period served to overcome a lack of perceived control by informing participants who were eligible to donate. Perceived difficulty was also abolished because expressing willingness required only the checking of a box. Simply, we placed a hypothetical card in hand, thus removing any barrier related to the "how to" of registration.

> Consideration #1: In line with TPB, maximizing PBC (perceived difficulty and perceived control) among people who hold positive attitudes toward donation can increase donation willingness.

Before moving forward, we should make a quick note on participants' perceptions of kiosks. Participants reported (a) an overall positive response to the idea of organ donor kiosks, (b) a general willingness to use kiosks as a means of registration, and (c) some concern for privacy. Suggested locations for placing the kiosks included malls, libraries, doctor's offices, community centers, universities, and airports.

An Unexpected Opportunity

Shortly after focus group completion, an opportunity arose to place kiosks throughout a stadium hosting a Phoenix Suns basketball game. Moreover, prior to tipoff, a donor recipient would take center court with the Suns mascot to direct attention to the kiosks. To be sure, focus group participants did not suggest a basketball game as a kiosk location. Also, there was no opportunity to set up intercepts to assess why registration did or did not occur. We were also unable to survey game registrants and nonregistrants to understand for whom the kiosks were most attractive. Nevertheless, because the DNAZ was going to place the kiosks at the game with or without our ivory-tower blessings, we "chose" to learn whatever we could within the given parameters.

We knew that a registration kiosk, in and of itself, would not be able to influence perceptions of eligibility. Thus, we did not expect a repeat of the outcomes obtained in the focus groups. We did expect, however, that focus groups would be replicated in one way—the kiosks would serve to abolish most issues caused by not knowing how to register. From a TPB perspective, even though the kiosks would not address perceived control issues, such as perceived ineligibility, the kiosks would address perceived difficulty by providing an immediate and complete registration mechanism. To highlight this fact, "Register Here" posters were placed on top of the kiosks. We anticipated the kiosks at the basketball game could serve as the metaphoric card in the hand. With an average of 19,000 fans attending each game, even a 5% registration rate could add nearly a thousand registrants. If even 1% signed up on the kiosk, the result would be 190 registrations per game.

Our expectations for kiosk success were heightened by consideration of Bagozzi's (1996) investigation into blood donation. This study found that high emotional arousal—granted a factor incongruent with assumptions of rationality undergirding TPB—leads to an enhancement of positive blood donation beliefs while minimizing the negative ones. If the basketball game served to increase emotional arousal, the registry would be the beneficiary. Adding to the anticipation for substantial registration numbers, the Suns were victorious (www.espn.com), thereby increasing positive affect, possibly leading to increased helping behavior (Isen, 1970).

We had hoped for a 5% registration rate, and, when registrations for the event were tallied, there was indeed a "5" in the results. However, this was not ".05" indicating a 5% rate, nor was it ".05" as in the cutoff point for statistical significance. In a stadium filled with people, with 80–90% likely supporting organ donation, and kiosks nearby where these people can immediately register without any difficulty, we obtained a registration rate of .0005. A DNAZ employee reported that less than 10 people registered at the kiosks that evening.

As mentioned earlier, the opportunity to place kiosks at the game did not come with the opportunity to set up an evaluation to assess why people did not register. We hesitated to make much out of a one-time trial, but we also did not want to repeat mistakes that could be corrected. Follow-up interviews with the DNAZ employees at the game revealed an unanticipated issue: The kiosks and even the pre-tipoff presentation were by and large unnoticed. People passed the kiosks;

they did not notice the kiosks. Apparently, the fans' minds were on the game, and the kiosks did enter their consciousness.

> Consideration #2: Removing issues related to perceived difficulty among people who hold positive attitudes toward donation does not necessarily lead to an increase in registrations.
> Consideration #3: A kiosk that can facilitate registration behavior is irrelevant if no one notices it.

The next item on our grant plan was a feasibility study. Although the basketball game was not part of the original research plan, several process-related concerns were alleviated as a result of those efforts. There was minimum trouble traveling with and setting up the kiosks, and the kiosks did work as planned for those rare few who chose to register. Nevertheless, there was still a need to assess what problems would arise if kiosks were left at the same location for an extended period of time. We also looked to learn from the basketball game and not place kiosks in a context where they are competing for attention with a professional sporting event.

After re-reviewing focus group suggestions as to locations for kiosk placement, we decided to place kiosks in locations where a 5-minute time investment would not have to be weighed against a Phoenix Suns game. The locations were St. Joseph's Hospital. Phoenix Civic Plaza, Arizona State University West, City of Phoenix City Hall, several library branches, and the Arizona Mills Mall. To draw attention to the kiosks, we held different events such as news interviews and radio remotes. Phoenix Mayor Phil Gordon issued a challenge to other mayors to educate their citizens to make them aware of donation and to sign up on the donor registry. The mayor used this press conference to sign up on one of the all-in-one kiosks. At Arizona State University West, a radio remote was utilized to draw attention. Moreover, the Register Here poster placed on top of the kiosk was expected to assure potential donors that registration was immediately available. These posters were unsuccessful at the basketball game; however, we reasoned the posters were more likely to be noticed at a library than at a basketball game.

Retaining faith that increasing information via the kiosk would lead to increased attitude–behavior consistency, we anticipated favorable results. Recall that 50% of participants wanted to register at the end of our focus groups. Also consider that Donate Life America reports that 36.3% of individuals designate themselves as donors when offered the opportunity at the DMV. If 2,500 people visit a Phoenix library each day, even a 3.0% registration rate would lead to 75 registrations a day, 27,375 per year. Our hopes were high.

Registration was low. A university-based radio remote resulted in less than five registrations. Moreover, from April though December, 58 people registered on the university-based kiosk. That works out to approximately one registration per

5 days. At city hall 103 people registered from April to January—slightly more than 11 per month. Forty-three signed up at a library kiosk during a 5-month stretch. At another library, one that boasts daily attendance of 2,500, less than 100 people registered from July through December—less than .0003%. The only silver lining was that there were no technical issues, although we figured that could be due to lack of use.

The results were perplexing. A potential donor might not have had sufficient time to act on positive attitudes toward organ donation at the basketball game; this was likely not the issue for most at the library. Investing 5 minutes of one's time during a professional sporting event could be problematic, but 5 minutes at the library could not have been so costly for all potential donors as to warrant blame. It was certainly possible and likely that the kiosks went unnoticed at a basketball game, but there was a radio station broadcasting from one of the kiosks, and still registrations could be counted on one hand.

> Consideration #4: Registration kiosks are a far cry from a magic bullet for increasing registration rates.

A magic bullet, kiosks are certainly not. However, knowing the financial resources spent on the kiosks motivated us to maximize the potential. The next phase of the grant was well suited for the task. This phase involved determining if registration rates could be increased through the use of theoretically derived messages displayed in the form of posters sitting atop the kiosks. Even if only a handful of people registered, we sought to increase that number to one and a half, or even two, handfuls. After reviewing research specific to organ donation and message variation (e.g., Smith, Morrison, Kopfman, & Ford, 1994; Winkel, 1984), we reviewed the social psychological literature and settled on four different appeals. To ensure effects were not unique to any one operationalization of a particular appeal, four different exemplars were used for each poster. With the help of our partners at DNAZ, a total of 16 different posters were created and tested using four different location types to make sure results were not unique to any one location (see Siegel, Alvaro, Crano, et al., 2008, for a complete account of this project).

The design was a 4 (location) × 4 (appeal) × 4 (exemplar) quasi-experimental design conducted in different naturalistic settings (hospital, library, university, and community college) examining different message appeals (counterargument, emotional, dissonance, and motivating action), each using exemplar variations (excuse, picture, quiz, and cartoon bubble) with the outcome measure being the number of actual registrations on the donor registry. Also, for each setting (hospital) or location type, there were four locations (i.e., four different hospitals) to allow for greater representativeness.

The study lasted 16 weeks. With a completely counterbalanced design in mind, appeals were switched every 2 weeks, and exemplars were switched weekly.

Changing the posters on 16 kiosks in four disparate locations on a weekly basis (enduring 100°F+ Arizona temperatures) was not easy. The DNAZ staff struggled to adhere to the demanding schedule—as well as to contain their resentment during weekly conference calls. Fortunately the results made it worthwhile—or so we still keep telling them.

Results indicate two key findings. First, the average registration counts on the kiosks adorned with the theoretically derived messages were three times higher than those with the basic Register Here message.

> Consideration #5: There is a reason why people in advertising have jobs. The message matters—all messages are not equal.

Moreover, of the four tested messages, substantial variance was revealed. The most successful message, defined by the number of registrations occurring when a specific poster was atop the kiosk, was the counterargument appeal—one easily interpreted as targeting perceived control. This appeal informed potential donors that they were not too old or too sick and that most religions support donation. In a broad sense, this is as close to the focus group context as we have been able to get: Perceived control was addressed via the poster, and perceived difficulty was addressed via the ability to register via the kiosk. This was nearly twice as effective at motivating registrations as the dissonance message (one basically pointing out the discrepancy between one's beliefs and one's actions).

> Consideration #6: Increasing perceived control (e.g., informing individuals that they are eligible to donate) could increase registration rates.

Also noteworthy is that the counterargument message was not the only one that led to more registrations than the other conditions. For example, the emotional appeal resulted in 25% more registrations than the dissonance appeal. When the kiosks were placed at hospitals, the emotional action was twice as effective as the motivating action. Recall that this is not a small commitment—we are not talking about signing a petition, we are talking about making one's organs available to others. Yet, the right message doubled, even tripled, registrations.

> Consideration #7: Even though donation is a high-commitment behavior, it is more vulnerable to persuasive messaging than might be expected.

A Radio Campaign

The final planned activity of the grant involved implementing a general market radio campaign to alert Tucsonans to the presence of the kiosks and the online registry while motivating listeners to register. Event-based messages, such as the announcement at the basketball game and the radio remote, were not successful at drumming up registrations. We hoped a radio campaign introducing the kiosks to the masses would lead to conversations about donation, thus leading to more favorable subjective norms for most, leading to an increase in registrations.

We met with our partners at DNAZ, and the kiosk posters were rewritten into copy for radio ads. One spot read, "Think your religion opposes organ donation? Ask your religious or spiritual leader, and you'll find out no major religion opposes organ donation. Sign up at azdonorregistry.org or at any public library." Another read, "Think you are too old or sick to be an organ donor? Most likely, you're wrong. Just about everyone is eligible to donate. Let a doctor decide. Sign up at azdonorregistry.org or at any public library."

For 2 weeks, the Tucson radio market was saturated with 10-second spots on six stations. Listeners were encouraged to go to the Donor Registry Web site or to find a registration kiosk placed at city libraries. As an analysis plan, we set our sights on an interrupted time series design with the concentrated campaign serving as the interruption and the weekly number of registrations throughout Tucson serving as the outcome measure. The short duration of the campaign did not allow respectable comparisons between the four different message appeals but gave the greatest potential for witnessing a spike in registrations as a result of the campaign.

Surely, if we tripled registrations at the kiosks with some theoretically based messaging, similar growth in registrations could be expected for this phase of the project. A postcampaign telephone survey indicates that "saturation" of the market was lacking: Only 20% recalled hearing the ads. Nevertheless, 20% of all of Tucson is still a large audience: There were approximately 400,000 adults living in the city of Tucson when the campaign aired. Put another way, there is reason to expect approximately 80,000 people heard the donor registry radio ads.

Data indicate no change in the rate of overall registrations in Tucson during or after the radio campaign. During the month of the campaign, in all of Tucson, a total of 136 people registered via the Donor Registry Web Site. Fifty-nine specifically mentioned a particular radio station or the radio in general as motivating the registration. We hoped the radio ads would motivate registrations. They did not.

We were again perplexed by the results. Thoughts of our funder's belief that sometimes more is learned by finding out what does not work than finding out what does kept us warm at night. If this was truly the case, we expected to be able to write an encyclopedia when this project was over. Being gluttons for punishment, we took advantage of one more unexpected opportunity.

A Workplace Campaign

Much like the basketball game, a workplace campaign was not part of the original project blueprint, but an opportunity arose toward the end of the project period. A set of hospitals, working with DNAZ, offered to send e-mails to their staff that could contain a message about the registry and a hotlink. The low cost and staffing needed to implement this activity made it impossible to resist. As with the radio campaign, the project team met, and workplace e-mail messages, which would include a hotlink to the registry, were created based on the kiosk poster message appeals.

Staff at the four hospitals received three e-mails over a one-month period. Each hospital received a different appeal. For example, one hospital received three e-mails, all using an emotional appeal; another three e-mails all using a dissonance appeal. The original hope was to implement a counterbalanced design much like the kiosk poster study; however, finding additional organizations willing to participant within the short time remaining in the project was problematic. The result was another one-time trial. Even if one appeal appeared to motivate the most registrations, there are myriad variables at the hospital level that can be responsible other than the message itself. Nevertheless, a gross-level assessment of the utility of the e-mail and hotlink approach for increasing registrations was feasible.

The number of registrations obtained via three e-mails to approximately 7,500 workers was 191. Certainly not a huge number, but our attention was drawn to the finding that the number of registrations that occurred as a result of the e-mails was greater than the number of registrations that could be claimed by the entire radio campaign. Moreover, sending three e-mail messages to 7,500 employees resulted in twice as many registrations as placing a kiosk at a university for 9 months and launching with a radio remote.

Analyzing Project Outcomes

The number of kiosk-based registrations never matched our high expectations. As mentioned earlier, the kiosks were clearly not a magic bullet. There is no theoretical reason to question the goal of increasing attitude–behavior consistency via increasing PBC; there is also no reason to question the kiosks ability to facilitate registrations; mechanically the kiosks work. We were left with much to contemplate. We mulled over the following: (a) Basketball fans did not notice the kiosks or register; however, (b) 50% of focus group participants expressed a willingness to donate at the end of the 2-hour session; (c) placing registration kiosks on college campuses, libraries, and even hospitals had little registration impact; but (d) the right persuasive message tripled registrations when placed as a poster on top of all-in-one kiosks; with (e) the counterargument message being most effective; (f) behavior appeared to be changed via posters to a greater extent than would be expected with such a high commitment behavior; but (g) a radio campaign blitz using the same messages had no impact on registrations; however, (h) a hotlink in an e-mail sent to 7,500 people resulted in just about the same number of registrations as a radio campaign. We considered the results in the context of social psychological theory and theories specific to helping behavior.

A compilation of results, pontifications, and frustrations were placed on a white board. We looked for patterns. What were these results telling us? At first, nothing revealed itself. We stood like mall-goers fascinated by one of those 3D posters where a space ship becomes visible if only one can relax their eyes and look beyond the poster. We stared for hours and even left the board full of our musings up overnight with the lab door open—on the off-chance a janitor receiving therapy from Robin Williams would come in and solve our problem.

No such luck. Fortunately, after eating some questionable leftovers found in the office refrigerator, we noted that four factors appeared to be heavily exerting influence on registration rates: (a) an immediate and complete registration opportunity, (b) information (particularly about eligibility), (c) focused engagement, and (d) favorable activation.

Immediate and Complete Registration Opportunity: "A Card in Hand"

This construct refers to the ability of potential donors to start and complete the registration process within whichever context they find themselves when motivated to register. In the focus group studies, the participants only had to check a box to register. Workers receiving the e-mail only needed to click a link. In those situations, the card was metaphorically placed in hand.

Consider two different approaches used to motivate registration. In the e-mail study, registration was literally one click away. The radio campaign may have motivated listeners to register, but think about how far most potential donors would have been from a registration mechanism at the time the message was heard and registration was motivated.

These two studies were certainly not set up with the intention of testing the importance of providing an immediate and complete registration mechanism, but a study conducted by Sanner, Hedman, and Tufveson (1995) offers support for the possibility that our findings are not spurious.

Sanner and colleagues (1995) used a quasi-experimental design to assess the impact of an information-based campaign and/or the impact of being mailed a donor card on registration rates. This study featured four communities. One received an information-based campaign focused on organ donation, another received no campaign but received organ donor cards in the mail, another received both the information campaign and the cards, and another received neither. If an immediate mechanism for registration did not matter, there would be no difference in donor registration rates between those in the community receiving only the information campaign and those in the community receiving the information campaign plus a donor registration card. This was not the case; the null hypothesis took a beating. In the community receiving only the informational campaign, donor registration rates were not impacted. However, registration rates quadrupled in the community receiving both the campaign and the card. Four times as many registrations resulted from placing a card in hand. More to the point, there was a 240% increase in donor registration in the community that received nothing more than a card in hand.

Information (Particularly About Eligibility)

The results of the kiosks–poster study (Siegel, Alvaro, Pace Jones, et al., 2008) clearly indicate the importance of providing registrants with eligibility information. No matter how the data are analyzed, the posters informing potential donors that they are "not too sick" and "not too old" which clearly hits upon TPB's perceived controllability resulted in more registrations than any other poster. This approach was not topped regardless of the location or the exemplar. In some contexts, the counterargument approach resulted in three times as many registrations as another approach. Moreover, the discussion on eligibility and false beliefs that occurred during the focus group can certainly make a case for deserving some of the credit in participants' willingness to register when the groups concluded.

To be clear, Sanner et al.'s (1995) study clearly indicates that information alone will not lead to increased registrations; however, as will be discussed, none of the constructs are intended to work solo—it is the simultaneous presence of all aspects of the model that is posited to increase registration rates.

Focused Engagement

The focus group participants had it; anyone reading the workplace e-mail had it. Close to the entire basketball arena did not have it, nor did the majority of the people at the libraries housing kiosks. *Focused engagement* refers to the activation of donor- and registration-related beliefs and attitudes and the presence of active contemplation regarding the registration act. Remember, TPB does not predict that all beliefs and attitudes will influence behavior. Only those that are *activated* will. A person may believe that registration is desirable, but if this belief is not thought about, it is nearly irrelevant.

We consider the lack of focused engagement the crux of the failure of the kiosks at the basketball game. We do not believe that 19,000 people noticed the registration opportunity offered by the kiosks and chose not to register. We failed to get the vast majority of the fans focused on the topic of donation, and as such, registration was not even contemplated. The same goes for the 2,500 daily library visitors. Library attendance might be 2,500 people on a given day, but that is not the same as 2,500 people noticing the kiosks and deliberating whether to register.

Favorable Activation

An immediate and complete registration mechanism might be provided at the same time that focused engagement occurs, but this will not always lead to registration. Donation is unique in that attitudes toward donation are commonly ambivalent (Parisi & Katz, 1986). This refers to people having not just positive attitudes about donation but negative ones as well. Not everyone thinks happy thoughts when they imagine dying, leaving their loved ones, and/or their organs being removed from their body. As mentioned, only accessible beliefs influence attitudes. If a person is thinking about his or her own death rather than the lives being saved, it would not be considered favorable for registration.

Earlier, we noted surprise that one kiosk poster can have such a strong effect on registrations compared to another poster. Our surprise was due to knowledge of attitude research indicating that, when it comes to behaviors leading to high levels of commitment, a persuasive message is expected to face greater scrutiny and therefore be less powerful (e.g., Crano & Prislin, 2008). If people have highly ambivalent attitudes about donation, it would explain the surprising strength of one poster to influence behavior over another: One poster activated one set of beliefs and attitudes, and another poster a different set. A recent study by Hirschberger, Ein-Dor, and Almakias (2008) truly brings the point home.

Hirschberger et al.'s (2008) study involved handing participants a flyer asking about either death concerns (mortality salience condition) or about back and muscle pain (comparison condition). Then, 15 meters away, research assistants solicited those receiving flyers to sign an organ donor card. Of those receiving the "pain" flyer, 17.6% registered; of those given the "death" flyer, 5.2%. On one hand, this study supports the notion that an immediate and complete registration mechanism, coupled with focused engagement, can motivate registration of donor intent. More than 17% registered for no reason other than the opportunity was provided while focused engagement was motivated by a direct interpersonal offer to register. On the other, this study drives home the importance of favorable activation. An unfavorable activation pattern can cut registrations in third.

An IIFF Model of Donor Registration?

For the reasons we have just laid out, we suspect that registrations are more likely to occur with the simultaneous presence of an immediate and complete registration opportunity, information, focused engagement, and favorable activation. Put another way, "IIFF these factors are simultaneously present, registrations will come." Not to be forgotten is that this proposed model is the result of post hoc assessment of a series of studies not implemented as a model-building exercise. This is not the end but the beginning; We are not even close to the end of the beginning.

The first step has to be a mental exploration as to why the simultaneous presence of these four variables impacts registrations as it does. Knowing the "why" is critical if other variables are going to be considered without randomly selecting among the universe of variables with the hope of stumbling upon another relevant factor.

We have previously argued that living donation campaigns would be significantly different from nonliving campaigns because vested interest is so much higher when the person in need is a loved one rather than someone you do not know (Siegel, Alvaro, Lac, Crano, & Alexander, 2008). Revisiting this argument led to a parsimonious explanation of why the IIFF model is even necessary.

When someone is vested in an outcome or activity, it means the individual has deemed that behavior and/or outcome as being of high importance *and* of great personal consequence (Crano, 1983, 1995, 1997). If registering to be a donor were something for which people were highly vested, an immediate mechanism placed in hand would not be necessary. If people were highly motivated to become donors, they would seek out the registration mechanism. This does not seem to be the case. The need to proactively correct misperceptions that hinder perceived control, such as a lack of eligibility, can also be construed as existing primarily due to a lack of vested interest. If someone won a million dollars but had to be eligible to collect, there is no question he or she would take proactive steps to investigate eligibility. This rarely happens when it comes to donor registration. Why? Much vested interest in the money, less vested interest in donation. Moreover, if this were a topic in which people were vested, it would be salient without prompting. There would be no need to encourage focused engagement; it would occur on its own. This, again, does not seem to be the case.

Recall that TPB indicates that only accessible beliefs influence attitudes, subjective norms, and PBC. Three of the factors of the IIFF model (immediate and complete registration mechanism, information, and focused engagement) might be best construed as what is necessary to make attitudes and behavior match when the outcome is not one in which the individual is highly vested.

This leaves favorable activation. The lack of vested interest can be stretched to explain why the behavior can be cut in third by a mention of death or tripled as a result of posters placed on top of kiosks, but the construct of attitude ambivalence offers a more parsimonious explanation. For some topics, people hold primarily positive or primarily negative attitudes. In these instances, making the topic top of mind is akin with making positive thoughts about the topic top of mind. This is unlikely the case when it comes to donation. This is due to potential donors likely holding both positive and negative attitudes toward an object (Parisi & Katz, 1986); as such, the issue of activation is particularly important. This reflects a situation attitude that researchers refer to as attitudinal ambivalence (Cacioppo, Gardner, & Berntson, 1997; Thompson, Zanna, & Griffin, 1995).

If all thoughts about becoming a registered donor were positive, then any accessibility of attitudes related to the topic would be good accessibility. However, this is not the case. Thoughts of donation can certainly bring to mind pleasurable images of a life being saved; they can also bring to mind images of death, which we know from Hirschberger et al.'s (2008) study can severely impair registration behavior. As such, the simultaneous presence of an immediate and compete registration mechanism, information, and focused engagement may be irrelevant if the activation pattern is not favorable.

Altogether, this very post hoc assessment leads us to believe that the presence of the constructs in the IIFF model might be a necessary addition to any intervention seeking to increase the incidence of a behavior where vested interest is low and attitude ambiguity is high. Organ donor registration is the prototype of such a behavior.

Future Directions

Two avenues of future research are envisioned. Experimentally testing each aspect of the IIFF model—ensuring each construct impacts registration rates as we suspect—is one. The other involves experimentally assessing the accuracy of the underlying mechanisms providing the rationale for the model. These two avenues are expected to lead to the third: the discovery of additional factors that influence donor registration.

First, experimentally testing each aspect of the model is paramount. Experimentally assessing the importance of a "card in hand" can be accomplished by randomly assigning groups of potential donors to receive a presentation on registration availability with or without a registration card provided at the end. The importance of information, particularly about eligibility, can easily be tested by randomly assigning potential donors to receive information about one topic, such as eligibility, whereas the others learn about another topic as long as it is void of any discussion on eligibility. Focused engagement studies can assess different ways of motivating deliberation of registration contemplation. If engagement is experimentally tested such that some participants are motivated to deliberate registration but another group is not and registration rates are assessed, the construct's importance or lack thereof will be revealed. Priming different beliefs about donation and assessing the influence of priming one set of beliefs versus another on donor registration rates can test favorable activation.

Equally important, if not more so, is the second recommended avenue of research: testing the underlying mechanisms thought to be responsible for the importance of the IIFF constructs in donor registration behavior. Figuring out the "why" will provide guidance for successfully operationalizing these constructs across intervention contexts and for more refined theory building. As we have noted and again stress—this is but the beginning of an explanation of organ donation registration behavior.

Lastly, if the IIFF model does predict donor registration behavior, and an explanation for the influence is derived, the next step would be investigating other variables that should also be part of the model.

In Closing . . .

Our objective with this chapter was to lay out a series of studies that have led to our current belief that interventions seeking to increase donor registrations have the greatest likelihood of success if the following four constructs are *simultaneously* present: (a) an immediate and compete registration mechanism, (b) information (particularly about eligibility), (c) focused engagement, and (d) favorable activation: the *IIFF model of registration behavior*: Tests of the model are warranted and encouraged.

Acknowledgments

The authors wish to thank Sara Pace Jones, Stacy Underwood, and the entire Donor Network of Arizona team for their invaluable contributions to the implementation of the projects discussed herein.

The projects discussed here were funded by grants from HRSA, Division of Transplantation grant (H39 OT 00021-01, R39OT01148) awarded to Sara Pace Jones, PI. The opinions expressed herein are those of the authors and do not necessarily represent those of the funding agency.

References

Ajzen, I. (1991). The theory of planned behavior. *Organizational Behavior and Human Decision Processes, 50*, 179–211.

Ajzen, I. (2002). Perceived behavioral control, self-efficacy, locus of control, and the theory of planned behavior. *Journal of Applied Social Psychology, 32*, 665–683.

Ajzen, I., & Fishbein, M. (1980). *Understanding attitudes and predicting social behavior.* Englewood Cliffs, NJ: Prentice Hall.

Alvaro, E. M., Jones, S. P., Robles, A., & Siegel, J. T. (2005). Predictors of organ donation behaviors among Hispanic Americans. *Progress in Transplantation, 15,* 149–156.

Alvaro, E. M., Jones, S. P., Robles, A. S., & Siegel, J. T. (2006). Hispanic organ donation: Impact of a Spanish-language organ donation campaign. *Journal of the National Medical Association, 98,* 28–35.

Bagozzi, R. P. (1996). The role of arousal in the creation and control of the halo effect in attitude models. *Psychology & Marketing, 13,* 235–264.

Cacioppo, J. T., Gardner, W. L., & Berntson, G. B. (1997). Beyond bipolar conceptualizations and measures: The case of attitudes and evaluative space. *Personality and Social Psychology Review, 1,* 3–25.

Crano, W. D. (1983). Assumed consensus of attitudes: The effect of vested interest. *Personality and Social Psychology Bulletin, 9,* 597–608.

Crano, W. D. (1995). Attitude strength and vested interest. In R. E. Petty & J. A. Krosnick (Eds.), *Attitude strength: Antecedents and consequences* (pp. 131–158). Mahwah, NJ: Erlbaum.

Crano, W. D. (1997). Vested interest, symbolic politics, and attitude-behavior consistency. *Journal of Personality and Social Psychology, 72,* 485–491.

Crano, W. D., & Prislin, R. (2008). *Attitudes and attitude change* (Frontiers of Social Psychology series). New York: Psychology Press.

Fishbein, M., & Ajzen, I. (1975). *Belief, attitude, intention, and behavior: An introduction to theory and research.* Reading, MA: Addison-Wesley.

Gallup Organization. (1993). *The American public's attitudes toward organ donation and transplantation.* Princeton, NJ: Gallup Organization.

Gallup Organization. (2005–2006). *2005 national survey of organ and tissue donation attitudes and behaviors.* Washington, DC: Gallup Organization.

Greenberg, J., Pyszczynski, T., Solomon, S., Rosenblatt, A., Veeder, M., Kirkland, S., et al. (1990). Evidence for terror management theory II: The effects of mortality salience on reactions to those who threaten or bolster the cultural worldview. *Journal of Personality and Social Psychology, 58,* 308–318.

Hirschberger, G., Ein-Dor, T., & Almakias, S. (2008). The self-protective altruist: Terror management and the ambivalent nature of prosocial behavior. *Personality and Social Psychology Bulletin, 34,* 666–678.

Isen, A. M. (1970). Success, failure, attention, and reactions to others: The warm glow of success. *Journal of Personality and Social Psychology, 15,* 294–301.

Parisi, N., & Katz, I. (1986). Attitudes toward posthumous organ donation and commitment to donate. *Health Psychology, 5,* 565–580.

Sanner, M. A., Hedman, H., & Tufveson, G. (1995). Evaluation of an organ-donor-card campaign in Sweden. *Clinical Transplantation, 9,* 326–333.

Siegel, J. T., Alvaro, E. M., & Jones, S. P. (2005). Organ donor registration preferences among Hispanic populations: Which modes of registration have the greatest promise? *Health Education and Behavior, 32,* 242–252.

Siegel, J. T., Alvaro, E., Lac, A., Crano, W. D., & Alexander, S. (2008). Intentions of becoming a living organ donor among Hispanics: A theoretical approach exploring differences between living and non-living organ donation. *Journal of Health Communication, 13,* 80–99.

Siegel, J. T., Alvaro, E., Crano, W. C., Lac, A. Ting, S., & Pace Jones, S. (2008). A quasi-experimental investigation of message appeal variations on organ donor registration rates. *Health Psychology, 27,* 170–178.

Smith, S. W., Morrison, K., Kopfman, J. E., & Ford, L. A. (1994). The influence of prior thought and intent on the memorability and persuasiveness of organ donation message strategies. *Health Communication, 6,* 1–20.

Thompson, M., Zanna, M., & Griffin, D. (1995). Let's not be indifferent about (attitudinal) ambivalence. In R. E. Petty & J. A. Krosnick (Eds.), *Attitude strength: Antecedents and consequences.* Hillsdale, NJ: Lawrence Erlbaum.

Trafimow, D., Sheeran, P., Conner, M., & Finlay, K. A. (2002). Evidence that perceived behavioural control is a multidimensional construct. *British Journal of Social Psychology, 41,* 101–121.

Weber, K., Martin, M. M., & Corrigan, C. (2007). Real donors, real consent: Testing the theory of reasoned action on organ donor consent. *Journal of Applied Social Psychology, 37,* 2435–2450.

Winkel, F. W. (1984). Public communication on donor cards: A comparison of persuasive styles. *Social Science and Medicine, 19,* 957–963.

Yzer, M. C., Hennessy, M., & Fishbein, M. (2004). The usefulness of perceived difficulty for health research. *Psychology, Health and Medicine, 9*(2), 149–162.

20

There's Nothing So Practical . . .
Theoretical Translations and
Organ Donation

William D. Crano

In one of the most revered dictums of 20th-century social science, Kurt Lewin (1964) wrote that there is "nothing so practical as a good theory" (p. 169). Even though it is honored more in the breach than in practice, this aphorism has survived because it is true. In reading the impressive work summarized in Siegel and Alvaro's important book, Lewin's maxim came to mind repeatedly. The relevance of theory in this admittedly and justifiably applied area of endeavor, organ donation, should be continually reinforced, and this is one of the central goals of this chapter. As considerations of theory recurred in my contemplation of the various (and uniformly excellent) chapters of this volume, so too will the importance and relevance of theory serve as the leitmotif in my brief commentary, assessment, and appreciation of the work contained here.

The Problem

Imagine a situation in which the majority of the population believes in the appropriateness of a particular behavior, but only a miniscule fraction of this majority actually acts on the belief. From a rationalist point of view, this incongruity between attitude and action would seem a rare occurrence, for certainly we all act on our beliefs. However, this lack of correspondence between beliefs and actions is exactly the fix in which many of those involved in organ donation research find themselves. Most people with even a shred of humanity believe that organ donation is a good thing, and that helping one's loved ones (or even strangers) via organ donation is a positive good. Yet, many appear enormously reluctant to act on this widely accepted belief by enrolling as donors, even though they presumably will have little use for their organs after death. With living donation the cost–benefit analysis may require greater contemplation, but even in this instance the odds should favor the altruistic alternative. The established lack of congruence between a well-accepted belief (organ donation is a good thing) and a belief–congruent action (donating organs for transplantation) is puzzling, and our failure to understand the dynamics of this relationship has retarded the potential contributions that social and behavioral scientists have been able to make to this vital arena of human action. The good news is that the lack of correspondence between attitudes and actions is not unique to the realm organ donation. The failure of people's beliefs to anticipate (or cause) their overt actions is far more common than we might assume on first consideration. In fact, this problem, which is a central feature of much research on organ registration and donation, has for many years been the focus of extensive study in the fields of communication and persuasion (Crano & Prislin, 2006). Clearly, organ donation researchers have much to gain by careful consideration of the mountains of research that have been amassed over the years in the study of attitude–behavior consistency—or inconsistency, as is often the case.

Quashed Assumptions

Early researchers on attitude and attitude change had for many years accepted as an article of faith that attitudes predicted or anticipated—some went so far as to say caused—actions. We assumed, naïvely perhaps, but with no little hope, that people acted in rational and predictable ways, despite research that popped up occasionally that suggested otherwise—LaPiere's (1934) overcited study comes instantly to mind. We assumed if we knew people's beliefs, we could predict their behaviors with reasonable accuracy. This fantasy (some would call it a hallucination) came to a screeching halt in the late 1960s, with the publication of Wicker's (1969) influential review of the literature, which shattered the comforting myth of simple, unmoderated, attitude–behavior consistency and instead laid bare a surprising lack of correspondence between verbal measures of attitudes and corresponding behavior. Wicker (1971) was to reinforce his observations with a later study in which some earlier identified moderators of attitude–behavior consistency were threatened, if not entirely debunked.

As might be expected, the field was quick to respond, and it did so with vigor. Although most acknowledged that it was perhaps naïve to assume a one-to-one association between a belief and a corresponding behavior, the underlying assumption that attitudes are functionally related to actions seemed impossible for most of us to relinquish. Rather, attitude investigators attempted to delineate the contexts and conditions that fostered, or retarded, the causal linkage between attitudes and acts. Work on this issue has been intense for the past 40 years or so, with various periods of ebb and flow, and the overall results have been encouraging. The activity level may be gauged by the slew of meta-analyses that have been devoted to one or another feature of the attitude–behavior consistency question. I have found 11 at last count—those of Glasman and Albarracin (2006) and Kraus (1995) are particularly noteworthy, in my view.

A Resurgence of Faith

The general finding advanced in these meta-analytic compilations is that attitudes do indeed predict actions, but they do not do so uniformly, they do not do so all the time, and they certainly do not do so under all conditions and circumstances. The meta-analytic studies counsel caution in extrapolating too far, in assuming that an idea that deserves to be right is, indeed, correct. From Wicker to today, we now know about a host of variables whose presence or absence will have much to say about the effect of attitudes on actions. Variables as diverse as the groups to which one belongs (Terry, Hogg, & White, 2000), group norms (Smith & Terry, 2003), the extent of knowledge about the attitude object (Fabrigar, Petty, Smith, & Crites, 2006; Wood, Rhodes, & Biek, 1995), one's direct experience with the attitude (Fazio & Zanna, 1978a, 1978b), the accessibility of attitude-relevant information (Kallgren & Wood, 1986), vested interest in the outcome of behavior that logically follows from the attitude (Crano, 1997; Crano & Prislin, 1995; Sivacek & Crano, 1982), the tendency to introspect (Wilson, Dunn, Kraft, & Lisle, 1989), and other individual differences (Jaccard, Helbig, Wan, & Gutman, 1990; Zanna, Olson, & Fazio, 1980) have all been shown to affect the likelihood that a specific attitude will inform an action, and this litany of moderators is a mere surface scratching. If the reader (and the writer) had sufficient time, space, and patience, the list could have been extended almost indefinitely. Clearly, attitudes can affect actions. Whether or not they do so is in large part dependent on a complex web of (probably) interdependent moderators that can spell the success or failure of any attempts at capitalizing on the attitude–action bond.

In light of the mountain of results that has been uncovered from the late 1960s onward, one might infer that Wicker was wrong—that, contrary to his assertions, there is indeed a clear link between measured (verbal) attitudes and correspondent behaviors. However, this reaction would be the result of overdefensiveness and an oversimplified understanding of the science. To be sure, attitudes do anticipate actions. Results of nearly a dozen meta-analyses are difficult to gainsay. But at least on one level, it is equally clear that Wicker's indictment was right on target. It is patently incorrect to assume that attitudes cause behaviors—without first acknowledging one or a number of factors that play into this statement. Yes, attitudes cause behavior, but only under circumscribed conditions about which we are not yet entirely informed. Wicker's critique forced attitude researchers, past and present, to sharpen their vision and to specify with greater certainty and clarity the conditions that affect the attitude–action bond. There is no doubt that attitudes do, indeed, affect behavior, but just as certainly attitudes' effects are moderated by a host of factors whose full extent has yet to be plumbed. At a minimum, those of us engaged in research on attitudes and their relation to behavior owe Wicker a debt of gratitude for forcing us to come to grips with the complexity of the topic we have chosen to understand. The lesson we should take home from this debate is straightforward, if not thorny: Life's complicated—(learn to) live with it.

Utility of Theory

These observations counsel a renewed appreciation of the utility of theory. The various moderators of attitude–behavior consistency were not drawn from thin air, but from a close theoretical consideration of the factors that might affect the attitude–behavior linkage. This area of research owes a greater debt to the facilitating force of theory than perhaps any other subfield of persuasion research. Without a good theoretical basis, choice of moderator would have been more a result of whimsy than informed scientific logic, and progress would have been retarded, if not halted entirely. The study of attitude–behavior consistency has made massive strides precisely because of its symbiotic relationship with theory. This relationship has allowed us to make important discoveries about the nature of people's policy choices (Lehman & Crano, 2002), health decisions (Siegel, Alvaro, Lac, Crano, & Dominick, 2008), and even the schools to which we will send our children (Crano, 1997). Without a firm theoretical base, these and other important factors that impinge on people's lives would not have been predictable.

This stress on theory is not accidental, nor is it necessarily a general mantra that is brought out whenever important research is discussed. It is directed toward a potential opportunity for enhanced growth in the social analysis of donor behavior that became evident in my reading of the chapters that constitute the substantive heart of this volume. There is no doubt that the work is done well. It could be improved, however. The stress in one of the chapters on proper measurement and evaluation (see Fischer, this volume) is exemplary and well worthy of emulation. Clearly, all we do is founded on the bedrock of proper design, measurement, and analysis. The field would do well to attend closely to fundamental design principles (see, Siegel et al., 2008) in its quantitative *and* qualitative renderings, and this chapter provides a useful and accurate road map for progress.

Proper methods and analyses, however, are not sure prescriptions for progress. Without proper theoretical grounding, research does not cumulate—at least not very quickly—and many of the important insights and implications that might have been gained by the research are likely to be missed. Opportunity costs aside, theory-free approaches are nearly as likely to mislead as to point in the right direction. Blind alleys are certainly possible with theory-based research, but they are almost inevitable with purely empirical studies devoid of theoretical backbone.

The Research Cycle

Guided by Campbell's orientation (and continual exhortations), my colleague Marilynn Brewer and I (Crano & Brewer, 2002) depicted the research process as cyclical, in which insights from the laboratory were taken to the field where they were to be tested in the cold light of the real world, and then brought back to the laboratory for further refinement and modification, and so on (Campbell, 1987, 1989, 1990, 1994, 1996; Campbell & Stanley, 1963). The nonrecursive nature of this process makes it impossible to assign primacy to laboratory or field as contexts for study, or to applied or basic research, and this is precisely the point. Rather, by conceiving research as a cyclical process, we emphasize the mutual interdependence of laboratory and field, the critical importance of both basic research and applications. To overemphasize one at the expense of the other is as shortsighted as it is common.

Social psychology often has been criticized for focusing so much of its energy on laboratory research, on internal validity, at the expense of application or generalizability. This critique is proper, and many, though not all, in the social psychological community have made important efforts to remedy the imbalance. Much remains to be done, but the building blocks are in place: The federal government is applying appropriate pressure in the form of funding quid pro quos, more of our best graduate schools are beginning to suggest that getting one's hands dirty with applied research is not a sign of intellectual mediocrity, and policy makers are beginning to take seriously the results of behavioral research and use them in developing intervention programs designed to ameliorate important social problems. Given this system of prods and rewards, it is conceivable that social psychology may finally make major returns on the social investments that have been made by the general society. As a field that has been strongly supported for many years by public funds, it is certainly arguable that payback time has come.

On the Other Hand

An emphasis opposite to that which characterized the progression of social psychology from a pure laboratory orientation to a greater concern for the application of its products appears evident in the research summarized in the present volume. Although the work reported here is excellent, its contribution to basic theory development, and the consequent creation and refinement of techniques that might advance our understanding of donor decision-making processes, could be accelerated. This is not to demean the work but rather to ask more of its architects. Put most simply, in this field, there appears to be an overemphasis on application at the expense of basic science, on field over laboratory, and on meeting immediate rather than long-term objectives. If we accept the cyclical nature of research—at least research that will pay the greatest dividend—then this trend does not bode well.

The motivation for this apparent overemphasis on application is understandable. It has everything to do with the utter urgency of the issues under consideration. The research conducted by the various chapter authors in this monograph truly is a matter of life and death, and any delays in bringing the fruits of investigation to the fore must be experienced by its authors as intolerable. Yet, an overemphasis on the application of tactics of influence at the expense of understanding how and why the tactics work, a rush to the field without the growth of proper theory, ultimately and perhaps even in the short run will retard progress and cost more than it saves.

It seems clear to me that the central focus of those in the Health Resources Services Administration (HRSA) who are concerned with organ transplantation is not the development of refined theory, but improved service delivery. In the present instance, this improved service centers on increasing the pool of potential organ donors. This is as it should be. However, if we consider this problem from a mid- to long-term perspective, we must come to the conclusion that there may be many ways to increase the donor pool. HRSA seems to have adopted a reasonable tactic of identifying variables that affect people's decision making, and importing it to the arena of organ donation. Typically, this "transplanted" research will not have been developed originally with affecting organ donation as its goal, but its transition into that context is not viewed as an important impediment. This strategy hinges on an important (if unvoiced) assumption, namely, that the translation of research results from one area of investigation are readily transferrable to the field of organ donation. If this is so, then a persuasion tactic that works when selling soap will be effective in persuading people to join an organ donation registry. The translation assumption has been supported on numerous occasions, as is evident in the published literature, but it has failed frequently as well, and these failures do not show up in the literature. These failures are costly and avoidable. A greater emphasis on the development of underlying theory and tactics specific to the donation decision would help us avoid costly unsupportive research outcomes.

A Reformist Prescription

Forty years ago, Campbell (1969) published an important paper that he titled "Reforms as Experiments." The gist of his argument is summarized in the first sentence of his paper:

> The United States and other modern nations should be ready for an experimental approach to social reform, an approach in which we try out new programs

designed to cure specific social problems, in which we learn whether or not these programs are effective, and in which we retain, imitate, modify, or discard them on the basis of apparent effectiveness on the multiple imperfect criteria available. (Campbell, 1969, p. 409)

The prescription for research that Campbell voiced in his "Reforms" paper is even more fitting today than it was when first presented. We have an unprecedented opportunity to understand the fundamental processes involved in organ donation if only we have the courage and foresight to take advantage of it. Why not use the talent that is clearly available in this area of study to mount an aggressive and wide-ranging campaign designed to attack the issue of organ donation on two fronts? The first is to retain a strong emphasis on what works—that is, to continue to import tactics from related fields of persuasion to help mitigate the unconscionable and incomprehensible gulf between those in need of organs and those willing to part with them after death—in other words, we must keep doing what is being done. The second goal is to facilitate the development of basic theory specific to organ donation. The central aim of this goal is not just to facilitate organ donation, but also to understand the process itself—why do people volunteer organs? What stops them from doing so? What are the most effective ways to overcome resistance? How can we boost voluntary donation behavior? This goal will require support for research that is not immediately applicable, but that has the promise to help redirect efforts in ways that will maximize the contribution of applied field studies in the near future. These goals are not incompatible. In fact, they are mutually interdependent. The roadmap for this "reformation" is not entirely discernable at this point, but there are a number of guidelines that we might consider in seeking the proper path.

A Road Map

First, we must recognize the important contributions the behavioral sciences have made to this issue. Although a relative newcomer to the table, support of this type of research has resulted in real progress. The literature suggests that the bulk of the support for research of this type is devoted to the application and dissemination of interventions whose utility has been demonstrated in other areas of research. Less support appears to have been dedicated to research leading to an understanding of how and why the interventions succeeded or failed. There is no denying the success of this model—much has been accomplished—but imagine the gains that might have been realized if greater emphasis had been laid on understanding the fundamental processes involved.

The reformist orientation would facilitate our moving away from a purely intervention-based strategy, which in other fields has resulted in faddish research that fails to add much, if anything, to cumulative knowledge. When the novelty of an intervention becomes the central determinant of the apparent worth of a project, the fight has been lost. Time after time and in field after field, research guided by an interventionist (vs. theoretical) orientation has proved disappointing. Such an orientation may result in some flashy findings, but they do not add up, and they do not provide useful insights going forward. Though titillating, these studies, some of which are even highly cited, rarely add to our real understanding of the phenomena they purport to investigate.

Campbell's (1969) suggestion that we evaluate our social interventions based on "the multiple imperfect criteria available" is of exceptional importance, and should be observed religiously in research on organ donation. This apparently simple and reasonable suggestion requires that we move away from a disquieting regularity in this field, which involves the use of a single "gold standard" measure. Much research on organ donation is characterized by dependence on an admittedly important but unitary outcome measure. Given the emphasis of this field, we are consumed with the question of whether or not people joined a donor registry, or pledged to donate an organ or two, in response to our experimental or quasi-experimental interventions. This use of a simple dichotomous measure is understandable, but it can unduly limit our research horizons. At the most obvious level, such a measurement choice negates the possibility of our using many of our most sensitive higher order inferential statistical techniques. This is a loss. More importantly, it distances the research from many theories whose indicators were developed in frank acknowledgment of the fact that although actual outcome behavior often is difficult, if not impossible, to obtain, proxies for the sought-for outcomes can be developed and can prove exceptionally useful. Ajzen and Fishbein's theory of planned behavior is a case in point (Ajzen & Fishbein, 2000, 2005). Much of the research undertaken with this model does not admit to ready behavioral observation. An anti-HIV campaign, for example, that has as its goal the practice of safe sex usually does not allow for direct behavioral observation of its success or failure. However, as has been shown repeatedly (e.g., Ajzen, Brown, & Carvajal, 2004; Armitage & Conner, 2001; Sheeran, 2002), experimental use of behavioral intentions as proxies provides a strong indication of actual behavior. This is not to counsel moving completely to less direct measures. The study of organ donation research does have its gold standard—registration as a donor—and it obviously should be used. However, to tie the field to a single indicator will limit the variety of research that will be undertaken, and this could prove costly. Nearly a half-century ago Campbell and Stanley (1963) advised social science to wean itself from its overdependence on the "interview," which they understood to be respondents' self-reports of their thoughts and likely actions. This was good advice, even if greater dependence on such variables is now being suggested. This advice does not amount to throwing out the baby with the bathwater, but rather for an expansion beyond the signature on the donor registration card. This simple expansion will broaden the palette on which our research may be drawn, and in the long run may allow for a deeper understanding of the processes we must come to know.

The expansion of measures and measurement processes has other advantages as well. At a minimum, it connects the research to other active subfields that have taken advantage of indirect measures that are less likely to be subject to social desirability biases. In addition, expanding from the common dichotomous measurement approach opens the way for a multiple operationistic orientation that fosters triangulation of methods and measures (Crano, 1986). The advantages of this approach for construct validity are difficult to overemphasize.

Another advantage realized when following Campbell's (1969) "reforms as experiments" prescriptions is the expansion of the research paradigms and the variables that now will enter into consideration. For example, on the variable front, we know from other areas of research that targeting our persuasive attacks to the inclinations of our receivers is a good strategy. In research on tobacco prevention, for example, Siegel and colleagues found strong differences in susceptibility to antismoking messages as a function of the usage status of their audience (Siegel, Alvaro, & Burgoon, 2003), just as did Crano and colleagues (Crano, Gilbert, Alvaro, & Siegel, 2008; Crano, Siegel, Alvaro, Lac, & Hemovich, 2008) in their studies of adolescent marijuana and inhalant abuse. If we develop similar filters for openness to donation, the success of our efforts at moving individuals from hesitant nondonor to cooperative donor would be enhanced.

The expansion of vision occasioned by adopting Campbell's reformist orientation would undoubtedly open the field to a more varied methodological armamentarium. This area of research seems naturally amenable to quasi-experimentation and secondary data analysis operations. The more widespread support and consequent adoption of these techniques would pay enormous dividends to the field. In addition to using established methods of quasi-experimentation (Shadish, Cook, & Campbell, 2002), the study of donor behavior could encourage the development of new investigative forms. The problems and difficulties of research in this area are well documented (e.g., see Quinn, this volume), but it is in contexts such as these that creative developments occur. We develop new methods of inquiry when the old ones prove insufficient.

The gains to be realized from the opportunistic use of secondary analysis of existing data sets also are readily apparent. In her chapter in this volume, Ganikos described a number of available databases that have been used to great advantage. It seems evident that even greater use could be made of these invaluable resources. Demographic variations, alone, would prove interesting, but even more interesting when associated with differences in donor volunteerism in response to theory-based mass-mediated interventions. The pieces are in place. The support necessary to realize these gains would not be great, but the advances well could be.

Some Inherent Advantages

In part, my sanguinity in raising these speculative but promising proposals is fostered by the built-in research advantages that already are in place in this research area. The availability of digital databases, whose exploitation could pay enormous dividends in terms of understanding and targeting, has already been mentioned. In addition, owing to HRSA's fostering of a strong interdependence between the practitioner community and researchers, there exists a level of appreciation between these groups that is truly rare. In no other area of which I am aware is the connection between researcher, evaluator, and client so tight and so cooperative. This interdependence among the major players in the research game is reflected in the diversity of the players—medical doctors, nurses, members of OPOs, psychologists, communication scholars, evaluators, methodologists, and others. There is clear evidence in this volume of exceptional cooperation among workers across all of these specializations. There is clear cooperation among the members of the research community at the national level, which no doubt has been facilitated by HRSA's practice of encouraging interaction among the various interested parties in the donor equation. These interactions clearly are responsible for the obvious collaboration and collegiality among scientists—as evidenced by this book itself—and between scientists and practitioners. Whoever developed this approach should be given a medal. It serves as a model of what can be done if the right people are running the show.

Concluding Observations

The message that I would like to impart in this brief overview is simple. Clearly, the study of organ donation has made enormous strides in a relatively short time period. There can be little doubt that this progress was fueled by the severity of the problem that research on donation is designed to address. The facts are simple but stark. There are now more than 100,000 Americans awaiting a transplant, and yet countless organs that might be used are being wasted, not because their former owners were unwilling to donate them, but because they never got around to ensuring that they would be used in altruistic support of needy others. The simple combination of these two facts could not be more frustrating, even to those who are not directly in need of a transplant. This is a reality that cries out for change.

Although the gains that we have witnessed in this field, many of which are described in this volume, are truly remarkable, we are now at a point at which progress can be accelerated if the appropriate decisions are made. A more direct adoption of Campbell's reformist orientation would expedite progress, and it would foster adoption of many of the factors for improvement that have been suggested throughout this chapter. The "reforms as experiments" orientation would demand a considerably greater emphasis on theory development than is evident to this point. It would foster a wider view of relevant variables, measures, and methods of research that could be used in securing the knowledge necessary for massive advance. It would encourage the use of designs congruous with the demands and shortcomings of the research context. Politically, this reformist approach could be viewed by policy makers even more favorably than present programs. Adoption of the implications of Campbell's reforms to the donor arena would prove consistent with the requirement that results be shown quickly. At the same time, the new approach would provide for an accumulation of knowledge that in the long run would prove invaluable. The insights derived from studies carried out under this regime would have the further advantage of contributing meaningfully to other areas of social import, and to methodological developments that would have widespread repercussions for social research in general. It seems a win-win proposition. As depicted in this book, the study of the social forces that govern organ donation is off to a great start. Let's not blow it.

References

Ajzen, I., Brown, T. C., & Carvajal, F. (2004). Explaining the discrepancy between intentions and actions: The case of hypothetical bias in contingent valuation. *Personality and Social Psychology Bulletin, 30*, 1108–1121.

Ajzen, I., & Fishbein, M. (2000). The prediction of behavior from attitudinal and normative variables. In E. T. Higgins & A. W. Kruglanski (Eds.), *Motivational science: Social and personality perspectives* (pp. 177–190). New York: Psychology Press.

Ajzen, I., & Fishbein, M. (2005). The influence of attitudes on behavior. In D. Albarracin, B. T. Johnson, & M. P. Zanna (Eds.), *The handbook of attitudes* (pp. 173–221). Mahwah, NJ: Lawrence Erlbaum.

Armitage, C. J., & Conner, M. (2001). Efficacy of the theory of planned behaviour: A meta-analytic review. *British Journal of Social Psychology, 40*, 471–499.

Campbell, D. T. (1969). Reforms as experiments. *American Psychologist, 24*, 409–429.

Campbell, D. T. (1987). Selection theory and the sociology of scientific validity. In W. Callebaut & R. Pinxten (Eds.), *Evolutionary epistemology: A multiparadigm program.* (pp. 139–158). Dordrecht, the Netherlands: Reidel.

Campbell, D. T. (1989). Fragments of the fragile history of psychological epistemology and theory of science. In B. Gholson, W. R. Shadish, Jr., R. A. Neimeyer & A. C. Houts (Eds.), *Psychology of science: Contributions to metascience* (pp. 21–46). New York: Cambridge University Press.

Campbell, D. T. (1990). The Meehlian corroboration–verisimilitude theory of science. *Psychological Inquiry, 1*, 142–147.

Campbell, D. T. (1994). The social psychology of scientific validity: An epistemological perspective and a personalized history. In W. R. Shadish & S. Fuller (Eds.), *The social psychology of science* (pp. 124–161). New York: Guilford.

Campbell, D. T. (1996). Unresolved issues in measurement validity: An autobiographical overview. *Psychological Assessment, 8*, 363–368.

Campbell, D. T., & Stanley, J. C. (1963). *Experimental and quasi-experimental designs for research*. Boston: Houghton, Mifflin.

Crano, W. D. (1986). Research methodology: The interaction of substance with investigative form. In V. P. Makosky (Ed.), *The G. Stanley Hall Lecture Series* (Vol. 6, pp. 9–38). Washington, DC: American Psychological Association.

Crano, W. D. (1997). Vested interest, symbolic politics, and attitude-behavior consistency. *Journal of Personality and Social Psychology, 72*, 485–491.

Crano, W. D., & Brewer, M. B. (2002). *Principles and methods of social research* (2nd ed.). Mahwah, NJ: Lawrence Erlbaum.

Crano, W. D., Gilbert, C., Alvaro, E. M., & Siegel, J. T. (2008). Enhancing prediction of inhalant abuse risk in samples of early adolescents: A secondary analysis. *Addictive Behaviors, 33*, 895–905.

Crano, W. D., & Prislin, R. (1995). Components of vested interest and attitude-behavior consistency. *Basic and Applied Social Psychology, 17*, 1–21.

Crano, W. D., & Prislin, R. (2006). Attitudes and persuasion. *Annual Review of Psychology, 57*, 345–374.

Crano, W. D., Siegel, J. T., Alvaro, E. M., Lac, A., & Hemovich, V. (2008). The at-risk adolescent marijuana nonuser: Expanding the standard distinction. *Prevention Science, 9*, 129–137.

Fabrigar, L. R., Petty, R. E., Smith, S. M., & Crites, S. L., Jr. (2006). Understanding knowledge effects on attitude–behavior consistency: The role of relevance, complexity, and amount of knowledge. *Journal of Personality and Social Psychology, 90*, 556–577.

Fazio, R. H., & Zanna, M. P. (1978a). Attitudinal qualities relating to the strength of the attitude-behavior relationship. *Journal of Experimental Social Psychology, 14*, 398–408.

Fazio, R. H., & Zanna, M. P. (1978b). On the predictive validity of attitudes: The roles of direct experience and confidence. *Journal of Personality, 46*, 228–243.

Glasman, L. R., & Albarracin, D. (2006). Forming attitudes that predict future behavior: A meta-analysis of the attitude-behavior relation. *Psychological Bulletin, 132*, 778–822.

Jaccard, J., Helbig, D. W., Wan, C. K., & Gutman, M. A. (1990). Individual differences in attitude-behavior consistency: The prediction of contraceptive behavior. *Journal of Applied Social Psychology, 20*, 575–617.

Kallgren, C. A., & Wood, W. (1986). Access to attitude-relevant information in memory as a determinant of attitude-behavior consistency. *Journal of Experimental Social Psychology, 22*, 328–338.

Kraus, S. J. (1995). Attitudes and the prediction of behavior: A meta-analysis of the empirical literature. *Personality and Social Psychology Bulletin, 21*, 58–75.

LaPiere, R. T. (1934). Attitudes vs. actions. *Social Forces, 13*, 230–237.

Lehman, B. J., & Crano, W. D. (2002). The pervasive effects of vested interest on attitude-criterion consistency in political judgment. *Journal of Experimental Social Psychology, 38*, 101–112.

Lewin, K. (1964). Field theory and the phase space. In D. Cartwright (Ed.), *Field theory in social science: Selected theoretical papers by Kurt Lewin* (p. 169). New York: Harper & Row.

Shadish, W. R., Cook, T. D., & Campbell, D. T. (2002). *Experimental and quasi-experimental designs for generalized causal inference.* Boston: Houghton, Mifflin.

Sheeran, P. (2002). Intention-behavior relations: A conceptual and empirical review. *European Review of Social Psychology, 12,* 1–36.

Siegel, J. T., Alvaro, E. M., & Burgoon, M. (2003). Perceptions of the at-risk nonsmoker: Are potential intervention topics being overlooked? *Journal of Adolescent Health, 33,* 458–461.

Siegel, J. T., Alvaro, E., Pace-Jones, S., Crano, W. C., Lac, A., & Ting, S. (2008). A quasi-experimental investigation of message appeal variations on organ donor registration rates. *Health Psychology, 27,* 170–178.

Siegel, J. T., Alvaro, E. M., Lac, A., Crano, W. D., & Dominick, A. (2008). Intentions of becoming a living organ donor among Hispanics: A theory-based approach exploring differences between living and nonliving organ donation. *Journal of Health Communication, 13,* 80–99.

Sivacek, J., & Crano, W. D. (1982). Vested interest as a moderator of attitude-behavior consistency. *Journal of Personality and Social Psychology, 43*(2), 210–221.

Smith, J. R., & Terry, D. J. (2003). Attitude-behaviour consistency: The role of group norms, attitude accessibility, and mode of behavioural decision-making. *European Journal of Social Psychology, 33,* 591–608.

Terry, D. J., Hogg, M. A., & White, K. M. (2000). Attitude-behavior relations: Social identity and group membership. In D. J. Terry & M. A. Hogg (Eds.), *Attitudes, behavior, and social context: The role of norms and group membership* (pp. 67–93). Mahwah, NJ: Lawrence Erlbaum.

Wicker, A. W. (1969). Attitudes versus actions: The relationship of verbal and overt behavioral responses to attitude objects. *Journal of Social Issues, 25,* 41–78.

Wicker, A. W. (1971). An examination of the "other variables" explanation of attitude-behavior inconsistency. *Journal of Personality and Social Psychology, 19,* 18–30.

Wilson, T. D., Dunn, D. S., Kraft, D., & Lisle, D. J. (1989). Introspection, attitude change, and attitude-behavior consistency: The disruptive effects of explaining why we feel the way we do. In L. Berkowitz (Ed.), *Advances in experimental social psychology* (Vol. 22, pp. 287–343). San Diego, CA: Academic Press.

Wood, W., Rhodes, N., & Biek, M. (1995). Working knowledge and attitude strength: An information-processing analysis. In R. E. Petty & J. A. Krosnick (Eds.), *Attitude strength: Antecedents and consequences.* (pp. 283–313). Hillsdale, NJ: Lawrence Erlbaum.

Zanna, M. P., Olson, J. M., & Fazio, R. H. (1980). Attitude–behavior consistency: An individual difference perspective. *Journal of Personality and Social Psychology, 38,* 432–440.

Author Index

Subject Index